POLITICAL TRIALS

POLITICAL TRIALS:

Gordian Knots in the Law

RON CHRISTENSON

Transaction Books
New Brunswick (U.S.A.) and Oxford (U.K.)

Library of Congress Catalog Number: 86-1066
ISBN: 0-88738-076-X
Printed in the United States of America

Library of Congress Cataloging in Publication Data

Christenson, Ron.
  Political trials.

  Bibliography: p.
  Includes index.
  1. Trials (Political crimes and offenses).
2. Political crimes and offenses.   3. Trials
(Political crimes and offenses)—United States.
4. Political crimes and offenses—United States.
I. Title.
K543.P6C56   1986   345′.0231   86-1066
ISBN 0-88738-076-X   342.5231

For Kate, Rolf, and Abbey

Contents

Acknowledgments

The framework for the book is a 1983 article by the author, "A Political Theory of Political Trials," reprinted by special permission of the *Journal of Criminal Law and Criminology*, © by Northwestern University School of Law, Vol. 74, No. 2. Also, from *The Trial of the Catonsville Nine*, by Daniel Berrigan, © 1970 by Daniel Berrigan, S.J., reprinted by permission of Beacon Press.

Preface

This book began with a simple question raised by a student in my Jurisprudence class: What is a political trial? My response was the generally accepted standard answer, that political trials are attempts by regimes to control opponents by using legal procedure for political ends. It was based on a book for which I have immense respect, Otto Kirchheimer's *Political Justice*. But my response satisfied neither me nor my students. With the trials of the Chicago Eight, the Boston Five, the Catonsville Nine, and Dennis Banks and Russell Means fresh in our minds, and after having had Leonard Weinglass, William Kunstler, Russell Means, and later Fr. Daniel Berrigan on campus as guest lecturers, the standard response to the question seemed vastly oversimplified. More questions about law and politics are raised by certain trials than we can encompass by saying that they involve the attempt of those with power to swat their opponents.

In subsequent semesters of the Jurisprudence class I invited my students to explore the problems raised in political trials by considering, along with the theories of law of H. L. A. Hart and Ronald Dworkin, such issues as are contained in Aeschylus' *Oresteia*, the trials of Socrates, Jesus, John Lilburne, and the Nuremberg defendants, Robert Bolt's play *A Man for All Seasons*, and Samuel Butler's satire of a trial in *Erewhon*. In each instance we asked ourselves: Is this a political trial? What is the difference between what is properly law and what is properly politics? What can the courts do when faced with a case which questions the legitimacy of the law itself? Is the fundamental difficulty that law and politics operate according to diametrically opposite premises: power is its own authority in politics, but the rule of law is legitimate only when might does not make right? Can the law be something more than an instrument of those who hold power— whether direct power, hidden economic power, or subtle social influence? Finally, can we have political trials within the rule of law?

I wish I could recall who in my class asked the question in the first place. I would tell that student, now probably a decade after graduation, that I have a better response: Chapter 1 of this book, with the other nine chapters as elaboration. The law's delay is nothing compared to the academy's.

In addition to my students who ask questions, I must thank those teachers of mine, such as Howard Lutz, Karl Meyer, Arthur L. Peterson, and Mulford Q. Sibley, who encouraged questions from students. "Certain

1

questions are put to human beings," Leo Tolstoy has taught us, "not so much that they should answer them but that they should spend their lives wrestling with them."

I am fortunate to be teaching at a college which is a community of good will. Cheerful colleagues have provided an informal and running conversation about the questions raised by political trials. They include Howard Cohrt, William Dean, Richard Elvee, Tom Emmert, Marleen Flory, Will Freiert, Michael Haeuser, Norma Hervey, Douglas Huff, Conrad Hyers, Byron Nordstrom, Garrett Paul, David Wicklund, and especially Don Ostrom. Charles Walcott was a dependable driver and listener. I was given time and assistance to work on the project by a leave from Gustavus Adolphus College and a National Endowment for the Humanities Fellowship for College Teachers. The first version of this project was presented at the 1982 meeting of the Academy of Criminal Justice Sciences in Louisville, Kentucky, and received the Anderson Outstanding Paper Award. Versions of chapters 4 and 9 were presented at the 1983 ACJS meeting in San Antonio, Texas. I appreciate the comments of the critics, especially Otis Stephens and Philip Rhoades. I am grateful to several people for their dedicated service in editorial, typing and detail work: Dalia Buzin, Lisa Bushmann, Janine Genelin, Janice Handler, Diane Jensen, Joyce Johnson, Omo Kariko, Joan Kennedy, Julie Lloyd, Nancy Pautz, and especially Saralyn Kriesel. Melody Decker and the staff of the Clerk's Office in the Federal District Court in St. Paul were helpful and patient while I spent a month in their office reading the Wounded Knee transcript.

I am particularly indebted to Ralston Deffenbaugh, Jr., now director of the Office on World Community of the Lutheran World Ministries, who was an observer for the Lutheran World Federation at the SWAPO trial of Aaron Mushimba and others in Namibia. Chapter 3 is his. I wrote it entirely from his materials and notes. In some places I simply used his words. Ralie, in addition to being coauthor of chapter 3, provided encouragement for the project from the start.

My loyal critic throughout has been my wife, Kathryn, from whom I have learned many things including much about writing. Finally, I value having had the opportunity to work with an editor of the stature of Irving Louis Horowitz.

Ron Christenson

1

What Is A Political Trial?

Are political trials necessary? Do they reflect something about the nature of politics and law which makes them inevitable in every society? Or are political trials a disease of both politics and law? Predictably, totalitarian regimes employ political trials—some sensational, most secret—to accomplish the obvious ends of total power: total control of a total population. Stalin's purge trials and the Nazi Peoples' Court were juridical nightmares, demonstrating that corrupted absolute power tends toward absolute self-justification. Do such "trials" have anything in common with other trials which must also be called political, including the Wounded Knee trial, the trials of the Boston Five, the Chicago Eight, and the Berrigan brothers, or even of Galileo, Joan of Arc, and Socrates? Do political trials make a positive contribution to an open and democratic society? This book concludes that they do. Political trials bring together for public consideration society's basic contradictions, through an examination of competing values and loyalties. They are not incompatible with the rule of law, and are best understood by examining the questions they raise.

Questions of Law and Politics

What is a political trial?[1] Are political trials better classified as law or as politics? If they are totally political, why have a trial? Since the courts are part of the "system," are all trials, therefore, political? Or, because in every political trial the accused is charged with a specific violation of the criminal code, are no trials political? Is the designation "political trial" pejorative, used when justice seems impossible, or is it merely descriptive, used when more is at stake in a trial than a transgression of the criminal code?

Most attempts to designate a trial as political become mired in the quicksand of motive, in the argument that the prosecution, the judge, even the entire court system, are "out to get" the defendant, or conversely, that the defendant and his lawyers are using the court as a platform in their program to undermine the legal system and accomplish their political goals. Such judgments are fine instances of the genetic fallacy. Legal and political

3

assessments, when based on a guess at motives, become quagmires. Motives are always numerous and various, and they generally operate at odds with each other. In both law and politics, however, we must make judgments. If we refuse to make judgments, believing that one motive is as good or as bad as another, we will land either in the cynical position that law is the will of the stronger and therefore all trials are political, or in the naive, Panglossian position that none are.

We might sidestep the difficulties of definition by beginning with the ingenuous assumption that we can recognize political trials when we see them. If we can point to a number of trials and say with some confidence that these, if any, are political trials, we might more easily understand the nature of law and politics that precipitates such trials. The trial of Socrates for corrupting the youth of Athens and the trial of Jesus for blasphemy and sedition are most likely to be generally recognized as political trials. We could follow these two classic examples with others: the Inquisition (both the medieval and Spanish versions), the 1431 trial of Joan of Arc for heresy and witchcraft, the 1534 trial of Thomas More for "maliciously" remaining silent when asked about Henry's supremacy in religion, the 1633 trial of Galileo for heretically suggesting that the earth moved around the sun, or the many treason and sedition libel trials in England's Puritan revolution. Are there more certain examples of political trials than those of two kings, Charles I in 1649 and Louis XVI in 1792? Would anyone suggest that the trial of the Irish patriot Robert Emmet or of the treasonist Lord Haw-Haw (William Joyce) after World War II were not political trials? What about the trials of Alfred Dreyfus, Sacco and Vanzetti, or Julius and Ethel Rosenberg?

These trials, and more, come to mind when political trials are mentioned. Most of the above defendants have come to us in the judgment of history as heroes unjustly prosecuted. Yet in each case an argument can be made that under the circumstances the prosecution was understandable, even reasonable, and the judgment sensible if not just.

In 399 B.C., while Athens was recovering from the disastrous Peloponnesian War, the democratic leaders Anytus and Meletus recognized that Socrates, who had associated with the oligarchic faction, was a threat to the postwar reconstruction. Two of his students, Alcibiades and Critias, had been ruthless while in power. Socrates, meanwhile, was undermining what small faith the youth had in democracy.[2] Likewise, Jesus presented an internal threat to Rome. Judea was difficult to govern with its mix of nationalist extremists inclined toward terror, such as the Zealots, and such religious fanatics as the Essenes or the followers of John the Baptist. The elders in the Sanhedrin, who had authority in Jewish law, regarded Jesus as a threat to the delicately balanced political relationship with the Roman governors. Further, he was a peril to Jewish law. His activities during Passover, driving the merchants and money-changers from the Temple in Jerusalem, were a forewarning to both the Sanhedrin and Rome. Removing such a troublemaker and blasphemer from the scene, one hailed by the mob as "King of Israel that cometh in the name of the Lord," could be defended as best for imperial and community interests. The full force of Rome, in fact, did move against the next generation in Jerusalem (70 A.D.).[3]

Similar sensible arguments can vindicate other notable political prosecutions. Joan was given every chance by her examiners to acknowledge that her "voices" were not superior to the authority of the church. She was admonished to return to the way of salvation but persisted in her heresy.[4] The interrogation of Thomas More was designed to secure his compliance, not his execution. Henry VIII and Thomas Cromwell desired the assent of More, the ex-chancellor, to the new policy of supremacy and to the revised order of succession after Henry's marriage to Anne Boleyn. When Henry learned that Pope Paul III had intervened by elevating More's fellow prisoner, John Fisher, to cardinal, he exploded. Only then did he set in motion the machinery that led both More and Fisher to their death.[5]

Galileo was admonished in 1616 by Cardinal Bellarmine that the church expected only obedience, not "absolute assent." He was not forbidden from entertaining his opinions as a probability or from discussing them with his peers. At his 1633 trial it was revealed to Galileo that even the inquisitor Firenzuola had "no scruple in holding firmly that the earth moves and the sun stands still." Nevertheless, the issue of the trial was not the scientific truth but the church's authority.[6]

Charles I had been waging war against Parliament, which tried him. Louis XVI, likewise, conspired and intrigued with foreign powers to bring about a war and "be really king again."[7] Robert Emmet was a leader in an insurrection which resulted in the assassination of Lord Kilwarden and Colonel Brown.[8] William Joyce collaborated with the Nazi propaganda machine.[9] Charles, Louis, Emmet, and Joyce, in different ways, all attempted to bring down the state by force.

With the perspective of time, the postwar trials of Dreyfus, Sacco and Vanzetti, and the Rosenbergs can be seen as products of hysteria: anti-Semite, antiforeign, and anticommunist. Nevertheless, at the time, highly respected leaders of opinion looked into the cases and put the weight of their influence behind the convictions. The French General Staff was intractable in its support of the court-martial of Captain Dreyfus, and the entire French society was divided. France had lost Alsace and Lorraine to Germany; Dreyfus had been born in Alsace, and it was evident that someone assigned to the General Staff had passed information to the German

Military Attaché Schwartzkoppen.[10] A distinguished committee composed of Harvard president Lowell, MIT president Stratton, and Judge Grant, advised Governor Fuller against clemency for Sacco and Vanzetti.[11] The Supreme Court, in a six-to-three decision, refused to stay the execution of the Rosenbergs.[12] President Eisenhower refused clemency, explaining that "the Rosenbergs have received the benefit of every safegaurd which American justice can provide. . . . I can only say that, by immeasurably increasing the chances of atomic war, the Rosenbergs may have condemned to death tens of millions of innocent people all over the world."[13] If the passage of time has brought the consensus of considered opinion to a different conclusion in each of these cases, we have, after all, the advantage of historical distance and hindsight.

As the Dreyfus, Sacco and Vanzetti, Rosenberg, and many other cases illustrate, political trials have served societies in crises by providing a method of righting their psychic balance. Revenge is among the most ancient and persistent of political motives. A just trial may bring the revenge cycle to a halt, but an unjust trial will encourage the wronged faction to "get even" and "right the balance," next time in their favor. In the sixteenth and seventeenth centuries the English partisans swung the pendulum of revenge, taking turns to demonstrate by trial and execution the treason of their opponents and generally ending with a show of their own perfidy.

Two trials from the French Revolution are examples of how in political trials societies seek a balance of injustice. First Louis XVI and then thousands of others were made to pay during the Reign of Terror for the sins of the ancien régime. Likewise, after the fall of Robespierre, Gracchus Babeuf and his followers in 1797, during the Directory, paid for the excesses of Robespierre's Committee of Public Safety. Louis and Babeuf were accused of treason: plotting against the revolution in one case and advocating revolution in the other, but for French society the significance of their trials reached far beyond even these expanded indictments. Louis represented the old order and was guilty of being king. "Louis must die," Robespierre told the convention trying Louis, "because the nation must live."[14] Babeuf represented the Jacobins and was guilty of being a revolutionary. In trying Babeuf the Directory sought to prove the same that Robespierre had in the trial of Louis: that Babeuf was an enemy of the people. To make their point, Babeuf was pulled through the streets to his trial in an iron cage, the same indignity the Austrians had earlier inflicted on the French.[15]

Not all political trials contrive to set up scapegoats. It is the thesis of this book that certain political trials are creative, placing before society basic dilemmas which are clarified through the trial. These trials become crystals for society. In them we can see the issues we must face and can better understand the choices we must make. But trials are not chess games which proceed according to exact rules, rigorous though the rules of evidence may be. Trials are, first and foremost, stories.

This book is written from the conviction that law is more than a system of rules. It emerges out of a tangled maze of stories. The rules are there to be found and are important. But they are found by lawyers and are important mainly for lawyers. Lawyers often set aside the stories. Law students and lawyers search for the law, even in our common-law tradition, by reading through appeals court opinions to find the rule, where the court says "We hold that. . . ." Given the vast number of cases, it becomes necessary to treat their accumulation as a code book full of holdings which become rules, and it becomes convenient to regard the one hundred-plus volumes of *Corpus Juris* as the literal embodiment of the law. Yet the wisdom of the common law is in the stories.

No matter how distilled the stories become and how thick the code books, the spirit, if not the body, of the law is in the stories. Certain stories, that is. They are the ones that shape our thinking about the dilemmas of law, influence our sense of justice, and change our morality. They do more. They provide society with a crucible for defining and refining its identity. These are the political trials. They are less useful for lawyers to build their cases upon than they are as the common possession for all society to use in clarifying what it stands for and why.

Aesop ended his stories with a moral tag. Would we remember or even care about any of his fables if they were distilled to a compendium of the moral tags? The message is contained in the tale of the frogs who asked for a king, the hare and the tortoise, the fox and the grapes, or the lion and the vixen. When we repeat an Aesopian story we can get the point across without employing the tag, and if we do want to include it we have to look it up to get it right.

What is the moral of the story of Hamlet? We learn the most from stories with no moral tag. Is there a moral to the story of John Peter Zenger, who was tried and acquitted in 1735 for seditious libel when he published articles critical of the New York governor? Seen from the lawyer's perspective the Zenger trial might carry the restriction, "good for this day only." The Zenger trial, as Leonard Levy demonstrates, is not important as a precedent.[16] The legacy of suppression continued long after Zenger's acquittal. Yet Zenger's case shaped American thinking about censorship and freedom of the press. It did more than any other single event to fix the meaning of the First Amendment. We can see even greater significance in the trials of Socrates, Jesus, Joan of Arc, and Galileo, none of which embodies legal precedents. They are vital because of their stories, not because of their rules and precedents.

The law, on the other hand, needs rules and codes. If the law were only stories, we would be lost in a house of mirrors. Wherever we looked we would see only ourselves, most of the time in grotesque distortion, and we would never find our way out. A painting without a title can pass judgment at a show, probably win a prize. While the artist may let us draw our own conclusion without the help of a tag, a judge, lawyers, and anyone concerned with law must have rules and codes in common. Art might do nicely without a canon, although this proposition itself has for centuries been an issue of dispute. The nature of law requires that it be a public standard. If it is not, it is not law.

Law is a combination of story and rule. H.L.A. Hart defines law as the union of primary and secondary rules. The primary rules give us our sense of obligation; the secondary rules correct uncertainty, provide modes for change, and offer remedies for inefficiency in the law.[17] This book will amend Hart's definition by arguing that law is the union of primary stories and secondary rules. Certain trials present stories of such consequence that society's common understanding of basic issues of politics derives from them. We change the rules of law accordingly as our understanding is revised by these stories. That is what makes the stories primary and the rules secondary. Most trials do not embody such paradigmatic and society-shaking stories. Few do, but those few present such basic dilemmas as to engage our common deliberation as a public. These trials compel us to examine our fundamental values and perhaps revise them. Such primary trials become our teachers.

We learn from political trials great and small. Certain trials, for instance the Chicago Eight trial or those of the Rosenbergs or Sacco and Vanzetti, characterize an era. We can see a generation's conflicts in one trial, and we understand the generation by understanding the trial. Other trials define a nation, and one or two—Socrates' and Jesus'—represent all Western civilization. Many other political trials, on the other hand, are mere specks when viewed against the landscape of history. The list of political trials in the appendix contains both those of world-historic primacy and those that are not. Likewise, certain chapters will give considerable attention to what might be historically insignificant trials. The Karlton Armstrong trial, for example, hardly ranks as important when set beside the trials of Thomas More, John Lilburne, or John Peter Zenger. Yet Armstrong's trial rates an entire chapter, and the others do not. Such apparently inequitable treatment implies no relativity of judgment. Some of the lesser trials provide either convenient instances or clear examples of the issues raised in political trials. The Armstrong trial is a vivid contrast to the trials of dissenters who acted from conscience, although Armstrong's defense was an indictment of the Vietnam War. The cases selected for attention in this book, in short, provide a way of untying knotty problems.

Gordius is said to have tied a knot so convoluted and tight that whoever was skillful enough to untie it would command all Asia. Many made the attempt, but none untied the knot. When Alexander the Great failed, he whipped out his sword and cut the knot.[18] Political trials present Gordian knots. While a court may cut through the issues with a rule in a sharp decision—the defendant may be convicted or acquitted—the dilemmas of responsibility, morality, representation, or legitimacy remain. The story and its dilemma continue no matter how the court decides.

This book concerns itself with political trials within the Western tradition. Given the long history of that tradition and its global influence, this is hardly a small bite. Certain features of the legal and political institutions of the West combine to produce political trials which in other traditions, such as the Chinese, would not be as clearly defined. In the Western tradition legal institutions are set against other institutions, distinguished from, although strongly influenced by, custom, morality, religion, economics, and politics. The tension between the legal and other institutions, especially the political, is further tightened in the Western tradition by the acceptance of the rule of law. The state is bound and limited by the law.[19] Those who possess power cannot use it arbitrarily. As a consequence of our relative legal autonomy plus the rule of law holding those with power accountable, political trials appear regularly and seemingly naturally. Further, political trials, as this book seeks to demonstrate, assist in the organic growth of the body of law. In crises the tension between reality and ideals, between the stable and the dynamic, between the immanent and the transcendent, produces change. Much of this change comes in courtroom confrontations when each side attempts to persuade not only the judge and jury but all society and even history. The Western legal tradition, as Harold Berman delineates it, has a built-in mechanism for change: "The law is not merely ongoing; it has a history. It tells a story."[20] If, in short, political trials are primarily a Western phenomenon, as products of a fundamental inner logic within that tradition, they are integral to it and contribute to its development.

A Typology of Political Trials

Political trials differ from ordinary trials in the questions they raise. Criminal trials with no political agenda naturally raise difficult questions of law. Matters of due process, from controversies over search and seizure or the *Miranda* rights to whether the death penalty is a cruel and unusual punishment, can hardly be dismissed as easy cases. However, ordinary cases do not involve the dual legal and political agendas that political trials simultaneously address. More precisely, ordinary trials within a constitutional framework operate from a legal agenda with only a trace, if any, of the political agenda. Conversely, partisan trials proceed according to a fully political agenda with only a façade of legality (although the legalism might be turgid). Political trials within the rule of law juggle the two agendas.

The distinction between political trials within the rule of law and partisan trials which substitute political expediency for law is not new. At root it is Aristotle's, paralleling his basic classification of constitutions. Aristotle found that a polity guided according to the common good, in which authority is exercised for the benefit of all members of society, is fundamentally different from one controlled in the interest of the rulers alone, in which those with power use it to their own advantage and not society's. Regardless of the number holding power, whether one, few, or many, the key is the purpose of power: the common good or a partisan advantage. Constitutions of the former type Aristotle called "*right* constitutions," and the latter "*wrong* constitutions, or perversions of the right forms."[21] The perverted forms are despotic, modeled after a master/slave relationship, while the right forms follow from an association of equals. So it is with political trials. Partisan trials carry the stamp of despotism, while political trials within the rule of law presume that all are equal before the law. They are fair trials despite their political agenda.

A further classification of political trials would categorize them into four types according to the basic issues of politics brought into question: (1) Trials of public responsibility. The nature of the public realm is at issue and the underlying questions are of two types: For an official in corruption cases, where is the line drawn between private life and public duty? For an accused in cases involving insanity, where is the line between actions of public responsibility and those for which a person cannot be held responsible? In both the question is what things are public and what are private? (2) Trials of dissenters. Here the correctness of both public policy and methods of dissent is at issue. The dissenter asks: Is the policy immoral? The dissenter in turn is asked: Is the dissent appropriate? (3) Trials of nationalists. A more basic issue, the nature of representation, is raised here, and the questions become: Is the government representing one people yet ruling another? Does this national group represent a distinct people? (4) Trials of regimes. The most fundamental issue of politics, the nature of legitimacy, is undertaken when one side asks: Was the former government legitimate? The other side responds by asking: Is the court legitimate?

We should note the progression from the issue of the relationship of public and private realms, to judgments about policy and dissent, to conflicts over representation, and finally to the critical matter of legitimacy. This escalation from a political trial of a rather common variety to the rare breed puts the court, the law, and the political order in increasing difficulty. Each type presents a Gordian knot tied successively tighter. The chart on the following page illustrates these types.

Political trials which proceed within the rule of law have their corresponding partisan trials. Trials of corruption can become mere trials of revenge. This is apparently what happened to Anne Boleyn and Marcus Garvey. Trials of dissenters can become a convenient way to eliminate the opposition, as the trials of Socrates, Thomas More, and others who have questioned public policy illustrates. Trials of ethnic nationalists, from the Spanish Inquisition against the Jews to the "terrorist" trials in South Africa today, can become a step in the establishment of domination or elimination. Finally, a trial of a regime has the capacity for being purely partisan, victor's justice. The issue in all partisan trials is the same: expediency in the use of power.

Any attempt to arrive at a typology involves a Procrustean effort to fit unique cases into a few pigeonholes. More than one political question can be raised in a given trial. Dissenters are often nationalists, and nationalists dissent. From John Lilburne and Peter Zenger to Lech Walesa, challengers of entrenched power raise many questions. How, for instance, should we categorize those in the Soviet Union? Some dissent on religious grounds, others for classically liberal reasons, and still others as nationalists. Yet the Soviet authorities treat them all as cases of insanity. As the director of the Institute of Forensic Psychiatry, G. Morozov, put it: "Why bother with political trials when we have psychiatric clinics?"[22] Nevertheless, to understand the nature of political trials, we must classify and arrange them in some logical order. Grouping them according to the issues they generate in the political sphere recognizes that, acknowledged or not, the political agenda is inescapably present in many trials.

Synopsis

The chapters in this book are of two types: those that explore trials raising issues of partisanism, responsibility, dissent, representation, and legitimacy, and those that take an intensive look at one trial. The latter chapters are an attempt to tell the story of a specific trial in detail. Although in the general chapters certain trials will be focused upon, they will be used as illustrations of the issues analyzed. Three trials—the SWAPO trial in 1976, Karlton Armstrong's in 1973, and the Wounded Knee trial in 1974—will provide in-depth accounts that go beyond serving as examples.

TYPES OF POLITICAL TRIALS

Trials Involving	Political Trials within the Rule of Law	Partisan Trials
PUBLIC RESPONSIBILITY	Issue: the Public Realm Questions: What is private? What is the nature of public responsibility? Corruption cases: For an official, where is the line drawn between private life and public duty? Examples: Francis Bacon (1621) Judge Otto Kerner (1973) Watergate (1973) Insanity cases: Where is the line between actions of public responsibility and those for which a person cannot be held responsible? Examples: Daniel McNaughton (1843) Charles Guiteau (1881) Dan White (1979) John Hinckley (1982)	Issue: Power and Expediency Question: Is this political revenge? Corruption cases Examples: Anne Boleyn (1536) Marcus Garvey (1925) Insanity cases Examples: Soviet psychiatric prisoners
DISSENT	Issue: Rightness of Policy, Methods of Dissent Questions: Is the policy immoral? Is the dissent appropriate? Examples: John Lilburne (1649) John Zenger (1734) Catonsville 9 (1968) Karl Armstrong (1973)	Issue: Power and Expediency Question: Is the trial designed to eliminate opposition? Examples: Socrates (399 BC) Thomas More (1532) Alfred Dreyfus (1894) Stalin Trials (1936-38)
NATIONALISTS	Issue: Representation Questions: Does the government represent all? Does the nationalist group represent a distinct people? Examples: Robert Emmet (1803) Panther 21 (1970) Wounded Knee (1974)	Issue: Power and Expediency Question: Is the trial designed to further the domination over an ethnic group? Examples: Jesus (30 AD) Joan of Arc (1431) Spanish Inquisition (1478) Sacco & Vanzetti (1921) Nelson Mandela (1962) SWAPO (Aaron Mushimba, 1976)
REGIMES	Issue: Legitimacy Questions: Was the former government legitimate? Is the court? Examples: Mary, Queen of Scots (1586) Pres. Andrew Johnson (1868) Nuremberg (1945)	Issue: Power and Expediency Question: Is this victor's justice? Examples: Charles I (1649) Louis XVI (1792) Iranian Tribunal (1980)

A partisan trial is a spurious legal proceeding but an authentic political event. Its one agenda is political, and its one purpose is expediency. The Inquisition, the Gunpowder Plot trials, the Dreyfus trial, and the trials in Hitler's Germany, Stalin's Soviet Union, and in South Africa provide examples in chapter 2 of how useful to those in power a show trial can be. In 1976 six members of the South West Africa People's Organization (SWAPO) were tried under South Africa's Terrorism Act following the assassination of Chief Elifas, a hereditary chief in Namibia. A detailed examination of this trial provides, in chapter 3, a case study of a partisan trial.

Certain trials raise the question: What is the nature of public responsibility? Where the trial involves possible corruption or other scandal, the issue requires that we draw the line between private life and public duty. Lord Chancellor Francis Bacon, tried in 1621 for taking bribes, provides the classic example, and the Watergate cases furnish recent examples. Insanity cases, especially those of assassins, raise another problem with responsibility: the difficulty of judging when a person can and cannot be held responsible. The John Hinckley and Dan White cases, as well as the trial of Charles Guiteau, who assassinated President Garfield, and the important case of Daniel McNaughton, will provide examples. This is the topic for chapter 4.

In chapter 5 the question of conscience and the law is raised. The trial of Socrates is the classic of this type, and the 1649 trial of John Lilburne demonstrates the wide diversity of issues such trials might touch. Other examples include the trials of Thomas More, Roger Williams, Anne Hutchinson, John Peter Zenger, the Boston 5, the D.C. 9, and the Berrigans. Because conscience is the focus in trials of dissenters, a frequent controversy involves jury nullification. When dissenters act out of frustration instead of conscience, as illustrated in chapter 6 with the trials of Fritz Adler (who assassinated the Austrian prime minister) and Karl Armstrong (who bombed the Army Math Computer Center at the University of Wisconsin), the argument about the immorality of the policy and the rightness of the act is undermined.

The nature of representation, the relationship of the part to the whole, arises when nationalists are tried. In chapter 7 the trial of Jesus is presented as a classic example, but other clear-cut nationalist trials include those of Joan of Arc, the Spanish Inquisition, Martin Luther, Irish nationalists, Gandhi, the Black Panthers, and Angela Davis. A detailed examination of such a trial is the topic of chapter 8, which is about the trial of Dennis Banks and Russell Means for the Wounded Knee takeover. The most difficult of all trials to rein in with the rule of law are those of regimes, the topic in chapter 9, because they undertake the most fundamental question of both law and politics: legitimacy. Such trials as those of Charles I, Louis XVI, and the Nazi leaders at Nuremberg. They take law back to its origins in the rejection of self-help and confront politics with the test of its limits in the rule of law.

The conclusion, chapter 10, will present a jurisprudence of political trials. Given the political questions that arise in political trials, what is law? Most of the dilemmas involved in political trials can be contained in the phrase *law and order*. Political trials alone will not resolve the dilemmas. But through certain political trials we may develop a sounder understanding of law, politics, and history. Political trials, by challenging us with basic tensions of politics, indirectly change both politics and law—indirectly and continually.

Notes

1. Attempts to define political trials are valuable but ultimately unsatisfying. The near-definitive work, Otto Kirchheimer's *Political Justice*, suggests that political trials are those in which "the courts eliminate a political foe of the regime according to some prearranged rules." Otto Kirchheimer, *Political Justice: The Use of Legal Procedure for Political Ends* (Princeton, Princeton University Press, 1961), p. 6: see also pp. 46-49, 419. Both Judith Shklar and Theodore Becker follow Kirchheimer's lead. Judith Shklar, *Legalism* (Cambridge, Mass., Harvard University Press, 1964), p. 149. Theodore Becker, "Introduction," in Becker, ed., *Political Trials* (Indianapolis, Bobbs-Merrill, 1971), pp. xii-xiii. For a discussion of the range of definitions of political trials, see Norman Dorsen and Leon Friedman, *Disorder in the Court: Report of the Association of the Bar of the City of New York, Special Committee on Courtroom Conduct* (New York, Pantheon, 1973), Ch. 5. See also Fowler Harper and David Haber, "Lawyer Troubles in Political Trials," *Yale Law Journal*, Vol. 60 (1951), 1-56; Nathan Hakman, "Political Trials in the Legal Order: A Political Scientist's Perspective," *Journal of Public Law*, Vol. 21 (1972), 73-125; Stephen Schafer, *The Political Criminal: The Problem of Morality and Crime* (New York, Free Press, 1974); Michal Belknap, ed., *American Political Trials* (Westport, Conn., Greenwood, 1981); Austin T. Turk, *Political Criminality: The Defiance and Defense of Authority* (Beverly Hills, Sage, 1982).
2. A.E. Taylor, *Socrates* (London, Peter Davies, 1932)), Ch. 3; I.F. Stone, "I. F. Stone Breaks the Socrates Story," *New York Times Magazine* (April 8, 1979, 22ff.
3. See Matthew 26-27; Mark 14-15; Luke 22-23; John 18-19; see also S. G. F. Brandon, *The Trial of Jesus of Nazareth* (New York, Stein & Day, 1968), Ch. 4, 5.
4. W. P. Barrett, *The Trial of Jeanne d'Arc: A Complete Translation of the Text of the Original Documents* (London, George Routledge, 1931), pp. 270-279; Albert Bigelow Paine, *Joan of Arc: Maid of France*, 2 vols. (New York, Macmillan, 1925). Vol. 2, Pt. 9, Chs. 1-27.
5. G.R. Elton, *Policy and Police: The Enforcement of the Reformation in the Age of Thomas Cromwell* (Cambridge, Cambridge University Press, 1972), pp. 400-420.

6. George de Santillana, *The Crime of Galileo* (Chicago, University of Chicago Press, 1955), Chs. 11-12.
7. Michael Walzer, ed., *Regicide and Revolution: Speeches at the Trial of Louis XVI* (Cambridge, Cambridge University Press, 1974), Ch. 5.
8. Thomas Howell (comp.), *A Complete Collection of State Trials and Proceedings for High Treason and Other Crimes and Misdemeanors from the Earliest Period to the Year 1783* (London, R. Bagshaw, 1809-1826), vol. 28, pp. 1169-78. Hereafter cited as State Trials.
9. Rebecca West, *The New Meaning of Treason* (New York, Viking, 1964).
10. Nicholas Halasz, *Captain Dreyfus: The Story of a Mass Hysteria* (New York, Simon & Schuster, 1955).
11. Felix Frankfurter, *The Case of Sacco and Vanzetti* (Boston, Little, Brown, 1962); Francis Russell, *Tragedy in Dedham: The Story of the Sacco-Vanzetti Case* (New York, McGraw-Hill, 1962); Brian Jackson, *The Black Flag* (New York, Routledge & Kegan Paul, 1981).
12. *Rosenberg v. United States*, 346 U.S. 273 (1953).
13. Walter Schneir and Miriam Schneir, *Invitation to an Inquest* (Garden City: Doubleday, 1965), p. 248. See also Ronald Radosh and Joyce Milton, *The Rosenberg File: A Search for the Truth* (New York, Holt, Rinehart, & Winston, 1983).
14. Walzer, *Regicide and Revolution*, p. 138.
15. Edmund Wilson, *To the Finland Station* (Garden City, Doubleday, 1953), p. 72. See also David Thomson, *The Babeuf Plot: The Making of a Republican Legend* (Westport, Conn., Greenwood, 1975).
16. Leonard W. Levy, *Freedom of Speech and Press in Early American History: Legacy of Suppression* (New York, Harper Torchbook, 1963), p. 133. See also Paul Finkelman, "The Zenger Case: Prototype of a Political Trial," in Belknap, ed., *American Political Trials*.
17. H. L. A. Hart, *The Concept of Law* (Oxford, Clarendon, 1963), Ch. 5.
18. Thomas Bulfinch, *Bulfinch's Mythology* (New York, Modern Library, n.d.), p. 44.
19. Harold J. Berman, *Law and Revolution: The Formation of the Western Legal Tradition* (Cambridge, Mass., Harvard University Press, 1983), pp. 7-10.
20. Ibid., p. 9.
21. Aristotle, *Politics*, Bk.3, Ch. 6, Sec. 11, trans. by Ernest Barker (New York, Oxford, 1958), p. 112.
22. Zhores Medvedev and Roy Medvedev, *A Question of Madness* (New York, Knopf, 1971), p. 67.

2

Partisan Trials:
The Question of Expediency

In 1717 a satirical poem directed at the late Louis XIV, his mistress, and the new regent made the rounds of French society. One day, while the 22-year-old Voltaire was sauntering through the royal gardens, he happened upon the regent, the Duke of Orleans, who challenged him:

> I bet you, M. Arouet, I will show you something you have never seen before.
>
> What is that, Monseigneur?
>
> The inside of the Bastille.
>
> I take it as seen.

The next morning Voltaire was awakened by an official who served him with a *lettre de cachet*, searched his room thoroughly, arrested him, and hustled him off to the Bastille. He was not allowed to contact family members, friends, or a lawyer. For eleven months Voltaire was kept in the infamous prison, neither charged with a crime nor tried.[1]

Had the regent been as swift to try Voltaire in a fair trial as he was to arrest him, he and the other authorities would have learned that, contrary to the report from their spy Beauregard, Voltaire was not the author of the offending poem. On the other hand, had the brilliant young playwright been subjected to a partisan trial, the result would have been a long term in the Bastille. A partisan trial, in all likelihood, would not have discovered that Voltaire did not write the satire. He was capable of writing it; he had written other imprudent and impudent verses, and he might have written it. For a partisan trial, as for indefinite detention without a trial under the *lettre de cachet*, the truth, guilt, or innocence is irrelevant. A partisan trial, for the purposes of justice, is the same as no trial at all. But partisan trials do serve other purposes.

Partisan trials have only one agenda, power, and one issue, expediency, which serves as the substitute for justice. They are outside the rule of law, often enveloped within an ideological wonderland. If most ordinary trials

16

operate from a legal agenda with no political overtones, partisan trials are the opposite: only a political agenda covered with a thin veneer of legality.

Inquisitorial Procedure

The Inquisition, it should be no surprise, is a prototype of the partisan trial. To the inquisitor, "eager to destroy the foxes which ravaged the vineyard of the Lord," H.C. Lea observes, "the task of exploring the secret heart of man was no easy one." Recognized judicial procedure, which might prevent injustice and discover the truth, necessarily was set aside. It was replaced by the inquisitor's assumption of omniscience. "Human frailty, resolved to accomplish a predetermined end, inevitably reached the practical conclusion that the sacrifice of a hundred innocent men was better than the escape of one guilty."[2]

Inquisitorial procedure was simple. If simplicity and certainty are legal virtues, partisan trials come with high recommendation. The inquisitorial process began with an oath, a promise to answer all questions asked, to betray all heretics known, and to perform all penance imposed. Refusal to take the oath revealed that the person was a heretic, defiant and obstinate, who required correction. Although not all heretics were easily discovered at the point of the oath, this first step was a big one. The English adopted the practice in the Star Chamber procedures employed by the Tudor and Stuart regimes. Its abuse there prompted the framers of the American constitutional system to insure against the inquisitorial oath in state bill of rights and in the Fifth Amendment's protection against self-incrimination.[3]

After the oath came the confession. A person mentioned in a prisoner's confession as a heretic would be the subject of a secret investigation. When evidence was collected against this next person, by now prejudged as guilty, he or she would be arrested or summoned to appear. Then the process would begin another cycle with the inquisitorial oath.

If either impenitent or caught in a heresy at the examination, the prisoner would be delivered to the secular authority for execution. But the confession was encouraged because it was central to the inquisitorial process. With it came conversion and repentance. The indispensable proof of sincerity, although not of truth, in the confession was the repentant heretic's willingness, even eagerness, to denounce others as suspect heretics, especially a pure-hearted betrayal of family and friends. Refusal to name names showed the heretic was undeserving of mercy.[4]

The prisoner of the Inquisition was interrogated and pressured to prove his or her sincerity. Yet the opposite virtue was the mark of a skillful inquisitor. Deceit and torture were tools an inquisitor could employ without scruple to produce a confession. The examiner might, for instance, pretend to read from pages of evidence or tell the prisoner that others have incriminated him. A jailer might use what is now called the "Mutt and Jeff technique" of feigning compassion, urging the prisoner to confess because the inquisitor is merciful and will take pity on him. The inquisitor might promise that after a full confession the prisoner will be allowed to return home, all done with the mental reservation that whatever is done for the conversion of heretics is merciful and that all penances are mercies. Spies could be employed, or the prisoner might find his or her family admitted to the cell to overcome reticence. A prisoner refusing the confession desired by the inquisitor might be sent back to the cell for an indeterminate time— days, weeks, months, years, even decades. In 1319 a Guillem Salavert, for example, was brought forth for sentencing after making unsatisfactory confessions in 1299 and 1316. Apparently his 1319 version met the inquisitorial standards of acceptability because his penance took into account his twenty years' imprisonment. Finally, torture, which saved the trouble and expense of long imprisonment, could be used to secure a speedy confession.[5]

Heresy itself was difficult to spot with any certainty. For this reason a new crime was invented by the Inquisition that was easier to recognize and more certain: suspicion of heresy. Trying the suspicion of heresy made such straight sailing for the Inquisition that it could be divided into three recognizable degrees: light or simple, vehement, and violent suspicion. Entering the house of a known heretic, for instance, could escalate a light suspicion into a vehement one.

Evidence of heresy, including rumor and gossip, would be sought out and carefully recorded. While the tales of an informer and floating chatter might not provide solid proof of heresy, they were the substance of suspicion of heresy. Senator Joseph McCarthy did not invent his techniques.

Obstacles on the path of conviction were removed by holding that a witness could revoke his or her testimony if it had been favorable to the prisoner, but if it had been adverse, the revocation was null. While for ordinary crimes witnesses had to be of good repute, for heresy and its suspicion the Inquisition knew no standards. Overall, the inquisitor held to the assumption that whatever could not be explained favorably would be taken as adverse proof. In probing the heart of a heretic or a suspected heretic, the inquisitor operated with such wide discretion that, as H. C. Lea put it, his "temper had more to do with the result than proof of guilt or its absence."[6]

Gunpowder Plot Trials

The early-1950s were not the only McCarthy era. Other ages, when international threats produced internal intrigue and witch hunts, have had partisan trials to cinch the benefits of foiling and trying insidious conspirators. Such partisan trials make truth the cat's paw of power.

A clear example is in the use made of the 1605 Gunpowder Plot by the Stuart regime. There was a plot against the life of King James, and it nearly succeeded. But the trial of the plotters had a sequel which served the regime's interests fully. England's rivals were the other two superpowers of the time, Spain and France. To those running England, Catholicism was a subversive un-English ideology. Jesuits were the agents of a vast international conspiracy against England. The plots that William Cecil (Lord Burghley), Elizabeth's close advisor, and his son Robert Cecil (the Earl of Salisbury), James's advisor, each saw against the crown were real enough. The plots involving Ridolphi and Thomas Howard, the Duke of Norfolk, Babington and Mary, Queen of Scots, the Earl of Essex and Sir Walter Raleigh, contained elements of genuine treason. They followed a pattern, as C. Northcote Parkinson demonstrates: a nucleus of conspirators with contacts in Spain or France, a public crisis putting the monarch in danger, a timely intervention, and a public trial and execution. "Each plot," Parkinson concludes, "was put to good use by those in power."[7]

The Gunpowder Plot, far more ominous than the others, followed the pattern exactly. Guy Fawkes was captured in the most dramatic fashion: outside the door leading to a cellar directly beneath the throne in the House of Lords near midnight on November 4, 1605, the eve of King James's speech from the throne. In the cellar the guards found thirty-six barrels of gunpowder hidden under some coal and wood, enough gunpowder to destroy the entire House of Lords, killing everyone assembled, including James I. Fawkes, moreover, was carrying certain incriminating items: pieces of kindling, a fuse, a lighted dark lantern, and in an age when hardly anyone carried one, a watch. He was hustled off to Whitehall for an interrogation by Robert Cecil, by other members of the Privy Council, and by King James himself in the royal bedroom. Although Fawkes readily admitted his intention—swearing in a rage that had he been discovered in the cellar he would have blown up the House of Lords, the guards, and himself—he nevertheless gave his name as John Johnson and refused to name others.

Fawkes's refusal to cooperate with his interrogators provided his accomplices two days' time to make their escape from London. Gradually, after the use of torture, Fawkes confessed the details of the plot and the names of the others involved. The sheriff of Worcestershire caught them riding west toward Wales. Four leaders were killed in a fight, and the others were either arrested then or captured soon.

After the survivors were returned to London and the Tower, they confessed fully to the plot. They readily admitted their own guilt, as Fawkes had, and admitted that they were Catholics. Nevertheless, they were interrogated much longer than would seem necessary. Robert Cecil delayed their trial until he had obtained evidence which would incriminate a priest, or better yet, a Jesuit. After two months of questioning in the Tower, during which the plotters denied any such suggestion, the one servant among them, Thomas Bates, avowed something which proved to be the wedge Cecil needed. It was enough for Cecil to order the arrest of the superior of English Jesuits, Fr. Henry Garnet.[8] It was the only wedge Cecil found, but it proved large enough. We will return to Fr. Garnet.

The Gunpowder Plot nearly succeeded. Had it done so, it would have killed James I, members of the royal family, noble lords, and members of the House of Commons. The plot failed because Cecil had been tipped off. He read a mysterious letter that Lord Monteagle, a Catholic, received. It advised Monteagle, "as yowe tender youer lyf to devyse some excuse to shift youer attendance at this parleament for god & man hath concurred to punish the wickedness of this tyme." It warned "they shall receyve a terrible blowe this parleament and yet they shall not seie who hurt them." Finally, it instructed him to burn the letter. He did not burn it but took it immediately to Cecil. A few days later the guards caught Fawkes outside the cellar door at the House of Lords.[9]

A dozen days after Bates had implicated Fr. Garnet and the Jesuits—after, that is, Cecil got the anti-Catholic wedge he wanted—Fawkes, Bates, and the six other conspirators were put on trial in Westminster Hall. They were the survivors of thirteen who had earlier laid the plot. The original central figure was a major landholder from Warwickshire, Robert Catesby, who had been killed in the battle after the plot had been discovered. Killed with him was Thomas Percy, a friend of the royal family who, had the gunpowder exploded as planned, was to have kidnapped five-year-old Prince Charles. John and Christopher Wright, friends and former schoolmates of Fawkes, had been involved with Catesby in the 1601 Essex plot. They were also killed in the battle with the sheriff. Francis Tresham, a cousin of Catesby's, died in the Tower a month before the trial. Since his sister was Lord Monteagle's wife, he might have been the author of the tip-off letter.[10]

A controversy in the aftermath of the Gunpowder Plot, similar to ones that followed the Sacco and Vanzetti and the Rosenberg trials, is whether or not Guy Fawkes and the others were framed. Fr. John Gerard, S.J., wrote in 1897 *What Was the Gunpowder Plot?* He argued that the traditional story was false, that Cecil, the Earl of Salisbury, invented the entire plot to pin it on the Jesuits and all Roman Catholics. The noted historian Samuel Gardiner, in the same year answered Gerard with *What Gunpowder Plot Was*, a point-for-point analysis of the accusation that Salisbury originated the plot for his own purposes. Gardiner concluded that the traditional account, that the plot was the work of Catesby, Fawkes, and the others, was sound. Gardiner found that, while the government acted, in the main, in a straightforward manner, its theory that the Jesuits originated the plot "was undoubtedly false." Fr. Garnet and the other Jesuits probably knew about the plot and "did not look upon it with extraordinary horror, neither did they take such means as were lawful and possible to avert the disaster," but the plot itself was real enough. Parkinson, on the other hand, marshals evidence that the Monteagle letter was actually Cecil's, written after a betrayal of Catesby by Percy and produced at Monteagle's door dramatically in time for Fawkes to be arrested on the eve of the king's speech. Cecil then arranged to doublecross Percy by having him silenced when he was not taken alive.[11] While it is difficult to conclude that Fawkes and the others were framed in the Gunpowder Plot, it is equally difficult to ignore the partisan use Cecil made of the plot against the Jesuits and the Roman Catholics of England.

The eight who were tried were Ambrose Rockwell, at twenty-seven the head of an ancient and wealthy Suffolk family that had never left the Catholic faith; Sir Everard Digby, also at twenty-seven one of the largest landholders in the Eastern Midlands; Robert and Thomas Winter, two brothers in their thirties, cousins of Catesby and Tresham; John Grant, a Warwickshire Catholic married to a sister of the Winter brothers; Robert Keyes, related by marriage to Rockwood; Thomas Bates, Catesby's servant; and finally, Guy Fawkes, the technical expert, a former Protestant from York who had learned his skills with explosives during his years as a volunteer in the Spanish army.[12]

Together, the thirteen conspirators were young (only Percy was over forty), wealthy, and connected to each other by family or, in Bate's case, employment. Only Fawkes and Digby were outsiders. Most had been involved in one or more of the treasonous plots. Catesby, the two Wrights, Grant, Tresham, and, interestingly, Monteagle were part of the 1601 Essex rebellion. Catesby, Christopher Wright, Thomas Winter, Fawkes, and again Monteagle were part of a 1602 intrigue to arrange with Phillip III for Spain to invade England. Monteagle, however, became an ardent supporter of the king when James I took the throne in 1603.[13] Cecil's agents were undoubtedly keeping a close eye on all. Perhaps to demonstrate his loyalty Monteagle hurried to Cecil when he received the mysterious letter, which may not have been a surprise to Cecil.

When the indictment was read at the opening of the trial, the first persons named as "false traitors" were Fr. Henry Garnet and two other Jesuits, who were not on trial. After the Jesuits the eight actually on trial were listed. Garnet and the other Jesuits were given top billing as the evil

geniuses who "did maliciously, falsely, and traitorously move and persuade" Fawkes and the others that "the king, nobility, clergy, and whole
community of the realm of England (papists excepted) were heretics . . .
accursed and excummunicate . . . and that it was lawful and meritorious to
kill our said sovereign lord the king, and all other heretics" to advance and
enlarge the authority and jurisdiction of the bishop of Rome and restore
the Romish religion to England. This was Cecil's wedge. Fr. Garnet is
mentioned in the indictment twelve times, nearly as often as those on
trial.[14]

Attorney General Sir Edward Coke, in our day regarded as the preeminent jurist of English common law, was the prosecutor. The Gunpowder
Trial was not the first time he had served as the royal hatchetman. In the
cabals at court Coke lined up with Cecil and even married into his family.
Coke had cooperated with the Earl of Essex in the 1594 prosecution of Dr.
Roderigo Lopez, Queen Elizabeth's physician, a foreigner and a Jew, one
who appears to have been suitable for framing as part of a Spanish plot to
poison the queen. The Lopez trial helped Essex demonstrate that he was
vigilant and that the threats from Spain, Catholics, and Jews were real.
"Worse than Judas himself," Prosecutor Coke cried as he trounced on
Lopez at the trial.[15] When Essex, in turn, was tried for his rebellion and
when Sir Walter Raleigh was tried in a scandalous proceeding for treason in
conspiracy with Spain to put Arabella Stuart on the throne, Coke again was
the prosecutor. In the Raleigh trial (1603) Coke indulged in regretable
tactics and bombast, at one point denouncing Raleigh as "the absolutest
Traitor that ever was."[16]

Coke's experience in persuading judges and juries that treason can be a
vague matter of intention and that evidence of treason could be equally
insubstantial served him well in the Gunpowder trial. Undoubtedly, Guy
Fawkes and his fellow conspirators could have been convicted on any definition of treason, narrow or wide. They had all worked diligently to position thirty-six kegs of gunpowder directly beneath the throne, and they
were caught red-handed. But Coke, and behind him Cecil, reached for
more than the conviction of the Gunpowder eight. He pushed the definition of treason far beyond what he needed, and he painted a picture of
treason more vividly than necessary to convict the eight in the dock:

> It is treason to imagine or intend the death of the king, queen, or prince. For
> treason is like a tree whose root is full of poison, and lieth secret and hid
> within the earth, resembling the imagination of the heart of man, which is so
> secret as God only knoweth it. Now the wisdom of the law provideth for the
> blasting and nipping, both of the leaves, blossoms, and buds which proceed
> from this root of Treason; either by words, which are like to leaves, or by
> some overt act, which may be resembled to buds or blossoms, before it

cometh to such fruit and ripeness, as would bring utter destruction and desolation upon the whole state.

He probably surprised no one when he identified that such roots were "all planted and watered by Jesuits and the English Romish Catholicks."[17]

In Coke's tale of the Gunpowder Plot the gunpowder activities were a subplot to a theme of Jesuit provocation. Some believe, he claimed, that the lay Catholics were "either desperate in estate or base . . . without religion, without habitation, without credit, without means, without hope." On the contrary, they were "gentlemen of good homes, excellent part, howsoever most perniciously seduced, abused, corrupted, and jesuited." Others have the opinion that the conspirators were men without religion, but, charged Coke, "I never yet knew a treason without a Romist priest." In this plot, he asserted, "there are very many jesuits . . . seducing jesuits; men that use the reverence of religion, yea, even the most sacred and blessed name of Jesus, as a mantle to cover their impiety, blasphemy, treason and rebellion, and all manner of wickedness. . . . Concerning this sect, their studies and practices principally consist of two *dd's*, to wit, in deposing of kings, and disposing of kingdoms."[18]

Robert Catesby, the leader of the plot, had been instructed in the conspiracy, according to Coke's version, by Jesuits who told him that it was "both lawful and meritorious." With Thomas Bates's statement given under interrogation in the Tower, Cecil and Coke had the link between Catesby and the Jesuits that they wanted. When, as Coke told the story, Catesby suspected his servant, Bates, knew about the plot against the king, Catesby took Bates in, swearing him to secrecy and requiring him to receive the sacrament and to go to confession with Fr. Tesmond, a Jesuit. The priest, according to Coke, told Bates to keep the plot a secret, that it was for a good cause, "and thereupon the Jesuit gave him absolution."[19] The eight in the dock accused of the Gunpowder Plot offered no defense, were found guilty, and were hanged.

In the followup trial of March 1606, Cecil and Coke delivered their knockout punch. The trial of Fr. Henry Garnet allowed Coke to amplify the warning about the Catholic and Jesuit threat. It began with a reading of the overblown indictment from the Guy Fawkes trial. Coke reviewed the various plots against Queen Elizabeth, the invasion by the Spanish Armada, as well as the Gunpowder Plot, blaming them all on Catholics led by Jesuits. Apart from Coke's diatribe, the trial reveals that Fr. Garnet knew about the plot against King James, but his defense was that he was bound to keep the secrets of confession. When asked "if someone confessed today that he meant to kill the king tomorrow, would he conceal it," Fr. Garnet responded that he would. When accused of being in secret league with

Catesby, Fr. Garnet replied that he did what he could to stop the plotters and "went into Warwickshire with a purpose to dissuade Mr. Catesby." After further questioning Fr. Garnet said, "My lord, I would to God I had never known of the Powder-Treason."[20] Garnet's equivocation and his defense of equivocation found reflection in *Macbeth*, which dates from the summer of 1606. The porter enters to answer the door:

> Knock, knock! Who's there, in the devil's name? Faith here's an equivocator, that could swear in both the scales against either scale; who committed treason enough for God's sake, yet could not equivocate to heaven: O, come in equivocator [Act II, scene 3].

Cecil's agenda for the trial was clear. He could use the trial to pin all of England's difficulties on Catholics led by Jesuits. He revealed his intentions in a letter:

> Whether Garnet lives or dies is a small matter, the important thing is to demonstrate the iniquity of Catholics, and to prove to all the world that it is not for religion but for their treasonable teaching and practices that they should be exterminated. It is expedient to make manifest to the world how far these men's doctrinal practice reacheth into the bowels of treason, and so, for ever after stop the mouths of their calumniation that preach and print our laws to be executed for difference in point of conscience.[21]

Garnet was convicted and executed. One side saw him as a martyr who refused to reveal a secret confided to him in confession, but the other side held the levers of power and was able to use the trial as prime anti-Catholic propaganda, placing Fr. Garnet in a Mephistophelian role. The Lord Chief Justice spoke to Fr. Garnet toward the end of his trial, summing up more the expedient dictum than any conclusion derived from the evidence: "You are in every particular of this action, and directed and commanded the actors: nay, I think verily you were the chief that moved it."[22]

Coke's extended metaphor that treason is a tree with poison roots that bears the fruit of destruction and desolation itself bore tyrannical fruit seventy-two years later. Among the consequences of claiming that the Gunpowder Plot was the work of Catholics led by Jesuits was the Popish Plot of 1678. Anti-Catholic sentiment in the 1670s was stirred by fears of a strong France and of a return to "Popery" when James, Duke of York, took the throne. A reign of terror against Catholics was initiated by Titus Oates, who presented a pack of lies as the Popish Plot. As Oates told it, he had a scoop on a vast conspiracy to murder King Charles II, invite a French invasion, massacre Protestants, and establish the Roman Catholic Church in England. Parliament and most of the public believed Oates, many in

Parliament because it conveniently served the Whig cause and many of the public because it looked like another Gunpowder Plot caught just in time. While Oates became a hero and was granted a lifetime pension, Catholics were persecuted. The infamous Judge George Jeffreys of the Bloody Assizes presided over the trials. Fourteen went to their death on the perjured testimony of Titus Oates.[23]

The Dreyfus Case

The most important partisan trial of modern times is the Dreyfus case. In 1894 the French General Staff discovered that the German military attaché in Paris had come into possession of various secret documents. Captain Alfred Dreyfus, who had been assigned to the General Staff, was arrested and tried by court martial, condemned, and exiled for life to Devil's Island.

The truth, which we now know, is that Count Ferdinand Walsin-Esterhazy, a major in the French Army, had sold the documents to the Germans. But the General Staff pounced on Dreyfus, who was from Alsace and a Jew, as the spy. Major Herbert Henry ignored evidence implicating his friend Esterhazy, forged documents that he placed in Dreyfus's file, and leaked "information" to the anti-Semitic newspaper *La Libre Parole*. Evidence emerged revealing that Esterhazy was the spy, a year and a half after Dreyfus had been arrested, but the army suppressed it and discharged Lt. Colonel Georges Picquart who had uncovered it. When Picquart showed General Charles Gonse his discovery that Dreyfus was innocent, the general replied: "For me truth is what the Minister of War and the Chief of the General Staff tell me is true. If you keep silent, no one need find out anything."[24]

That Alfred Dreyfus was finally exonerated fully and restored to his military position was due to the persistence of Picquart; the dogged work by Alfred's brother, Mathieu; the exposé, *J'Accuse!*, written by Emile Zola and published by George Clemenceau; and the massive political effort by the Dreyfusards led by Clemenceau. France had not been so divided since the French Revolution a century earlier. As the Gunpowder Plot proved to be a prelude to the 1640 Puritan Revolution, so the Dreyfus Affair offers, as Hannah Arendt characterizes it in her *Origins of Totalitarianism*, "a foregleam of the twentieth century."[25]

For arriving at the truth, as the Garnet and the Dreyfus trials demonstrate, a partisan trial is worse than no trial at all. That, of course, is exactly what makes such a trial useful. Guilt, innocence, the truth, and the rule of law are irrelevant. What is relevant in a partisan trial, and the only relevant agenda, is political expediency. Expediency can manufacture a lie that those in power can market as a substitute for truth. Fr. Garnet could be billed in the show trial as the evil mastermind of a deep-laid Jesuit intrigue. Because all Catholics would blindly follow the Jesuit lead, all Catholics could be suspect. The actual events of the Gunpowder Plot and the activities of Guy Fawkes and his fellow conspirators became secondary to the machinations of Fr. Garnet. Until the truth in the Dreyfus case was finally unearthed, Captain Dreyfus was cast by the anti-Semite faction in the same demoniacal role.

Such trials become overheated kitchens for innovative partisan chefs. A teaspoon of evidence which may be true will be blended with a barrel of "facts" and assumptions made up for the occasion. The mixture is allowed to rise in the heat of an exaggerated public imagination. After baking in an indictment, it is served up with official decorum at the trial. Bates's mention of his confession was all Cecil and Coke needed to prove the treason of Jesuits and the "iniquity of Catholics." In the Dreyfus case the anti-Semite cause had even less than that in the cupboard. After Dreyfus was arrested he was required to provide endless samples of his handwriting. One small piece of writing which could compare with the itemized list of documents written by the spy and given to the German attaché was all they needed to convict Dreyfus. After a week of writing Dreyfus had not demonstrated that his handwriting was the spy's. The experts identified every scribble from Dreyfus as his, and every bit that was not his was also properly identified. Further, during an exhaustive questioning Dreyfus did not slip-up even once. All this lack of evidence might have been conclusive of Dreyfus's innocence in a trial within the rule of law. But in a partisan trial it became conclusive of his guilt. The prosecutor cited it as proof that Dreyfus was a supercriminal, clever and without a conscience, unable to be undone, as lesser criminals would be, under intense questioning.[26] It showed "how dangerous he must be."

The Hitler and Stalin Trials

Hitler operated from the premise that the big lie needed a dash of truth to give it the flavor of credibility, but, given that, the people would more easily swallow a big lie than a little lie. Hitler and Goering were angered when the German Supreme Court acquitted three of the four Communist defendants accused of setting the Reichstag Fire in 1933.[27] The Supreme Court decision led Hitler and the Nazi leaders to ensure that henceforth jurisdiction over political crimes, those involving "insidious attacks against the government," were removed from the ordinary courts to special courts. In 1934 an additional court was established by Hitler and Goering, the notorious Peoples' Court, controlled by the Nazi Party and the Gestapo.

Clearly instruments of terror and propaganda, five of the seven Peoples' Court judges were chosen from the party, the S. S., or the military. Defense lawyers were "qualified" Nazis who seemed resolved to outdo the prosecution in castigating the accused. The Queen of Hearts, best known for her shrieks, "sentence first, verdict afterwards," and "off with her head," was a wise jurist compared with Nazi judge Roland Freisler. No appeals were allowed. Rather, Hitler and Goering retained the right to quash the criminal proceedings in the event the result were unfavorable.[28] Partisan courts such as the Peoples' Court operate at the center of propaganda and on the fringe of terror, waging psychological warfare more against the entire population than against the accused on trial.

In the trials following the Russian Revolution, continuing throughout the Stalin era, the courts operated on the premise that under the new revolutionary order the question of guilt was irrelevant. Guilt was itself declared to be a bourgeois concept, unworthy of the new order of justice. N.V. Krylenko, the prosecutor general, sculptured, as he put it, "a new law and new ethical norms." The tribunal became "an organ of the class struggle of the workers directed against their enemies," acting in the "interests of the revolution . . . having in mind *the most desirable results* for the masses of workers and peasants." Defendants are "carriers of specific ideas," and the court must recognize this fact in judging a defendant: "*Only one* method of evaluating him is to be applied: evaluation from the point of view of class expediency." Individual guilt is replaced by class expediency. "We protect ourselves," Krylenko concluded, "not only against the past but also against the future."[29]

Roland Freisler in Nazi Germany and N.V. Krylenko in Stalin's U.S.S.R. were mistaken if they thought that their jurisprudence was new or that their courts could create a new order. It is more accurate to say that their legal standard, expediency, was the oldest law. In a crisis or tyranny it is the most commonplace. In all circumstances it is the most tedious. It is not new, however. Freisler and Krylenko do not give us a creative idea about law, only a restatement of the operative motto of all tyrannies: justice is the interest of the stronger. The people of the small island of Melos faced this standard when powerful Athens demanded that they submit or be destroyed. The Athenians state the principle of Freisler and Krylenko advocated with flat clarity: "The standard of justice depends on the equality of power to compel and that in fact the strong do what they have the power to do and the weak accept what they have to accept."[30]

The one-sidedness of a partisan trial and its lack of contradiction encloses it within an ideological wonderland, not too different from what Alice found. In challenging the prosecution at a partisan trial, the accused stands no chance of seriously contesting the indictment, much less persuading the court. Nikolai Bukharin, for example, was charged with leading a conspiratorial group (the bloc of rightists and Trotskyites) to sabotage and dismember the U.S.S.R. and undermine its defense capacity. In the 1938 show trial, Bukharin challenged public prosecutor Andri Vyshinsky's strategy of using those in the dock to verify the "evidence" presented during the preliminary investigation. Bukharin wedged his protest between the demand that he cooperate as a condition for being allowed to appear in court and his desire that he set his political ideas on record for future generations. Although he was cut short by Vyshinsky whenever, by way of his confession, he explained his heretical views, he was the only defendant who refused to play the evil conspirator role cast for him. Even then, Bukharin was only partially successful, for, as George Katkov concludes, "in the process he found himself ensnared in a net of equivocation and ambiguous phrases, so that instead of defending what he believed to be the truth, he upheld that most powerful weapon of the very tyranny to which he had fallen victim—institutionalized mendacity."[31]

The legacy of partisan justice under Stalin, part of the long tradition from the czars, continues on in Soviet psychoprisons. Trials, after all, can result in courtroom challenges such as at Bukharin's trial or at the trial of writers Andrei Sinyavsky (Abram Tertz) and Yuli Daniel (Nicolai Arzhak) in 1966.[32] Much safer for the police state is partisan psychology. A sane person who opposes the system puts his or her word against the state's. One side is wrong or at fault, and it might be the state. But if the dissident is mad, no one can be blamed, certainly not the state. Challenging the authorities over a question of truth or justice becomes a symptom of a paranoid personality. A leading Soviet psychiatrist suggested that "dissidence may be caused by brain disease."[33] Zhores Medvedev, a biochemist, was diagnosed as suffering from "incipient schizophrenia" and "paranoid delusions of reforming society." His split personality was manifested in his combining scientific and publicist work, in his overestimation of his personality, and in his poor adaption to the social environment.[34] Andrei Sakharov, Soviet officials declared in 1984, is "a talented, but sick man." The evidence, of course, is in his article published in America urging a buildup of nuclear weapons in the West. He was sent into exile to Gorky "for his own peace of mind." There he will receive the proper Soviet medical attention: "Soviet medics are taking all necessary measures to restore his health."[35]

Soon after Sakharov was sent into exile his wife, Yelena Bonner, was tried for "slandering the Soviet state." Her defense lawyer was selected by the KGB, and the trial was in a courtroom from which her friends and relatives were excluded but which was packed with KGB personnel who uttered abuse about her.[36] Whether dissidents are declared mentally ill and punished by partisan psychotreatment or are sent through partisan courts and punished as political offenders, the result is the same. Soviet law operates with a dual system. Ordinary crimes are handled by courts within a rule of law, but political prosecution is carried out with prerogative justice. Police states are dual states: a prerogative state operates with arbitrary standards with political expediency as its aim, while coexisting with it is an ordinary state guided by formal rules in nonpolitical cases.[37] The formalism of the ordinary courts provides a quasi rule of law for daily conflicts and regular crimes. The dual state reflects the accepted and safe attitude of authoritarianism: A good citizen will attend to his or her job and family while allowing all political matters to be taken care of by the authorities. Justice can be expected in the ordinary courts for ordinary cases, but when a political question arises the prerogative courts will provide only partisan justice. This dualism in the law was as characteristic of the Tudor-Stuart government as it is of the Soviet. By excluding the political cases from the rule of law such regimes shut their eyes to anything they might learn from those who challenge them, refusing to acknowledge that dissidents might be able to teach society. In the long run this might be the Achilles' heel of authoritarianism. Partisan justice does not teach, only propagandize.

South African Trials

South Africa today provides all too many examples of both internment without trial and partisan show trials. The Terrorism Act allows any police officer above the rank of lieutenant colonel to detain indefinitely anyone he has reason to believe is a terrorist or has information about terrorists. Under this law, as Section 6.5 provides, "no court of law shall pronounce upon the validity of any action taken under this section, or order the release of any detainee."[38] Other laws, such as the Internal Security Act, allow the minister of justice to ban or detain for 180 days whomever he "is satisfied" constitutes a danger to "the security of the State or the maintenance of public order."[39] These South African versions of the *lettre de cachet* (incidentally, not the only point of resemblance to prerevolutionary France) permit the government to silence its critics as well as stop revolutionaries by putting any of its opponents away quietly.

We have no way of learning exactly how many people in South Africa are at any one time being held incommunicado under the Terrorism Act and its several legal look-alikes. The figures offered by the minister of law and order are under some suspicion, but in 1983 he told Parliament that since 1967 a total of 4,140 have been in detention. The records kept by the Institute of Race Relations and the Council of Churches put the annual number of detainees at 453,[40] and some suggest it is much higher. We do know that many of those detained are Black leaders, journalists, trade unionists, churchmen, teachers, and students. We also come to know, after the fact, the names of those who die in detention, in the hands, perhaps at the hands, of the Security Police. Steve Biko, a founder of the South African Student Organization (SASO) and a leader of the Black Peoples' Convention (BPC), and Dr. Neil Aggett are two of the fifty or seventy-five who have died while held incommunicado, and we know of the circumstances of their deaths only because of persistent inquiry.[41]

If the Security Police, without being checked by the courts, may subject whomever they wish to an indefinite detention, why have a trial at all? South Africa, certainly, has had a number of celebrated trials, such as the 1956–1961 Treason Trial when ninety-one were put on trial, the 1964 Rivonia Trial of Nelson Mandela and other African National Congress (ANC) leaders, or the 1976 trial of the SASO/BPC leaders. There have been frequent less celebrated trials and always the possibility of a trial. Although such trials under the Terrorism Act or Internal Security Act are notable for their partisan quality, not all of those accused are convicted. The five-year Treason Trial ended in 1961 with an acquittal. Nelson Mandela, on the other hand, has spent the past two decades in the infamous Robben Island after his conviction. The answer to the question of why have a trial at all will best be found in a close-up examination of a trial. That is the topic for the next chapter.

It should be noted, before we make a careful inquiry into a given trial, that South Africa, perhaps because of its deep divisions within, has had a history of partisan trials. Until the party of the Afrikaners took over in 1948, Afrikaners were frequently the defendants. These trials are now looked back upon with nationalistic reverence, for they give evidence to the Afrikaners that they were a persecuted nation. In 1815 a frontiersman, Frederick Bezuidenhout, was summoned by the British authorities to answer charges of cruelty in his treatment of a Khoi servant. In the attempt to arrest him Bezuidenhout was killed while he resisted. The incident prompted a revolt against the British. After the revolt of frontiersmen was suppressed, a two-judge Special Commission banished thirty-two of the rebels from the Eastern Cape and sentenced six to be hanged at Slagter's Nek.[42] They are now Afrikaner martyrs.

After the Boer War at the turn of the century, the bitter-enders among the Afrikaners resented the decision of the South African government, led by former generals and Afrikaner moderates Louis Botha and Jan Smuts, to enter World War I on the side of the hated British. When the Afrikaner diehards' revolt of 1914 was put down, most of the leaders received mild sentences. But a minor leader, Jopie Fourie, who had been in the South

African defense force, was sentenced to death. In his address to the court Fourie recalled the Slagter's Nek executions and foretold his own role as an Afrikaner martyr: "The little tree planted today and watered with my blood will grow and bring forth wonderful fruit for our people."[43]

During World War II former Olympic boxer and popular Afrikaner Robey Liebbrandt went to Germany for training, returned to South Africa in a German submarine, and attempted to organize the overthrow of the government. He was convicted of treason and sentenced to death. Ironically, Liebbrandt's trial itself may have helped in accomplishing his objective: Smut's government in 1948 was voted out of office, the Nationalist Party was voted in, and the key issue was the decision to enter the war on the side of the British. Soon after the Nationalist Party took over, Liebbrandt was released.[44]

The Afrikaner nationalists turned the tables in 1948. Since then most of the significant trials have been of African nationalists. It is to one of those trials that we now turn.

Notes

1. See S. G. Tallentrye, *The Life of Voltaire*, 2 vols. (London, Smith, Elder, 1903), Vol. 1, pp. 24-25.
2. H. C. Lea, *The Inquisition of the Middle Ages: Its Organization and Operation* (New York, Harper & Row, 1969, originally published 1887), p. 154.
3. Leonard W. Levy, *Origins of the Fifth Amendment: The Right against Self-Incrimination* (London, Oxford University Press, 1968), Ch. 2, 12.
4. Lea, *Inquisition of the Middle Ages*, pp. 160-163.
5. *Ibid.*, pp. 169-183.
6. *Ibid.*, p. 187.
7. C. Northcote Parkinson, *Gunpowder, Treason, and Plot* (New York, St. Martin's, 1976), pp. 14-22.
8. Donald Carswell, ed., *The Trial of Guy Fawkes and Others* (London, William Hodge, 1934), Introduction, pp. 40-41.
9. Parkinson, *Gunpowder*, pp. 68-73.
10. Carswell, *Trial of Guy Fawkes*, p. 53; Samuel Gardiner, *What Gunpowder Plot Was* (New York, Greenwood, 1969; originally published 1897), pp. 121-125.
11. Gardiner, *What Gunpowder Plot Was*, pp. 198-199; Parkinson, *Gunpowder*, pp. 66-73.
12. Carswell, *Trial of Guy Fawkes*, pp. 16-20.
13. *Ibid.*
14. *State Trials*, Vol. 2, pp. 160-164.
15. Catherine Drinker Bowen, *The Lion and the Throne: The Life and Times of Sir Edward Coke* (Boston, Little, Brown, 1956), pp. 90-94.
16. *State Trials*, Vol. 2, p. 9; Bowen, *Lion and Throne*, Chs. 15-16.
17. *State Trials*, Vol. 2, pp. 167-168.
18. *Ibid.*, p. 171.
19. *Ibid.*, p. 175.

20. *Ibid.*, pp. 255-256. See Gardiner, *What Gunpowder Plot Was*, pp. 193-199, for a discussion of Fr. Garnet's position.
21. Philip Caraman, *Henry Garnet, 1555-1606, and the Gunpowder Plot* (New York, Farrar, Straus, 1964), p. 376.
22. *State Trials*, Vol. 2, p. 256.
23. Sir John Pollock, *The Popish Plot: A Study in the History of the Reign of Charles II* (Cambridge, Cambridge University Press, 1944); Winston S. Churchill, *The New World*, Vol. 2, *A History of the English-Speaking Peoples* (New York, Dodd, Mead, 1956), Ch. 23; Levy, *Origins of the Fifth Amendment*, pp. 316-320.
24. Nicholas Halasz, *Captain Dreyfus: The Story of Mass Hysteria* (New York, Simon & Schuster, 1955), p. 68. See also Alfred and Pierre Dreyfus, *The Dreyfus Case* (New Haven, Yale University, 1937).
25. Hannah Arendt, *The Origins of Totalitarianism* (New York, Meridian, 1958), p. 93.
26. Halasz, *Captain Dreyfus*, pp. 37-43.
27. William L. Shirer, *The Rise and Fall of the Third Reich* (New York, Crest Books, 1959), pp. 267-273. See Georgi Dimitrov, *The Reichstag Fire Trial* (New York, Howard Fertig, 1969); Fritz Tobias, *The Reichstag Fire*, Introduction by A.J.P. Taylor (New York, G. P. Putnam's Sons, 1964).
28. Shirer, *Third Reich*, pp. 369-378, 1389-1397.
29. Aleksandr I. Sozhenitsyn, *The Gulag Archipelago*, Vol. 1, trans. by Thomas P. Whitney (New York, Harper & Row, 1973), pp. 306-309. See Lon L. Fuller, "Pashukanis and Vyshinsky: A Study in the Development of Marxian Legal Theory," *Michigan Law Review* 47 (1949), pp. 1157-1166; Stephen J. Powell, "The Legal Nihilism of Pashukanis," *University of Florida Law Review* 20 (1967), pp. 18-32.
30. Thucydides, *History of the Peloponnesian War*, trans. by Rex Warner (Baltimore, Penguin, 1954), Bk. 5, p. 90.
31. George Katkov, *The Trial of Bukharin* (New York, Stein & Day, 1969), p. 192. For a transcript see Robert C. Tucker and Stephen F. Cohen, editors, *The Great Purge Trial* (New York, Grosset & Dunlap, 1965).
32. See Max Hayward, trans. and ed., *On Trial: The Soviet State versus "Abram Tertz" and "Nikolai Arzhak"* (New York, Harper & Row, 1967). See also John E. Turner, "Artist in Adversity: The Sinyavsky-Daniel Case," in Becker, ed., *Political Trials*, pp. 107ff.
33. Vladimir Bukovsky, *To Build a Castle: My Life as a Dissenter* (New York, Viking, 1979), p. 362. See Harvey Fireside, *Soviet Psychoprisons* (New York, Norton, 1979); Amnesty International, *Torture in the Eighties* (London, 1984), pp. 220-222; *Amnesty International Report, 1982* (London, 1983), pp. 286-288.
34. Zhores Medvedev and Roy A. Medvedev, *A Question of Madness* (New York, Knopf, 1971), p. 175.
35. Walter Reich, "To Soviets, Sakharov Really Is Crazy," Minneapolis *Star-Tribune*, August 12, 1984, p. 27A.
36. Louise I. Shelley, "Yelena Bonner meets Soviet Justice System," Minneapolis *Star-Tribune*, September 21, 1984, p. 13A.
37. See Ernest Fraenkel, *The Dual State: A Contribution to the Theory of Dictatorship* (New York, Octagon, 1969).
38. Quoted by John Dugard, *Human Rights and the South African Legal Order* (Princeton, Princeton University, 1978), p. 118.

39. *Ibid.*, p. 121.
40. *Survey of Race Relations in South Africa, 1983* (Johannesburg, South African Institute of Race Relations, 1984), p. 549.
41. Donald Wood, *Biko* (New York, Paddington, 1978): *Rand Daily Mail* (Johannesburg), June 15, 1982.
42. Dugard, *South African Legal Order*, pp. 208-209, 228.
43. *Ibid.*, p. 237.
44. *Ibid.*, p. 211. Newell M. Stultz, *Afrikaner Politics in South Africa, 1934-1948* (Berkeley, University of California Press, 1974), Ch. 8.

3

The SWAPO Trial: A Partisan Trial

With Ralston H. Deffenbaugh, Jr.

Assassination of Chief Elifas

Chief Filemon Elifas, a hereditary chief in Namibia, was assassinated on a Saturday night in August 1975, just as he stepped out the door of a drinking establishment into the darkness. A gunman had been waiting in ambush and pulled the trigger when the chief was framed against the light of the door. The gunman fled into the African night and was never found.

Whether one person or more were involved in the assassination of Chief Elifas is a matter of dispute. But because Chief Elifas was a favorite of the South African government neither the police nor supporters of the South African rule in Namibia were hindered by the absence of information about the killing. The Windhoek *Advertiser*, a major newspaper in the capital city, carried a banner headline: "Chief Elifas Assassinated," and charged that "there is little doubt that he was the victim of a political murder, perpetrated by his many enemies who have regarded him through the years as a puppet of the South African government."[1] The South African government had even less doubt that it was a political crime, for it immediately acted to rout the leadership of the South West Africa People's Organization (SWAPO), Namibia's most influential political party. SWAPO is militantly proindependence and set against any solution for Namibia imposed by South Africa. Both the press and the government were certain they knew the motive for the murder of Chief Elifas and that it was the result of a SWAPO plot, no matter who the killer happened to be.

Together with the African nationalist organizations in South Africa, SWAPO sees the ethnic isolation of apartheid as a form of racist domination and seeks to prevent South Africa's bantustan policy of separate tribal "homelands" from spreading into Namibia with an independence settlement. Unlike the American Indian Movement (AIM), which desires greater ethnic autonomy, even to the point of creating a separate Lakota nation-state, SWAPO wants less ethnic identity. If AIM listens to the voices from the traditional society of the past as its members find their identity in a technological society, SWAPO looks to the African nations north of them for leadership in making Namibia a modern independent democratic nation with citizens in control of their own destiny. Both AIM and SWAPO are nationalist movements, but what differences they have reflect not disparate values as much as the contrasting societies within which they operate. If Russell Means and Dennis Banks were to meet the leaders of SWAPO, they would find much to discuss and, it would seem, a common agreement on the fundamentals of politics.

Namibia is the only territory in the world for which the United Nations has direct responsibility, yet there are no UN personnel in the country. Formerly a colony known as German South West Africa, Namibia was conquered by South African forces in World War I. Following that war, South Africa retained control under a League of Nations mandate which permitted the territory (then called South West Africa) to be ruled as an integral part of South Africa. After World War II, South Africa applied to the UN to annex the territory, but the request was rejected. South Africa continued to rule Namibia (as the rest of the world now calls it) as if it were a province, subjecting the country to the apartheid system and to South African law in spite of the mandate's having been revoked by the General Assembly in 1966 and of the fact that the continued presence of South Africa in Namibia was ruled illegal by the International Court of Justice in 1971. Beginning in 1977, South Africa has recognized the right of Namibia to independence but has opposed free elections overseen by the UN. It is generally understood that South African resistance to such elections derives from an accurate estimate that SWAPO would win hands down. But this takes us temporarily beyond the story of the 1975 assassination and the 1976 trial.

Soon after the Elifas murder, vigilantes forcibly broke into the homes of SWAPO leaders. Instead of taking action against the vigilantes, the government put the victims in detention. Over the next two and a half months, fifty-four persons were known to have been detained in a wave of arrests by the police, but estimates by reliable sources put the actual total detentions as high as 200.[2] The detainees were held incommunicado and the incidents were not reported publicly.

Nine months after Chief Elifas was assassinated, a court sentenced two SWAPO members, Aaron Mushimba, twenty-nine, and Hendrik Shikongo, twenty-eight, to death by hanging. Two nurses who had contributed money to SWAPO, Rauna Nambinga, twenty-eight, and Anna Nghihondjwa, twenty-three, went to prison for seven and five years respectively. This SWAPO trial from mid-February to mid-May 1976, was billed in the press as the Elifas murder trial. Yet the murderer was not present. Although the prosecution introduced thirty-two witnesses, most of whom presented details of the assassination, at the end of the trial the police had little better idea of who the assassin was than when they had arrived on the scene and found the body. None of the four sentenced in May was accused of pulling the trigger. None of them was accused of belonging to a conspiracy which plotted Chief Elifas's death. Except for Hendrik Shikongo, none of the four was accused of having anything to do with the murder of Chief Elifas. Shikongo was charged and convicted of providing the mysterious assassin(s) with a ride to the scene of the murder, but the state's case, purporting to show that he knew his passengers intended to harm the chief, is murky. The trial of the four SWAPO members and the assassination of Chief Elifas remain two unrelated events. What matters and makes all the difference is that each of the defendants was a member of SWAPO and was charged under South Africa's Terrorism Act.

For anyone who lies awake at night thinking of how orderly life would be under a police state, the South African Terrorism Act is a dream come true. The police have enough discretion under the Act that they can charge anyone who does anything "with intent to endanger the maintenance of law and order" as a "terrorist". Given police provocation, which needs to be little more than mild irritation, terrorist suspects can be detained indefinitely, held incommunicado for interrogation, and dragged through a terrorist trial which carries a maximum sentence of death.[3] The detention itself is, naturally, punishment. The law allows the police to make use of all those techniques of coercion imagined and practiced by inquisitors and Star Chamber prosecutors that the protection of habeas corpus was designed to prevent. Because the Act provides that "no court of law shall pronounce upon the validity of any action taken . . . or order the release of any detainee," the police interrogators need fear no correction from a court.[4] The writ of habeas corpus might seem arcane to the police in such circumstances.

Once the police-and-vigilante dragnet had put behind bars those SWAPO members they thought were troublemakers, and had satisfied themselves— for there is no one else they must satisfy—that they detained a group of terrorists, the police could begin the task of sorting the detainees into state witnesses and accused. More than likely any of the detained, or nearly anyone picked at random off the street, could serve as the accused. In order to convict anyone of terrorism, the state must prove that he or she "with intent to endanger the maintenance of law and order . . . takes any steps to undergo . . . encourages or procures any other person to undergo any training which could be of use to any person intending to endanger the maintenance of law and order, and who fails to prove beyond a reasonable doubt that he did not undergo . . . or encourage . . . such training." Further, the burden of proof is shifted to the accused to demonstrate that he or she "did not intend . . . to commit any act likely to have any of the above results." Even if a person is charged with hampering any person "from assisting in the maintenance of law and order" or with encouraging "the achievement of any political aim" which will "embarrass the administration of the affairs of the State," the accused has the burden of proof.[5]

With the possibilities contained within the wording of the Terrorism Act any assiduous police interrogator would have his imagination set ablaze. After the state has proved that the accused has committed an act which is likely to result in, for instance, obstructing traffic or embarrassing the authorities, or some other typically terrorist crime, the burden shifts to the defendant who must show not only that he or she did not intend "to endanger the maintenance of law and order" but that he or she did not intend *any* of the results of the Act. It becomes the defendant's task to prove his or her innocence beyond a reasonable doubt.

Suppose we take as an illustration that most common of all murders, a man who kills his wife's lover. The state would first prove that the accused did dispatch the paramour and that would be murder in some degree but not terrorism. All the state must do to accomplish a terrorist conviction is prove that the murder was likely to produce one of the various forbidden results. By the magic of the Terrorism Act a domestic murder could be converted into terrorism. The Act is used selectively, but the fact is that many activities which could not be considered crimes are, under its aegis, terrorist acts. A priest theoretically commits "terrorism," although no other crime, when he exhorts his flock to follow the ways of the Lord, because that might result in encouraging social change in cooperation with an international institution, the Roman Catholic Church. A political cartoonist might satirize the government, causing it embarrassment, and thereby be guilty of "terrorism."

What prevents overly diligent policemen from filling the jails with detained "terrorists" and every restless prosecutor from demonstrating his continual vigilance to his superiors and to the press, is that the Terrorism Act cannot be instituted unless authorized by the Attorney General.[6] Ordinary crimes, daily life, and courtroom regularities are thus not usually undermined by the application of the Terrorism Act, but when the minister of justice and the attorney general determine that someone or some group stand in disfavor with the government, they can send down thunderbolts of vengeance by invoking the Terrorism Act. When they do, those rounded up have scant shelter from the power of the police and their legal lightning bolts. The detained might be released after a few days and never find out why they were held in the first place. Or, they might be kept for months and put through aggressive interrogation until they either agree to become government witnesses or find themselves in the dock accused of terrorism.

Parallel to the Terrorism Act and even broader in scope is Proclamation R.17, which applied only to Ovamboland in northernmost Namibia, the largest of the areas the South African government designated to become a "homeland." This regulation provided that whenever the commissioner or *any* member of the police "is satisfied that any person" has committed an offense under its provisions or "has reason to suspect that any person has or has the intention to commit such an offense," he may arrest without a warrant, may question, or may detain that person until the commissioner or policeman "is satisfied that the said person has answered fully and truthfully all questions put to him which have any bearing upon the said offense or intended offense." As for seeing a lawyer, R.17 decrees that no person so arrested or detained, "without the consent of the Minister or person acting under his authority," shall "be allowed to consult with a legal advisor in connection with any matter relating to the arrest and detention."[7] Unlike the Terrorism Act, the decision to detain someone is not limited to high-ranking police officers. Under R.17 the lowliest policeman, who in Ovamboland are often poorly trained tribal police, could arrest anyone without warrant and detain that person until the policeman "is satisfied" that the detainee has answered all questions fully. Again, as with the Terrorism Act, there is no possibility of any objective test of bona fides of the arrest, but it is completely within the discretion of the policeman or his superiors. Some of the 1975 detainees were held under the Terrorism Act, some under R.17, but it is unknown which persons were held under which law. But it made little difference because the conditions of detention were the same and the authority under which the person was being held was only a function of the frame of mind of the policeman, if indeed he thought of it at all.

The wave of detentions following the assassination of Chief Elifas netted, among others, the principal of a Lutheran seminary in Namibia, a seminary instructor, and six Lutheran pastors, none of whom could have been involved in the Elifas murder. They had been, however, outspoken against apartheid. "We can only conclude," wrote the general secretary of the Lutheran World Federation, Carl H. Mau, Jr., in an open letter to Prime Minister B. J. Vorster, "that the South African government is engaging in a systematic attack upon the Christian churches in Namibia of a kind that is intolerable and an offense to the world community of Lutheran churches."[8]

The Griswold Investigation

Irwin Griswold, long-time dean of the Harvard Law School and more recently the solicitor general of the United States, was engaged by the

Lutheran World Federation to investigate the plight of the detainees, visit them if possible, and recommend a course of action. He arrived in South Africa in mid-November. His first stop was a visit with the then minister of justice and police, James Kruger, an interview which someone of lesser stature would have never obtained. Griswold noted for Kruger the seriousness of the problem: holding so many people incommunicado for so long and without charge, making it impossible to arrange for counsel or to conduct a defense investigation, and prompting rumors about duress and torture. Kruger explained that the police investigation had not yet concluded and that things were more difficult in South Africa than in the United States, but, he agreed, Griswold would be allowed to see "the accused" with a security officer present. After telling Griswold that the trial would begin December 1—a real piece of news—Kruger vigorously asserted that Griswold's trip to inquire after the detainees had nothing to do with the fixing of a trial date and that he "had records to prove that." At the close of the interview Kruger summoned the head of the South African Police, General Prinsloo, and the head of the feared Security Police, General Geldenhuys, as well as a Security Police officer, Colonel Schoon. To this gathering of police state worthies Kruger explained the circumstances of Dean Griswold's visit and arranged for General Geldenhuys and Colonel Schoon to accompany him to Namibia.[9]

In a Windhoek prison Griswold saw four nurses from a Lutheran hospital in the northern area of Ovamboland: Rauna Nambinga, Anna Nghihondjwa, Hendrina Shaketange, and Naimi Nombowa. With an interpreter and his distinguished police escorts Geldenhuys and Schoon present, Griswold saw each woman separately, explaining why he was there, asking if she was treated well, and telling her that the Lutheran bishop sent his love and that everything that could be done to assist the detainees was being done. He told them that he did not know what they would be charged with, if anything, but if they were they would have excellent counsel. Finally, he asked each of the detained women if she wished to tell him anything. None answered more than a few phrases, although Nambinga said she was worried about certain statements she made to the police, and Nghihondjwa expressed concern for her husband whom she had married only a few days before she was arrested. After the interviews Geldenhuys told Griswold: "I do not think these women should be charged. They were used. . . . I will recommend that they not be charged."[10] They remained in prison nevertheless, and, in fact, three of the four were charged and stood trial.

The next stop for Griswold and the two most dreaded police officers in the country was the Windhoek police station where they called upon three men: Andreas Nangolo, Aaron Mushimba, and Hendrik Shikongo. Like the women, the male prisoners said little. Nangolo, however, said that they were not well treated and that "we have no right to speak what we want to say. If I tell you the truth, I may commit a crime. How much of what I say would put me in trouble? What I want to say is this. If you are really sent by the L.W.F., please do pray for us and for our people here, because we are not well treated. People in detention as well as on the outside. That's all." Mushimba told Griswold that he had been beaten and asked why they had nothing like newspapers to read. Shikongo said that they had previously been in solitary confinement but were not now.[11] The brevity of their answers, considering that Griswold was a complete stranger in the company of the highest-ranking Security Police officers in South Africa, is not surprising. What is striking is the bravery they exhibited in saying as much as they did under such strained circumstances.

Later all three men were charged and stood trial. Griswold was not allowed to see those detainees who were being held to be witnesses. When he protested this, saying it was not in accord with the understanding reached with the minister of justice, he learned that literally it was in accord because he had asked to see the "accused," not the "detainees." Geldenhuys assured him that he could "practically guarantee" with a 99.9% certainty that none of the persons Griswold did not see would be charged. When Griswold produced a list of known detainees and inquired about each of them, he learned that all but five had been released and that the five were being held in Ovamboland as witnesses. The police would not volunteer any names of others who might be detained but were not on Griswold's list.[12] Although Griswold avoided contact with the press, news stories giving Minister Kruger as the source appeared, telling how some thirty prisoners were to be flown from distant places to Windhoek in order to be interviewed by the visiting American jurist.[13]

Griswold was the first outsider ever allowed access to any Terrorism Act detainees. Although the Security Police limited and shaped the visit, as well as talking maximum publicity advantage, events moved rapidly following Griswold's brief visit. The seven prisoners he saw were given reading material and allowed visits from their families. A charge sheet was published two days after Griswold left. Court was set to convene in order to hear pleas on December 1. The church leaders engaged the Windhoek law firm of Lorentz & Bone to represent the seven accused.

Trial: Openings

Six of the seven detainees Griswold visited were charged under the Terrorism Act as "members and/or active supporters of the South West Africa Peoples' Organization . . . guilty of the crime of participating in terrorist activities." Aaron Mushimba, a traveling bicycle salesman, was charged with giving R380 ($437 RI then equalled $1.15), a Landrover, and some blankets to Victor Nkandi of SWAPO. Andreas Nangolo was said to have given a Landrover to Usko Nambinga, the brother of Rauna, for use by SWAPO. Hendrik Shikongo, in the only accusation which touched the Elifas murder, was charged with transporting Nicodemus Mauhi and two unknown men from SWAPO to the Onamugundo bottle store where Elifas was shot, knowing that they intended to harm Chief Elifas. Rauna Nambinga was accused of visiting Angola and giving a SWAPO supporter a dress, soap, and sanitary napkins, and of collecting R10 ($11.50) for SWAPO from two other nurses and giving her brother, Usko, the money for SWAPO. Naimi Nombowa and Anna Nghihondjwa were accused of being terrorists because of R10 donations to SWAPO. SWAPO, it should be known, is a legal political party in Namibia, but the peculiarities of the Terrorism Act make that fact irrelevant.

The South West Africa Division of the Supreme Court of South Africa, the highest trial court of the territory, convened at 10 A.M. on December 1, 1975, to begin the first formal proceedings in *The State v. Aaron Mushimba and Five Others*. A peaceful and well-disciplined group of Blacks gathered on the steps of the Windhoek Supreme Court Building to sing SWAPO songs and display placards declaring "SWAPO Will Win," "Freedom Now," and "Illegal Regime [Has] No Right to Try the Just Cause."[14] When the doors opened, the demonstrators filed inside to the seats designated for non-Whites. Inside and outside the police were busy taking photos.

Presiding was Judge J. H. Badenhorst of the S.W.A. Division. Flanking him were two assessors who help a judge weigh the facts but not the law. Appearing for the state was Advocate J. C. H. "Chris" Jansen, an ambitious young prosecutor specially brought up from Grahamstown in the Cape Province to try this case. The defense was represented by Advocate Hans Berker, an older lawyer from an established German family in Windhoek. He was instructed by an attorney, Colin du Preez, from the firm of Lorentz & Bone. The six accused, together with a policeman and the court interpreter, sat in a dock facing the bench. The only Black court official was the interpreter. Instead of a bailiff or marshal to serve the court, as would be usual in U.S. practice, regular uniformed South African policemen, indistinguishable from those who make arrests, were used as court officials in this case. Their presence detracted from an appearance of impartiality.

Both sides proposed January 19, 1976 to the judge as an agreed-upon date for the trial to begin. Judge Badenhorst rejected that suggestion and proposed December 17 or 19 because the defendants had already been in jail for three months, and two and a half weeks should be enough time for the defense to prepare. Advocate Berker objected strenuously, reminding the court that they had been charged only a few days previously and that there were many witnesses in Ovamboland who must be interviewed before the defense would be ready. Jansen for the prosecution requested that the trial be held in the coastal resort town of Swakopmund. No reasons were given, but it was assumed that the state believed Swakopmund's small size and isolation preferable to Windhoek, the capital, with its 70,000 population, and with demonstrations more likely. The defense objected, citing the inconvenience of transportation and legal research in Swakopmund. After a tea break Judge Badenhorst announced that the trial would begin February 16 in Swakopmund. Court adjourned.

Two Security Police officers, Col. Willem Schoon, one of Griswold's guides, and Lt. Gert Dippenaar, had been assigned to the case immediately after the murder of Chief Elifas. State advocate Jansen was brought into it shortly after Griswold arrived and, by then, had only to decide whom to prosecute, whom to use as witnesses, what the charge sheet should say, and how the trial preparation should be done. The basic groundwork had been done by the police and handed to him.[15]

By contrast, the defense began its trial preparation much later and with only the charges, a statement taken by the police from each defendant, and a list of thirty-one prospective state witnesses, i.e. people with whom the defense could not tamper. Church leaders instructed Lorentz & Bone to engage David Soggot, a leading Johannesburg advocate, but he was planning the defense in the terrorism trial of the leaders of the South African Student Organization and the Black Peoples' Convention (SASO/BPC), another major South African trial. The defense then turned to Dr. Wilfred Cooper of Cape Town as senior counsel. Advocate Berker would stay on as junior counsel.[16] David Soggot was able to assist in the investigation, although not in the trial, before he was called to Pretoria for the SASO/BPC trial.

In their interviews in prison the four defense lawyers, Cooper, Soggot, Berker, and du Preez, found culture a greater barrier than language. In an apartheid society why should six Blacks, already held for several months under the hostile care of the police, immediately trust and confide in four White strangers just because the latter had been hired by a church that the prisoners did trust? Besides, who could say that the police might not place an informer among the lawyers, a fear that, as it turned out, was well founded. Although Nangolo and Mishimba were Windhoek businessmen and Nangolo had been a South African policeman, their dealings with White society's European assumptions could not overcome the cultural differences and the master/servant mentality of South Africa. For the other four who had lived their lives in rural Ovamboland, the barrier was especially difficult. After a week of consultation the lawyers had the stories in

general terms and perceived that there were no major legal questions—
only the problem of dragging out the evidence and slogging through the
facts. Considering the circumstances, the defendants' spirits and morale
were remarkably high.[17]

The Terrorism Act, in addition to its other nightmares, thwarts defense
efforts with a catch-22 option. With the burden of proof placed upon the
defendant, witnesses in this case would be essential for any kind of defense.
Prospective witnesses named in the charge sheet or mentioned by the accused, assuming they could be found, might incriminate themselves and
endanger others in SWAPO if they did testify for the defense. Those outside, if found, would not return to Namibia. Those in Namibia would
neither come forth nor cooperate if found. Active SWAPO supporters and
guerrillas regarded the law illegal, the court a fraud, and the government
occupation of their homeland illegitimate. Counsel did fly to London to
interview David Meroro, the SWAPO national chairman who slipped
through the dragnet after the murder of Chief Elifas, but he was tense and
uncommunicative, providing nothing useful for the defense. A trip to
Zambia proved similarly unsuccessful.[18]

Through Lutheran and Anglican church people, the lawyers were able to
arrange consultation with witnesses in the home of a Finnish missionary.
Throughout the consultation a police vehicle drove around and around the
house, hardly providing a setting which would inspire openness. After the
lawyers had left, the assistant to the Lutheran bishop received a call from
the chief minister of Ovambo who asked why the church was cooperating
with terrorists and their defense lawyers in covering up the murder of Chief
Elifas.[19]

The trial opened in Swakopmund on February 16, 1976, in a politically
charged atmosphere that would not favor the defendants. A young White
farm couple living along the road between Windhoek and Swakopmund
had been murdered with automatic weapons on the eve of the trial. This
brutal murder intensified the anti-SWAPO feeling. Furthermore, the defense lawyers grimly awaited the state's case, about which they were in the
dark. Their own files were pitifully thin, containing mainly the accounts
given them by their own clients. The defense investigation had run into
dead ends down nearly every avenue of inquiry. Their single consolation
was a promise from the prosecuter that he would not ask for the death
sentence.

Small groups of Blacks began to gather early in the morning outside the
modern two-story glass and concrete courthouse located next to the man-
sion of the administrator for South West Africa, close to the police station,
and two blocks from the sea shore. By 9 A.M. a fairly large demonstration
with placards and songs was in progress, but by 9:50 the singing ended as

the demonstrators filed into the courtroom to take spaces behind the rows allotted to Whites. Most Blacks were not admitted but remained outside in a sandy lot on the hot, sunny north side of the courthouse. During lunch break they resumed the demonstration, but when they did not disperse quickly enough for the police, the crowd was rushed with swinging batons and dogs.

In the courtroom the six accused sat in the dock facing the judge's bench. Nearby was a Black court interpreter who would translate the proceedings from Afrikaans to Ovambo. Seated at a table directly in front of the dock were the counsel: Cooper and Berker for the defense and Jansen for the state. But seated between Cooper and Jansen at the counsels' table, as though he too were an advocate, was Lt. Dippenaar, the investigating officer. Seeing the security policeman who interrogated them in prison now watching from the counsels' table, next to their own counsel in fact, must have confused the witnesses and troubled the accused.

At precisely 10 A.M. a South African policeman cried out in Afrikaans: "Silence in the Court!" In strode Judge J. J. Strydom, an associate justice of the South West African Division, wearing his red criminal trial robes. Contrary to the expectation of the defense, he was without assessors. The charge was read, translated, and the six accused pleaded not guilty. Throughout the trial, as is custom, the accused were referred to as "Accused No. 1" or "Accused No. 2" instead of by their proper names. When their names were used, only the first name was mentioned, not their family names. In speaking to Blacks the Afrikaans familiar second person *jy* was used, but when speaking to Whites, the formal second person *u* was employed.

Trial: Prosecution Witnesses

Prosecuter Jansen's brief, ten-minute opening address revealed that the trial would be not so much against the six accused as against SWAPO, with the accused serving as scapegoats for the organization. It was clear to the defense that the trial would be intensely political. The opening state witnesses shed no light on the assassination of Chief Elifas and little directly on the accused. Aaron Mushimba and Andreas Nangolo had been charged with purchasing and delivering two Landrovers to SWAPO for use in overthrowing the government. The first eight state witnesses testified to the details of the purchase and to an incident ten days after the assassination of Chief Elifas when South African Army soldiers had been fired upon from the same Landrover Mushimba had purchased. For the duration of the trial the blue Landrover was parked outside the courthouse by the police. What use had been made of the other Landrover, the one purchased by Nangolo, was never clarified in the trial. Under cross-examination the defense was unable to learn more about the shooting incident because it was all a "matter of state security." The crucial connections were, for the defense, imperceptible: between those who shot at the soldiers and the murderers of Chief Elifas and between either of these and the defendants.

When the state turned its attention to the crime at hand, the murder of Chief Filemon Elifas, the spotlight had shifted to Hendrik Shikongo, who was the only one of the six accused who was charged with having any involvement in the murder. He was charged with having given three men a ride to the scene of the murder knowing that they intended to harm the chief. Chief Immanuel Elifas, who succeeded his brother as chief of the Ondonga tribe of the Ovambos, told the court that he had accompanied his brother to Thomas Nangombe's bottle store and that Shikongo had come in and bought a hipflask of whiskey for the chief. The chief, however, was angry at Shikongo and reprimanded him for giving him a face full of dust on the previous day when Shikongo drove away in his Ford pickup. After the scolding from the chief, Shikongo left. About five minutes later the chief walked out the door and was shot. The intimation encouraged by the prosecution is that Shikongo left in order to signal the assassin.

The trial was lent a police-state mood by the appearance as state witnesses of seven persons who had been arrested under the Terrorism Act. They took the stand while still detained in the absolute control of the police. Under the watchful eyes of Lt. Dippenaar, who had held and interrogated them for more than three months and who now sat at the counsels' table only a few feet away, they took the stand knowing they would return to Dippenaar's control following their testimony. Naturally, these witnesses were under extreme stress. Their stories, as cross-examination revealed, were shaky. In spite of the defense request that the witnesses be admonished not to discuss the case outside the court, Lt. Dippenaar was seen in the lobby during adjournment with witnesses in an insistent whisper, as though prepping them.

The appearance as a state witness of Sam Shivute, a well-known senior SWAPO official who had served as secretary for Northern Namibia, caused the audience to stir. He told the court that shortly after 11 P.M. on the night of the Elifas murder, about two hours after the shooting, Hendrik Shikongo told him how he had driven two unknown SWAPO leaders to the store where the chief had been murdered. Coming from such a highly placed SWAPO leader, this testimony was damaging. Under severe cross-examination by Cooper, Shivute was asked if the police had offered to release him from detention if he gave evidence that Shikongo had identified the mysterious pair as SWAPO members.

Cooper: But you on your own volition told the Police that Hendrik said that the two
     men were members of SWAPO?

Shivute: Yes, Hendrik said to me that those two persons were members of SWAPO, but I myself to tell the truth cannot confirm that they were members of SWAPO.

Cooper: Mr. Shivute, you understand my question without an interpreter. My question is very simple. Did you of your own volition tell the Police that Hendrik said the two unknown men were members of SWAPO?

Shivute: I myself did not tell them, but I only told them what Hendrik said.

Cooper: So it was of your own volition that you told the Police?

Shivute: It was only during the questioning.

Interpreter (in Ovambo): Did you say that of your own volition. Were you not forced to say it?

Shivute: (in Ovambo): I do not understand what he wants to say

Interpreter (in Ovambo): The story which you have now told here, is that of your own volition that you told it?

Shivute: (in Ovambo): It does not mean that it is of your own volition. It depends whether a person is in detention and upon the method of his interrogation or the circumstances of his interrogation.

Interpreter (in Afrikaans): It was merely during the interrogation.[20]

On the day following the Elifas murder Shivute was arrested and interrogated time and time again by Lt. Dippenaar. He had been held in solitary confinement from his arrest in August until the trial in February.

Elizabeth Namunjebo, known as Queen, a 38-year-old mother of four and a salesperson in a general store, was the third state witness who, at the time of her testimony, was under detention. She had been a SWAPO member for several years and was an acquaintance of Mushimba and Shikongo. In her testimony she connected the blue Landrover with Mushimba, Mushimba with SWAPO member Victor Nkandi shortly before the Elifas murder, and Nkandi with Shikongo on the day of the murder, a string of circumstances. More significantly, she claimed that Shikongo had come to her home on the night of the murder after she was in bed asking if she had seen his friends and telling her, "We killed the chief." During the cross-examination she could remember few details beyond those she gave in her direct testimony, and she revised and contradicted some of them. She admitted, further, that about two months before the Elifas murder she had been arrested for possessing ammunition and a SWAPO card and that after she talked with Mushimba about her legal problems he arranged for a lawyer. Although she could remember little of these events, she related with exactness the phone calls in which Mushimba inquired about Victor Nkandi. As for Shikongo's words, "we killed the chief," she revised her recollection under cross-examination to "the chief is finished," and then to "the chief is finished; we killed him."

Two of the seven detained who took the stand for the state revealed in their testimony far more about police methods than about either the accused or the Elifas murder. Two frightened nurses, both in their twenties, were brought in by the state to tell about SWAPO meetings at which the accused nurses—Rauna Nambinga, Naimi Nombowa, and Anna Nghihondjwa—had each contributed R10 ($11.50) to the SWAPO cause and about a visit across the Angola border with supplies of sanitary napkins and soap for those Namibians who had fled the country. During cross-examination the first nurse told how the soldiers had surrounded the hospital one day in October and arrested her and nine other nurses. Soon after her arrest she made a statement, but it was torn up and she was told by her interrogators that it was not the truth. Cooper asked her when she had been last interrogated. After having been asked the question three times and admonished not to be silent, she blurted out that it had been earlier in the day by Lt. Dippenaar. At that point Dippenaar, sitting directly in front of the witness at the counsel table, stood up and left the room. She said that he had told her she must say in court what she had said in her "acceptable" statement that had not been torn up by the police. Although her statement was under oath, she did not know the meaning of perjury. She said she had to tell the truth and proceeded to revise her "acceptable" story under questioning by both Cooper for the defense and the judge.

The second nurse, Kaino Malua, had a similar but even more revealing account of police methods while she was cross-examined by Cooper.

Cooper: When were you interrogated?

Witness: From the 21st to the 23rd (of October)

Cooper: Were you interrogated continuously during this period?

Witness: Yes, I was interrogated those days.

Cooper: By whom?

Witness: By the Police.

Cooper: And did you make a statement to the Police?

Witness: Yes.

Cooper: Were the Police satisfied with the first statement you gave them?

Witness: No, they were not satisfied with it, since they tore up the other papers.

Cooper: Now, after they had torn up the papers what did the Police do then?

Witness: They interrogated me again.

Cooper: For how long?

Witness: Yes, it was a long time, because it was a whole night. I did not sleep that night.

Cooper: Which night did you not sleep? The 20th, 21st, the 22nd, the 23rd?

Witness: Between the 22nd and the 23rd.

Cooper: Now how were you able to remain awake all night, Kaino?

Witness: I was suspended from 3 o'clock in the afternoon to 1 o'clock at night, hoisted, shall I say, by my right arm and my feet could not touch the floor.

Cooper: How were you hoisted by your right arm, could you explain to the Court?

Witness: My arm was fastened as I indicate, it was chained, and the chains fastened to the light (fan light?).

Cooper: The witness now shows with her right hand that her right hand was extended or stretched?

Witness: Yes, it was stretched.

Cooper: Above her head?

Witness: Yes, as I now show.

Cooper: That is above your head?

Witness: Yes.

Cooper: You say that a chain was fastened to the wrist of your right arm?

Witness: Yes.

Cooper: To what was the chain then attached?

Witness: Something which hangs above like this.

Cooper: You have not shown that you are stretched. When the chain was then attached, where were your feet?

Witness: I was not altogether on the plank, I did not altogether touch the plank.

Cooper: Did you stand comfortably?

Witness: I could not stand comfortably as I stand today, since I was in the air, and my feet did not touch the ground and the floor.

Cooper: For how many hours were you fastened in this manner?

Witness: From 3 o'clock until 1 o'clock at night.

Cooper: Now can you tell the Court why the Police did that?

Witness: They said that I was not telling the truth, but I then said that I was telling the truth.

Cooper: After you were fastened like that, did the Police again take a statement from you?

Witness: Yes.

Cooper: And were the Police satisfied with the statement?

Witness: Yes.

Cooper: And was the statement given under oath?

Witness: Yes, I gave it under oath, although it was not correct.

Cooper: In what respect was it not correct?

Witness: Yes, I gave it under oath and I swore to it because they considered it to be correct.

Cooper: But what appears in the statement is not correct?

Witness: Some of it is the truth, but other is not the truth.

Cooper: Why then did you take the oath for this statement, of which parts were not the truth?

Witness: I swore the oath because they believed that everything was the truth.

Cooper: Now which parts of your affidavit were untrue?

Witness: I cannot remember.[21]

Of the thirty-three prosecution witnesses, two SWAPO members refused to cooperate. Both Victor Nkandi and Axel Jackson Johannes were under detention and told the court that they would not testify until they had each been put in the dock as an accused. Judge Strydom read the provision of the criminal code which specifies a sentence of up to twelve months for such refusal, reminding them also that after twelve months' imprisonment they could again be brought before the court and if they continued to refuse to testify, they might receive another twelve-month sentence. "According to the laws of the country," the judge explained, "it is the duty of a person called upon to testify to answer to lawful questions and a person who refuses to answer lawful questions breaks the law." Johannes responded: "As I have told the Court, I have spent 200 days in gaol, if I have then done something, if I have then transgressed anything, then I must appear before the Court, then I must be prosecuted. Because I do not know of a law that a witness may be locked up. I see that witnesses are always at large." The judge interpreted the Terrorism Act, telling Johannes that it "is a law that authorizes the authorities to detain witnesses until they have given evidence." When asked by the judge whether he persisted in his attitude, Johannes, like Nkandi before him, replied that he did, and the judge sentenced him, as he had Nkandi, to twelve months in prison.[22]

When Security Police lieutenant Gert Dippenaar was called to testify, he left his seat at the counsel's table and walked around to the witness box with a confident and eager manner. As the major investigator of the Elifas murder, he covered the details of the location of the vehicles at the bottle shop, the interrogation he had conducted of those people at the scene, and the contents of the blue Landrover. He determined that when he had arrived about two hours after the killing, two vehicles had left, one of which belonged to Hendrik Shikongo or, as he put it on the stand, "connected with the name of Number 3." In the morning he saw to it that Shikongo was arrested. Among the documents found in the Landrover Mushimba had purchased, according to Dippenaar, were a draft constitution of SWAPO; the SWAPO membership card of Ruben Hauwanga (the brother of Shikongo's girl friend); a green, red, and blue SWAPO flag; a seventy-page manual on the use of a 75mm recoilless antitank gun; four letters in the Kwanyama dialect telling about guerrilla activities; maps; an appointment book; and a memo book. The appointment book had an entry for August 16, 1975, the day of the assassination, which read: "This is the day of death for Chief Elifas." The memo book had an entry for the same day reading: "Today is a great day to remember for all the people of Namibia as we see the death of Chief Elifas at 8:30 P.M. by SWAPO soldiers. Four brothers are fulfilling this task.[23]

Among the expert witnesses introduced by the prosecution was a Security Police translator who provided the court with the lyrics from several SWAPO songs found on tapes taken from Elizabeth (the Queen) Namunjebo. She said they had come to her from the Usko Nambinga, a SWAPO organizer and brother of the accused Rauna Nambinga. The defense objected that the tapes were hearsay, but the prosecution persuaded Judge Strydom that they should be admitted because they mentioned killing Chief Elifas, proving that SWAPO was responsible for the murder. Some of the verse on the tapes which were played for the court and translated from Ovambo include the following that the prosecution offered as evidence of terrorism:

> *Namibia, our whole land is in slavery, SWAPO will come.*
> *Have weapons ready to attack the black Boers.*
> *Throw out the Boers with our weapons.*
> *Elifas, the dawn has come and you're still asleep.*
> *We Namibians must unite.*
> *We are the men from the bush who fight for freedom.*
> *The Lord is the conqueror.*
> *Tell Ndjoba and Elifas we'll settle accounts with them.*
> *We'll come dancing. We'll come with cannons. We'll bury them.[24]*

Colonel Willem Schoon, the Security Police officer who accompanied Griswold, testified, if that is what it can be called, by reading from cover to cover the September-December 1975 issue of the English-language SWAPO publication *Kalahari Pilot*. (The *Pilot* is one of many names under which SWAPO's *Namibia News*, is published in London and banned in South Africa, appeared in Namibia.) One story in the magazine was about the mass arrests, complete with photographs of Aaron Mushimba and Sam Shivute, and another told of guerrilla activities. But the relevance of Col. Schoon's giving an oral rendition of the entire magazine, including stories such as "Successful UK start to SWAPO Women's Tour," was neither questioned by the judge, objected to by the defense, nor explained by the prosecution.[25]

The final prosecution witness, the thirty-third to appear, was the government's expert on SWAPO, Petrus Ferreira. He had been a captain in the Security Police, but in 1970 he had left to join a governmental department he preferred not to name (the dreaded and supersecret Bureau of State Security, BOSS, as cross-examination later revealed). He told at length of the 1957 origins of SWAPO, its development, its goals to free South West Africa from White domination and separate development, and its methods, including the military. Because Ferreira was a surprise witness, Cooper rose to say that the defense was not in a position to cross-examine him at the time. By bringing in Ferreira, Cooper charged, "what the State has done to put SWAPO into the dock as an accused." Judge Strydom refused to acknowledge the charge because all of the accused were members of SWAPO and they were charged with having given aid to terrorists.[26] Nevertheless, in order to give the defense time to find documents and hold consultations with experts on SWAPO, the judge granted a two-week adjournment.

This was the second adjournment and one which presented the defense with a dilemma. During the first adjournment, ten days following the testimony of Gert Dippenaar, the defense made a trip to the scene of the crime in Ovamboland to find out, among other matters, if Shikongo's truck could be seen from inside the bottle shop, as witnesses interrogated by Dippenaar had claimed. The defense found that it would be practically impossible to see his truck, but Judge Strydom, after some delay, refused to grant the defense application to recall several witnesses.

The second adjournment presented the defense with a question unrelated to the circumstances of the Elifas murder: Should they try to defend SWAPO as well as the accused? Ferreira's testimony raised a dilemma as intrinsic to political trials as it is potentially inimical to the rule of law. By presenting experts qualified to refute Ferreira, the defense would accept the premise that his testimony was relevant, suggesting that the six accused were part of the SWAPO terrorist designs that he outlined. But by playing down Ferreira, arguing that his testimony was irrelevant, the defense would risk having the court accept it, nevertheless, unchallenged. Further, given the Terrorism Act, any genuine authority on SWAPO would, by testifying, put himself or herself in a position of either being used as an unwitting spy or being arrested as a terrorist. Because Ferreira's testimony had received a considerable amount of press coverage that portrayed SWAPO as a violent Communist-inspired organization with a lust for power, the state would win no matter which strategy the defense employed.

The defense decided to use the cross-examination to attempt to discredit Ferreira as an expert while maintaining that what he said about SWAPO was irrelevant as far as the six accused were concerned. The lawyers had, before deciding on a course of action, visited several of the SWAPO leaders held on Robben Island, South Africa's top-security political prison for Blacks, as well as various academics. On the stand Ferreira admitted that none of his testimony had been based on personal knowledge. Much of his research on SWAPO relied on periodicals, press statements or speeches by SWAPO leaders, and books by Mao Tse-tung and Che Guevara. The writings of Mao and Guevara, incidentally, are banned by the government of South Africa. Concerning an incident Ferreira had emphasized in his direct testimony, the disturbances surrounding the forced removal of Windhoek's Blacks, he was unaware that an official governmental investigation had laid the responsibility not on SWAPO but on the Herevo tribe. As for a 1971-1972 strike, which he had claimed had been organized by SWAPO leaders, Ferreira could cite no source beyond saying it was "delicate information" from an undercover source whose life would be in danger if his name were revealed. Ferreira, moreover, had not been in the locations where the strikes had occurred.[27]

Ferreira was the last prosecution witness. The defense applied for the discharge of Andreas Nangolo on the ground that there was no evidence by which a reasonable man could convict him of handing the Landrover he had purchased over to a "terrorist." It was not proved, Cooper argued, that Nangolo had any knowledge of Usko Nambinga's alleged subversive activities because it had not been shown that the vehicle had been used by Nambinga or anyone else for such purposes, much less that Nangolo intended that it should be. Jansen contended that the key to the case against Nangolo was that Nambinga was a terrorist, as proved by his false signature, a name which means "fighter for the Lord," on the purchase document. Judge Strydom dismissed the defense motion, concluding that while the state might have a weak case, still a reasonable person could find Nangolo guilty.[28]

Trial: Defense Witnesses

All of the thirteen defense witnesses testified to the particulars of either the Elifas murder at Thomas Nangombe's bottle store or, for the accused who took the stand, the particulars of their own activities, but in no case about SWAPO. Most of the defense witnesses offered what they knew concerning the whereabouts of Hendrik Shikongo and his truck at the time of the murder. A storekeeper, for instance, detailed the sequence of events after he drove into the parking lot at Nangombe's shop on the night of the killing. He had seen Shikongo leave and walk to his truck which was parked near the store (not near the pumps as the prosecution witnesses had said) and drive away; he, the shopowner, had had a drink with Chief Elifas and several others; and after he returned to his own car, he heard three shots and saw a person run between two buildings carrying a gun. Although he neither saw Elifas leave nor noticed who was running with the gun, he did hear the shots and see the flashes—all after Shikongo had left. Such information was apparently of little interest to Lt. Dippenaar who had interrogated the shopkeeper but had not taken a statement from him.[29]

Dr. Thomas Ihuhua, a local medical doctor, testified that Elizabeth (the Queen) Namunjebo had on the day of the murder requested that he give two friends rides to the bottle store. After he said he could not, she asked permission to borrow his car. He told her his wife needed it. Several days later, after the murder, she had asked him to forget her request.[30]

Shikongo and the three accused nurses, Rauna Nambinga, Naimi Nombowa, and Anna Nghihondjwa, took the stand to testify on their own behalf. Shikongo spent four days in the witness box chronologing his movements of the day before, the day of, and the day after the Elifas assassination, emphasizing the details about the two strangers Elizabeth Namunjebo had asked him to transport to the bottle store. While he was getting a haircut and having several little girls wash his truck, he received a message to phone Elizabeth. When he returned the call she asked him to come by her store in order to help some visitors with a ride and told him that she could not give him the whole message over the telephone. He met the two strangers who were with his friend, Nicodemus Mauhi, at Elizabeth Namunjebo's store. The two strangers had not given their names, although Shikongo introduced himself to them. Elizabeth told him that they had come to speak with the chief and that they were in a hurry. Shikongo drove Nicodemus Mauhi and the two to the bottle store, parking his truck near the stoop. Since the chief's car was there, they went inside. Shikongo got into a brief but heated argument with the owner, Thomas Nangombe, over an incident of the previous day when, as Nangombe saw it, Shikongo had spun his wheels and thrown dust at Chief Elifas. Nangombe kicked Shikongo out, telling him not to return. While he was waiting for Mauhi and the other two, he went to a repair shop to have his turn signals fixed and then returned to pick up his three riders. Since he could not enter the bottle shop, Shikongo stopped his truck and waited along the road. While waiting he heard gun shots, became frightened, and drove off to Elizabeth's. He told her that there had been some shooting, and that he then went to a café where he saw some friends. While there someone came in at 10 P.M. with the news that the chief had been killed. From the café Shikongo went to see his girlfriend, Helena Hauwanga, who returned with him to his home where they spent the night together.[31]

In the morning Shikongo returned to Elizabeth Namunjebo's to inquire after his riders whom he had left behind when he heard the shots.

Shikongo: When I got there and knocked on her door she answered me quickly. She opened the door and called me into the sitting room. I greeted her and she greeted me. She said to me that she had just heard that the chief was dead. I did not ask her where she had heard that, I told her that I had also heard about that. I asked her if Nicodemus and his two friends had come. She answered and said that she had not seen them and that they were not with her. She just said, "We will just see what happens." We didn't talk much longer. I told her I was going back home.

Cooper: Did you do so?

Shikongo:Yes

Cooper: Elizabeth testified in this court and said that on the Saturday night, when you were at her house you said to her, "We killed the chief." What do you say about that testimony?

Shikongo: I did not say that and those words are not the truth.[32]

Shikongo's cross-examination at the hands of Jansen was, needless to say, severe. Although his story remained basically unaltered, Jansen raised minor inconsistencies with those of prior witnesses, which Shikongo insisted on maintaining. The items were not important in themselves, but they served to cast doubt on the reliability of both Shikongo and the defense witnesses whom he persisted in contradicting.

Jansen turned to Shikongo's SWAPO membership and the aims of SWAPO. Shikongo had joined in 1965, but he said that although he was a member he did not know everything about what SWAPO did. What he did know was that all the people of Namibia wanted freedom and that SWAPO was and is the organization which stood in favor of getting freedom.

Jansen: SWAPO wants freedom. What kind of freedom does SWAPO want?

Shikongo: Freedom so that we in this country may live in peace.

Jansen: Yes? We would now be living in peace were it not for SWAPO, but go on. Peace, is that now the only goal of SWAPO, you want to have peace?

Shikongo: To me, as I see it, there's not anyone who is free.

Jansen: Do you mean by that that besides peace you also want to have freedom?

Shikongo: That is correct.

Jansen: Now I want to hear from you what type of freedom you want to have.

Shikongo: The freedom we want to have is that people in the country must be free and each one must look upon another as their brothers.

Jansen: Brothers. What do you mean by brothers?

Shikongo: The brotherhood which I speak of is that each one must look upon the other one as a person. It must not be "what is this one and what is that one?" but that you look upon each other as a person.

Jansen: And how will you attain that freedom?

Shikongo: In the peaceableness which comes from the United Nations. . . .

Jansen: How will the freedom from the United Nations come?

Shikongo: I don't know how it will come from the United Nations, but I reckon it will be given peacefully.

Jansen: If the South African government does not want to meet the demands of the United Nations, how will it happen then?

Shikongo: That I am not able to say.

Jansen: Has SWAPO not thought about that?

Shikongo: Your Honor, I am not all of SWAPO. I am just a member of SWAPO. What has been spoken of and decided, I do not know what it is.[33]

Jansen's cross-examination intensified when he turned his question to the events surrounding the Elifas assassination. Jansen submitted and of course Shikongo denied that he and, among others, Aaron Mushimba, Axel Johannes, Usko Nambinga, and Nicodemus Mauhi, had planned either to kidnap Chief Elifas and take him to Zambia or to shoot him. Moreover, that they were working in coordination with another SWAPO team which was planning to kidnap or kill others. Jansen contended that an attempt had been made against Chief Elifas on Friday, August 15, when Shikongo's truck kicked up sand at the chief, but it had failed. On Saturday, as Jansen's thesis had it, Shikongo tried to ascertain where Elifas would be that evening. When a different SWAPO team had failed to find their victim and had arrived at the bottle shop, "then and there it was decided that the forces would be put together and Elifas would be shot dead."

Shikongo: I do not know of all that stuff.

Jansen: I submit also that then you and your Ford pickup and Victor Nkandi with the blue Landrover—Exhibit 1 before the Court—waited behind the shop complex of Thomas Phillipus.

Shikongo: That is not so.

Jansen: And that Nicodemus and the four men ran past your vehicle and climbed in the Landrover and were taken in it to Odibo.

Shikongo: I do not know. If it was so, I do not know; I did not see a Landrover as it is here now described.

Jansen: Lastly, I just want to submit you had constant knowledge that evening Chief Minister Elifas would either be kidnapped or killed.

Shikongo: That is not so.[34]

Unfortunately for the state's case, these words had come from Advocate Jansen, not from his witnesses.

Judge Strydom was disturbed that Shikongo did not go directly to the police to report the shots he had heard. It seemed, the judge observed, that any innocent person under the circumstances would have gone to the police at the first opportunity. Shikongo answered that while he had not gone to the police, he had stayed at his house, thinking that if the police wanted him they would find him there.

The three accused nurses, Rauna Nambinga, Naimi Nombowa, and Anna Nghihondjwa, took the stand as defense witnesses. Although each admitted that she was a SWAPO member, it was obvious that none of the nurses could have had anything to do with the Elifas murder. They had heard SWAPO organizers, including Rauna's brother, Usko, speak; they had contributed money (R10, or $11.50) and such items as soap, and they had visited refugees across the border in Angola. But they maintained that their contributions and their visits to the refugees were because of the pity they felt for the refugees, not because of any wish to overthrow the government or aid terrorists.[35]

Trial: Final Arguments

The final arguments presented to a South African court are lengthier and more detailed than those presented to a court in the United States. Although some written material is given to the court at the time of the arguments, the bulk of the case is made orally. The written material, called the "Heads of Argument," is organized in outline form. The prosecutor's heads were sixty-two pages long, and the defense's amounted to eighty-seven pages. Each side was allowed to respond to the other's heads. One of the defense's responses had to be made by telex because it received part of the state's heads at the last minute. The arguments in court took five days, two days for the state to present and three days for the defense.

Jansen's detailed summary stressed that, as he would have the judge see the testimony, the state witnesses were almost invariably honest and reliable, their inconsistencies the understandable result of human fallibility, while the defense witnesses were generally either irrelevant or deliberately misleading. Aaron Mushimba, he argued, was a SWAPO organizer who

purchased the Landrover which Victor Nkandi had used at the assassination and other SWAPO terrorists used later. Under the law, he reminded the court, after the state had made the connection between Mushimba and an "act" of terrorism, the burden of proof shifted to Mushimba to show he did not commit the act.

Hendrik Shikongo came in for the most attention in Jansen's summary. The evidence showed, Jansen argued, that he had angrily kicked up dust at Chief Elifas with his truck, that he arranged with Elizabeth and Nicodemus to transport the two "strangers," that he knew both of them, that he went inside the bottle shop to make sure Elifas was there, that he waited outside for the gunmen after the shots were fired, and that he told Elizabeth, "The chief is finished, we killed him."

The case against the three nurses, according to Jansen, was clear: The money had been collected for the use of SWAPO terrorists whose aim was to overthrow the government by force. Jansen told the court that the case against Andreas Nangolo, however, had not been proved. Although he had helped in negotiating for the car purchase, he had not been present when the purchase document was signed. Judge Strydom, after an adjournment, held that because there was insufficient evidence of the "act" of terrorism, the charges against Nangolo would be dismissed. When a policeman escorted him to a place in the gallery, even Advocate Jansen was among those who shook his hand. Nangolo had been imprisoned for over seven months.

Cooper began the final argument for the defense by commenting on several general features of the case. The state, he pointed out, had made no allegation of a conspiracy among the members of SWAPO to which the accused were a party. No admissible evidence showed that SWAPO was even implicated in the assassination of Chief Elifas, and, indeed, the court remained in the dark as to the identity of the assassin or assassins. The state, in fact, failed to call various witnesses who were on the scene at the time of the murder, and it was strange, Cooper commented, that no statements were taken from certain witnesess later called by the defense. The implication of Cooper's observations was that the state was more interested in trying and convicting SWAPO than in solving the Elifas murder.

As for the case against Shikongo, Cooper contended that there was "no shred of evidence" that Nicodemus and the two men intended to abduct or harm Chief Elifas or that Shikongo knew of any such plan. The same can be said for the prosecutor's speculation that a plot to abduct various leaders existed and that Shikongo knew of it and participated in it. If there wa' such a conspiracy, Cooper suggested, it was curious it was not mentioned i the indictment but only raised by the prosecution near the end of the tria The state failed to prove, Cooper argued, that Shikongo knew that t' purpose of Nicodemus and the two strangers was to kidnap or harm Ch

Elifas. Since direct evidence supports neither the contention that they intended to kidnap or harm the chief nor the accusation that Shikongo knew that they did, Shikongo could not be convicted.

Cooper submitted that the evidence of both Festus Shaanika, another prosecution witness, and Elizabeth Namunjebo should be rejected because it was in some respects improbable and, in others, untrue. What Shaanika said on the stand conflicted in the details of circumstances, time, and place not only with what Shikongo acknowledged but with what the state's own witnesses, Gabriel David and Sam Shivute, had mentioned. Cooper asserted that Shaanika, who testified for the state while under detention since August 21, had motives for not disclosing the true facts: He was a close friend of Nicodemus, he also had transported the alleged assassins, and his movements were consistent with someone shadowing Elifas.

Elizabeth Namunjebo, Cooper contended, was "a figure who would not have been out of place in the French Revolution." Although she denied any knowledge of a plot to kill Elifas, as well as any knowledge that Nicodemus had wanted to speak with Elifas, she had spent a great deal of time with Nicodemus the several days before and including August 16 making arrangements for him. Although she denied asking Shikongo to take Nicodemus and the two strangers to the bottle shop, she had made a similar request of Dr. Ihuhua only a few hours before Shikongo said she asked him. She too had motives for falsely incriminating Shikongo: She had charges involving the illegal possession of ammunition, medicine, and SWAPO membership cards hanging over her, and she was the mother of four children who had been, at the time of her testimony, in detention for six months.

Overall, Cooper observed, the probability was that Shikongo had given Nicodemus and the other two rides out of a matter of chance. His activities on August 16 were not those of a man intent on aiding a murder plot. If he had assisted, he certainly would not have worn a SWAPO button. He would have had no reason to return to Elizabeth's, since he would have known the murderers had made a safe getaway. If he had been part of a plot, he would have tried to flee the country instead of seeking out his girl friend, Helena, and spending the night with her in his own house.

Advocate Berker summarized the argument concerning Aaron Mushimba. He noted that the state must prove, but had not, that Mushimba handed the Landrover over to Victor Nkandi with the intent that Nkandi give it to persons whose object was to overthrow the government. Furthermore, the state must prove that Mushimba acted with the intent of endangering the maintenance of law and order. The only evidence, Berker pointed out, that Mushimba had handed the vehicle over to Nkandi was the testimony of Elizabeth Namunjebo that she had seen Nkandi driving a

similar Landrover and that Mushimba had asked her over the phone whether Nkandi had passed by in a blue Landrover. There was evidence neither of Mushimba's intent, nor that Nkandi was a terrorist, nor, if the Landrover did go from Mushimba to Nkandi, how it came to the possession of the unidentified persons who fired upon the South African army patrol.

The circumstantial evidence the state must rely upon, since it had no direct evidence, Berker argued, allowed for more possibilities than the inference that Mushimba's purchase of the vehicle was a terrorist act. Another reasonable inference, for example, would be that Mushimba delivered the Landrover to Nkandi for delivery to Nkandi's brother in Ovamboland. In any case, the state, Berker charged, failed to make a prima facie case against Mushimba.

Cooper took the final defense arguments in the case against the three nurses. He summarized the charges, noting that the state made no allegation of conspiracy or of any connection with SWAPO beyond mere membership. Cooper noted that all five of the state witnesses were detained for various periods after October 20, 1975, and that two were in detention until after they testified. Each of the five appeared fearful and apprehensive, which was hardly surprising when it is considered that they had been rounded up by armed soldiers, intensely interrogated, and in at least one case tortured. In short, he argued, the evidence given by the state witnesses was vague, contradictory, and inconsistent, in contrast to the satisfactory and corroborated testimony of the defendants. The state had failed, Cooper submitted, to prove the elements of a terrorist act beyond a reasonable doubt which, in turn, did not engage those provisions of the Terrorism Law that shift the burden of proof to the defendant to show he or she did not intend to endanger the maintenance of law and order or to accomplish any of the other results mentioned in the law. All that was proved concerning both the defendants and the state witnesses was that they had given their donations in compassion with the intention of helping persons in need.

Trial: Judgment and Sentencing

On May 11, the day Judge Strydom had announced that he would deliver his judgment, the courtroom was packed before 9 A.M. After the "White" half of the gallery had accommodated those Whites who wanted to attend, the remainder was opened to Blacks. Even so, many Blacks were not able to get into the courtroom and milled about outside in the hot sun. The police prevented several of the better-known local SWAPO leaders from entering, despite their having been near the head of the line. Outside, before the court was called to order, demonstrators peacefully sang SWAPO songs and chanted slogans.

Justice Strydom's judgment, given orally in Afrikaans, lasted from 9 A.M. until 3 P.M. with a twenty-minute morning tea break and an hour lunch break. It fills ninety-four pages of the transcript.

In the first hour and a half Judge Strydom summarized the evidence relating to SWAPO, from the oral testimony and documents to weapons and songs. He noted that all the defendants were members of SWAPO and that it had not been declared an unlawful or prohibited organization. Some of his findings were almost eccentrically quaint: "Despite SWAPO, according to their exhibits, claiming or proclaiming that it is an organization which enjoys world-wide recognition, I do not find here any profession of God, who through his omnipotence and guidance controls the destiny of things and people."[36] He accepted the evidence given by the state's expert on SWAPO, Petrus Ferreira, saying that the defense had advanced no evidence in contradiction. Although the defense contended that SWAPO had an internal wing whose leaders have declared themselves against violence, the judge observed, none of these leaders gave evidence. Although he acknowledged the validity of Cooper's argument that membership in SWAPO alone could not cause the court to find that the accused desired forceable overthrow of the government, Judge Strydom also accepted the documents found in the Landrover as evidence and concluded that:

> According to the uncontested evidence SWAPO has no right to existence. It is a militant organization which desires the overthrow of the Government and Administration of the Territory of South West Africa by force of arms and terrorism. An appreciation of what SWAPO actually is, what its objectives are, and what it does, is necessary for a true determination of the probabilities when judging the Accuseds' alleged deeds, which might otherwise appear to have been innocent.[37]

In discussing the cases of Mushimba and Shikongo, the court recognized that the defense had called attention to the fact that because witnesses had been held in detention, at times in solitary confinement, with persistent interrogation, "the psychological condition of the person interrogated becomes so influenced that he imagines and later believes and says things happened, which in fact are untrue and flights of the imagination."[38] He even quoted from another case to underscore the point that the court "has a duty to reject the evidence of any witness if it has grounds for believing that his relationship with the police made the reliability of his evidence, when viewed in the light of all relevant circumstances, suspect."[39] After saying this Judge Strydom commented that the state witnesses were intelligent, withstood cross-examination well, and did not give the impression of telling a fabricated story. The court accepted the version as told by Elizabeth Namunjebo, Festus Shaanika, and Sam Shivute, as well as Lt. Dippenaar and the other state witnesses.

The court gave a detailed critique of the defense witnesses and Shikongo's own testimony. One witness, he said, did not take the defendant's case far; another could not have much weight given to his testimony; a third had been faulty in the recollection of a detail; Dr. Ihuhua's testimony was irrelevant; yet another witnesses's testimony was a lie; Shikongo's girl friend's evidence had no probability of being considered true, and others did not refuse the state's case. As for Shikongo himself,

> He gives the impression of an arrogant and presumptious young man. At an early stage grave suspicion arose in regard to his story that he was an innocent victim of a calculated cunning scheme on the part of Elizabeth. The fact of the case is that Nicodemus came from Odibo near the Angolan border with two SWAPO soldiers to Ondangwa. It is a reasonable possibility that their purpose included the use of their Tokarev self-loading pistols of which four were indeed used at the scene where Chief Minister Elifas was shot dead and others wounded. Nicodemus and his companions had two basic considerations in this undertaking, namely self-protection and a successful attack, for both of which transport and prior arrangements were essential. To suggest that Nicodemus and his companions would rely on Elizabeth's possible arrangements on such a loose basis as Accused 3 suggests is simply laughable. To assume also that Nicodemus and his companions would not make use of someone in order to precisely establish the whereabouts of the Chief Minister is equally laughable.[40]

The court found that Shikongo's response to the court's question as to why he had not reported to the police was "evasive" and "strongly blanketed by lies." If Shikongo's story were true, observed the court, "it is incredible that he did not react as any normal citizen would. A normal citizen would immediately hasten to the Police, not only to dispel any suspicions upon himself, but to offer help in order to trace the persons guilty of so brutal a murder. . . . My total impression of Accused 3's account is that it is a fabrication made up to fit in with the State case as adduced."[41]

As for the case against the three nurses (Rauna Nambinga, Naimi Nombowa, and Anna Nghihondjwa), or as the court called them, "Accused 4, 5, and 6," Judge Strydom said that their defense was elementary. That they had given assistance for charitable and humanitarian reasons, he regarded as "sheer nonsense."

> The Chief Minister made appeals over Radio Ovambo to the people who had been lured out of the country by false pretenses, to return. Those who remained beyond the border were therefore training as terrorists. People who suffered misery there as described by the Accused were simply too lazy to

walk a few kilometers back to their Fatherland, unless they were terrorists, but apart from their starved, ill appearance, torn clothes, bare feet, the Accused could give no clear and acceptable description of these people. All three accused gave the Court the impression of being intentionally vague, and of concealing the truth. . . . The Court has no doubt that these stories are cooked-up, mealy-mouthed lies.[42]

The court concluded that the state had proved that the elements of the act of terrorism had been committed by Nambinga and Nghihondjwa who had donated their R10 after having visited SWAPO soldiers in Angola and therefore knew who would receive the money. Nombowa, however, gave her R10 before visiting Angola, which led the court to entertain a reasonable doubt as to her knowledge when she contributed the money.

Shikongo's participation in the murder of the chief minister, Judge Strydom determined, provided irrefutable evidence that he had the intent to endanger the maintenance of law and order. The only major point to be considered with respect to Mushimba, Judge Strydom concluded, was whether he handed the Landrover over to Victor Nkandi, and that, based on the evidence of Elizabeth Namunjebo, had been proved beyond a reasonable doubt. The court apparently assumed that Nkandi delivered the vehicle to those who fired on the soldiers since the point was not considered. The court noted that Landrovers were particularly suited for terrorist activities, that Mushimba knew Nicodemus Mauhi, that Mushimba as an officer in SWAPO was "aware of what was going on," and that SWAPO was militant and violent. The final failure of Mushimba was in not offering to testify on his own behalf:

> The true position is that, in cases resting on circumstantial evidence, if there is a *prima facie* case against the accused which he could answer if innocent, the failure to answer it becomes a factor, to be considered along with the other factors; and from that totality the Court may draw the inference of guilt. The weight to be given to the factor in question depends upon the circumstances of each case.[43]

Therefore, the court announced, it found Aaron Mushimba, Hendrik Shikongo, Rauna Nambinga, and Anna Nghihondjwa guilty. Naimi Nombowa was not found guilty. The defendants must have been prepared for such a result. They had little reaction, just a smile and a shrug from Mushimba to his family in the gallery.

The court then adjourned for a quarter-hour before the late-afternoon session which had been requested by Prosecutor Jansen, who wanted to call two witnesses-in-aggravation of sentence. The first was Colonel Carel Coetzee of the South African Police who testified that he was investigating seven terrorist cases, which he briefly described. The second witness was

Colonel Willem Schoon of the Security Police who had testified earlier by reading an entire issue of a SWAPO publication into the record. In this encore appearance he read a long report into the record. It was a list of fifty-nine "terrorist" incidents in Ovamboland over the past nine months, all attributed by the police to SWAPO. While the murder of Chief Elifas and other terrorist-type crimes, such as exploding landmines, were included on Schoon's list, many of the acts were of the following sort: "On February 7, Phillipus Ndoya's store was robbed of nearly R4,000"; on February 10, "terrorists stole just under R1,000 from Tolve Joel's shop"; and "On March 11, the shop of an Ovambo woman, Ferresia Kolamoni, was robbed near Ohauwanga. R100 worth of goods was taken." Colonel Schoon concluded by saying "SWAPO terrorists are responsible for all these cases we are presently investigating. We, in fact, have evidence to prove that SWAPO are [sic] guilty of these acts."[44]

On the next day defense attorney Cooper's cross-examination of both witnesses-in-aggravation lasted a total of three minutes. Both witnesses admitted that their evidence was based on documents, not personal knowledge, and that no accused were before any court as a result of these incidents. Cooper then announced that the defense would present no witnesses in mitigation of sentence. Instead, he made an argument for mercy. The accused in this case, he said, were not criminals in the usual sense, for their acts were not motivated by personal gain but by their political involvement. Alluding perhaps to the experience of many Afrikaner Nationalists, among them Judge Strydom and Prime Minister Vorster, who had both been detained during World War II as Nazi sympathizers, Cooper noted that the criminals of today are often the patriots of tomorrow. "We've seen this in our own country since 1945."

He asked the court to deal with the sentencing dispassionately and to note that all of the accused were first-offenders and relatively young. Mushimba, Cooper pointed out, had a wife and two small children, and there was no evidence that he had actively participated in a terroristic act or that the Landrover had been used in the assassination of Chief Elifas. Shikongo, said Cooper, was a lively young man who should not be punished for the deeds of others. He was not a party to the killing, and there was no suggestion that he knew his passengers were armed. Cooper asked that the court not feel a sense of frustration because the person in court was not the main culprit. Nambinga and Nghihondjwa, Cooper noted, were young women trained to serve society. Nghihondjwa had been married shortly before being arrested. Both had been heavily influenced by older people found by the court to be terrorists. In conclusion, Cooper observed that the witnesses called by the state created the impression that it was calling for vengeance. "But vengeance is mine, says the Lord," Cooper reminded the court. He said that it is easy for one to be *kragdadig* (an Afrikaans expression implying a powerful wrath), but the history of South Africa, since the turn of the century and the harsh treatment of Afrikaners during the Boer War by their British captors, had demonstrated the counterproductiveness of *Kragdadigheid*.

Advocate Jansen, in his remarks, told the court that terrorism in South West Africa was on the increase and that SWAPO was accountable. Shops had been robbed, people kidnapped and killed, with innocent people the victims. The security of each citizen was at stake. The sentence, he urged, must serve not only as a punishment for a deed done but also as an example to others. "Accused No. 1" had purchased a Landrover which was later used to fire on the South African Army. "Accused No. 3" had taken the murderers of Elifas to their goal with full knowledge of their aims. "Accused Nos. 4 and 6" had given knowing aid to terrorists. He asked the court, therefore, to impose the most severe sentences.

In rebuttal Cooper argued that the two witnesses-in-aggravation had relied only on documentary evidence to testify to events which were not before the court but which had happened for the most part after the accused had been arrested. It would be unfair to hold these events against the accused. He finished by asking the court to deal with the accused according to their merits and punish them according to their deserts. The court adjourned for an hour and a half to consider the sentence.

When court was reconvened, policemen lined the walls of the gallery while the defendants stood. Judge Strydom read his four-page judgment. After noting that the Terrorism Act provided for sentences ranging from imprisonment to death, he gave a detailed overview of the evidence of terroristic incidents introduced by the two witnesses-in-aggravation of sentence. He was deeply affected by this evidence and held it against the four accused standing before him:

> It is a foreign and barbarous outrage to murder and to injure innocent men and women under the banner of liberation of the oppressed. . . . The Accused heard this evidence—it was led yesterday afternoon. They have had the whole night to consider what they were engaged in and how obviously incensed is the peace-loving and orderly community of South West Africa and Ovambo at these incidents.

> Notwithstanding this, they have elected not to give any evidence or to indicate even a glimmer of remorse, dissociation or even severance. This evidences an evil disposition which is still being maintained.[45]

The court said that three factors were normally taken into account in sentencing: (1) the offense, (2) the offender, and (3) the interests of the community. In cases of terrorism, he said, the interests of the community demand preference, not as a demand for retribution but to set up a deterrent against further acts and to prevent citizens from taking the law into their own hands.

The guilt of Nambinga and Nghihondjwa, the court said, was aggravated by their moral assistance to terrorists, by the size of their gifts (20 percent of their month's salary), and by the voluntary nature of their acts. But their youth, the deception and temptations by Usko, Nicodemus, and Gabriel, and the fact that the authorities had not seen fit to act formally against SWAPO, were all mitigating factors. Rauna Nambinga was sentenced to seven years' imprisonment, and Anna Nghihondjwa to five.

A world of difference, Judge Strydom observed, existed between the cases of Accused 1 and 2 and Accused 4 and 6. "Terrorists who murder a Chief Minister and carry out an attack on the South African Defense Force can expect no mercy from a Court. This is an evil which must be wiped out, roots and all. Law and order must be maintained. . . . The Court finds no mitigation for imposing a sentence other than that for high treason."[46]

The clerk rose at this point to ask the accused whether they had anything to say to explain why the death sentence should not be imposed. Aaron Mushimba said that he had not known of these terroristic events and did not participate in any of them himself. He had bought the Landrover for his friend and did not know what he would do with it. He said that he did not want to violate the law or harm anybody and asked for mercy. He was not a person to kill others, and he had a family. Hendrik Shikongo said that it was correct that he had taken Nicodemus and the two others in his truck, but he had not known their purpose. No one had asked him to help the escape. He was not guilty of murder, and he had not intended to kill anyone or endanger the maintenance of law and order. He asked for mercy, that he might receive only imprisonment. Judge Strydom responded that he had no authority to give mercy.

A policeman in the front of the courtroom rose and chanted in Afrikaans, "Hear ye, hear ye, hear ye! Silence in the court as the sentence of death is read!" Judge Strydom's face flushed and his eyes opened wide as he looked through the two men standing in front of him as he condemned them: "Accused No. 1 and No. 3, the sentence of this Court is that you be taken to the place of custody and that you will hang by the neck until you are dead."

As the death sentence was read some family members began to wail. The two men standing before the judge, after they heard their fate, held up their hands with fists clenched. The gallery answered the clenched fists. The four prisoners were taken out of the courtroom quickly. A crowd milled outside at some distance from the court building which was ringed with attack dogs and armed paramilitary police in battle dress.

"First S.W.A. Political Leaders to Hang," announced the headline in the Windhoek newspaper, and the story began: "Swakopmund. Two SWAPO members, one of them an important official of the organization's internal wing, were given death sentences yesterday—the first political leaders to die on the gallows in the history of modern South West Africa, unless a petition to the Chief Justice succeeds."[47] The defense immediately moved for leave to appeal. They asked that they be allowed to appeal the convictions and that the record be changed to reflect error on the part of the court in not going to Ovamboland for an inspection *in loco* and in not recalling certain state witnesses for further cross-examination. Without adjourning to consider the motion, Judge Strydom stated that he did not see "a reasonable prospect," which is the legal standard, that a higher court would find differently than he. He denied the application and adjourned court.

Spying Incident and Appeal

The next step for the defense was an appeal directly to the chief justice of South Africa. But before this effort could be mounted, events in the offices of Lorentz & Bone took an unexpected turn. A few days after the end of the trial, a Mrs. C. M. de Beer, confidential secretary to Attorney du Preez, told him that she had been approached during the trial and asked to help spy for the Security Police. The approach had been made by Mrs. Elsie Ellis, the 27-year-old office receptionist/telephone operator. Mrs. de Beer said that she had not revealed this earlier because the Security Police had threatened her with detention if she told anyone. This threat alone, apparently, was enough to precipitate a miscarriage, which she had had shortly afterward.

A meeting of the entire Lorentz & Bone staff was called that day. An announcement was made that there had been a highly confidential leak and that Mrs. Ellis had been discharged. Any others who had been approached by the Security Police were asked to identify themselves. A clerk, B. R. S. Mautschke, spoke up to say that one of the partners in the firm, Anthony Smit, had asked him if he were willing to convey information to the Security Police, and that he had refused to become an informer. He said that he had been present, moreover, on several occasions when Smit talked with Captain A. T. C. (Attie) Nel of the Security Police about cases undertaken by Lorentz & Bone, including the Mushimba trial at Swakopmund. An office boy, Andrew Pike, also reported that in mid-May Mrs. Ellis had confessed to him that she had been spying for the Security Police and that Smit was also involved. The partnership between Smit and Lorentz & Bone was dissolved forthwith and the decision was made to file a motion with the Supreme Court for a special entry into the record of the Mushimba trial.

The defense team had had suspicions early in the trial that they were being spied upon. The main cause for their uneasiness was an encounter with the ubiquitous Lt. Dippenaar in a bar. He had been drinking substantially. When he invited Attorney Colin du Preez to join him and du Preez put a question to him, Dippenaar bragged that he knew everything that was in the defense files, including who was paying the defense fees.

All these details were aired in a five-day hearing which began June 16, 1976. Justice Strydom was on vacation after the lengthy trial. The matter was an urgent one, and rather than wait for Strydom's return, he was replaced by Justice M. J. Hart, his colleague. Appearing for the applicants were Wilfred Cooper and Hans Berker, who had conducted the trial, as well as an advocate from Johannesburg, I. A. Maisels, Q. C. The Attorney General of South West Africa, J. E. Nöthling, represented the state. Each side introduced eight witnesses, including the principals, Mrs. Ellis, Mrs. de Beer, Attorney Smit, and Captain Nel.

Judge Hart delivered his opinion on June 25. He noted at the outset that he had read neither the record nor the judgment in the trial itself, and that neither the conduct of the learned trial judge nor the events of the trial were challenged, but that "common justice and humanity required that the hearing proceed and that a decision on the application be reached with the least possible delay."[48] The matter before him, he observed, was "unique in South African legal history, and indeed, fairly unique in the legal history of many other systems."[49] The issue was the breach of the privilege existing between attorney and client. He found that for the past four years there had been "a type of conspiracy between Mrs. Ellis and Capt. Nel to obtain confidential information from the offices of the defense attorneys, which establishes an exception to the Hearsay Rule, thus rendering such evidence [as conversations or, for instance, confessions to the office boy] admissible."[50] A wild card, such as the law of conspiracy, can at times be played against even the police.

Judge Hart was impressed by Mrs. de Beer as a witness, finding her "both intelligent and truthful," but was incredulous at the testimony of Mrs. Ellis, who, he thought, "left the witness-box . . . thoroughly discredited." Mrs. Ellis, it was revealed, had been a police informer since 1972, consistently associating with Capt. Nel, to whom she had given copies of documents in the Swakopmund trial, including such crucial items as a coded message from David Meroro, the exiled SWAPO leader in London, Hendrik Shikongo's statement, and other defense material. Witnesses recalled that Mrs. Ellis especially volunteered to type several of the critical statements. Mr. Smit, the erstwhile partner, had violated his professional fealty by becoming an informer for Capt. Nel. Smit had unsuccessfully attempted to recruit a clerk as a coinformer but did provide Nel with facts about the case, such as a visit of counsel to London, the sources of fees payable, and how information about SWAPO had been gathered, activities which Judge Hart called "sordid." Capt. Nel, he said, was evasive in his testimony, but the Security Police is a dangerous organization, and "it is equally dangerous for members of this branch to disclose the sources of their information." The court found Lt. Dippenaar to be candid and most probably unaware of the source of his information beyond Capt. Nel. The court concluded that the privilege between attorney and client had been seriously breached and the special entry must be made.[51] This allowed the defense to include in its appeal to South Africa's highest court all the details of the spying.

Appeal to the Supreme Court of South Africa, located in Bloemfontein, Orange Free State, was granted, and, a year to the day (February 15-16, 1977) after the Swakopmund trial opened, they heard the case. Cooper and Jansen faced each other as adversaries once again. On the bench were Judge Kotze, Judge Hofmeyr, and Chief Justice Rumpff. Both the merits of the Swakopmund trial and the attorney-client privilege were argued.

The Supreme Court's decision was handed down on March 17, 1977, in a 28-page opinion written in Afrikaans by Chief Justice Rumpff. The Swakopmund trial was not touched upon, only the attorney-client privilege issue. The opinion began with an expression of understanding, although not sympathy, for the acts of the authorities dealing with SWAPO's "dual existence. . . . an organization which ostensibly envisages peaceful political changes and is not banned, whilst there is an external wing of the party which advocates a militant policy and which also enjoys internal support, and which infiltrates terrorists into the Country." In a climate where innocent people are murdered, it is not surprising that "some people are violently anti-SWAPO and are prepared to place authority and order above any other consideration. The question which arises in this case is whether a breach of the privilege between client and legal advisor upon such an attitude can result in a conviction of an offense being set aside."[52]

The court noted that only one of the accused, Shikongo (still carrying his trial appelation, "Accused No. 3"), had been charged with being connected with the murder, and that he "was not charged with having murdered Chief Elifas, nor with being an accessory to the murder. The other five Accused were charged with acts which had no connection whatsoever with the murder of Chief Elifas." The erroneous impression that the trial concerned the murder of Chief Elifas "must have placed all the Accused, except Accuse No. 3, in an unfavorable light and which gave a wrong complexion to the case."[53]

After recounting the facts of the leak involving Ellis, Smit, Nel and Dippenaar, the court concluded: "From the date when instructions to defend were received until the end of the case, the Security Police, through the medium of Captain Nel and Mrs. Ellis, completely penetrated the defense and the privilege was simply eliminated. . . . In my view, the complete elimination of the privilege is not only an irregularity, but an extremely gross irregularity, which, so far as it concerns privilege, can scarcely be surpassed." Justice Rumpff traced the breach from Nel to Dippenaar, who had acted virtually as Prosecutor Jansen's junior counsel working in the closest cooperation with him, creating a channel "which ran from the office of the defense to the Prosecutor in the case." Although Jansen was unaware of the channel, that it "was directly linked with the proceedings and during the entire period of the proceedings," is beyond doubt.[54] The judgment of the Supreme Court, concurred in by Judges Hofmeyr and Kotze, was that "the Appellants' protection by privilege before and during the trial totally disappeared as a result of the conduct of the Security Police, that as a result thereof the trial did not comply with what is required in this regard by justice, and that, accordingly, justice was not done."[55] The convictions and sentences were set aside.

All four accused were released directly from their prisons in Pretoria and returned to Namibia. Victor Nkandi and Axel Johannes, upon expiration of their one-year contempt sentences for refusing to testify, were immediately redetained. Lt. Dippenaar returned to Ovamboland to continue the investigation into the Elifas murder.

In the SWAPO trial both the legal and political agendas of the South African government failed. The question of who murdered Chief Elifas was not solved, and SWAPO was not discredited. If the government had been serious about the legal agenda, those who were tried would not have been indicted. Others, perhaps the real killers, might have been caught and tried. The preoccupation of the government with the political agenda did not, in the end, bear the fruit they wanted. They could not use the trial to justify banning SWAPO as an organization. They played with a wild card, South Africa's Terrorism Law, which allowed the government a maximum of discretion in arresting, accusing, and trying nearly anyone they wished, but they did not win. The murder of Chief Elifas was a potential wedge, similar to the one Robert Cecil employed in the Gunpowder Plot trial against Jesuits and all Catholics. The Elifas wedge might have served to demonstrate the perniciousness of SWAPO and all Nambian nationalists. But in spite of the odds, it did not. Not all partisan trials turn out as the government desires. Sometimes those with power overreach.

Notes

1. Windhoek *Advertiser*, August 18, 1975, p. 1.

2. *Namibia News* (September-December 1975), p. 6; also Dr. J. L. de Vries (president, Evangelical Lutheran Church of Namibia), interview, November 19, 1975.
3. Terrorism Act, No. 83 of 1967. See Albie Sachs, *Justice in South Africa* (Berkeley, University of California Press, 1973), pp. 251-253; Anthony Mathews, *Law, Order, and Liberty in South Africa* (Berkeley, University of California Press, 1972), p. 151ff; John Dugard, *Human Rights and the South African Legal Order* (Princeton, Princeton University Press, 1978), pp. 117-121, 253-255, 260-264. The main provisions of the Terrorism Act are now part of the omnibus Internal Security Act.
4. Terrorism Act, Sect. 6.
5. *Ibid.*, Sec. 2.
6. *Ibid.*, Sec. 8.
7. Proclamation R.17, Regulations for the Adminstration of the District of Ovamboland, Republic of South Africa Government Gazette, February 4, 1972.
8. Letter to Prime Minister B. J. Vorster, September 18, 1975.
9. The account of Dean Griswold's visit is based on his report, "Journal and Report of a trip to South West Africa at the Request of the Lutheran World Federation, November 13-15, 1975" (unpublished report, 1975).
10. *Ibid.*
11. *Ibid.*
12. *Ibid.*
13. Windhoek *Advertiser*, November 20, 1975, p. 1.
14. *Ibid.*, December 1, 1975, p. 1.
15. Interview with Chris Jansen, Swakopmund, May 12, 1976.
16. South Africa follows the English in having a split bar. A client consults an attorney, du Preez of Lorentz and Bone in this case. Attorneys who cannot appear before the trial court engage generally two advocates for all litigation. Advocates are of two types, Senior Counsel (in England called Queen's Counsel—QC) who wear silk robes, and Junior Counsel. In this case Cooper served as Senior Council and Berker as Junior, although he was older and more experienced than Cooper.
17. Interview with Colin du Preez, conducted by Ralie Deffenbaugh, Windhoek, December 11, 1975.
18. Interview with David Soggot, conducted by Ralie Deffenbaugh, Windhoek, January 14, 1976.
19. Interview with Pastor K. Dumeni, conducted by Ralie Deffenbaugh, Windhoek, February 8, 1976.
20. Trial Record, pp. 334-335.
21. *Ibid.*, pp. 432-440.
22. *Ibid.*, pp. 575-578.
23. *Ibid.*, pp. 614-638; Windhoek *Advertiser*, March 3, 1976, p. 7.
24. *Ibid.*, pp. 539-557. Cornelius Ndjoba was the chief minister of Ovambo.
25. *Ibid.*, pp. 612-613.
26. *Ibid.*, pp. 803-805.
27. *Ibid.*, pp. 829-872.
28. *Ibid.*, pp. 885-893.
29. *Ibid.*, pp. 903-926.
30. *Ibid.*, pp. 977-978.
31. *Ibid.*, pp. 1038ff.

32. *Ibid.,* p. 1062.
33. *Ibid.,* pp. 1066-1067.
34. *Ibid.,* pp. 1166-1168.
35. *Ibid.,* pp. 1196-1262.
36. Judgment in *State v. Mushimba and Others* (May 12, 1976), p. 5.
37. *Ibid.,* p. 36.
38. *Ibid.,* p. 48.
39. *State v. Hassim and Others,* p. 73.
40. Judgment in *State v. Mushimba and Others,* p. 73.
41. *Ibid.,* pp. 73-74.
42. *Ibid.,* p. 80.
43. Quoted by Judge Strydom from *State v. Letsoko and Others,* 1964 (4) S.A. 768 (AD), in Judgment in *State v. Mushimba and Others,* p. 93.
44. Windhoek *Advertiser,* May 14, 1976, p. 5.
45. Sentence in *State v. Mushimba and Others,* p. 2.
46. *Ibid.,* p. 4.
47. Windhoek *Advertiser,* May 13, 1976, p.1.
48. Judgment of Mr. Justice Hart, *Aaron Mushimba and Others v. the State.* Supreme Court of South Africa, South West Africa Division, June 25, 1976, p. 4.
49. *Ibid.,* p. 2.
50. *Ibid.,* p. 19.
51. *Ibid.,* pp. 20-25; Windhoek *Advertiser,* June 28, 1976, p. 1.
52. *Mushimba and Others v. the State,* Supreme Court of South Africa 1977, pp. 1-2.
53. *Ibid.,* p. 3.
54. *Ibid.,* pp. 17-19.
55. *Ibid.,* p. 28.

4

Trials of Corruption and Insanity:
The Question of Responsibility

Responsibility is the garden variety issue in political trials. It blooms forth from all quarters with many variations. In this chapter we will examine two types, corruption cases and insanity cases, but responsibility is the issue in diverse political trials. For instance, the parallel libel suits filed against CBS and *Time* by Generals William Westmoreland and Ariel Sharon, respectively, turn on the responsibility of the generals and of the media. While the legal agenda in both trials involved the formulation of responsibility for actual malice under the tangle of doctrine deriving from the *New York Times v. Sullivan* case, another agenda addressed a broader issue of responsibility. What was General Westmoreland's responsibility in advising or misleading the president on enemy troop strength? What responsibility did General Sharon have for encouraging the Sabra and Shatila massacres? What responsibility had CBS and *Time* for accuracy? Each of these libel trials reached beyond the issues presented in the courtroom toward more basic political questions: What was the United States doing in Vietnam? What was Israel doing in Lebanon? What were CBS and *Time* doing in shaping public opinion? That these matters were not settled, that all sides, in fact, claimed victory while they left the legal knot as perplexing a conundrum as ever, should be no surprise.

Likewise, the Bernard Goetz subway vigilante case extends the issue of responsibility far beyond an ordinary urban shooting. It concerns responsibility at its most basic level, self-help. The widespread discussion of whether Goetz was justified in shooting four young men who approached/ threatened him on the New York subway rapidly spread across the country. It was hotly debated not only on television but in rural communities by people who had never been to New York or to any large city. The question of responsibility in the Goetz case touches each citizen at the Hobbesian level of fear in a city where life is felt to be "solitary, poor, nasty, brutish, and short" (*Leviathan*, Ch. 13), because of the danger from either muggers or vigilantes.

Some trials raise important political questions not because of the causes involved—there may be none—but because of the individuals. When powerful political figures are tried for bribery or for a breach of ethics, standards of conduct for all public officials are brought to the surface. The lines between what is and what is not allowed are explored in the courtroom and by the media. Whether the verdict comes out guilty or not guilty, the trial itself serves to educate.

In bribery trials the court and the public face a question of responsibility: Where is the line between private life and public duty? The specific facts about the deals cut by an Adam Clayton Powell, Marvin Mandel, Daniel Flood, or the Abscam congressmen fade rapidly in our minds, but the pattern stays. Even when the case does not come to trial but the media have devoted attention to it and a trial looms as a threat, we recognize the problem of influence and its consequences. This happened when the details of payments made to Spiro Agnew were brought to light. The bribes he took as a county executive, as governor, and as vice-president were instructive not only about one person's iniquity but about the reach of monied influence in all politics.

G. Gordon Liddy, Maurice Stans, John Mitchell, John Ehrlichman, and H. R. Haldeman were not accused of taking bribes. They did not illegally enrich themselves. If they had a cause it was nothing beyond loyalty to the president. But their trials for the break-in at the Watergate and its cover-up, for arranging "hush money" payoffs, destroying documents, and lying to various investigative bodies taught important lessons in the responsible use of power and in temptations for its abuse. What they did in service to the president challenged the rule of law. Which takes priority, loyalty to the president or to the law?

When loyalty to the president and the rule of law become irreconcilable, a deeper question arises: legitimacy. Even if White House advisors, cabinet members, and a vice-president are brought down, their trials seem small when compared to the trial of a president. Legitimacy surfaced as an issue during the Watergate inquiries, became the subject for the House Judiciary Committee as it considered the impeachment articles, and would have been the focus for the pending trial of President Nixon by the Senate. It is a question fundamentally different from the issue of responsibility, which will be covered in a later chapter, chapter 9.

Responsibility is raised in another way in trials not of public officials who take bribes or abuse their office but of citizens who commit public acts for which they may not be responsible. In these contrasting trials the political questions arise because the victim is a powerful figure. In the John Hinckley trial the court, especially the jury, must contend with a knot of responsibility even more difficult than taking bribes or abusing power. Hinckley had no cause, nor did he attempt to enrich himself. He admitted he pulled the trigger, but he maintained he was not guilty because of insanity. Yet since his victim was President Reagan, the trial was inescapably political.

Trials of Political Scandal

If there ever was a classic trial for corruption, it would be the trial of Lord Chancellor Francis Bacon in 1621. Bacon, one of the founders of modern science, had published his critique of Aristotle, the *Novum Organum*, the previous year. His influential *Advancement of Learning* had been published nearly two decades earlier. As a politician he had served in Parliament for nineteen years and, with the accession of James I, became the solicitor general, then the attorney general, a member of the Privy Council, Lord Keeper of the Great Seal, and finally the powerful right hand of the king, Lord Chancellor. His affluence increased with his power, but so did his enemies. A bitter rival throughout their parallel careers was Edward Coke. Coke served on the committee investigating Bacon and was the first to substitute the word *bribe* for "gift" or "gratuity."[1] Bacon's impeachment by Parliament for taking bribes must be viewed as an attack also on King James. James, who was not above taking gratuities, gifts, or bribes himself, acknowledged that "if I were . . . to punish those who take bribes, I should soon not have a single subject left."[2]

On the advice of James, Bacon confessed to twenty-three counts of corruption, admitting that he took gifts from litigants but denying that he had been influenced. The House of Lords condemned him to pay a ruinous fine of £40,000, to be imprisoned in the Tower during the king's pleasure, and to be barred from holding office. Granting a full pardon, James released Bacon from the Tower after four days and remitted the fine. Although his scholarly career continued, Bacon's political career was at an end. Before he died, he wrote in his notebook about his trial: "It was the justest censure in Parliament that was these 200 years."[3]

History reveals no lack of trials for misuse of public authority for private ends. Every generation has its Watergate, Abscam, or Teapot Dome cases, and many similar cases involving lesser officials, calling our attention to the temptations of power and the question of where the line is drawn between private life and public duty. The dilemmas inherent in holding public office arise not only from the influence that those with power have for shaping policy toward special interests while claiming that they are acting in the public interest, but also from their vulnerability to the bad publicity of false charges.

For example, in 1971, Secretary of the Treasury John Connally urged President Nixon, as taped conversation reveals, to "satisfy dairymen" in order to secure their financial support for the 1972 election. In 1975, Connally was tried for accepting $10,000 in illegal gratuities from the Associated Milk Producers in return for his efforts to obtain an increase in the milk price support. The major prosecution witness was a lawyer from the Milk Producers, Jake Jacobsen, who had been granted immunity from prosecution by the federal authorities in return for his testimony. Connally was acquited, but Jacobsen was arrested by the Texas authorities for misuse of $825,000 in a savings and loan firm for which he was an officer.[4] Was Connally the victim of a "con job" by Jacobsen, or did Connally merely "beat the rap?"

When public officials are tried on charges of corruption, public confidence in the judicial system is often at stake. Judge John Sirica became *Time* magazine's Man of the Year for upholding the integrity of the law in the Watergate cases. Conversely, federal Court of Appeals judge and former Illinois governor Otto Kerner was convicted of taking a bribe of racetrack stock in return for favors to racetrack owners while he was governor. Although he had an unimpaired reputation and insisted that he was innocent, it was important to demonstrate to the public, as a *New York Times* editorial pointed out, that not even so powerful an official as Kerner was beyond the reach of the judicial system, especially when the system is often accused of being stacked in favor of the elite and against the lowly.[5] The prosecutor, incidentally, was James R. Thompson, who later became the Illinois governor partially because of his reputation for being tough on crime, gained somewhat in the Kerner case.

A trial for corruption can easily become partisan. Anne Boleyn's trial for adultery and incest in 1536 is an example. Although Anne had borne a female child to Henry VIII, she incurred Henry's sharp displeasure when a baby boy was born dead. Henry's eye was also attracted toward a maid of Anne's, Jane Seymour. He accused Anne of adultery, and he referred the matter to the Privy Council. Faithfully, the members of the council reported that Queen Anne had committed adultery with five members of the court, including her own brother. The five, plus Anne, were sent to the Tower, tried in Westminster, found guilty, sentenced to death, and executed. Before the month was out Henry married Jane.[6] Like all partisan trials, Anne Boleyn's lacks significant political or legal questions. It operated wholly within the political agenda set by Henry's will. Just as the Privy Council and the court at Westminster had obliged Henry, the archbishop obliged Henry by annulling his marriage to Anne and declaring their child, Elizabeth, a bastard. Henry wanted Anne out of his way, and the only question was how it could be accomplished.

Trials for corruption which operate within the rule of law present difficult entanglements of fact, legal issues, ethical judgments, and trial-by-media. From the trial of Francis Bacon to Watergate and Abscam a mesh of problems ensnare the courts and the public. Who did what? Which witness can be believed? Was there criminal intent? Were the defendants entrapped? Did the media bias the jury? Are the judge and lawyers politically ambitious? These and other similar questions arise in each case. Unlike a partisan trial, in which such potential embarrassments can be sidestepped, these matters arise because of the rule of law.

The Agnew Scandal

Although the affair involving Vice-President Spiro Agnew did not result in a trial, the entire scandal is instructive for understanding the issues of political trials. The vice-president's resignation in a cloud of incrimination was not directly connected to the Watergate happenings. But such a resignation by someone so high in government was a first in our history. The resignation came in the midst of the controversy over President Nixon's Oval Office tapes and shortly before the "Saturday Night Massacre" when Special Prosecutor Archibald Cox was fired. It was a dress rehearsal for Watergate and President Nixon's resignation.

After a criminal investigation revealed that Agnew had taken at least $100,000 in bribes on Maryland contracts, he resigned as vice-president on October 10, 1973, pleading no contest, which is equivalent to a guilty plea, to a charge of income tax evasion. That charge was a result of a plea bargain which many regarded as a generous offer from the Justice Department. Given the looming impeachment of President Nixon himself, it is likely that such generosity toward the vice-president resulted from the thought that it was more important to remove Agnew from office than imprison him. Instead of trying Agnew on bribery and extortion charges, Attorney General Elliot Richardson recommended to the court that the bargain should be accepted to avoid inflicting "serious and permanent scars" upon the nation.

> It is unthinkable that this nation should have been required to endure the anguish and uncertainty of a prolonged period in which the man next in line of succession to the presidency was fighting the charges brought against him by his own government.

Richardson urged, further, that "out of compassion for the man, out of respect for the office he has held, and out of appreciation for the fact that by his resignation he has spared the nation the prolonged agony that would have attended upon his trial," the judge not send Agnew to prison.[7]

Judge Walter E. Hoffman accepted the plea bargain after he pointed out that although the sentence was his responsibility, he would not disregard "the national interests, and the consequences flowing from any sentence." He admitted that "generally speaking, where the defendant is a lawyer . . . . I resort to the practice of imposing a fine and a term of imprisonment." But because of the strong recommendation by the attorney general and since he was "persuaded that the national interests in the present case are so great and so compelling," Judge Hoffman approved the plea bargain and did not send Agnew to prison.[8] In this case the two agendas—the legal one involving bribery by a lawyer and the political one concerning the national interest and Agnew's office—worked to Agnew's favor.

Should those in high public office be held to a stricter account than others? Does their responsibility increase because they are in the public eye, hold a public trust, are models for all public servants, and therefore represent the integrity of the legal and political system? That was the answer in Judge Kerner's case. Or do important public officials, because they have the public's attention, deserve more generous treatment to avoid the public's anguish over a trial and imprisonment? That was the answer in Agnew's case. The difference lies in the special nature of the presidency. Agnew got off easy. Nixon, but no one else, was pardoned. The president and his second possess the special trait of speaking as the nation's legitimate representatives.

The Agnew case would have held an important enough place in the history of our time even if it had not by coincidence happened during Watergate. As it was, the Agnew affair served as an interlude in the Nixon tapes crisis and as a prelude to Nixon's own resignation.

The Watergate Trials

The term *Watergate* has expanded. From the name of a group of apartments and offices on the shores of the Potomac River in Washington, it has come to mean a series of scandals during 1972-1974. Both the building and the scandals, it might be noted, are mazes. Beyond the Nixon administration scandals, "Watergate" has bequeathed to our language the suffix *gate* meaning political scandal. "Watergate" is our supreme political scandal. It is also a vivid lesson in the rule of law.

A year before the Watergate break-in the Watergate wheel was set in motion. Publication in June 1971 of the Pentagon Papers, obtained from Daniel Ellsberg by the *New York Times*, caused a wave of anxiety to roll through the White House. When the Supreme Court refused to halt their publication, President Nixon and his staff resolved to stop the leaks which made their publication possible and to find out as much as they could about Ellsberg.[9] Other wiretapping and covert political operations had been started earlier, but in mid-1971 the paranoia intensified. Within a month of the Pentagon Papers crisis the "plumbers' unit" was established in the White House and G. Gordon Liddy was hired. When the 1972 campaign was organized Liddy shifted from the White House to the Committee to Re-elect the President. In both places he put his skill in clandestine jobs to use.[10]

The Watergate break-in was on June 17, 1972. The cover-up story concocted by John Mitchell, Jeb Magruder, John Dean, and several others held up through the November election of 1972. They would admit to authorizing Liddy to use $250,000 for intelligence-gathering, but they would claim that the break-in was Liddy's scheme.[11] After the January 1973 trial of Liddy and James McCord, in which the jury found them guilty on all counts of the break-in, Judge John Sirica delayed sentencing because, as he told them, he was not satisfied that "all the pertinent facts that might be available" were produced in the trial.[12] Sirica's pressure worked. On March 23 he read a letter in open court in which McCord revealed that political pressure had been applied to keep the defendants silent, that perjury had been committed at the trial, and that others were involved.[13] This quickly ended the cover-up. Within a few days the news was out that McCord had told the Senate Watergate Committee that Mitchell, Magruder, and Dean were the ones involved, and within a few more days Dean and then Magruder began negotiating with the prosecutors. That set in motion the 1974 cover-up trial of John Mitchell, H. R. Haldeman, and John Ehrlichman.

During the Liddy-McCord break-in trial another trial was progressing in Los Angeles: Daniel Ellsberg and Anthony Russo were being prosecuted for the theft of the Pentagon Papers. At first it seemed that the Ellsberg-Russo trial was unrelated to the Watergate trial. But on April 27, 1973, it became known that the judge in the trial, Judge W. Matthew Byrne, had been twice contacted by John Ehrlichman to discuss the possibility that Byrne might accept the FBI directorship. The burglary at the office of Ellsberg's psychiatrist prompted Judge Byrne to dismiss all charges and declare a mistrial. The additional knowledge that Ehrlichman had met with the judge during the trial to offer him a job provoked heightened speculation about White House motives.[14]

A week after Judge Byrne declared a mistrial in the Ellsberg-Russo case the nation's attention was captured by the Senate Watergate Hearings (the Senate Select Committee on Presidential Campaign Activities), chaired by Senator Sam Ervin and televised gavel-to-gavel from mid-May to August

1973. Congressional hearings and political trials in the United States raise the same political questions but operate from contrasting models. Hearings by Congress are akin to the inquisitorial model, except that they are generally far from secret. Trials under the accusatorial system commence with a detailed indictment and advance according to stringent rules of relevancy and protection against self-incrimination toward a verdict from an unbiased jury. In contrast to trials and more akin to grand juries, Congressional hearings arise from a general matter to be investigated and proceed with informal rules and few protections for the witnesses toward a recommendation which is often a vector of political forces. The Ervin Committee was charged by the Senate to investigate "illegal, improper, or unethical activities . . . in the presidential election of 1972," given authority to subpoena anyone who it believed would have knowledge of such activities, and asked to recommend legislation to safeguard the electoral process.[15] Mainly it informed the nation about Watergate.

After the Ervin Committee had heard from James McCord, Maurice Stans, and Jeb Magruder, it found that it then had before it a head-on collision between John Dean's testimony that President Nixon had participated in the Watergate cover-up and a White House denial. Dean's testimony, while trenchant, pitted his credibility against the president's, a contest Dean would have difficulty winning.[16] But with the revelation by Alexander Butterfield, which was the bombshell of the hearings, that Nixon had taped his Oval Office conversations, the confrontation rapidly shifted to the president vs. the committee and then to the president vs. the courts. This struggle began in July 1973 and ended a year later when the Supreme Court said in a unanimous decision that the tapes would have to be turned over to Judge Sirica's court for the cover-up trial. On August 9, 1974, Nixon resigned.

While the battle over the White House tapes raged, the White House backed-and-filled. Nixon kept his distance by saying such things as "let others wallow in Watergate, we are going to do our job."[17] While, in short, the legitimacy of the Nixon administration drained away, two recent cabinet members were put on trial. Not knowing what was coming up later during 1974 the press billed the Spring 1974 trial of former attorney general John Mitchell and former commerce secretary Maurice Stans "one of the most extraordinary criminal cases in the nation's history" that promised to be "a courtroom drama unparalleled in the last half century."[18] Mitchell and Stans were charged with taking a secret $200,000 from financial manipulator Robert Vesco in return for their influence on the Securities and Exchange Commission which was investigating Vesco. The jury found Mitchell and Stans not guilty on all nine counts.[19] Vesco himself, before the indictment came from the grand jury, had skipped the country.

If the Mitchell-Stans trial had not been called "the trial of the century," the Plumbers' trial might have qualified. It involved one of President Nixon's closest advisors, John Ehrlichman, and the black bag team that operated out of the White House (Bernard Barker, G. Gordon Liddy, and Eugenio Martínez). They were tried for the break-in at Dr. Fielding's office (Daniel Ellsberg's psychiatrist) with testimony offered by another close advisor to Nixon, Charles Colson. The Plumbers' trial coincided with the impeachment hearings in June and July 1974. It was upstaged.

Neither the Mitchell-Stans trial nor the Plumbers' trial were a "trial of the century." They were nearly forgotten when the national attention was drawn to the House Judiciary Committee impeachment hearings and Nixon's resignation. While the Mitchell-Stans and the Plumbers' trials involved corruption, the misuse of power, and the issue of responsibility, the impeachment hearings touched the legitimacy of the Nixon administration. Because we understand human nature or think we do, we can fathom matters of corruption and the misuse of power, although when those in high places are put on trial, it is a public drama to watch the mighty being humbled. But legitimacy is mysterious, and the office of the president embodies that mystery. The impeachment hearings and the higher drama at the White House captured our deeply felt sense of the symbolic. In politics legitimacy has primacy.

The long-anticipated cover-up trial of John Mitchell and presidential aides H. R. Haldeman and John Ehrlichman came as an anticlimax after the Nixon resignation. Their trial had to come after the tape question was resolved, but the Supreme Court in resolving it precipitated Nixon's fall. The Watergate cover-up trial revealed that those closest to President Nixon were engaged in cover-up activities as soon as the break-in had been discovered: attempting to arrange to get the burglars out of jail and out of the country, making secret hush-money payoffs, approaching the CIA for covert funds, destroying documents, lying to the FBI investigators, and committing perjury before the Senate Committee and the grand jury.[20]

Not only were those who broke into the Democratic Headquarters caught red-handed, but so were the advisors closest to Nixon and, with the full verification of Dean's story on the tapes, Nixon too. The scandal was their reckless disregard for the law, not that they had enriched themselves. The trials of the Nixon administration higher-ups and especially the Ervin Committee hearings, since they were televised, served as a national classroom in the meaning of responsibility in a democracy. Like students in a large class, the public was a bystander whose ideas and opinions the participants on all sides took into account while making decisions. Public opinion polls kept a running record of the changing sentiment. The early reactions to Watergate were predictable, as the Langs in their study of the battle for public opinion during Watergate show: "Hints of wrongdoing by one's own party usually encounter more skepticism than hints about similar wrongdoing by the other side. But in a major scandal, which overrides at least temporarily the normal political divisions, the symbolic issue dominates. As the alleged offenses by Nixon and his entourage came to be perceived as inadmissible deviations from the public order, there arose a demand for some form of punishment, the desire to see justice done, expressed as an essentially disinterested concern for order. The almost universal acceptance of Nixon's resignation signifies just such an identification with the rule of law to a point where it overrides normal political allegiances."[21]

Did the media pillory the Watergate defendants? Or, on the other hand, did the press uncover the scandal and smite the evildoers? In either case, whether the media coverage was akin to a witch hunt or to David slaying Goliath, the issue is the place of the media in the rule of law. If the media creates caricatures of those involved in a trial and portrays the courtroom as a stage for a melodrama, then, whatever the legal agenda, the political agenda will be inevitably partisan. One view of the role of the media would have it that such a result is the only result we can expect: "Misinforming merely abuses the audience; boring loses the audience."[22] The Watergate story, as Raymond Price sees it in retrospect, was an ideal one to tell with drama and fiction: "High stakes, fast action, famous stars, mystery, suspense, confrontation, good guys, and bad guys. Further, it was the best kind of story, from a newsman's standpoint: not a one-day story, but a building story, the sort that engages the audience's interest and holds its attention, promising a continuing series of dramatic denouements." Such stories, Price notes, win journalistic prizes, yield fame and fortune, and build journalistic legends. "All this, and Nixon too," Price remarks.[23]

Maurice Stans, in looking back at the Watergate events, argues that most of those punished and defamed were innocent victims. The combination of ambitious politicians and prosecutors plus the "media binge" produced, in Stans's judgment, "a relentless search for wrongdoers" comparable to the Salem witch trials.[24] While he acknowledges that the Watergate trials did bring some guilty to justice (such as Liddy, although he was "exorbitantly punished"),[25] Stans finds that some of the guilty got off easily (those given immunity for their testimony) and many undeserving innocent were punished. "Without having played any part in Watergate or its coverup," Stans asks, "why in the world was I so victimized by it?"[26]

The "media binge" Stans sees behind the Watergate hysteria was to him most evident in the "range of despicable tactics" employed by Woodward and Bernstein of the *Washington Post*. They and the rest of the journalists created a climate in which accuracy was sacrificed for sensationalism.[27]

This high excitement permitted the prejudices of the Ervin Committee to exercise arbitrary power over him and the other victims. While there was no connection between the Vesco matter and Watergate, the prosecutors, the Ervin Committee, and the media linked the two events with the suggestion that Stans was guilty in both. Senator Ervin, Stans asserts, had two categories of witnesses: "guilty with penitence" or "guilty wthout penitence."[28] In short, from Stans's viewpoint, the hearings and trials of Watergate were beyond the limits of the rule of law and functioned as partisan trials. As he finished his testimony before the Ervin Committee Stans appealed to the committee to take account of the "innocent victims of this tragedy." He, together with others in the Nixon administration and campaign, "believed in my President. . . . All I ask, Mr. Chairman and Members of the Committee, is that when you write your report you give me back my good name."[29]

G. Gordon Liddy represents an extreme Watergate position. His ideas, as well as his actions, are a straightforward challenge to the rule of law. Liddy rejected its limits and denounced those who took it seriously. If some of the others involved in Watergate were ad men and ambitious politicians with a willingness to use Machiavellian tactics to advance the cause of Nixon's reelection, Liddy was a Nietzschean who approached politics as a terrorist would. The others were drawn into the Watergate quagmire out of loyalty to Nixon, but Liddy viewed the entire world as a power jungle where only those who fought survived. While the others would later regret and repent, Liddy not only justified what he had done but regretted only that he was restrained from doing more. He gloried in his aggressive stance. The others saw Watergate as dirty but necessary politics; Liddy viewed Watergate as a skirmish in a war.

The prime example of the internal war the Nixon administration faced, as Liddy looked at the situation of the early 1970s, was the bombing of the Army Math Center at the University of Wisconsin (a case which will be covered in chapter 6). He saw this bombing as part of the "thousands of bombings, burnings, riots, and lootings of the '60s, to say nothing of the murders of police just because they were police, the killing of judges, and the general disintegration of social order."[30] To fight this trend Liddy, while working for the White House, masterminded a series of battle plans. ODESSA was the coordinating group for a variety of clandestine projects which included discrediting Daniel Ellsberg, perhaps with drugs which would befuddle him when he made a speech, because he was the person "who had been made a hero by the press . . . now the symbolic personification of all the leakers."[31] After he was shifted from the White House to the Committee to Reelect the President, Liddy drew up elaborate plans under the code name GEMSTONE. These included details for kidnapping demonstration leaders, drugging them, and holding them in Mexico until the Republican Convention was over; spying on the Democratic candidates with bugs and even chase planes to eavesdrop on airplanes and buses; using prostitutes in a houseboat wired for sound during the Democratic Convention; promoting a variety of counterdemonstrations; and finally, employing a sabotage team to destroy the air-conditioning equipment at the Democratic Convention. John Mitchell told Liddy the million-dollar budget for GEMSTONE was too much, that he should return with "something more realistic," and that he should burn his charts.[32] When Jack Anderson wrote a column in which, in Liddy's judgment, an intelligence source abroad had been compromised, perhaps to the point of threatening the agent's life, Liddy developed a plan to assassinate Anderson.[33]

Most of Liddy's extravagant battle plans were rejected by his superiors, although the two break-ins for which he was convicted—Ellsberg's psychiatrist's office and the Watergate—had been approved. To Liddy such projects, including assassinations, were not justified out of blind obedience to authority. Blind obedience would lead, he suggests, to justifying genocide, as the Nazis did. Liddy's code, by contrast, was built on the distinction between an action which is evil in itself (genocide or the sexual assault of a child) and an action which is wrong only because a law prohibits it (driving through a stop sign). Liddy was willing to propose and carry out an assassination of Jack Anderson provided it was "a) an order from legitimate authority; b) a question of *malum prohibitum* (wrong only because the law prohibits it); and c) a rational response to the problem."[34] Assassinating Anderson, Liddy explained, would not be a matter of retribution for what he had written in his column but a preventive measure. Fortunately, the one condition not met was (a); he did not receive an order. But the other two conditions, in Liddy's estimation, were in place.

Liddy's argument for the ODESSA and GEMSTONE projects and for political assassination is vigilante justice. The regular legal process, Liddy reasoned, was not bringing Ellsberg to justice, and the media was making him into a culture hero. The same thing he saw was happening to the anti-Vietnam War demonstrators. Jack Anderson was not being stopped by the regular processes. Even the FBI, in which Liddy had begun his career, was unwilling to undertake the measures necessary. Liddy justified his projects because the law was not effective in halting the illegal activities of the dissidents and the media. Justice Louis Brandeis had this to say about agents of the government using criminal methods in order to control crime:

> In a government of laws, existence of the government will be imperiled if it fails to observe the law scrupulously. Our Government is the potent, the

omnipresent teacher. For good or for ill, it teaches the whole people by its example. Crime is contagious. If the Government becomes a lawbreaker, it breeds contempt for law; it invites every man to become a law unto himself; it invites anarchy. To declare that in the administration of the criminal law the end justifies the means—to declare that the Government may commit crimes in order to secure the conviction of a private criminal—would bring terrible retribution. Against that pernicious doctrine this court should resolutely set its face.[35]

This would apply to Liddy while employed by the White House. His activities as an agent for the Committee to Reelect the President would be even more clearly from a terrorist's book.

Liddy's code was the code of war, not the rule of law. He agreed with Stewart Alsop who described him as engaging in war, not politics. Throughout, Liddy viewed himself as a loyal and professional soldier who would not engage in indiscriminate terror in which civilians would be injured but who would not hesitate to employ discriminate terror against the enemy. Like a soldier, he was willing to accept the consequences of his own actions, well illustrated by his refusal to provide details and information in exchange for a lighter sentence and by his suggestion to John Dean that if the administration wanted him killed all Dean had to do was to tell him on which street corner to stand.[36]

Woven through the various books written by the Watergaters are themes which present Watergate as a moral lesson. Liddy's story follows the Nietzschean pattern of aristocratic and heroic self-assertion. His autobiography is titled *Will*. Once a sickly and fearful child, he tells how he drew upon a family heritage and his capacity to test himself to become a belligerent FBI agent, county prosecutor, Watergate spy, and prisoner. His one grandfather was a football star, the other a pugilist and stevedore; an uncle was an FBI agent who helped catch Dillinger, and his father was a successful lawyer who was knighted by the king of Sweden as a member of the Royal Order of the North Star. Young G. Gordon did such things as climb a tree during an electrical storm and eat a rat. Although he was a lawyer, Liddy's code throughout was a challenge to the rule of law. After being tried, convicted, and serving a prison term, he left prison in triumph.

By way of contrast, the narratives of Jeb Magruder and John Dean are moral odysseys. They tell about their journeys through the mazes of power toward a wisdom learned in painful experience. Their titles also suggest their themes: Magruder's *An American Life: One Man's Road to Watergate* and Dean's *Blind Ambition: The White House Years.* Magruder and Dean begin in what they see as mundane but yet successful careers and are raised to the realms of power. Both describe the excitement and awe of their first visits to San Clemente where they had their job interviews and were admitted into the presence of Nixon. After he is hired Magruder thinks: "This was the chance I had been waiting for all my life. The Magruder family had, over the years, known its ups and downs, but now I was one of the Magruders who was on the way up, all the way to the top."[37] The moral stumbling block was, of course, Watergate. "Slowly, steadily, I would climb toward the moral abyss of the President's inner circle," Dean related, "until I finally fell into it, thinking I had made it to the top just as I began to realize I had actually touched bottom."[38] The hearings and trials were a moral purging. When Magruder decided to talk to the prosecutors, he felt he was "sick of lying, to my wife, to my friends, to the press, even to myself. The strain was just too much." Once he made the decision he changed: "I felt a tremendous sense of relief, I felt almost happy, to be finished with the cover-up and all its lies. I felt as if I'd been seized by madness for a long time and suddenly I had become sane again."[39] Magruder and Dean left the Watergate experience humiliated but wiser.

The Watergate defendants, especially those who wrote books, appealed to the public through the political agenda. The most vivid example of this is H. R. Haldeman's petition two days before Nixon resigned. Haldeman, on behalf of the Watergate defendants, urged that Nixon grant clemency to everyone convicted for Watergate crimes. After submitting that all the acts they had done were either done at the president's direction, with his knowledge and approval, or for his benefit, not for their own enrichment, Haldeman suggested that such clemency "permits the wrongs and rights to be adjudicated in the 'court of history' rather than in the highly prejudiced political crucible of Washington, D. C. courts." He went on to suggest that such an act would add "to the image of Richard Nixon" by demonstrating that he "seeks to do justice when he knows the judicial process cannot or will not."[40]

The political agenda of Watergate contained what historian Daniel Boorstin calls "the conscience of the marketplace—the people's feeling of outrage at the violation of common decency, of legal and constitutional rules."[41] Whether the "court of history," to use Haldeman's term, will turn that outrage in favor of the Watergate defendants remains to be seen. Thus far, the D. C. courts have expressed the conscience of the marketplace in favor of the rule of law and against those who used the power of the White House to violate it. Boorstin distinguishes the *conscience* of the marketplace from the *judgment* of the marketplace, which is lynch law.[42] The former is the rule of law, while the latter is partisan justice. While the jury of history is always out, although it comes in with continual verdicts, in the first decade after Watergate the verdict seems clear: The Watergate defendants violated the law and were properly convicted. The victor is, therefore, neither a person nor a party but the rule of law.

The Insanity Plea in Politically Related Trials

In certain dramatic political trials from time to time the insanity plea is invoked and a public outcry arises. The reaction against John Hinckley's successful insanity defense in 1982 nearly equaled the original stir in 1981 over his attempted assassination of President Ronald Reagan. The same outrage has been felt before over similar events and trials. If we look at only a few of the more sensational trials involving political victims and the insanity plea, some understanding of the public's ambivalence on the issue of responsibility might emerge. We can begin with the 1800 trial of James Hadfield for shooting at King George III but missing him (plea accepted). In 1812 John Bellingham assassinated Prime Minister Perceval and was executed (plea not accepted). Edward Oxford in 1840 shot at Queen Victoria and missed (plea accepted). The centerpiece trial of the insanity plea is the Daniel McNaughtan case (plea accepted). McNaughtan was tried for killing the secretary to Prime Minister Peel. Other notable cases involving the insanity plea include the 1881 trial of Charles Guiteau for assassinating President Garfield (plea not accepted), the 1979 trial of San Francisco supervisor Dan White for killing Mayor Moscone and Supervisor Harvey Milk (diminished capacity accepted), and the Hinckley trial.

Before we examine some of the above trials, another important case deserves mention. In 1945 Ezra Pound might have been tried for treason but he was not. Because of the insanity plea, the nation was spared seeing one of its most influential poets tried and perhaps given the death penalty. The Pound case illustrates how the insanity plea can be used in a partisan way to the advantage of the accused. In contrast to the political use of law and psychiatry in the Soviet Union, American psychiatrists shielded Ezra Pound and protected him from retribution at St. Elizabeths Hospital where he was free to work, hold salons with major figures in American literature, and engage in considerable political activity with some leading extremists. Pound, one of the preeminent poets of the twentieth century, broadcast some three hundred speeches, largely anti-Semitic and pro-Axis diatribes, over Radio Rome during World War II. He also wrote speeches for others and worked on propaganda slogans, doing all he could for the Axis cause. After the war he was indicted for treason and for creating dissension between the United States and its allies, and racial prejudice and distrust of the American government among the American people, all while in the employment of the Italian government of Mussolini.[43] For doing much less and being primarily a victim of circumstances, Iva Toguri d'Aquino, known as "Tokyo Rose," was convicted of treason and sentenced to prison.[44]

Spearheaded by Ernest Hemingway and Archibald MacLeish, who was an assistant secretary in the State Department, Pound's defenders rallied *the* names in American letters: T. S. Eliot, Robert Frost, Allen Tate, William Carlos Williams, as well as publisher James Laughlin, reviewer-poet Dudley Fitts, and psychiatrist-poet Merrill Moore. Pound had written to the attorney general saying that he would use his treason trial to expose Roosevelt and the Jews, but the old-boy-writer network arranged for a lawyer, Julien Cornell, who convinced Pound to acquiesce in a plea that he was unfit for trial because of insanity. Dr. Winfred Overholser, who oversaw the diagnosis with three other psychiatrists, was a leading authority in psychiatry, an officer in the American Psychiatric Association, the superintendent of St. Elizabeths Hospital, a close friend of Merrill Moore, and an admirer of Pound's work. In his twelve years at St. Elizabeths under Overholser's protection, Pound received his best friends—the leading figures in literature—regularly, wrote some of his important work, contributed a prodigious supply of articles to political and literary journals, carried on a vast correspondence, and conducted brisk political activities with his disciple John Kasper who was an organizer for the White Citizens Council.[45] While at St. Elizabeths he received, thanks again to some influence by his friends, the Bollingen Prize and, some believe, could well have won the Nobel Prize.[46] In short, the decision that Pound would not be tried for treason, as was to be the case with Iva Toguri d'Aquino, and that he would be sheltered within a charmed circle living a charmed life at St. Elizabeths, quite unlike what happens in the Soviet Union, were both judgments of expediency. The question of insanity introduces a maximum of discretion into the law which, in turn, opens the door to partisanship.

The basic legal test for insanity as a criminal plea comes in the aftermath of the trial of Daniel McNaughtan. In one way it resembles the Pound case: The prosecution pulled punches at the trial. He too was saved by the insanity plea. McNaughtan had killed Edward Drummond, the secretary to Prime Minister Robert Peel, and his trial in the Old Bailey had created a stir. But, like the Hinckley trial, the public stir of the trial was not nearly as great as, when McNaughtan was acquitted on grounds of insanity, the uproar which swept the country. Queen Victoria expressed her displeasure in a letter to Peel, suggesting that Parliament establish a rule on which judges would instruct juries. Both McNaughtan and Edward Oxford, who had shot at her three years earlier and also had been acquitted on grounds of insanity, were, as Queen Victoria saw it, "perfectly conscious and aware of what they did!"[47] The McNaughtan rule, written by the House of Lords, is the result. Its nucleus is that the jury should decide whether or not the accused "was labouring under such a defect of reason from disease of the mind, as not to know the nature and quality of the act he was doing, or if he did know it, that he did not know that what he was doing was wrong."[48] If the jury finds the accused was conscious that the act was one he/she ought not to do, the jury's verdict can be guilty. Otherwise, if the test is met, the verdict should be not guilty by reason of insanity.

Daniel McNaughtan was a Glasgow woodturner actively involved in the Chartist movement during a time of severe economic depression. The Chartists had led various strikes, riots, factory sabotage, and work stoppages against the policies of Peel and the Tories which had kept prices high and wages low. The London Police, called Bobbies in honor of Peel, were at times mobilized against the Chartists. Glasgow was also a center for Chartism and police harassment. McNaughtan had intended to assassinate Peel in the summer of 1842 when Queen Victoria, Peel, and their entourage visited Scotland, but the opportunity did not present itself then.

McNaughtan traveled to London, where he was seen loitering around the government offices, especially near Downing Street. In the days before television and newspaper photographs, it is understandable how, in spite of careful stalking, McNaughtan mistook Peel's private secretary, Edward Drummond, for Peel. On January 20, 1843, Drummond left the prime minister's residence, made the rounds of the Treasury and Admiralty, and was walking near Charing Cross when McNaughtan came up from behind and shot him. Drummond died five days later. When the police officer at the station asked McNaughtan if he knew who it was he had shot, McNaughtan replied, "It is Sir Robert Peel, is it not?"[49]

Richard Moran, in a careful investigation of McNaughtan's life and crime, demonstrates that McNaughtan did not meet the test which carries his name. He was not insane, and, what is more, he attempted to assassinate Peel for political reasons. Both the expert and conventional wisdom about McNaughtan is that he was paranoid, imagining that Peel was persecuting him. Mistaking Drummond for Peel has been put down as part of his paranoia.

Moran found that at the time of his arrest McNaughtan was carrying a bank deposit receipt for £745. That is equivalent to a quarter of a million dollars today. Yet McNaughtan in the depressed economy had not done well in his Glasgow woodturning shop. He had sold the business for a mere £18, tools and all. We know that he had made several trips between Glasgow and London and had visited France. Shortly before the assassination he purchased two pistols and an expensive set of clothes, including a beaver hat. None of McNaughtan's finances were explored in detail at the trial, although both Peel and Queen Victoria remarked on his suspiciously large bank deposit. The prosecution told the court that the money had been saved by McNaughtan from his Glasgow shop. Moran, after examining McNaughtan's bank records and his family finances, asserts that McNaughtan had been paid to assassinate Peel.[50]

McNaughtan retained England's finest lawyers, and they were able to procure the testimony of nine prominent medical experts and other witnesses, eight brought down from Glasgow. This defense effort was financed by the £750 in McNaughtan's bank account. Alexander Cockburn, who presented the defense case, argued that while McNaughtan's delusions that he was being persecuted by the Tories and the Jesuits had a political and religious bias, they were nevertheless delusions, "phantoms of a disordered mind." The solicitor general, Sir William Follett, presented the case for the crown, concentrating on the deliberate preparations McNaughtan had made for his act, emphasizing the rational planning it involved. Moran, unlike either side at the trial, tracks McNaughtan through Glasgow and London, documenting the fact that Tory agents had been intimidating Chartists in Glasgow and that the priest of the only Catholic church in Glasgow, with McNaughtan's shop less that a hundred yards away, harangued against Chartists and cooperated with the Tories against them. Given Moran's findings, it is probable that McNaughtan was correct in his statement that the Tories were persecuting him. "It may well be," Moran observes, "that the only real delusion McNaughtan ever suffered from was the delusion that he had shot the prime minister."[51]

Why did all of this not come out at the trial? Moran's conclusion is that the McNaughtan trial "demonstrates how the insanity verdict can be used effectively to detain and discredit political offenders. By bringing in a verdict of not guilty on the grounds of insanity, the court said that the assassin McNaughtan was suffering from a 'morbid affection of the mind'; that there was no logical or political explanation for his behavior."[52]

Additional reasons for believing McNaughtan's claim that the Tories were after him can be found in the Lancaster trial of Feargus O'Connor and fifty-eight other Chartists. McNaughtan's trial and the Lancaster trial coincided, both coming in the first days of March 1843. A measure of the importance attached to the two trials is that, while Solicitor General Follett represented the crown in Old Bailey, his superior, Attorney General Sir Frederick Pollock, made the long journey to the north to represent the crown in the O'Connor trial. McNaughtan was not mentioned in Lancaster. Feargus O'Connor, the Chartists, and McNaughtan's involvement in the Chartist cause were not mentioned in Old Bailey. What the O'Connor trial does reveal clearly, however, is the extent and thoroughness of the informers who reported to the police on Chartist activities. The testimony introduced by Sir Frederick against O'Connor and the others detailed where they met, what they said to each other privately and in public, and what they did to advance the seditious conspiracy they were accused and, finally, convicted of in Lancaster. Unlike the prosecution in the McNaughtan trial, and contrary to Moran's hypothesis that the crown did not want to reveal the extent of its spy network, Sir Frederick put the police spies on the witness stand and asked them to read their notes and to tell all they did, saw, and heard.[53]

Attorney General Pollock made it clear in his efforts to prosecute O'Connor and the others in Lancaster that the government wanted to discredit the Chartists. Why did the solicitor general in the McNaughtan trial avoid this even better opportunity? What could bring more dishonor to the Chartists than evidence that McNaughtan was a Chartist? An answer might lie in the difference between the two trials, especially in the nature of the accusation and the contrasting personalities of the accused.

O'Connor and the other Chartists were classic dissenters who opposed the government openly with writings in the *Northern Star*, with speeches, mass rallies, the demands of their charter, and strikes.[54] They were charged with seditious conspiracy for inciting a work stoppage. Their trial could serve as a warning to other Chartists and could discredit the Chartist cause to the public as a violent movement led by irrational hotheads. Dissenters such as O'Connor, who operate in full public view to sway opinion, can be most easily discredited if they are portrayed as secret plotters intent on violence. Assassins, on the other hand, who might well be involved in plots and who always move in the shadows with violent intentions, will only be given a luster of respect if they are characterized as acting for political reasons. As we did with Oswald, Sirhan, and Ray, we prefer to believe that the assassin was a lone gunman, even better, a madman.

The groundwork was prepared, then, for Alexander Cockburn's insanity defense of McNaughtan. Lacking the evidence that the prosecution chose not to follow, Cockburn could argue that while McNaughtan's delusions that he was being persecuted by the Tories had a political bias, they were nevertheless delusions, "phantoms of a disordered mind," which had been established at the 1800 trial of James Hadfield who shot at the king but was found not guilty by reason of insanity. If the crown had chosen to open the door to the Chartists' activities McNaughtan had engaged in, seeking to convince the jury that McNaughtan was a paid assassin, Cockburn would have lost the case at the starting gate. But if such political matters were kept out, Cockburn would have only to place McNaughtan in the Hadfield framework. And he did.

After medical witnesses testified that McNaughtan was insane, Justice Tindal asked the prosecution whether the crown had any evidence in reply. When the solicitor general said he had none, Justice Tindal stopped the trial and told the jury that "the whole of the medical evidence is on one side, and that there is no part of it which leaves any doubt on the mind."[55] The jury found McNaughtan "not guilty on the ground of insanity."

McNaughtan spent the rest of his life, some twenty-one years, in mental hospitals. Feargus O'Connor and twenty-nine of the Chartists were found guilty of seditious conspiracy, but because of a legal technicality they were never called for judgment. O'Connor resumed his leadership of the Chartists, and in 1847 was elected to the House of Commons for Nottingham. Later in his life his mind gave way, and, like McNaughtan, he too ended his days in a mental hospital.

The 1881 trial of Charles Guiteau, who assassinated President Garfield, has been called the most celebrated American insanity trial of the nineteenth century. Guiteau, coincidentally like John Hinckley a century later, was an enthusiast of the news media. When Guiteau determined on his plan to assassinate President Garfield, he took care in selecting a pistol with an inlaid grip with a view to how it would look on display. On the morning of the assassination, July 2, 1881, Guiteau left a bundle of documents at the railroad station newsstand for the reporters in order to explain his act and provide them and the world with the proper biographical information. Among the papers was his "Address to the American People" in which he told why President Garfield was a traitor imperiling the life of the Republic under the manipulation of Secretary of State Blaine. He saw the need for "removing the President." Earlier he had written to the Chicago papers with the suggestion that they would find use for information about him. He sent the editors his autobiography with the puff that "the story of my life is pointed and graphic, and reads like a romance, and tells of my acquaintance with public men, and of my attempted removal of the President." He also included, for their further edification, a volume he wrote and published on his theology (*The Truth: A Companion to the Bible*). After the assassination, Guiteau, now in the limelight as a national figure, increased his own infatuation with his public image. Guiteau, for instance, asked a photographer to pay a $25 royalty for the use of his photograph, told the court during the trial that he was magnanimously *not* charging for his autograph, and expected that after his acquittal he would make some $30,000 a year on the lecture circuit. In letters to President Garfield following his election in 1880, Guiteau asked for an appointment to the United States mission in Vienna, recommending himself in part because he would soon be marrying a wealthy heiress, a wife suited to his station as a diplomat. In truth he had never met the woman he was convinced would marry him and assist in his diplomatic obligations, although he had seen her in church.[56]

The trial of Charles Guiteau became a battle of psychiatrists. Fourteen experts for the prosecution argued that Guiteau understood the nature and consequences of his act, reasoned coherently, and showed no signs of a hereditary insanity. When asked what, if not heredity, had caused his act of assassinating the president, Dr. Allen Hamilton, a specialist in mental illness, responded, "intemperance, sin." Guiteau objected to the use of the insanity defense, aguing that he had acted as God's agent to "remove" the president for the good of the country. Under cross-examination by the prosecutor J. K. Porter, Guiteau was asked: "Who bought the pistol, the Deity or you?" Guiteau: "I say the Deity inspired the act, and the Deity will take care of it." Porter: "Did it occur to you that there is a commandment, Thou shall not kill?" Guiteau: "If it did, the divine authority overcame the written law." Porter asked him how he could be sure it was God rather than the Evil One who instructed him. Guiteau replied, "I claim that I am a man of destiny. I want to tell you and the public that I am a man of destiny."[57]

Another building block of the defense was that "there was a strong hereditary taint of insanity in the blood" of Guiteau. The two leading defense experts, both neurologists, Dr. James G. Kiernan of Chicago and Dr. Edward Spitzka of New York, held that they saw a congenital disposition toward a lack of moral perception and control. Dr. Kiernan maintained that he could spot physical stigmata: "the asymmetry of the skull being identified with the symmetry of the brain." Spitzka concluded: "I am inclined strongly to believe and to affirm, as positively as science permits us to come to a conclusion, that it was a congenital moral defect."[58] The jury, not convinced by the insanity defense, declared Guiteau guilty, and he was sent to the gallows.

Two recent cases have called public attention to the use of the insanity plea or provisions in the law for diminished responsibility. The reactions to both illustrate the hold which the common sense standards, such as Queen Victoria's "perfectly conscious and aware" test, have on the public mind. In addition to the John Hinckley case, there is the reaction to the 1979 trial and light sentence of San Francisco supervisor Dan White and his 1984 release from prison. White was a 32-year-old army airborne veteran, a former policeman and, like his father, a fireman. On the board White was known for his hard line against legislation which would strengthen the rights of homosexuals. When he was elected he resigned his fireman's job but soon found himself in financial difficulty. To help his budget he joined with a partner in a sideline, a fast food potato franchise at Pier 39. The Hot Potato proved to demand more of his time than he could give it, forcing him to resign his supervisor's position. When he resigned he was met with pressure from his constituents, the policemen and firemen, to seek reappointment. After five days he gave in to the pressure and asked Mayor Moscone to reappoint him. Although the mayor told reporters that "a man has a right to change his mind" and seemed ready to reappoint White, liberals on the board, led by Supervisor Harvey Milk, pressured Moscone to appoint someone else. Moscone was planning a press conference to announce his decision when White received the news that Moscone was not planning to do what White thought he had promised. Several hours before the presss conference White went to City Hall, crawled through a window to avoid the metal detectors at the door, went to Moscone's office where he shot and killed him and, after reloading, went to Milk's office where he shot and killed him also. He fled, first to phone his wife, and finally with his wife to the police station where, a half hour after the shootings, he surrendered to an old friend on the police force and, a half hour later, gave a detailed confession.[59]

Prosecutor Thomas Norman presented the details of White's movements, noting that he took ten additional cartridges when he left home with his police service revolver, that, as witnesses testified, he seemed "normal, friendly," without a sense of urgency when he stepped into Supervisor Milk's office saying, "Say, Harv, can I see you a minute?"[60] The prosecution demonstrated White had a design and was aware of his activities.

White's defense attorney Douglas Schmidt, on the other hand, argued that White had "cracked" under financial and political pressures. "He had no intent at that time when he entered City Hall via a window to harm anyone, much less to kill the mayor or to kill Harvey Milk. . . . Dan White was a good man. He was a good policeman, he was a good fireman. . . . Good people—fine people with fine backgrounds simply don't kill people in cold blood." Psychiatrists for the defense testified that White suffered from manic depression or recurrent melancholia which affected his judgment, depriving him of the ability "to hold in mind" the intention to kill or the knowledge that it was wrong. The disease, the psychiatrists maintained, is partly "a biochemical problem in the brain" which can be aggravated by acute stress.

Dr. Martin Blinder, although he refused to make a pronouncement about whether White was mentally ill, made the observation that White's frequent episodes of deep depression were escalated by an excessive diet of junk food. This was enough to give the entire defense the popular label, the "Twinkie defense." Blinder's testimony was that White "placed a lot of emotional chips" on his reappointment to the Board of Supervisors. "When the Mayor pulled the rug out from under him, he fell down." Blinder characterized White as a person with rigid values which conflicted with his experiences in everyday life. He felt that the other board members "don't give a damn" about constituents, only themselves, but until he resigned from the board "he never had any relief from these tensions."[61]

The jury, under a rule akin to the insanity plea allowing for a finding of "diminished capacity" to make judgments, found that the slayings were committed without malice and that White was guilty of voluntary manslaughter, instead of the first-degree murder with which he had been charged. Riots broke out, City Hall windows were smashed, fires were set, and some 140 people, including sixty police, were injured.[62]

The same criticisms were raised in the White case as in McNaughtan's. The California voters in referendum removed the diminished capacity provision from the books, largely in reaction to the White verdict. The prosecution, as in the McNaughtan case, was criticized for pulling punches. They did not call to the witness stand a jailer who observed and was appalled by the chummy comaraderie Dan White had with the policemen, receiving something close to a hero's reception when he surrendered. Contrary to the testimony about White "cracking up," the jailer saw him as "perfunctory and businesslike, very controlled." A member of the City Charter Commission and a former policeman agreed that a factor in the trial which the prosecution did not open up was the police attitude toward gays and liberals: "There was clearly some sort of a deal cut not to hit on the political aspects of this case. Everybody in town knew from the early defense subpoenas—for most every politician in town—that this was going to be a political trial. The defense was going to show the tensions—gays, liberals, the changes in town—that were offending Dan White's sense of values."[63] Thomas Szasz, psychiatrist and gad-fly of his profession, charged that "according to the experts, there is no such thing as a political assassination in America. In America, only 'mental patients' kill political figures."[64]

The John Hinckley Trial

Szasz's critique was soon put to the test in the John Hinckley trial. Hinckley showed no hints of a political purpose. John Wilkes Booth, Leon Czolgosz, and Sirhan Sirhan may have been moved by extremist politics in their shootings of presidents Lincoln and McKinley and of Robert Kennedy, and McNaughtan may have had a cause to advance, but that cannot be said of Hinckley. Guiteau may have assassinated Garfield either out of his belief that he was God's agent or out of personal revenge, but Hinckley held nothing against President Reagan, nor against the office of president, and he made no claim of divine guidance. Add to these James Earl Ray who assassinated Martin Luther King, Jr., and President Kennedy's assassin, Lee Harvey Oswald, as well as Lynette Fromme and Sara Jane Moore who made attempts on the life of President Ford. Compared with these assassins, the one with the foggiest motives is Hinckley.[65]

Judge Barrington Parker told the jury in the Hinckley case that in addition to proving beyond a reasonable doubt Hinckley's guilt on the thirteen counts of the indictment, the prosecution also had the burden of proving his criminal responsibility beyond a reasonable doubt. Earlier, in his chambers, Judge Parker had read the draft of his instruction, which referrred to "the burden placed upon the government, namely, that it must prove beyond a reasonable doubt that the Defendant was sane." Roger Adelman, the assistant U.S. attorney, objected, saying, "Your Honor, we don't have to prove he was sane. We have to prove he was criminally responsible."[66] All parties agreed.

The jury subsequently heard the standard federal court definition of insanity from Judge Parker: "At the time of the criminal conduct the defendant, as a result of mental disease or defect, either lacked substantial capacity to conform his conduct to the requirements of the law or lacked substantial capacity to appreciate the wrongfulness of his conduct." He told them that everyone is presumed to be sane and responsible for his or her acts, "but that presumption no longer controls when evidence is introduced that he may have a mental disease or defect." Insanity does not require, moreover, a showing that the defendant was disoriented. He told the jury that in considering whether Hinckley had an abnormal condition of the mind which affected his mental or emotional processes and substantially impaired his behavior control that they may consider testimony "concerning the development, adaptation, and functioning of these mental and emotional processes and behavior controls." Unless the government established beyond a reasonable doubt that Hinckley was not suffering from a mental disease or defect and had substantial capacity on March 30, 1981, both to conform his conduct to the law and to appreciate the wrongfulness of his conduct, he instructed the jury, they should bring in a verdict of not guilty by reason of insanity.[67] In addition to those family members on the defense side and the police and FBI agents on the prosecution side, all of whom gave direct evidence, the jury heard from five experts for the defense and four from the prosecution who sought to explain the *why*. In brief, the defense experts—three psychiatrists, a psychologist, a radiologist, and a neurophysicist—analyzed Hinckley as suffering from schizophrenia driving him into delusions concerning Jodie Foster and the characters in the movie *Taxi Driver*, as well as John Lennon and his assassin Mark Chapman. The prosecution countered with experts whose analyses led them to see Hinckley as narcissistic, pampered, privileged, and self-centered, but not schizophrenic. He made, they suggested, a cool, rational decision to shoot and showed no remorse but was interested in the media coverage and his "shift from obscurity to notoriety."[68] He had personality disorders, they admitted, but not mental illness. The defense radiologist saw in a CAT scan that Hinckley's brain was shrunken, a condition sometimes associated with schizophrenia. No, replied the prosecution neuroradiologist, there was no evidence of abnormality in the CAT scan.[69]

An indication of the task the jury faced is provided by the testimony of Dr. Thomas Goldman, a psychiatrist who examined Hinckley's writings for psychological characteristics. In eight poems, a short story, a TV script, letters to his parents and grandparents, and in Hinckley's reactions to a novel and to the movie *Taxi Driver*, Goldman found a series of psychological themes which indicated that Hinckley suffered from a mental disease. In Hinckley's writings he found traits of isolation from society with a profound feeling that he did not fit in (in a poem called "Elephant Man"), fantasies of being famous like John Lennon but yet a failure at normal life (in a poem called "He Would Have Been a Genius"), disappontment with his psychiatrist Dr. John Hopper for not understanding him (in a poem called "The Quiet Psychopathic Types"), and a plea for help in a television script in which a teenage boy is arrested after shooting at cars along a freeway and one deputy remarks to another, "That boy need psychiatric attention and fast."[70]

"Son of a Gun Collector," a short story by Hinckley, portrays a conflict between a boy and his father in which the mother is sympathetic to the boy. When the boy shoots the father with the father's own weapon, he proclaims, "Now I'm the man of the house." Goldman discussed the story with Hinckley, who did not feel the story was about himself and became angry when the connection was made. Nevertheless, Goldman thought that Hinckley did identify with the boy but did not recognize the Oedipal theme in his own wishes.[71]

During cross-examination Goldman agreed that in his fantasy Hinckley had created an "all-evil prohibitive figure" who hated him, sought to destroy him, and denied him access to an idealized mother figure. The president became the prohibitive figure, and Jodie Foster assumed the mother role. Although Goldman admitted there was no direct evidence that Hinckley saw the president in that role, "I think there is evidence that he generally perceived people in power as keeping him away from the things that he wanted and keeps him from feeling like a whole person, a competent person, a person who could have what he wanted." Goldman agreed that this meant that he shot President Reagan because Reagan was denying him access to Jodie Foster: "He felt in some ways that that was so at the moment, at the time that he decided that he had to do it, yes . . . he was operating partly under that fantasy." Reagan represented, Goldman observed, "a type of figure which is the most important authority, the most powerful male available and someone, the elimination of whom would be sure to be impressive to Miss Foster."[72]

For the prosecution, on the other hand, psychiatrist Park E. Dietz told the jury that Hinckley's writings did not reveal mental illness and, as fiction, could not be used to judge his state of mind. "If we were to judge the mental state of an author by his poetry, our mental hospitals would be filled with the most distinguished poets in history," from Shakespeare to e. e. cummings. Dietz not only differed with the defense interpretation of the obvious themes in Hinckley's writings, but suggested that Hinckley picked up his ideas from the psychiatrists, the news media, and his lawyers, and embellished his description of his mental state when he shot President Reagan. He characterized his life, for instance, as "a movie starring me" with Ronald and Nancy Reagan "and a cast of doctors, lawyers and hangers-on." He asserted that "the movie ain't over, folks," suggesting that the last scene would show him taking Jodie Foster away from Yale and "from the world permanently." Dietz proposed that Hinckley picked up the notion of his life as a movie script from a defense psychiatrist who unwittingly provided him with ideas he might imitate.[73]

As to why Hinckley decided to shoot Reagan, the prosecution psychiatrists held the view that his choice demonstrated, not mental illness, but a desire for attention and fame. Sally A. C. Johnson told the jury that Hinckley showed a "logical reasoning process" when he picked his assassination target. He had stalked President Carter, but since Carter's popularity in the polls declined, he shifted to president-elect Reagan. Four or five times after the election Hinckley waited outside Blair House with a gun when Reagan was staying there. He based his decision on how powerful the person was. But even on those occasions he chose not to shoot. He was not driven by suicidal impulses and the distorted emotions from his inner world which compelled him to shoot at Reagan. Johnson concluded that Hinckley was not "a person compelled to shoot the President . . . that wasn't the case with John." "He functioned too well," Johnson testified, to fit the pattern of schizophrenia.[74]

In the Hinckley trial the judge and jury faced the problem Lord Patrick Devlin saw as the dialectic of trial by jury: "Hard cases make bad law; the jury is sometimes too frightened of the hard case and the judge of the bad law. This is the eternal conflict between law in the abstract and the justice of the case—how to do what is best in the individual case and yet preserve the rule."[75] Lord Devlin's observation about the nature of law is well illustrated in the insanity plea dispute.

Three problems arise with the insanity plea. The first is that we expect that it should be reduced to a formula. How many books on psychology and law, especially criminal justice textbooks, treat the insanity test as if it were litmus paper? The fact that there are several versions of the test, so goes the implication, merely means that in criminal justice, unlike chemistry, we have yet to find a reliable dye. If law is a set of rules and formulae to which the judge and jury have the task of fitting each case, law can be clearcut, the fog of discretion can be dispelled. Instead, because law develops from stories, not a periodic chart of the elements, we should look for lessons which converge to teach us, not formulae. When the law lords stated the McNaughtan rule in answer to questions about "the criminal responsibility of persons labouring under partial delusions," they spoke out of a tradition of law, not from the position of a committee writing rules for a new board game. If we think of the insanity standard as a formula, we might make the mistake of applying it in an all-or-nothing fashion, like the rules of baseball or Monopoly. But if it is understood as a consequence of a principle, a test in which the plumb line of experience is held up to the case at hand, the insanity test might not seem so confusing and contradictory.[76] What matters is our expectation of the law.

The second problem with the insanity defense is that the jury is exasperated by the conflicting testimony of experts. Much of the testimony of psychiatrists is a richness that the members of the jury do not need. The jury's verdict is not about the nature of the defendant's illness. Neither the symptoms, the causes, nor treatment concern them. Their decision must emerge from a question more subtle: Was the defendant responsible for the act?

The variety of mental states of which the human mind is capable resembles the shadings in the color spectrum. No compartments or divisions break the continuum from just this side of infrared to just this side of ultraviolet. So it is with the mind. When we look at a rainbow, however, we begin to pick out the separate colors. We cluster red, yellow, and blue, the primary colors, and sort out various combinations with orange, green, pink, or purple. People with a sophisticated eye for color will note aqua, peach, or chartreuse. In the same way, psychiatrists will see conditions of mental illness clustering around schizophrenia, manic-depression, paranoia, phobia, and other conditions, including milder categories of mental disorientation. A diagnosis may account for the mind's many blends, but a jury's judgment must be either/or. When experts testify about a defendant's mental state, we then ask the jury to reproduce, with their verdict, the rainbow in black and white.

Even if we revise the insanity plea to allow for, on the one side of the spectrum, a plea of diminished responsibility, or, on the other side, a guilty-but-insane verdict, or even if we abolish the special plea completely and return to the *mens rea* (criminal intent) standard, we have not essentially changed the jury's difficulty.[77] The former, a more tolerant test, allows the jury to reduce first-degree murder to manslaughter, as it did in the Dan White trial, by saying that the accused is sane but not fully responsible. Its reciprocal, the second and more restrictive test, permits the jury to say the accused is guilty but not fully sane. Returning the law to what it was before the Hadfield and McNaughtan tests, making mental illness no more an exculpatory claim than blindness, would abolish the insanity defense, [78] but it would not provide juries and judges with an automatic touchstone. All three reforms adjust the concept of a guilty mind (*mens rea*) to fit the circumstances, slackening up on it in the first, tightening it in the second, and pruning all except criminal intent in the third. The fundamental question remains that of responsibility, no matter how and in which direction we refine it.

The third complicating feature of the insanity defense is the ubiquity of a political agenda. Of the sixteen most important American asassination cases, most raise the question of insanity.[79] Of the most important insanity plea cases, most involve leading political figures: King George III (Hadfield), Prime Minister Peel (McNaughtan), presidents Garfield and Reagan (Guiteau and Hinckley), and we might also include Mayor Moscone and Supervisor Milk (Supervisor White). The persons involved make these cases important, and the insanity issues makes them hard. "Great cases like hard cases make bad law," wrote Justice Holmes. "For great cases are called great not by reason of their real importance in shaping the law of the future, but because of some accident of immediate overwhelming interest which appeals to the feelings and distorts the judgment. These immediate interests exercise a kind of hydraulic pressure which makes what previously was clear seem doubtful and before which even well-settled principles of law will bend."[80]

Although Justice Holmes wrote these remarks in a famous railroad case, we might say the same about the insanity defense in trials with a political agenda. That agenda, unlike its purely legal counterpart, will provide the "immediate overwhelming interest" to which Holmes refers. Yet, what is society to do when the hydraulic pressure of public opinion and events surrounding an assassination forces these hard cases into court? They must be resolved. If the results are perplexing, this reflects Justice Holmes's other reminder that "the life of the law has not been logic: It has been experience." As Holmes elucidates, the law develops out of "the felt necessities of the time" and other factors, "avowed or unconscious," which embody "the story of a nation's development through many centuries," not the "axioms and corollaries of a book of mathematics."[81] Political trials in general, and those involving the question of insanity in particular, provide a prime example of the law having its birth and life in experience.

Conclusion

Certainly, such trials as Watergate or Hinckley's might be called ordinary criminal trials. The defendants were charged with commiting acts which are crimes in anyone's book: bribery, perjury, breaking and entering, attempted murder. The accused in such trials do not seek to justify their actions as right either morally or legally. Unlike John Hinckley, for example, the assassin of President Anwar Sadat of Egypt claimed that his action was vindicated: "I am guilty of killing the unbeliever and I am proud of it."[82] Hinckley claimed no high cause, nor did John Mitchell or Spiro Agnew. When God's will or the dialectics of history are introduced to justify the action, a clear political agenda is added to the legal agenda. It becomes a full-scale political trial. Trials of scandal or insanity become political trials because of the people involved, either as defendant or as victim.

The public stir over who is involved creates a political trial and gives it importance. The trial itself might be conducted according to a strictly legal agenda. Perhaps no one seeks to use the trial as a political apologia. Yet the political agenda will be carried in the media and becomes inescapable in everyone's mind, including those in the courtroom. This is not to say that such trials are by nature partisan because of the media attention and an unspoken but evident political agenda. The rule of law is not incompatible with thorough and fair media coverage. Partisan trials can result from the lack of media attention, as the Star Chamber trials illustrate, as well as from irrepressible media. The rule of law is strengthened by responsible media, just as it is undermined by irresponsible ones. The same can be said for the bar, for the bench, and for all involved. The truth is that the law has life only when it is respected throughout society. The trials in this chapter illustrate this point.

Defendants in political trials are representative persons. The crisis they undergo in the trial is, vicariously, ours. We identify with their struggles— whether Stans's injured innocence, Magruder and Dean's repentence, Liddy's defiance, Goetz's fear and rage, or Hinckley's confused anguish. When journalists and others who tell the stories of political trials do their jobs responsibly, we as citizens learn the political intricacies, moral entanglements, even mental disturbances involved in public responsibility. Those who tell the story have the same obligation to answer to the requirements of truth as those who wield power have to answer to the requirements of the rule of law. As citizens in a democracy we must hold them both accountable.

If we, the public, are to be in a position to learn from the Watergate or the Hinckley trials, of necessity we will understand that such trials operate from two agendas, one legal and one political; in two different courts, the judicial and the historical; before two juries, the twelve in the jury box and the uncounted in public opinion; facing two judgments, the short run which might result in a prison sentence or other institutionalization and the long run which is the defendant's reputation and the public's sense of what is appropriate in politics. Few lessons can be learned from the purely legal agenda, but the wrong lessons will be learned from a partisan trial with only a political agenda. It is the tension between the two sides of political trials which produces valuable results.

The way we learn from political trials is as fundamental as anything in politics. Its clearest formulation is in Plato's cave analogy.[83] Plato asks us to picture a group of people who have lived all of their lives in a cave. All they know of the world comes from the shadows cast upon the wall. Because that is all they have ever known, that is all they are inclined to want to know. When one of the denizens leaves the cave and returns to it with the message that the world is different from what the shadows show, he is stoned to death. At the heart of the issue of responsibility, as Plato demonstrates, is the question: What is the real world?

If we learn from political trials only what we want to learn about responsibility, we will only reinforce our stereotypes because we will see only the shadows. Much depends on the media. If those who tell the story of Watergate or Hinckley tell us only what we want to hear as measured by the ratings, we will not be challenged to think. Politics itself and political trials, the miniature of politics, will be written with a soap opera script. On the other hand, if the media tell us what we might not want to hear, if they challenge our image of what the real world is, their ratings might fall and we will have killed the messenger. Is that the dilemma: either the illusion of truth or death to the messenger? Yes, if we are not responsible as citizens. No, if we recognize that we as citizens are as responsible for the rule of law and the statement of the truth as are judges, juries, lawyers, and news reporters.

The opposite of responsibility is cynicism. Cynical lawyers, politicans, and news managers presume that truth in politics and law is the image. This leads to the assumption made by those engaged in the Watergate cover-up that the rule of law can be replaced by directives about a public relations problem called Watergate. Plato made no such assumption. He saw that a democracy could degenerate to the point where citizens became drones, but he also saw that we have more potential.[84] The key is whether or not the public believed in standards of justice and truth which were not merely matters of public taste and preference. In short, is the rule of law possible? We might easily be misled, but we can be responsible.

Notes

1. Catherine Drinker Bowen, *Francis Bacon: The Temper of a Man* (Boston, Little Brown, 1963), p. 188. See also Jonathan L. Marwil, *The Trials of Counsel Francis Bacon in 1621* (Detroit, Wayne State University Press, 1976).
2. *Ibid.*, p. 190.

3. *Ibid.*, p. 209.
4. *New York Times*, April 4, 1975; April 15, 1975; April 18, 1975; August 7, 1975.
5. *Ibid.*, February 21, 1973, at 42.
6. James Anthony Froude, *The Reign of Henry the Eighth*, 3 vols. (London, Dent, 1909), Vol. 2, pp. 146-171.
7. Attorney General Elliot Richardson's statement to the U. S. District Court of Maryland, Judge Walter E. Hoffman, presiding, October 10, 1973, in David C. Saffell, ed., *Watergate: Its Effects on the American Political System* (Cambridge, Mass., Winthrop, 1974), pp. 147-148.
8. Statement by U. S. District Court Judge Walter E. Hoffman, *Ibid.*, pp. 149-150.
9. Peter Schrag, *Test of Loyalty: Daniel Ellsberg and the Rituals of Secret Government* (New York, St. Martin's, 1980), Ch. 7.
10. G. Gordon Liddy, *Will* (New York, St. Martin's, 1980), Chs. 15-22.
11. Jeb Stuart Magruder, *An American Life: One Man's Road to Watergate* (New York, Antheneum, 1974), Ch. 12; John Dean, *Blind Ambition: The White House Years* (New York, Pocket Books, 1976), Ch. 5.
12. John J. Sirica, *To Set the Record Straight: The Break-in, The Tapes, The Conspirators, The Pardon* (New York, W. W. Norton, 1979), p. 88.
13. *Ibid.*, p. 96.
14. Schrag, *Test of Loyalty*, Ch. 7; John Ehrlichman, *Witness to Power: The Nixon Years* (New York, Simon & Schuster, 1982), pp. 374-375.
15. Theodore H. White, *Breach of Faith: The Fall of Richard Nixon* (New York, Dell, 1975), p. 297.
16. Dean, *Blind Ambition*, Ch. 10.
17. Richard Nixon, *RN: Memoirs*, Vol. 2 (New York, Warner, 1978) p. 432.
18. Maurice H. Stans, *The Terrors of Justice: The Untold Side of Watergate* (New York, Everest House, 1978), p. 291.
19. Congressional Quarterly, *Watergate: Chronology of a Crisis*, Vol. 1 (Washington, Congressional Quarterly, 1974), pp. 46, 71-72.
20. See Richard Ben-Veniste and George Frampton, Jr., *Stonewall: The Real Story of the Watergate Prosecution* (New York, Simon & Schuster, 1977), Ch. 15.
21. Gladys Engel Land and Kurt Lang, *The Battle for Public Opinion: The President, the Press, and the Polls during Watergate* (New York, Columbia University Press, 1983), p. 300.
22. Raymond Price, *With Nixon* (New York, Viking, 1977), p. 186.
23. *Ibid.*, p. 187.
24. Stans, *Terrors of Justice*, p. 7.
25. *Ibid.*, p. 53.
26. *Ibid.*, p. 201.
27. *Ibid.*, Ch. 16.
28. *Ibid.*, p. 270.
29. *Ibid.*, p. 278.
30. Liddy, *Will*, pp. 194, 128.
31. *Ibid.*, pp. 146, 170.
32. *Ibid.*, p. 200.
33. *Ibid.*, pp. 207-213.
34. *Ibid.*, p. 210.
35. *Olmstead v. United States*, 277 U. S. 438 at 485 (1928).
36. Liddy, *Will*, pp. 299, 258.
37. Magruder, *American Life*, p. 10.

38. Dean, *Blind Ambition*, p. 21.
39. Magruder, *American Life*, p. 322.
40. Ehrlichman, *Witness to Power*, p. 408.
41. Congressional Quarterly, *Watergate*, p. 170.
42. *Ibid.*
43. E. Fuller Torrey, *The Roots of Treason: Ezra Pound and the Secret of St. Elizabeths* (San Diego, Harcourt Brace Javanovich, 1984), pp. 174-196. See also Stanley I. Kutler, *The American Inquisition: Justice and Injustice in the Cold War* (New York, Hill & Wang, 1982), Ch. 3.
44. See Kutler, *The American Inquisition*, Ch. 1. For accounts of the trials of Mildred Gillars ("Axis Sally") and others tried for treason after World War II see William G. Schofield, *Treason Trial* (Chicago, Rand McNally, 1964).
45. Torrey, *Roots of Treason*, Ch. 8.
46. *Ibid.*, pp. 234-235, 254-255. See George Steiner, "The Scandal of the Nobel Prize," *New York Times Book Review* (September 30, 1984), p. 38.
47. Richard Moran, *Knowing Right from Wrong: The Insanity Defense of Daniel McNaughtan* (New York, Free Press, 1981), p. 21. See also Nigel Walker, *Crime and Insanity in England*, Vol. 1, *The Historical Perspective* (Edinburgh, University Press, 1968), Ch. 5.
48. The Queen against Daniel McNaughton, *Reports of State Trials, New Series* (London, Professional Books, 1970 reprint), Vol. 4, p. 848. Hereafter cited as *State Trials, New Series*.
49. Moran, *Knowing Right from Wrong*, Ch. 2.
50. *Ibid.*, pp. 38, 87-90, Appendix E.
51. *Ibid.*, p. 40.
52. *Ibid.*, p. 115.
53. *State Trials, New Series*, Vol. 4, pp. 935-1230, esp. 966, 974, 992-996.
54. See Donald Read and Eric Glasgow, *Feargus O'Connor: Irishman and Chartist* (London, Edward Arnold, 1961).
55. *State Trials, New Series*, Vol. 4, p. 925.
56. Charles E. Rosenberg, *The Trial of the Assassin Guiteau: Psychiatry and the Law in the Guilded Age* (Chicago, University of Chicago, 1968). See also James W. Clarke, *American Assassins: The Darker Side of Politics* (Princeton, Princeton University Press, 1982), pp. 198-214.
57. *Ibid.*, pp. 139-141, 173.
58. *Ibid.*, pp. 148, 163-164.
59. San Francisco *Chronicle*, May 22, 1979, pp. A, B, 1, 18. White's confession is found in the *Chronicle*, May 4, 1979, pp. 8-9. See also Mike Weiss, *Double Play: The San Francisco City Hall Killings* (Reading, Mass., Addison-Wesley, 1984).
60. San Francisco, *Chronicle*, May 2, 1979, p. 16.
61. *Ibid.*, May 8, 1979, pp. 1, 14.
62. *Ibid.*, May 25, 1979, p. 4; *New York Times*, May 23, 1979, p. 6.
63. Warren Hinckle, Hinckle's Journal, San Francisco *Chronicle*, May 23, 1979, p. 6.
64. *New York Times*, August 4, 1979, p. 19. In his study of the sixteen assassination attempts since the one in 1835 on President Jackson, James W. Clarke concludes that "there is an unmistakable *political* bias toward a highly individualistic psychopathological explanation of the motives of assassins. Thus, at the official level there is a strong inclination to 'explain' assassinations in terms of the personalities of allegedly mentally ill individuals. To do otherwise would be

to risk acknowledging the rationality of some political grievances. . . . Second, this political bias has been supported by a *psychiatric* bias that tends to view any deviation from social norms as ipso facto evidence of pathology. . . . The combination of such political and psychiatric biases results in highly *reductionist* explanations of American assassinations." Clarke, *American Assassins*, p. 258. For a compelling account of psychiatrists on the witness stand as story tellers see Willard Gaylin, *The Killing of Bonnie Garland: A Question of Justice* (New York, Simon & Schuster, 1982).

65. For a discussion of these and other cases of assassins see Clarke, *American Assassins*.

66. *United States v. John Hinckley, Jr.,* 81-306, Criminal Docket, United States District Court for the District of Columbia, transcript, June 17, 1982, pp. 8713-8714, 8382. Hereafter cited as Hinckley Transcript.

67. *Ibid.*, pp. 8714-8716.

68. Washington *Post*, June 12, 1982, p. 47.

69. *New York Times*, June 2, 1982, Sec. 4, p. 19; June 4, 1982, p. 1.

70. Hinckley Transcript, May 24, pp. 4764-65, 4776-81, 4796-97, 4817-18.

71. *Ibid.*, pp. 4812-4815, 5152-56.

72. *Ibid.*, pp. 5236-41.

73. *Washington Post*, June 12, 1982, p. 47.

74. *Ibid.*, June 13, 1982, p. 45.

75. Lord Patrick Devlin, *Trial by Jury*, The Eighth Hamlyn Lecture, 1956 (London, Stevens, & Sons, 1966), p. 124.

76. See Ronald Dworkin, *Taking Rights Seriously* (Cambridge, Mass., Harvard University Press, 1977), Ch. 2, "The Model of Rules I."

77. For an advocacy of dimished responsibility and a critique of the guilty-but-insane position see Sheldon Glueck, *Law and Psychiatry: Cold War or Entente Cordiale?* (Baltimore, Johns Hopkins University Press, 1962), pp. 23-38.

78. For an advocacy of the abolishment position see Norval Morris, *Madness and the Criminal Law* (Chicago, University of Chicago Press, 1982), Ch. 2.

79. Clarke, *American Assassins*, pp. 259-266.

80. Northern Securities Company v. United States, 193 U. S. 197 at 400 (1904).

81. Oliver Wendell Holmes, Jr., *The Common Law*, in *The Mind and Faith of Justice Holmes: His Speeches, Essays, Letters, and Judicial Opinions*, ed. by Max Lerner (New York, Modern Library, 1943), pp. 51-52.

82. Minneapolis *Tribune*, November 30, 1981, p. 3A.

83. Plato, *The Republic*, 514-521.

84. *Ibid.*, pp. 555-561.

5

Trials of Dissenters:
The Question of Conscience

When dissenters are tried, so are the policies of a government. A trial of a dissenter brings into public light matters of morality or wisdom for all to see. If a genuine appeal to conscience is to be made, those who break the law do so in order to demonstrate that the law is wrong. A trial is the forum to air the issue. In such a trial the government is reluctant to have public attention focused on the question of rightness, only the legal issue surrounding the broken law. Yet the government needs to try dissenters in order to demonstrate that it is "doing something" about troublemakers, perhaps subversives, who are taking the law into their own hands. In such cases the government is eager to raise a moral question: the rightness of the law. Whether the defendants want to bring the question of wrong to the attention of the public or the government does, trials of dissenters are appeals to conscience.

Among fourteen people arrested for demonstrating against the navy's first Trident nuclear submarine in 1982 was Ruth Youngdahl Nelson, 78, the American Mother of the Year in 1973. The Justice Department quickly dropped the charges. Although President Reagan had declared an emergency in the Bangor, Washington area before the protest began, thereby increasing the penalty from a $1,000 fine or one year in jail to $10,000 and ten years, the government was, in all likelihood, not desirous of the media coverage her trial would have generated. As it was, the protest and arrest begat headlines such as "Mother of the Year Arrested in Nuclear Sub Protest." Mrs. Nelson and the other protesters, since they were challenging the Trident submarine as part of a first-strike nuclear policy, were disappointed to have their efforts in civil disobedience cut short when the charges were dropped.[1]

By contrast, the government arrested, prosecuted, and executed Ethel Rosenberg in spite of flimsy evidence. Whatever might be said about the evidence against Julius Rosenberg,[2] Ethel was the victim of J. Edgar Hoover's zealous crusade. Throughout the events of the Rosenberg case the government sought publicity. Klaus Fuchs had engaged in genuine and significant atomic bomb spying.[3] He confessed in England and set off a round of arrests in the United States. Hoover and the prosecution puffed out the Fuchs connection into a vast chimera around the Rosenbergs. What real evidence they had of Soviet espionage was magnified. Concerning Ethel they had none. After Julius had been arrested, Hoover told Attorney General J. Howard McGrath that "there is no question if Julius Rosenberg would furnish details of his extensive espionage activities it would be possible to proceed against other individuals . . . proceeding against his wife might serve as a lever in this matter."[4]

Robert Cecil and Edward Coke in 1605, like Hoover and the prosecutors in 1951, parlayed a real but limited Gunpowder Plot involving Guy Fawkes and a dozen conspirators into a colossus. Later in the century Titus Oates tied together another knot of lies in the Popish Plot. Both fed on the fear and prejudice in anti-Catholicism. Yet the basic facts in the original Gunpowder Plot were true. Fr. Henry Garnet, who had a tenuous connection with the actual Gunpowder plotters, was tried and executed as the mastermind of a treasonous plot against all England, boundless in reach and unfathomable in perfidy. Likewise, the Rosenbergs, with Julius's slender links to spy activities, were depicted by Judge Kaufman as

> putting into the hands of the Russians the A-bomb years before our best scientists predicted Russia would perfect the bomb has already caused, in my opinion, the Communist aggression in Korea, with the resultant casualties exceeding 50,000 and who knows but what that millions more innocent people may pay the price of your treason. Indeed, by your betrayal, you undoubtedly have altered the course of history to the disadvantage of our country.[5]

As the Gunpowder and the Rosenberg trials demonstrate, momentous trials of dissenters, after a passage of time, take on a life of their own. For a while, perhaps a long while, the intent of a Cecil and a Coke, a Hoover and a Kaufman might succeed. The specter of the Gunpowder Plot can be raised over and over against Catholics for two or more generations. In some quarters the meaning of Guy Fawkes Day is anti-Catholic to this day, although it has become for most Britons a civic celebration—the Fourth of July and Halloween in one. The Rosenberg trial and the trial of Alger Hiss served those who sought to discredit dissenters as subversive. It worked well during the 1950s and on occasion thereafter, but, while the debate surrounding the Rosenberg and Hiss trials continues,[6] the incantational effect of the trials works no more.

The symbolic struggle represented by the Rosenberg and the Hiss trials, and in the previous generation the Sacco and Venzetti trial, document the political profile of an era. Were Sacco and Vanzetti framed?[7] Or Hiss? Were the Rosenbergs? Were these trials part of a campaign to stir up a red scare hysteria? Apart from any of the facts in the cases, the answers to these questions have shaped the contours of politics since the trials. The political faith, belief, and, for many, dogmatics arise from the meaning such trials have generated. The Sacco-Vanzetti, Hiss, and Rosenberg trials are hardly the first, and the Gunpowder Plot trial was not the first either. At least since the trial of Socrates, trials of dissenters have shaped our sense of public morality. The life of their own which such trials achieve, independent of the facts concerning guilt or innocence, is our public reservoir from which we draw our conscience. We need real human beings, not abstract rules, in order to know what is right and what is wrong.

After Socrates

The demagogues in Athens tried Socrates in 399 BC for corrupting the youth. They sought to show how he was undermining democracy by his teaching. But the prosecution of Socrates backfired. His defense became an indictment of Athenian tyranny, a declaration of faith for liberal thought from his time to ours, and an expression of the ideals of Greek culture so powerful that we approach the ancient Greeks first through Socrates' *Apology*. Likewise, Galileo's 1633 trial by the Inquisition does for the natural sciences in Western civilization what the trial of Socrates does for the humanities. Just as Socrates lived and was tried at the dawn of our culture, so Galileo's life, time, and work represent the beginnings of modern science, and his trial gives us an understanding of its moral dimension. Both dissenters stand for the struggle of the independent mind against mindless orthodoxy. Our conscience is shaped by both.

Yet the fact is that Socrates had earlier made his peace with brutal tyrants and did not call them to account.[8] The stumbling block in the Galileo case is not that as an old man he was frightened and dragooned by the Inquisition to retract but that seventeen years earlier he was unable to offer any scientific proof of his position.[9] If Socrates once sided with tyranny and Galileo resorted to dogmatic claim instead of empirical evidence, does that destroy the significance of their trials for the causes of liberal thought and free scientific inquiry? Not if we recognize that the trials have a symbolic meaning far greater than any imagined at the time by the participants, especially the defendants. Nor does the truth of the causes represented by the trial of Socrates and Galileo depend upon the factual truth of the events surrounding the trial. We do need, nevertheless, the trials as fulcrums for judgment. As a consequence, our understanding of such trials parallels a problem in theology concerning the life, trial, and crucifixion of Christ. Should the New Testament account be demythologized?[10] Orthodox, fundamentalist, and liberal schools emerge to explain the historical facts, the myth, and the message (*kerygma*) about the trial of Jesus. How these conflicts are resolved determines how important issues of history and value are settled. The same is true with the trials of Socrates and Galileo and other dissenters including Sacco and Vanzetti, Alger Hiss, and the Rosenbergs. The October 1983 debate in New York between the team of Ronald Radosh and Joyce Milton, who argued that Julius Rosenberg was guilty of low-level spying but that the trial was unfair, and the team of Walter and Miriam Schneir, who maintained that the Rosenbergs were innocent, illustrates how central the interpretation of certain trials can be even three decades later. Tickets for the Rosenberg debate sold out a month in advance; the Town Hall was filled with a crowd of 1,500, and the sharp exchanges in the debate itself became national news.[11] It works both ways with political trials which become fulcrums on which our political judgments turn: The schools of interpretation decipher the trial, and the trial becomes a crucible for the cause. In this way our public judgment evolves.

Which trials are *that* important? Which become not merely attention grabbers but fulcrums? Apart from the trial of Socrates, which is *the* exemplar, other trials of dissenters become morally paradigmatic as movements develop the myths of their struggles. For the American labor movement, for instance, the trials of Eugene Debs, in 1895 for the Pullman strike and in 1918 for denouncing the government's persecution of dissent, plus the trials of Big Bill Haywood and other IWW organizers (1907, 1917, and 1918) provide insight into their cause, what they faced in their struggle, and how the modern labor movement has attained its identity because of them.[12] For the same reason attention has been drawn to the 1873 trial of Susan B. Anthony for daring to attempt to vote, a trial which provides the feminist movement with a sense of its struggle and identity. The civil rights movement, likewise, finds the expression of conscience in the trials of those who have protested against racial injustice, from John Brown's 1859 trial for raising a slave rebellion to Martin Luther King's 1963 trial for demonstrating in Birmingham, Alabama. Certainly the peace movement has no difficulty in listing its central trials with the trial of the Catonsville nine in 1968 heading the list. In such trials the trial itself acquires a symbolic value from which the movement finds its sense of mission and the rest of society learns its public values.

The poetry of movements comes from the inspired statements in trials. It emerges from the routine of legal process and the formality of legal language like prophetic scripture. For feminism Susan B. Anthony's stirring statement before sentence was pronounced provides a concise homily of the movement's purposes.[13] Eugene Deb's speech to the jury in his 1918 trial can be read as a capsule narrative of the legend of American radicalism and the rise of American labor.[14] Statements during their trials by Daniel and Philip Berrigan are poetic sermons on peace.[15] Martin Luther King's "Letter from Birmingham Jail" has become *the* classic on civil disobedience.[16]

The prototype of all such statements is Socrates' *Apology*. Just as Socrates told the Athenian court that his mission had been imposed on him by the god of Delphi,[17] so Anthony, Debs, the Berrigans, and King find that their dissent is required of them by a moral covenant contained in the Declaration of Independence, the message of Christianity, or both. Dissenters disobey the law, not because of a criminal desire for gain in wealth or power, but because they must obey a higher law. Their appeal is to the joint knowledge of conscience.

Dissenters, following Socrates' example, seek to teach their fellow citizens, not frighten or coerce them. Socrates characterized himself as a gadfly arousing, persuading, reproaching, and exhorting his fellow Athenians to do what was best for themselves: seek virtue, not private interest. Anthony said that her purpose "was to educate all women to do precisely as I have done, rebel against your man-made, unjust, unconstitutional forms of law, that tax, fine, imprison, and hang women, while they deny them the right of representation."[18] Debs told the jury in 1918 that his "purpose was to have the people understand something about the social system in which we live and to prepare them to change this system by perfectly peaceable and orderly means to what I, as a Socialist, conceive to be a real democracy."[19] The Berrigans and most dissenters would concur with Martin Luther King: "Just as Socrates felt that it was necessary to create a tension in the mind so that individuals could rise from the bondage of myths and half-truths to the unfettered realm of creative analysis and objective appraisal, we must see the need of having non-violent gadflies to create that kind of tension in society that will help men rise from the dark depths of prejudice and racism to the majestic heights of understanding and brotherhood."[20]

Finally, dissenters see that the way to change law is not by escaping from it or evading its impact but by urging that it be applied fully and by confronting its injustices. Although his friends had bribed the guards and arranged for his escape from death row, Socrates refused to leave. To do so would undermine the rule of law and deny the principles on which he built his life and teaching.[21] Anthony, like Socrates, told the judge that she had hoped for a broad interpretation of the Constitution "that should declare equality of rights the national guarantee to all persons born or naturalized in the United States. But failing to get justice—failing, even, to get a trial by a jury *not* of my peers—I ask not leniency at your hands—but rather the full rigors of the law."[22] King and the Berrigans have made statements similar to Deb's admission to the jury that he not only did what he was accused of doing but that it is what others should do and accept the consequences under law: "Yes, I was opposed to the war. I am perfectly willing, on that count, to be branded as a disloyalist, and if it is a crime under American law, punishable by imprisonment, for being opposed to human bloodshed, I am perfectly willing to be clothed in the stripes of a convict and to end my days in a prison cell."[23]

Thomas More, Roger Williams, and Anne Hutchinson

When Henry VIII in 1529 made Thomas More his Lord Chancellor he replaced the corrupt wheeler-dealer Cardinal Wolsey with a scrupulously honest lawyer. When Wolsey fell from royal favor, or perhaps tripped in his own maneuvers, Henry was attempting to rid himself of Queen Catherine in order to marry Anne Boleyn. He pushed ahead with his divorce plans without Cardinal Wolsey and without substantial help from More. Yet Lord Chancellor More spoke for King Henry to Parliament. As the king's good servant he presented Henry's case for the divorce, telling Commons, for instance, that "the King hath not attempted this matter of will for pleasure, as some strangers report, but only for the discharge of his conscience and surety of the succession of his realm."[24] Henry's position was that since Catherine bore him no male heir, only a daughter (the future Queen Mary), he would have to divorce her and remarry in order to insure the male succession. Although he refused to sign a petition to the Pope urging him to grant the divorce, More kept his opposition to himself. But when Henry moved against the Church's authority itself, denying bishops the power to seize heretics for instance, More immediately resigned. The day after the bishops submitted fully, agreeing to all royal demands, More handed Henry the Great Seal.[25]

The final break with Rome came in 1533. After this it was more difficult for such a prominent person as More to keep his dissent private. Henry determined to have More take the Oath of Supremacy acknowledging Henry to be head of the church. For his refusal he was sent to the Tower in April 1534 and tried and beheaded in July 1535. When faced with the charge of treason for refusing to give assent to royal supremacy over the church, More submitted that silence itself is no crime, that treason is an overt act, that even if silence were construed as an act the presumption must be that it means consent rather than the reverse, that a loyal subject when in doubt will refer to his conscience, and that a loyal subject by definition cannot harbor seditious thoughts in his conscience.[26] While More acknowledged the king's authority in secular matters and granted that the pope's temporal authority was limited by English law, he did not believe national law could restrict papal authority in the church.

More's trial in Westminster Hall is a clear-cut instance of a partisan trial, although More's answers to his accusers stand in today's light as an indictment of Henry's regime. Since he was accused of treason, he was presumed guilty. He was not given a copy of the indictment and did not hear it read until he appeared in court. He was allowed neither counsel nor the right to call witnesses. The trial was held before a special commission of Oyer and Terminer instead of a regular court, and, instead of being independent, it was packed with royal favorites. Although one of the disputed matters was More's opinion on the matter of Henry's marriage to Anne Boleyn, Anne's father, brother, and uncle were appointed to the nineteen-man commission. Thomas Cromwell, Henry's secretary and More's chief rival, and others close to the king were there too. They had all taken the oath and could be expected to think it only reasonable that More should as well.[27]

The issue in More's trial became the question of the obligation of conscience, a meaning which is not always clear. More had, after all, in speaking on behalf of the king told Parliament that Henry sought the divorce because of his conscience for the future of England, and Henry himself had told his Council that "I have asked the counsel of the greatest clerks in Christendom, and for this cause I have sent for this legate as a man indifferent, only to know the truth and settle my conscience, and for no other cause as God can judge. . . . These be the sores that vex my mind, these be the pangs that trouble my conscience, and for these griefs I seek a remedy."[28] Further, could not More's accusers, who had taken the oath, rest content with their consciences that in following their king they had done what was right?

What does conscience mean? More meant by conscience, according to G. R. Elton, "a recognition of . . . the truth established by a greater consensus than was available in one realm alone." More made it clear that by conscience he did not mean everyone's right to judge arbitrarily but, instead, the duty to accept a vision granted to the body of Christians. "And therefore," he told his judges, "I am not bound to conform my conscience to the council of one realm against the great council of Christendom." Thomas Cromwell, now in the position of speaking for the king, argued for "the conscience of the subject, the member of the community of England who owed a duty to obey the law made for that community by the King-in-Parliament," a duty Cromwell did not see as conflicting with divine law because the pope's authority rested on no scriptural authority.[29] Both More and Cromwell accepted the idea that conscience is a joint knowledge between an individual and the community. Both reject the notion that conscience is a private assertion of judgment. Where they differ is in the source of the community's knowledge: Does conscience derive from all Christendom or from a nation?

In England the prototypical conflict over religion and loyalty is the collision of Thomas More with Henry VIII. The equivalent in America are the clashes Roger Williams and Anne Hutchinson had with the Massachusetts orthodoxy. In all three struggles the central issues are the meaning of conscience and the rule of law. Although More was a devout Catholic whose mind operated in a medieval framework and Williams and Hutchinson were intrepid Puritans in tune with the revolutionary spirit of the seventeenth century, they would have agreed on the obligation of conscience and the necessity of opposing arbitrary authority.

As a teenager Roger Williams attracted the attention of none other than Sir Edward Coke, who at the time, around 1620, was doing battle on behalf of the common law against the claims of divine right by King James I. Coke and the Williams family were communicants of St. Sepulchre's in London, and young Roger took shorthand notes for Sir Edward of sermons and also of proceedings in the Star Chamber. Coke became the patron of Williams's education at Charterhouse School and then at Cambridge.[30]

Williams became a minister but refused his first call because the Boston church had not separated itself from the Church of England. Two years later, in 1633, after he had spent some time living among the Separatists at Plymouth, he was called to the Salem Church, and that is where his problems with the authorities in Massachusetts began. Given the precarious state of politics in England in the 1630s, the hostility of Charles I and Archbishop William Laud to Puritans wherever they might be, plus the attempt of the Massachusetts Puritans to prove that their colony was based on the Bible, was uniform in its worship, and was not separated from the king's church, it is hardly surprising that the magistrates reacted against Williams.

Williams attacked the very idea of a royal charter. He had written that the Indians, not the English king, were the only lords of the soil. The "great sin" was that "Christian Kings (so called) were invested with Right by virtue of their Christianity, to take and give away the Lands and Countries of other men." He accused the king with "a solemn public lie" in proclaiming himself the first Christian prince to discover "this land." Williams, one of the few in New England to regard the Indians as equal human beings with a culture as valid as the European, contended that because the Indians "hunted all the Country over" and twice a year burned off the underbrush they had proof of their property which was as good as the king's to his English forests.[31] The spread of such ideas could easily endanger the colony's royal charter.

But there is more. Williams also objected to the oath which required residents to swear their loyalty. By invoking the name of God an oath became an act of worship, Williams argued, which could not be forced upon the unregenerate without becoming a perversion of God's worship.[32] This idea, based on Williams's conviction that forced worship is idolatry, challenged the very assumptions of the Holy Commonwealth and threatened the covenant the orthodoxy had, to their satisfaction, established with God.

In October 1635 the General Court, which had requested that all of the Bay ministers attend because of the importance of the case, heard arguments in the trial of Roger Williams and pronounced judgment:

> Whereas Mr. Roger Williams . . . hath broached and divulged dyvers newe and dangerous opinions, against the aucthoritie of magistrates, as also writt letters of defamacon, both of the magistrates and churches here, and that before any conviccon, and yet mainetaineth the same without retraccon, it is therefore ordered, that the said Mr. Williams shall departe out of this jurisdic-con.[33]

We have no trial transcript, but the controversy was carried on in a battle of pamphlets between Williams and John Cotton. Williams did not return to England for his exile, as expected, but instead he founded the colony of Rhode Island.

Two years later Anne Hutchinson faced the Massachusetts General Court and met with the same judgment Williams had: exile. In England she had been an avid follower of the preacher John Cotton whose scholarship and eloquent sermons were attracting the attention of many beyond his church in Boston, Lincolnshire. The authorities soon had him denounced for nonconformity and Puritanism before the Court of the High Commission in 1632. Cotton put on a disguise, took an assumed name, and fled for his safety to Boston in New England. Anne Hutchinson and her family followed.[34]

The same ship which arrived with the Hutchinsons also brought a demand from King Charles I that the Massachusetts Bay Colony return its charter. This increased the pressure to prove to the English powers-that-be that New England knew how to handle dissenters and troublemakers. The trial was presided over by the founder of the Bay Colony, Hutchinson's nearest neighbor and chief accuser, John Winthrop. He told her that she was accused of troubling "the peace of the commonwealth and the churches here," of having spoken "divers things . . . very prejudicial to the honor of the churches and ministers," and of maintaining a meeting "in your house that hath been condemned by the general assembly as a thing not tolerable nor comely in the sight of God nor fitting for your sex."[35]

Hutchinson had supported her brother-in-law, Rev. John Wheelwright, who had challenged the orthodoxy with a sermon calling upon those under the Covenant of Grace (presumably the Hutchinsonians) to "come out against the enemies of the Lord, and if we do not strive, those under a Covenant of Works will prevail." The latter were legalists in the orthodoxy. Wheelwright had been sentencd to banishment by the General Court, and Hutchinson, among others, had presented a petition. Winthrop asked her why she countenanced the faction, "That's a matter of conscience, Sir," Hutchinson answered. Winthrop: "Your conscience you must keep or it must be kept for you." When asked what law she had broken, Winthrop replied, "the law of God and of the state." When she pressed him for a particular law, Winthrop answered that she had broken the fifth commandment, "Honor thy father and thy mother." She responded that she did honor her parents. But Winthrop understood that the "fathers of the commonwealth" had been dishonored.[36]

John Cotton was the major witness who spoke on Hutchinson's behalf. He was in a ticklish position because his ardent disciple was on trial, in large part, for ideas he had promoted, and yet he had difficulty endorsing any dissent from this particular orthodoxy. Massachusetts was, after all, what he had long worked for, a true Bible commonwealth. When asked about Hutchinson's attack on his colleague at the Boston church, the Rev. John Wilson (against whom she had led a walk-out during one of his sermons),[37] and about her claims that only Cotton and Wheelwright were able ministers, John Cotton admitted that he was uncomfortable at any such comparison. As for the issue in dispute with her opponents over the covenant of works, Cotton helped Hutchinson's defense by observing that what she said did not seem "so ill taken" and that he "did not find her saying they were under a covenant of works, nor that she said they did preach a covenant of works."[38]

If the defense had rested at that point, as Richard Morris shows, Hutchinson might have been acquitted, but following Cotton's testimony Hutchinson brought up an issue which hamstrung her case. She claimed that what she spoke from her conscience she knew to be true of "an immediate revelation" from God, just as Abraham had. To this she added a curse which unhinged her defense completely: "Take heed how you proceed against me, for I know that for this you go about to do to me, God will ruin you and your posterity, and this whole state!"[39] That ended it for Hutchinson. Even Cotton voted against her. She was banished "as being a woman not fit for our society."[40]

The argument raised by the Williams and Hutchinson trials did not end with their banishments. It continued on in an exchange of pamphlets between John Cotton and Roger Williams for another fifteen years. A treatise, *A Model of Church and Civil Power*, written by the ministers of Massachusetts and sent to the people in Williams's Salem congregation at the time of his trial, plus several letters and books by Cotton constitute the case for the prosecution. The heart of the argument for the orthodox cause was stated by Cotton:

> That government, which by the blessing of Christ doth safely, speedily, and effectually purge out such grievous and dangerous evils, as threaten the ruine of Church and State, that government is safely allowed, and justly and wisely established by any civil state.[41]

Williams and Hutchinson, whose errors were judged "fundamental, or seditiously and turbulently promoted," could not be tolerated because "evill it would be to tolerate notorious evill doers." Although Cotton argued that no one should be punished for his or her conscience, he likewise held that an evil doer can be punished "for sinning against his [or her] conscience."[42]

Williams published his *Bloudy Tenent of Persecution for Cause of Conscience* nearly a decade after he was banished, while he was in England to secure a charter for Rhode Island from Parliament. Williams insists that we not confuse persecution with punishment. The distinction between punishment and persecution depends upon the difference between government under a rule of law and arbitrary government. If the rule of law does not prevail, "the law of arms, the sword and blood" will. Government under the rule of law can enjoin obedience. Such a state does not require conformity in spiritual matters, only in civil affairs. Civic duties can be fulfilled not out of fear but out of conscience, since the sword of civil justice is "for the defense of Persons, Estates, Families, Liberties" and the "suppressing of uncivil or injurious persons or actions."[43]

Arbitrary government, according to Williams, enforces an idolatrous civil religion. When they extend the sword to "spiritual and Soul-causes, Spiritual or Soule punishment," the result is the bloody tenet of persecution. Even a true religion, if enforced with the civil authority as an established doctrine, is idolatry and comes under Williams's strongest condemation:

> Yea it is most wofully found evident, that the best *Religion* (like the *fairest Whores*, and the most *golden* and *costlie Images*) yea the most holy and onely true *Religion* and *Worship*, appointed by *God* himself, is a *Torment* to

that *Soul* and *Conscience*, that is forc't against its own *free love* and *choice*, to embrace and observe it.[44]

Punishment must be employed by governments under the rule of law for trangressions of civil order, such as murder and theft, which are "inconsistent to the . . . [relationship] of man to man," and are contrary to the common good. Williams would extend the civil authority's use of punishment beyond actions to lying and to advocating doctrines which violate the civil order, for example teaching the "abominable and most inhumane" practice of human sacrifice or urging wanton love "leading to ushering in *laciviousnesse* and *uncleanness*."[45] But persecution differs in kind from punishment. It is inflicted for some spiritual matter. A person is persecuted for conscience when he or she is punished for refusing to accept or obey an established doctrine.[46] Punishment aims at the preservation of justice while persecution aims at spiritual uniformity. Yet the nature of persecution is such that it tends to corrupt the language. Williams pointed out that those who persecute avoid the word *persecute*, masking the practice as punishment:

> *Christ* is a seducer of the people, a blasphemer against God, a traytor against *Caesar*, therefore hang him; Christians are schismaticall, factious, heretical, therefore persecute them; The Devill hath deluded *John Hus*, therefore crown him with a paper of Devils, and burne him.[47]

Just as Cotton and Winthrop cited the evils which befall a nation such as England when it did not follow the Biblical model of government, so Williams used England to illustrate the entanglements of hypocrisy that accompany the establishment of religion and the persecution of conscience:

> True it is, the *Sword* may make . . . a whole *Nation* of *Hypocrites*. . . . What a most wofull proofe hereof have the *Nations* of the Earth given in all *Ages*? And to seek no further than our *native* Soyle, within a few scores of yeeres, how many wonderful *changes in Religion* hath the *whole Kingdome* made, according to the *change* of *Governours* thereof, in the severall *Religious* which they themselves imbraced! Henry the 7. finds and leaves the *kingdome* absolutely *Popish. Henry* the 8. casts it into a *mound* half *Popish* halfe *Protestant. Edward* the 6. brings forth an *Edition* all *Protestant*. Queene *Mary* within few yeares defaceth *Edwards* worke, and renders the *Kingdome* (after her Grandfather Hen. 7 his pattern) all *Popish. Maries* short *life* and *Religion* ends together: and *Elizabeth* reveth her Brother *Edwards* Modell, all Protestant: And some eminent *Witnesses* of Gods Truth against *Antichrist*, have enclined to believe, that before the downfall of that *Beast*, England must once againe bow down her faire Neck to his proud usurping yoake and foot. . . . It hath been *Englands* sinfull shame, to fashion & change their *Garments* and

Religions with wondrous *ease* and *lightnesse*, as a *higher Power*, a *stronger Sword* hath prevailed; after the ancient patterne of *Nebuchadnezzars* bowing the whole world in one most solemne *uniformitie* of *worship* to his *Golden Image*.[48]

John Cotton made at least two additional claims: Persecution is in the *real* interest of the victims, for their own good, and the persecutors are the *real* victims. Williams regarded Cotton's argument that a person cannot be persecuted for conscience but only for "sinning against his conscience" as, to use Williams's words, "overturning and rooting up the very *foundation* and roots of all true *Christianity*." Since persecution oppresses both true and erroneous conscience, in Williams's opinion, it falls most heavily on those who are most godly and leads the persecutor to such arrogance "that he speaks so tenderly for his own conscience, hath yet so little respect, mercie or pitie to the like *consciencious* perswasions of other Men."[49] Orthodoxy which contains a justification of persecution soon substitutes its idolatry for the common good and becomes the agent for dissolving the bonds of society. It creates a nation of hypocrites by compelling a people to "forsake their Religion which their hearts cleave to."[50] It confuses the spiritual and civil realms by punishing a person both as a "heretick against the *church* [and] as a traitor against the king." And, instead of unifying society, it sets society against itself: "If this be the *touchstone* of all *obedience*, will it not be the *cut-throat* of all *civil relations*, *unions* and *covenants* between Princes and people, and between the people and people?"[51]

John Lilburne and John Peter Zenger

John Lilburne was the Tom Paine of the English Revolution in the seventeenth century. Lilburne, like Paine, wrote the most provocative and catalytic of all the many Puritan pamphlets. The difficulties his writings got him into make him a model dissenter. A century later in the colony of New York a printer, John Peter Zenger, was prosecuted for writings in his newspaper which parallel Lilburne's ideas in a trial which has similarities to Lilburne's. In both instances those in authority were faced with a dissenter who believed arbitrary power had to be checked with the rule of law. Their trials, Lilburne's in 1637 and 1649, Zenger's in 1735, pit two opposite views of government directly against each other. If those in authority are regarded as set apart from the rest of us and superior to us because of their public position, then criticism and, especially, dissent lessens their authority by disparaging their reputation. Dissent is, for this position, a scandal of government. That was the view, in general, of the prosecution. On the other hand, if those with public authority are agents of the rest of us, dissent is merely calling a servant to terms. Freedom of speech, for this position, is a necessity for self-government. Lilburne and Zenger represent this view.

Seventeenth-century England, more than New England, is the seedbed of modern political thought. While it cannot be said that daily life changed into a modern style in the seventeenth century, thought did. Certainly all shades of political opinion arose in the English upheaval: From the divine right theory of James I, the righteous despotism of Cromwell and his New Model Army, the scientific police-state absolutism of Thomas Hobbes, to the constitutional democracy of the Presbyterian and Whig parliamentary party, the radical democracy of Lilburne's Levellers, all the way to the communal communism of Gerrald Winstanley's Diggers and the chiliastic Fifth Monarchists's expectations of Christ's immenent return. Religious thought, in a day when religion was central, likewise ranged from the Roman Catholic, the former orthodoxy under an English cloud, to the Anglican and Presbyterian competing orthodoxies, to a wide range of dissenting sects of Baptists, Quakers, Seekers, Ranters, and Muggletonians.[52] The currents of change in any age of turmoil are most clearly disclosed in political trials. That is where the arguments of a generation are unleashed. In their wake comes legal evolution. In England before 1640 the trials conducted in the Star Chamber or the Court of the High Commission were treason or heresy persecutions of Puritan and other dissenting pamphleteers. After 1640 the political trials were directed against those close to the king: the Earl of Strafford and Archbishop William Laud. In 1649 the king himself was tried. After the 1660 Restoration those who once held authority held it again and tried the regicides. It meant a vicious reaction. In chapter 9 we will explore the difficulties created when a regime in power puts a regime out of power in the prisoner's dock. For now we must focus on a dissenter in the dock.

John Lilburne is a consistent dissenter. He objected to the abuse of power by the Stuart regime, by Parliament when it overthrew Charles, and by Cromwell when he did away with Parliament. He was by no means an anarchist. Lilburne held strong convictions about the rule of law, and that is the key to understanding him. He attacked Charles I for denying the rights in Magna Carta, such as trial by jury, but he was equally vigorous in his attack on the erstwhile dissenters, his former allies, when they put Charles on trial and denied him a trial by jury.

In 1637, when Lilburne was twenty-three, he was arrested for importing "factious and scandalous" books from Holland. He had visited Amsterdam, but his attempt to smuggle into London several thousand Puritan pamphlets by Dr. John Bastwick and William Prynne was betrayed by an agent provocateur. The several men who seized Lilburne shouted that they "had taken one of the notoriousest dispensers of scandalous bookes that was in the kingdom."[53] He was first clamped in the same prison which held Dr. Bastwick himself who, along with several other Puritans, had been sentenced to life imprisonment and had their ears removed by the king's executioner. At about the same time, William Prynne, the Puritan attorney who had written another of Lilburne's imports, referred to "Women Actors" as "notorious Whores" in a book approved by the licensing authorities six weeks *before* the queen took a role in a play. He was sentenced by the Star Chamber to life imprisonment, fined £5,000, expelled from Lincoln's Inn, disbarred, stripped of his Oxford degree, set in a pillory, had both ears removed, and was branded on his forehead with the letters *SL* (seditious libeler).[54]

Under an order from the Privy Council Lilburne was privately interrogated by the Attorney General's chief clerk, but little in the way of information came out of the questioning because Lilburne kept insisting that the questions were not "pertinent to my imprisonment." Questions about Dr. Bastwick and the others were irrelevant because, as he maintained, "I am not imprisoned for knowing and talking with such and such men, but for sending over books; and therefore I am not willing to answer you to any more of these questions, because I see you go about this Examination to ensnare me."[55]

Because he refused to cooperate, the next stop for young Lilburne was the notorious Star Chamber. That body had recently dealt with Bastwick and Prynne, a dim prospect. Lilburne and John Wharton, a bookseller in his eighties who had been arrested as Lilburne's accomplice in book smuggling, were tried. But the Star Chamber proceedings were not as smooth as those in power normally expected and hardly routine. Lilburne began his resistance to the Star Chamber by refusing to take the inquisitorial oath ex officio when offered the Bible. He first pretended not to see the Bible. Then he was instructed to take off his glove and lay his hand directly on the book. Finally, he was told he must swear:

What to do Sir?

You must sweare.

To what?

That you shall make true answer to all things that is asked you.

Must I so Sir? But before I sweare, I will know to what I must sweare.

As soon as you have sworne, you shall.[56]

Lilburne refused. He became the first person ever to refuse the Star Chamber oath.[57]

After four days in his cell to think about the Star Chamber oath, his refusal, and the whole matter of his book smuggling, Lilburne again refused to take the oath. Not surprisingly Lilburne and Wharton were declared "guilty of a very high contempt and offence of dangerous consequence, and evil example." Both the young Lilburne and the elderly Wharton were pilloried. Lilburne, in addition, was whipped through the streets of the city for about two miles, a walk which for his supporters who watched became akin to a religious pilgrimage. In spite of the pain as he was being whipped, Lilburne spoke to the crowd, keeping them spellbound with his story of the "inquisition oath." The warden gagged him, returned him to prison, and put him in irons in the dungeon. Yet during three years of imprisonment he managed to write and secrete out nine sharply worded pamphlets which were printed and distributed.[58]

After taking power one of the first acts of the Long Parliament was the freeing of "free-born" John Lilburne, declaring that the Star Chamber sentence had been "illegal, and against the Liberty of the subject . . . bloody, cruel, wicked, barbarous. and tyrannical." Soon after that they abolished the Star Chamber and the High Commission and forbid the oath ex officio.[59]

Controversy over the Star Chamber and the High Commission and the oath did not appear for the first time in Lilburne's trial. Puritans had rallied with lawyers a generation earlier in the cause of common law—the Puritans because it was a weapon against the orthodoxy and the lawyers because it returned law-making to the courts. The Petition of Right (1628), largely the work of the lawyer's lawyer Edward Coke, now no longer the royal hatchet man he had been in the Gunpowder trials, came close to abolishing the oath. It provided that "none be called to make answer, or take such oath, or to give attendance, or be confined, or otherwise molested or disquieted concerning the same, or for refusal thereof."[60] The full season of the oath ex officio came with Archbishop William Laud who employed it against dissenting Puritans.[61] Lilburne's secret Star Chamber trial and his public punishment, his defiant spirit and his trenchant pamphlets, nevertheless, contributed more than anyone else or series of events to the abolition of the Star Chamber oath and, in fact, to the establishment of the right not to be a witness against oneself.

Lilburne's 1637 confrontation with the Star Chamber was not his last trial, not even his most famous. After his release from prison Lilburne was made a captain in the Parlimentary Army. In 1642 he was taken prisoner by the king's forces and tried at Oxford for treason. He would have been executed had Parliament not threatened reprisals. He was later exhanged and given a major's commission, later a lieutenant-colonel's. He soon left the army because he could not enter Cromwell's New Model Army without taking another oath, the covenant.

Out of the army Lilburne wrote more pamphlets. His writing led him into more trouble with those in power, now his comrades-in-arms-and-in-prison. Early in 1645 he drew his pen to do battle against intolerance and in defense of freedom of conscience and speech, against, ironically, William Prynne, now a powerful member of the House of Commons. Prynne saw to it twice that Commons summoned Lilburne to answer before one of its committees, not too different from the Star Chamber, but both times he went unpunished. He was finally arrested when he was overheard in conversation saying certain scandalous things against the speaker of the House Lenthall. The person who reported him was none other than Dr. John Bastwick.

In his trial for disrespectful remarks Lilburne refused to answer questions unless the cause of his arrest were specified, a repetition of events which must have caused him some sense of déjà vu. He claimed the procedure was contrary to the privileges of free-born English and Magna Carta. After he spent three months in Newgate prison, Lilburne was released and the charges dropped.[62]

Lilburne spent two more years in prison, between 1645 and 1647, because of a controversy which began with a dispute over his back pay from his service in the army which rapidly became a matter of slander against the powerful Earl of Manchester. He was summoned before the House of Lords but refused to acknowledge its jurisdiction or to answer incriminating questions. His sentence to the Tower and fine were matters the House of Commons moved slowly on, but they finally did secure his release. His outpouring of pamphlets increased. When plans for the king's trial were taking shape, Lilburne not only refused to take part but argued that Charles I should be tried by a jury.

In March 1649, two months after Charles I had been tried and executed, Lilburne came out with *Englands New Chains Discovered*. It was his strongest attack on the denial of fundamental rights by Parliament and the army officers whom he labelled the "Grandees." When he was brought before the council of state, he refused to admit its jurisdiction or answer incriminating questions—déjà vu once again. For his refusal he was sent to the Tower for another stay. Somehow he managed to continue writing pamphlets and getting them out to a printer. One was an effort he made with several other Levellers, *An Agreement of the Free People of England*. This manifesto reads like a harbinger of the charges against arbitrary government found in the *Declaration of Independence* and the guarantees of rights in the Bill of Rights of the *United States Constitution*. It proclaims that God gave them the opportunity

> to make this Nation Free and Happy, to reconcile our differences, and beget a perfect amitie and friendship once more amongst us, that we may stand clear

in our conscience before Almighty God, as unbyassed by any corrupt Interest or particular advantages. . . . We the free People of *England*, to whom God hath given hearts, means and opportunity to effect the same, do with submission to his wisdom, in his name, and desiring the equity thereof may be to his praise and glory; Agree to ascertain our Government, to abolish all arbitrary Power, and to set bounds and limits both to our Supreme, and all Subordinate Authority, and remove all known Grievances.[63]

The pamphlet urged the recognition of a freedom of religion which would include conscientious objection, the securing of a protection against self-incrimination, and the insuring of provisions that government would take neither life, limb, liberty, nor estate without due process of law.

For writing his pamphlet Lilburne was accused of being a "false traitor, not having the fear of God before thine eyes, but being stirred and moved upon the instigation of the Devil, [who] didst endeavour not only to disturb the peace and tranquillity of this nation, but also the government thereof to subvert."[64] The indictment quoted Lilburne's writings, as did the attorney general, in order to establish that Lilburne "didst publish that the government aforesaid is tyrannical, usurped, and unlawful; and that the Commons assembled in Parliament are not the Supreme Authority of this nation." His writings had "the intent to stir up and raise forces against the Government with a mutiny in the army."[65]

John Lilburne's 1649 trial became the seventeenth-century version of the Chicago Eight trial with Lilburne playing all eight parts. He questioned the location of the trial: in Guild Hall instead of a regular court or Westminster Hall. He challenged the prosecution for approaching the bench alone: "Hold a while, hold a while, let there be no discourse but openly; for my adversaries or prosecutors whispering with the Judges is contrary to the law of England."[66] Or another time: "Not in hugger-mugger, privately or whisperingly."[67] His insistent objections and lengthy declamations were generally permitted by the judges, but occasionally they were as provoked to speak out as Lilburne: "I will not be outvoiced by you," Lord Keble admonished him, "our lives and our souls are upon it, therefore you shall have equity and justice."[68]

Like the Chicago Eight trial, Lilburne's is notable for the scope of legal issues he raised. Not only did Lilburne insist that the prosecutor have no "hugger-mugger" conferences with the judges, he sparred with the court over the right to counsel, the protection against self-incrimination, and the independence of the jury. Lilburne fought a running battle with the judges over what he believed was his "birth-right and privilege" guaranteed by the "good old Laws of England:" the right to consult with counsel. Judge Keble replied to Lilburne's demand by saying that the trial concerned only matters of fact, for which he needed no counsel, and "if matter of law do arise upon the proof of the fact, you shall know it, and then shall have counsel assigned to you."[69] Lilburne shot back: "You expect from me impossibilities; for, seeing I have been seven months in prison for nothing, and could not in the least know perfectly what would be laid to my charge, nor after what manner I should be proceded against." Besides, as he pointed out to the court, the form of the proceedings were not in English, his only language, but in Latin and French. Further, what was in English held "a great many snares, and a great many niceties in the practick," making the formal proceedings impossible for him.

> Therefore I beseech and most earnestly intreat you, to assign me counsel to consult with, before I be too ensnared: and, if you will not do it, and give me some reasonable time to prepare my plea and defence, then order me to be knocked on the head immediately in the place where I stand, without any further trial, for I must needs be destroyed, if you deny me all the means of my preservation.[70]

He was not allowed counsel, although a solicitor, Mr. Sprat, was in the courtroom ready to speak for Lilburne. When Sprat did speak up, he was silenced:

Lord Keble: Spare yourself; when your time comes, you shall speak.

Mr. Sprat: He asked leave for me first. And, Sir it is easy to prove the whole indictment to be a matter of law.

Judge Jermin: What impudent fellow is that, that dare to be so bold as to speak in the court without being called.[71]

Lilburne insisted that the laws of England insured that his words would not be used against him. "Sir," he instructed the court, "by Petition of right, I am not to answer to any questions concerning myself." A reading of the Petition of Right does not readily reveal the source of Lilburne's claim, but he was dogged. His insistence, in fact, made his trial a landmark in the establishment of the right. While in error, he helped forge a fundamental principle. When the attorney general mentioned that the accused had pled not guilty but had confessed, Lilburne jumped in: "No, Sir; you do me wrong, and abuse me. I never confessed any thing, neither did I plead Not Guilty; for my plea was conditional, grounded upon your promises, not to take any advantage of my ignorance in your formalities."[72]

Although Lilburne would tell the court his name, he refused to raise his hand. Even that, he surmised, might be used against him. "You demand I should hold up my hand at the bar," he told the court, "and I know not what it means, neither what in law it signifies." Judge Jermin explained that by raising his hand he would identify himself as the man called for and would signify "a pure innocent hand does set forth a clear unspotted heart; that so the heart and hand together might betoken innocency." Lilburne continued to resist. Judge Keble urged him: "Hear the Court, Mr. Lilburne, there shall be nothing of circumvention or interruption; but as you have professed to be a rational and understanding man in words, let your deeds so declare you." Lilburne replied, "Sir, I beseech you, do not surprize me with punctilios or niceties, which are hard things for me to lose my life upon. I tell you again, my name is John Lilburne, son of Mr. Richard Lilburne." At that Judge Keble lost his composure: "Talk not of punctilios with us, nor talk not of judges made by the laws; you shall not want law: but if you talk of punctilios here in this room, we will stop that language." After one more speech on the matter by Lilburne, in which he pointed out his disadvantage in not knowing the formalities of the law, Lord Keble gave in and said that they would be done with the issue in order to let the trial progress.[73] Score one for "ignorant" John Lilburne in his battle with the learned judges.

Lilburne maintained such a consistent adherence to the principle that he had a right not to give evidence against himself that when asked by the court to identify the original of a pamphlet he had handed to a soldier, Lilburne refused so much as to look at it. Judge Keble asked that the documents be shown to Lilburne, but Lilburne replied: "I am too old with such simple ginns to be catched; I will cast mine eyes upon none of your papers, neither shall I answer to any questions that concern myself. I have learned more law out of the Petition of Right, and Christ pleading before Pilate, than so."[74]

Lilburne insisted throughout the trial that the burden of proof rested with Attorney General Ned Prideaux, not with him. The opening of Lilburne's defense speech shows him to be the Puritan that he was: "You have done no more to me, than the Scribes and Pharisees did to Jesus Christ; and in my dealing with you, I have but walked in the steps of my Lord and Master Jesus Christ and his apostles." Lilburne used Jesus's trial to establish that he was right in insisting that the government had the burden of proof. When Jesus was called to answer, Lilburne reminded the court: "Pilate adjured him to answer him, whether he was such a one or no, well, saith he, thou sayest it: so say I, Thou, Mr. Prideaux, sayest it; they are my books, but prove it."[75]

In addition to the right to counsel and the protection against self-incrimination, a third major theme in Lilburne's 1649 trial is his insistence that the jury had authority to judge matters of law as well as fact. Lilburne wanted to quote Edward Coke's Institutes to the jury, but this led to another altercation with the judges, now over the role of the jury.

Lord Keble: Master Lilburne, quietly express yourself, and you do well; the jury are judges of matter of fact altogether, and judge Coke says so: But I tell you the opinion of the Court, they are not judges of matter of law.

Lilburne: The jury by law are not only judges of fact, but of law also; and you that call yourselves judges of the law, are no more but Norman intruders; and in deed and in truth, if the jury please, are no more but cyphers, to pronounce their verdict.

Judge Jermin: Was there ever such a damnable blasphemous heresy as this is, to call the judges of the law, cyphers?

Lilburne: Sir, I entreat you give me leave to read the words of the law, then; for to the jury I apply, as my judges, both in the law and fact.[76]

Lilburne's insistence on a type of jury sovereignty, while wide of the legal mark, might be understood as aimed at an important principle, namely, the independence of the jury from punishment for a "wrong" verdict. In 1670, when William Penn and William Mead were aquitted of speaking to an unlawful assembly in spite of pressure from the judge on the jury to find them guilty, the jury was fined and imprisoned, not an unusual practice then. Edward Bushell and three jurors appealed the punishment and won in the Court of Common Pleas which held that a jury could not be questioned or molested for their verdict.[77] The Bushell case is a legal movement, but Lilburne's trial, as we will see, is its foundation.

The right to counsel, protection against self-incrimination, and the independence of the jury were concerns of Lilburne in the trial, but the transcript reveals others which are also important. He challenged the "hugger-mugger" bench conference, as we noted, and he questioned whether the special Oyer and Terminer court was legal. He maintained that he had a right to be tried not by a "special prejudged, packed, over-awing" extraordinary court but by "the ordinary, universal and common trials at ordinary assizes-sessions." He cited Magna Carta, the Petition of Right, and the abolition of the Star Chamber as his authority.[78]

Lilburne also insisted that his arrest had been illegal: "Fetched out of my bed in terror and affrightment and led through London-streets with hundreds of armed men" instead of by "civil and magisterial officers." He listed several parliamentary declarations on the mode of arrest.[79]

Lilburne criticized the way in which he had been interrogated. Like the Star Chamber procedures which had been abolished, he had been taken before the Council of State, but he "saw no accuser, no prosecutor, no accusation, no charge or indictment," yet he was questioned nevertheless.[80] In addition, Lilburne wanted the trial to be open to the public (probably because he was a popular figure facing those he had criticized). When the trial began he insisted that the door remain open. One of the first issues he raised in the trial, after demanding that the proceedings be public, was the fact that, among other things, he had not been given a copy of the indictment. Another issue was that, in addition to needing a lawyer, he needed the authority to subpoena witnesses, time (perhaps ten days) to bring witnesses from distant places, and time to prepare his defense. After Lilburne raised these matters with the court, they were denied and the trial proceeded.[81]

Attorney General Prideaux taunted Lilburne in his address to the jury: "He will write, print, publish, bespatter, and reproach; yea, and raise tumults and rebellion in a clandestine way: but if we chance to question him therefore, he will not own it."[82] Prideaux read to the jury the text of the July 1649 law of high treason (which, incidentally, was passed by Parliament *after* Lilburne had been arrested) together with matching portions from Lilburne's writings. The new law described what a false traitor would be: "That if any person shall maliciously or advisedly publish by writing, printing, or openly declaring, that the said government is tyrannical, usurped or unlawful; or that the commons in parliament assembled are not the supreme authority of this nation," plus a long list of other offensive activities, "shall be taken, deemed and declared by authority of this parliament to be high treason."[83] It takes little more than a reading of the titles of Lilburne's works to see how he fits with the new treason law: "An Impeachment of High Treason against Oliver Cromwell, and his son-in-law Henry Ireton, esquires, members of the late forcibly dissolved house of commons; presented to public view, by lieutenant-colonel John Lilburne, close prisoner in the Tower of London, for his real, true, and zealous affections to the liberties of his native country."[84] This and other pamphlets contained compelling illustrations of what Parliament, Cromwell, and the Model Army intended to stop. Nevertheless Lilburne insisted that the new treason law was contrary to the law of England which required not one but two witnesses. He quoted Coke's Institutes: "Only upon direct and manifest proof, not upon conjectural presumptions, or inferences, or strains of wit."[85] Here again, as in his demand for due process, Lilburne's critique of the law of treason anticipates the United States Constitution in which James Madison drafted a definition of treason which was designed to be difficult to commit or be found guilty of transgressing.

After the jury had heard from both sides, after Lilburne presented all of his challenges and took time to explain each with a detailed knowledge of Coke and other legal authorities, and after the court turned down his demands and answered his charges at least to their own satisfaction, the jury retired at 5 P.M. to consider their verdict. By 6 P.M. they returned.

Clerk: What say you, (look upon the Prisoner) is he guilty of the Treasons charged upon him, or any of them, or Not Guilty?

Foreman: Not Guilty of all of them.

In an unusual entry in the trial transcript, the recorder described the scene which followed the verdict:

> Which No being pronounced with a loud voice, immediately the whole multitude of people in the Hall, for joy of the Prisoner's acquital, gave such a loud and unanimous shout, as is believed was ever heard in Guildhall, which lasted for about half an hour without intermission; which made the Judges for fear turn pale, and hang down their heads; but the Prisoner stood silent at the bar, rather more sad in his countenance than he was before.[86]

This situation might explain why Lilburne, in spite of his harsh language and challenges to the court's authority, not to mention his importunateness, was not cited for contempt. Unlike the Chicago Eight and their lawyers who received lengthy contempt citations from Judge Hoffman for their courtroom behavior, Lilburne received none. Nevertheless, he was not released after his acquittal but returned to the Tower. A grumbling public made demands for Lilburne's release, and two weeks later the Council of State finally ordered his discharge.

The 1649 trial was not Lilburne's last. He continued to churn out pamphlets. In 1651 the Rump Parliament, side-stepping the awkwardness of another public trial, summarily banished Lilburne. He left for Amsterdam and stayed until Cromwell had dissolved Parliament completely. In June 1653 he returned without permission, only to be indicted, arrested, and brought before a regular court and jury, not an extraordinary court as in 1649, at Old Bailey. Lilburne again demanded a copy of the indictment, assignment of counsel, and time to prepare his defense. Reluctantly perhaps, the court yielded. In insisting on these rights Lilburne had performed, according to James Fitzjames Stephen, "the feat which no one else ever achieved, of extorting from the Court a copy of his indictment in order that he might put it before counsel and be instructed as to the objections which he might take against it."[87] During the trial Lilburne challenged the act of Parliament by which he had been banished, claiming that either the Rump Parliament was an illegal body, therefore its act was null, or if legal, Cromwell had unjustly dissolved it. In either case, he argued, his banishment was void. Besides, he had been banished without a trial by jury. Further, following another of his 1649 arguments, the present jury could judge both law and fact. This 1651 trial, reported to be "even more stormy than the earlier one," came to the same result: not guilty. Even Cromwell's regiments sounded their trumpets and shouted their approval when they heard the verdict.[88]

Cromwell evidently did not know what to do with Lilburne. He was too popular to either release or to try again, a threat to a dictator whether at large or in the courtroom. Ignoring the writ of habeas corpus, Cromwell had Lilburne shifted from prison to prison and then exiled to Jersey, Guernsey, and the Isle of Wright. When, two years later, Lilburne became ill, Cromwell allowed him to return to die at the age of forty-three.[89]

John Peter Zenger's trial almost a century later raises some of the same matters as Lilburne's trials did, but not nearly as many. In spite of the attention in the American tradition given Zenger's trial—the trial was a preview of the coming revolution—Lilburne's conflicts remain the ones which most clearly define the most issues faced by modern dissenters. Nevertheless, Zenger's trial is important in the history of American political trials.[90]

When Governor William Cosby of New York sued his predecessor, Rip Van Dam, and then removed Chief Justice Lewis Morris who had ruled against him, Cosby prompted criticism and satire in a newspaper printed by Zenger. Chief Justice James DeLancey, whom Cosby appointed to replace Morris, did the governor's bidding by ordering that the offending issues of the newspaper be burned. Soon Zenger was arrested and tried.

Without going into the details of Zenger's 1735 trial, we can make note of the clash of issues in the trial. One theme which characterizes the Zenger case from beginning to end is the independence of the courts. The newspaper articles Governor Cosby took exception to were about his arbitrary removal of Justice Morris. When Zenger was arrested Justice DeLancey announced in the bail hearing that "if a jury found Zenger not guilty, they would be perjured."[91] Bail was set at an unprecedented £400, an excessive amount. Attorney General Richard Bradley, instead of going to a Grand Jury, filed an information against Zenger, which was then regarded as a high-handed way of avoiding the popular basis of a jury system.[92] When Zenger's lawyers. James Alexander and William Smith, objected to Justice DeLancey hearing the case, he disbarred (yes, disbarred) them. Zenger's court-appointed attorney, John Chambers, looked over the list of forty names the clerk of court chose as potential jurors only to discover an attempt to pack the Zenger jury: It included men in Governor Cosby's employ and others linked with him. Chambers was able to strike them and obtain a jury not composed of Cosby's friends. If anything, as Stanley Katz argues, the new jury represented the Morris majority in New York.[93] Finally, when the well-known Philadelphia lawyer, Andrew Hamilton, joined Zenger's defense, he urged the jury to render a verdict on the whole matter before them, to judge the law as well as the facts. The only question that the prosecution and Justice DeLancey wanted the jury to consider was whether or not Zenger had printed the paper. Hamilton admitted that Zenger had but argued that the real question before the jury was broader, extending to the truth of what Zenger printed. After Justice DeLancey told Hamilton that he "ought not to be permitted to prove the facts in the papers," Hamilton told the jury this:

> Then, gentlemen of the jury, it is to you we must now appeal for witnesses to the truth of the facts we have offered and are denied the liberty to prove. . . . You are citizens of New York; you are really what the law supposes you to be, *honest and lawful men*; and, according to my brief, the facts which we offer to prove were not committed in a corner; they are notoriously known to be true; and therefore in your justice lies our safety. And as we are denied the liberty of giving evidence to prove the truth of what we have published, I will beg leave to lay it down as a standing rule in such cases, *that the suppressing of evidence ought to be taken for the strongest evidence*; and I hope it will have that weight with you.[94]

The other major theme of Zenger's trial is freedom of press. Zenger faced the standard argument for suppression found in all oligarchies, today in the Soviet Union as much as in colonial New York: criticism of those who rule detracts from their rightful authority. The articles in the *Weekly Journal* which aroused Governor Cosby's wrath were written by James Alexander and William Smith, the attorneys whom Justice DeLancey disbarred. Much of what Zenger printed was satire. One of Cosby's henchmen was recognizable in a mock advertisement for a "large spaniel, of about 5 feet 5 inches high" who "has lately strayed from his kennel with his mouth full of fulsome panegyricks." The sheriff was identifiable as a monkey which "lately broke his chain and ran into the country."[95] Zenger printed a song sheet which cheered those who would "be brave for liberty and law,/ Boldly despise the haughty knave,/ that would keep us in awe." The song castigated the courts:

> *Though pettifogging knaves deny*
> *us rights of Englishmen;*
> *We'll make the scoundrel rascals fly,*
> *and ne'er return again.*
> *Our judges they would chop and change*
> *for those that serve their turn,*
> *and will not surely think it strange*
> *if they for this should mourn.*[96]

This was an obvious reference to Governor Cosby's removal of Justice Morris and the appointment of Justice DeLancey.[97]

Zenger was charged with seditious libel. This doctrine in the law developed after the zealous misuse of the treason law by the Tudors. The courts held that defamation of a public person was a more serious offense than when committed against a private person because, as Edward Coke explained it, then "it concerns only the breach of the peace but the scandal of Government."[98] This is exactly 180 degrees opposite the position the Supreme Court took in the 1964 *New York Times v. Sullivan case*. In the *Sullivan* decision those who criticize public officials are provided with an extra protection of the law because of "a profound national commitment to the principle that debate on public issues should be uninhibited, robust, and wide-open, and that it may well include vehement, caustic, and sometimes unpleasantly sharp attack on government and public officials."[99] While Zenger was tried for printing what was true, the *Sullivan* case allows factual error which is not malicious. Hamilton argued that "every freeman that lives under a British government on the main of America" has "a right—the liberty—both of exposing and opposing arbitrary power (in these parts of the world, at least) by speaking and writing the truth." He told the jury that the case of Zenger was not the cause of a poor printer but the issue of liberty versus arbitrary government: "Men who injure and oppress the people under their administration provoke them to cry out and complain; and then make that very complaint the foundation for new oppressions and prosecutions."[100]

Zenger was found not guilty by the jury. While his case is not the legal landmark many have assumed it must be, it can be seen as a clear confrontation by the colonists, as represented by the jury as well as Zenger and his lawyers, against the colonial government in the person of the judge and prosecution as well as Governor Cosby. The legal precedents from the Zenger case amount to little, for, as Leonard Levy demonstrates, the Zenger case "was like the stage-coach ticket inscribed, 'Good for this day only.'"[101] Zenger's trial is important largely because it symbolizes two opposing perspectives on government and dissent. Hamilton's position is given above. Justice DeLancey characterized the other in his instructions to the jury. The jury was to leave the question of law to the court (they, of course, did not), and they should heed the words of another judge, whom Justice DeLancey quoted:

> If people should not be called to account for possessing the people with an ill opinion of the government, no government can subsist, for it is very necessary for all governments that the people should have a good opinion of it. And nothing can be worse to any government than to endeavor to procure animosities; as to the management of it, this has been always looked upon as a crime, and no government can be safe without it be punished.[102]

In short, the contest in the Zenger trial, if pushed to the logical ends, is between one side which maintained that dissent undermines government and leads to anarchy and another side which argued that dissent is necessary to prevent arbitrary rule.

The Boston Five and the D.C. Nine

Dr. Benjamin Spock, the Rev. William Sloane Coffin, and the others known as the Boston Five were indicted in 1968 for doing essentially what John Lilburne and John Peter Zenger had done: saying things which might disrupt the military and bring about ill opinion of government. The Boston Five could not be charged, as Lilburne had, with treason, because the treason law had drastically changed in the Glorious Revolution of 1688 and the American Revolution. The American Constitution prevented anyone from being charged with constructive treason.[103] Nor could they be charged, as Zenger had, with seditious libel because that doctrine had been scrapped. The First Amendment's "Congress shall make no law abridging the freedom of speech" stands against it, and the Supreme Court has insured that seditious libel will not reappear by shaping their several interpretations of the First Amendment to be versions of Justice Holmes's requirement that the circumstances of the speech will "create a clear and present danger that they will bring about the substantive evils that Congress has a right to prevent."[104] But a charge of conspiracy against the Boston Five was possible.

In 1967, after the Vietnam War had been drastically escalated and the draft became a focal point of protest, a petition made its way around the country, especially on college campuses, gathering 28,000 signatures. "A Call to Resist Illegitimate Authority" was addressed "to the young men of America, to the whole of the American people, and to all men of good will everywhere." It declared that "an ever growing number of young American men are finding that the American war in Vietnam so outrages their deepest moral and religious sense that they cannot contribute to it in any way." It cited the Constitution and the United Nations Charter as a treaty to argue that the war was "unconstitutional and illegal." It maintained that the United States had violated treaties and principles of law in fighting the war, committing crimes against humanity for which the Nuremberg defendants were tried. It pointed to the religious tradition of opposition to unjust wars and argued that it was unconstitutional to withhold draft exemption from those opposed to the war. Finally, it called for resistance. Among those in the military, it reported "some are refusing to obey specific illegal and immoral orders, some are attempting to educate their fellow servicemen on the murderous and barbarous nature of the war, some are absenting themselves without official leave." Among those not in the military "some are applying for status as conscientious objectors . . . some are refusing to be inducted." "Each of these forms of resistance against illegitimate authority," it declared, "is courageous and justified. Many of us believe that open resistance to the war and the draft is the course of action most likely to strengthen the moral resolve with which all of us can oppose the war and most likely to bring an end to the war." It was signed by such notables as Robert McAffe Brown, Alexander Calder, Denise Levertov, Robert Lowell, Herbert Marcuse, Ashley Montegu, Martin Niemoller, Michael Novak, Conor Cruise O'Brien, Linus Pauling, Bishop James Pike, Edgar Snow, and Sol Yurick.[105] The call was sent out in a mass mailing together with a letter urging that people sign the petition and contribute money. The letter was signed by Noam Chomsky, William S. Coffin, Dwight Macdonald, and Benjamin Spock.[106]

Any of the 28,000 who signed the petition, any one of the 200 who were listed in the ads as signers, or, what might be more logical, the four who sent out the covering letter, might have been indicted as part of a conspiracy. Instead of charging a group who met together to plan out the writing and distribution of the petition and the various demonstrations, including draft-card turn-ins at the Justice Department, the government indicted as conspirators a group of five people who, for the most part, did not know each other. They were: Dr. Spock, the famous pediatrician; Rev. William Sloane Coffin, a World War II paratrooper, a member of the CIA in the early 1950s, Yale chaplain, and later the senior minister at New York's Riverside Church; Mitchell Goodman, organizer of demonstrations; Marcus Raskin, former White House advisor and one of the founders of the Institute for Policy Studies; and Michael Ferber, a Harvard graduate student and activist.

The jury found Ferber, who had not even signed the call, guilty along with Spock, Coffin, and Goodman, but it found Raskin, the author of the call, not guilty. The three-judge Circuit Court of Appeals held, two to one, that Ferber and Spock must be acquitted because neither counseled draft resistance; the former might have been part of a small conspiracy which he organized but not the large one, the two-judge majority noted, and the latter might have been a drafter of the call which summoned forth the large conspiracy but what he did lacked specific intent.[107] That left Coffin and Goodman, out of the 28,000 possible, who were not entitled to acquittals because they had counseled resistance to the draft, precisely what the call had urged in strong language.

The Appeals Court set the verdicts aside, ordering new trials for Goodman and Coffin and acquitting Spock and Ferber, because of Judge Ford's prejudicial error in the trial. He had asked the jury not only to come in with a verdict of guilty or not guilty but to fill out a questionnaire. The first of these "special findings" was: "Question No. 1. Does the Jury find beyond a reasonable doubt that defendants unlawfully, knowingly and willfully conspired to counsel Selective Service registrants to knowingly and willfully refuse and evade service in the armed forces of the United States in violation of Section 12 of the Military Selective Service Act of 1967?" The seecond question substituted the word *aid* for *counsel*, and the third substituted the word *abet*. There were ten questions in all, each requiring a "yes" or "no" answer from the jury.[108]

Judge Ford, apparently skittish over being reversed because of an unclear indictment and charge, sought to clarify the jury's verdict with his ten questions. "Suppose," he explained, "they found them guilty, and so forth, and found them guilty of counseling. I may be wrong on the definition of aiding and abetting, but if they found them guilty of counseling, that would be enough to sustain the verdict."[109] Instead of being sustained by the questions, it was the questions themselves which contributed to the Appeals Court decision to overturn. They held that while such questions might be appropriate in a civil trial, a jury in a criminal trial had one duty only: a verdict of guilty or not guilty. Judge Ford's questions amounted to judicial pressure. "Put simply," Judge Aldrich wrote in his opinion, "the right to be tried by a jury of one's peers finally exacted from the king would be meaningless if the king's judges could call the turn." For a precedent he cited the case which followed Lilburne's trial, Bushell's case (1670).[110]

The jury, all White and all male (thus no mother who had been guided by Dr. Spock), evidently had been influenced, not merely instructed, by Judge Ford. One juror, when asked after the trial why he had voted to convict, replied: "I knew they were guilty when we were charged by the judge. I did not know *prior* to that time—I was in full agreement with the defendants until we were charged by the judge. That was the kiss of death!" Another juror said: "The biggest discussion was not 'guilty or not guilty,' but what the judge meant by conspiracy. You can interpret that in a lot of ways. The judge did outline it very clearly, but it's not what an ordinary layman would call conspiracy."[111] Besides, the jurors, like most jurors everywhere, were conscientious, believing that no matter how sympathetic they might be with the defendants, their duty lay in following the judge's instructions. "You can't have juries deciding whether *laws* are right," as one juror put it, "there are certain laws on the books."[112]

The Boston Five trial and the appellate court opinion touch a matter near the core of what trials of dissenters are about: conscience. Dissenters want to reach the community with a message about how wrong the government is. Likewise, the government desires to demonstrate how dangerous the dissenters are. Both are issues of conscience, the moral knowledge of a community. The jury is the community in miniature. Consequently, the jury's authority is a central concern for both sides. The jury in the Boston Five trial refused to contemplate the thought that they might ignore the judge's instructions. Their standard of right and wrong in the law was shaped for them by Judge Ford.

The trial of the Dow Chemical demonstrators in 1970 raised the question of jury nullification, a matter that has been controversial in the law since the trial of John Lilburne. The D. C. Nine, as they were called, broke into the Dow offices in Washington one Saturday in March 1969. In the full view of media cameras, which they had invited, the anti-war activists threw papers out the windows, broke furniture, and spilled something like blood all about the Dow offices in protests of Dow's manufacture of napalm. After they were convicted, one of the issues of their appeal was whether Judge John Pratt had acted properly in refusing to instruct the jury that they could acquit the defendants without regard either to the law or to the evidence.

Although the Appeals Court reversed the convictions and ordered a new trial of the Dow Chemical protesters, it was not on the jury nullification issue but on Judge Pratt's refusal to allow the defendants to represent themselves. Nevertheless, the difference of opinion between two Appeals Court judges on the question of jury nullification crystallized not only the controversy over that issue but the wider issue on the nature of political trials. Judge Harold Leventhal acknowledged that in the American experience jury nullification has a distinguished history. Judge Leventhal referred to the Zenger trial as a leading example. Zenger's sympathetic jury refused to find him guilty of seditious libel. Another important example are the acquittals in the nineteenth century under the fugitive slave laws. Such leading Founders as John Adams and Alexander Hamilton expressed the idea "that jurors had a duty to find a verdict according to their own conscience, though in opposition to the direction of the court; that their power signified a right; that they were judges both of law and of fact in a criminal case, and not bound by the opinion of the court."[113]

But, as Judge Leventhal read American history, what was a "youthful passion for independence" settled down and "accommodated itself to the reality that the former rebels were now in control of their own destiny." Soon Justice Story's 1835 ruling against jury nullification carried the day. Story's opinion was that the jury's function was to accept the law as given by the judge and to apply it to the facts. As for jury nullification, according to Leventhal, "the old rule survives today only as a singular relic."[114]

Chief Judge David Bazelon disagreed with Judge Leventhal. "The sticking point," Bazelon argued, "is whether or not the jury should be told of its power to nullify the law in a particular case. . . . I see no justification for, and considerable harm in, this deliberate lack of candor."[115] Since Judge Pratt "emphatically denied the existence of a 'legal defense' based on 'sincere religious motives' or a belief that action was justified by 'some higher law,'" the trial judge in his instructions to the jury was not neutral on the matter of jury nullification.[116] He discouraged the jury from "measuring the defendants' action against community concepts of blameworthiness." This Bazelon called a "sleight-of-hand" which was based on a fear that "an occasionally noble doctrine will, if acknowledged, often be put to ignoble and abusive purposes—or, to borrow the Court's phrase, will 'run the risk of anarchy.'"[117] Bazelon suggested, by contrast, that a juror who is motivated by prejudice is more likely to ignore spontaneously the judge's instructions than is a conscientious juror who considers the case in the light of prevailing community values. Bazelon would prefer nullification arising out of knowledge than out of ignorance: "I simply do not understand the justification for relying on a haphazard process of informal communication."[118]

At the heart of the difference between judges Leventhal and Bazelon are contrasting views of juries and of the law. For Judge Leventhal the matter boils down to pluralism. If each jury is going to be assigned the role of a minilegislature, criminal law will be paralyzed. "It is one thing for a juror to know that the law condemns, but he has a factual power of lenity. To tell him expressly of a nullification prerogative, however, is to inform him, in effect, that it is he who fashions the rule that condemns. This is an overwhelming responsibility, an extreme burden for the jurors' psyche." Facing an unpopular verdict, a juror can tell his friends and neighbors that he was merely following the judge's instructions. But, to Leventhal, "an explicit instruction to a jury conveys an implied approval that runs the risk of degrading the legal structure requisite for true freedom, for an ordered liberty that protects against anarchy as well as tyranny."[119]

Judge Bazelon's position, by contrast, is that the jury is the "spokesman for the community conscience in determining whether or not blame can be imposed." Abuse is possible, Bazelon admitted, but the underlying problem is not the nullification doctrine but the prejudice which prompts it. A clear example would be the acquittal by a bigoted jury of a White who committed a crime such as lynching against a Black. The solution, Bazelon suggested, "is not to condemn the nullification power, but to spotlight the prejudice." The "revulsion and sense of shame fostered by that practice fueled the civil rights movement, which in turn made possible the enactment of major civil rights legislation."[120]

Judges Leventhal and Bazelon agree that jury nullification is legitimate. But they differ on whether or not the judge would inform the jury of their power. Like parents uncertain about what to tell their child about sex, judges Leventhal and Bazelon disagree on how much a judge should tell the jury. If Leventhal is correct, instruction from the judge is not necessary because the culture provides it and juries will assume their power when the occasion presents itself. The formal instruction from the judge is only part of it. The informal education of a jury comes from, as Judge Leventhal listed them, many sources: novel, drama, film, television, newspapers, magazines, conversation, history, and tradition. "Law is a system, and it is also a language, with secondary meanings that may be unrecorded yet are part of its life."[121] The same, of course, can be said of sex education. Judge Bazelon is of the opposite school, and if he is correct, responsible use of the jury's power is better than ignorant use. If Leventhal would argue that to inform juries would encourage irresponsible use of nullification, Bazelon makes the point that abuse will arise from misinformation. For Leventhal, to tell them would threaten the rule of law, while for Bazelon to tell them will strengthen it.

To turn back to the Boston Five trial, the defendants in that case did not accomplish the goal of persuading the jury and enlightening the public about their civil disobedience. The jury got from the attorneys a series of conflicting messages. James St. Clair, who in Boston defended Coffin and a few years later defended Richard Nixon before the Supreme Court in the Watergate tape case, developed the theme, that "we are not trying the war. We are not even trying the constitutionality of the draft act."[122] Instead, he suggested, consider Coffin's character: "Is it likely that a clergyman, chaplain of one of the major universities in the world, with a distinguished military record, who was a trusted employee of the CIA for a number of years, would enter into a criminal conspiracy?" St. Clair argued to the jury that Coffin did not participate in a particular demonstration of burning draft cards because he was opposed to that form of demonstration.

Likewise, Raskin's lawyer, Calvin Bartlett, listed the activities of the others, ten "lurid activities," with which Raskin had nothing to do—no demonstrations, no press interviews, no obstructing induction centers, no picketing, no draft card burning. Raskin, he observed, did not listen to the speeches of the others because "they were boring."[123]

From the lawyers for Goodman and Spock, by contrast, the jury heard an appeal to conscience. Ed Barshak for Goodman argued that it was against the background of the Vietnam War tearing apart the American people that the jury had to make its judgment.

> It is one thing for the Court to tell you what is the law of this, that and the other thing. . . . But what in fact is left over for free speech, what in fact is left over for the rights of us Americans depends upon how *you* find the facts. . . . There is a danger that juries could find facts in such a way that this tool of the

law called conspiracy will eat up the area that you and I and everyone has considered to be our right to associate with each other, to sign things, to go to meetings. . . . After you hear the rules, the question is whether or not you are going to characterize the defendants' actions factually as a criminal conspiracy or as allowed American conduct, allowed American association, allowed sitting down on the sidewalk for the purpose of violating a local ordinance, *you* are going to decide that, and nobody else can.[124]

Leonard Boudin on behalf of Spock challenged the concept of conspiracy as used in the trial. The call had been signed by thousands, including Robert McAfee Brown and Robert Lowell. "Either the document is meaningless, or it contains an implication of criminal intent on behalf of all of these distinguished men." Perhaps the call should be seen, Boudin continued, as a political platform, "a public manifest or tract, the kind that were so familiar in the days of Tom Paine, a campaign document, a statement of beliefs." Instead of emphasizing how his client was not involved, as the other lawyers had, Boudin stressed how the government had documented only a fraction of Spock's antiwar activities.[125]

If the jury heard an uncertain defense, they had no trouble picking up the prosecution's message. Assistant U.S. attorney John Wall told them that the issue in the trial was law and order versus anarchy. "If there is disagreement on policy, even on mortality," he stressed, "as long as we can go to the polling booth and vote, I submit that is the proper way to do things, if we are not going to have *anarchy*. A sincerity can't be a defense. It can't be. Beliefs cannot be accepted as justification for conduct in violation of the duly passed law of the land. To permit that justification would be to say that whatever a person says his beliefs are is superior to the law of the land and would permit an objector to be a law unto himself. *Anarchy!*"[126] This too is an appeal to conscience.

At a rally following the sentencing of the four of the Boston Five who had been convicted, Coffin denounced the trial as "dismal, dreary, and above all demeaning." It was demeaning because it was unworthy of the best of America. "I had little quarrel with being indicted; in a way I had invited it. But the invitation read clearly: to test out in court the legality of an undeclared war, the constitutionality of the draft law, and finally to test in court what is always and eminently worth testing—the limits of dissent guaranteed under the First Amendment. But what did the government do? It skirted the uncomfortable, it ducked the difficult, it refused the invitation." It was also demeaning to the defendants who faced the frustration of "having to argue a big case in a small way."[127]

The Berrigans

In three trials one or both of the activist Berrigan brothers have directed public attention to issues of war and civil disobedience. In 1967 Fr. Philip

Berrigan and three others were tried in Baltimore (the Baltimore Four) after they had poured blood over draft records in the Selective Service office. Less than a year later Fr. Philip Berrigan was joined by his Jesuit brother, Fr. Daniel Berrigan, and seven others (the Catonsville Nine) in a raid on another Selective Service office near Baltimore where they took some 600 draft records to a parking lot, burned them, and then said prayers and sang hymns until they were arrested. In 1980 both Berrigans and six others (the Plowshares Eight) went into a General Electric plant in King of Prussia, Pennsylvania, where they poured blood over blueprints and used household hammers to damage two MX missile nose cones. In each of these trials of their own choosing the defendants were found guilty, but they were able to challenge war symbolically.

In 1972 Fr. Philip Berrigan and six others (the Harrisburg Seven) were indicted and tried on charges of conspiring to kidnap Henry Kissinger and blow up the heating system in Washington federal buildings. This bizarre trial was not of the defendants' choosing, but it ended with a deadlocked jury.[128] The Harrisburg trial might be best seen as a harbinger of the Watergate events rather than as a trial of dissenters. Robert Mardian, who directed the Justice Department's internal security division under Attorney General John Mitchell and was tried along with him in the Watergate cover-up trial, was in charge of several initiatives, including the wiretapping of radicals without court approval and the conspiracy trial in Harrisburg. Shortly after the trial ended unsuccessfully for the government, Mardian resigned from the Justice Department to work in President Nixon's 1972 reelection campaign.[129]

The 1968 Catonsville Nine trial might in our time serve as the exemplar trial of dissenters. Frs. Philip and Daniel Berrigan were joined by Thomas Lewis, one of the Baltimore Four; a Christian Brother, David Darst; three former Maryknoll missionaries, Marjorie and Thomas Melville, and John Hogan; Mary Moylan, a nurse; and George Mische, a peace organizer. They were charged with destroying government property when they raided the Selective Service offices and burned the draft records. The prosecutor emphasized that the war in Vietnam was not an issue of the trial:

> I want it clearly understood that the government is not about to put itself in the position—has not heretofore and is not now—of conducting its policies at the end of a string tied to the consciences of these nine defendants. This trial does not include the issues of the Vietnam conflict. It does not include the issue of whether the United States ought to be in the conflict or out of it.

> But this prosecution is the government's response, the law's response, the people's response, to what the defendants did. And what they did was to take government property and throw flammable material upon it and burn it beyond recognition. And that is what this case is about.[130]

The defense, on the other hand, saw the Vietnam War as the only important issue in the trial. As William Kunstler told the jury:

> The trial of Socrates was not merely a question of a man sowing confusion
> and distrust among the youth in Athens; the trial of Jesus could not be
> reduced to one of conspiracy against the Empire.

> In the first place, we agree with the prosecutor as to the essential facts of the
> case. The defendants did participate in the burning of records.

> It is not a question of records which are independent of life. We are not
> talking about driving licenses or licenses to operate a brewery. We are talking
> of one kind of record. No others so directly affect life and death on a mass
> scale, as do these. They affect every mother's son who is registered with any
> Board. These records stand quite literally for life and death to young men.

> They wanted, in some small way, to throw a roadblock into a system which
> they considered murderous, which was grinding young men, many thousands
> of them, to death in Vietnam.

> Also, they wanted, as they said, to reach the American public, to reach you.
> They were trying to make an outcry, an anguished outcry, to reach the Amer-
> ican community before it was too late. It was a cry that could conceivably
> have been made in Germany in 1931 and 1932, if there were someone to
> listen and act on it. It was a cry of despair and anguish and hope, all at the
> same time. And to make this outcry, they were willing to risk years of their
> lives.[131]

When William Kunstler quoted Peter Zenger's attorney's exhortation
that the jury "make use of their conscience" to the Catonsville jury, Judge
Roszel Thomsen admonished Kunstler:

> You are urging the jury to make their decision on the basis of conscience.
> This morning, I said to you that if you attempt to argue that the jury has the
> power to decide this case on the basis of conscience, the court will interrupt
> to tell the jury their duty. The jury may not decide this case on the basis of
> conscience of the defendants. They are to decide this case only on the basis of
> facts presented by both sides.[132]

Daniel Berrigan asked the judge to consider whether or not his reverence
for the law did not require him:

> to interrupt and adjust the law to the needs of people here and now. I believe
> no tradition can remain a mere dead inheritance. It is a living inheritance
> which we must continue to offer to the living. So it may be possible, even
> though the law excludes certain important questions of conscience, to in-
> clude them none the less; and thereby, to bring the tradition of life again for
> the sake of the people.[133]

Judge Thomsen responded during a colloquy outside the hearing of the jury that as a man he was moved by what the defendants said, but as a judge he must say that the "basic principle of our law is that we do things in an orderly fashion. People cannot take the law into their own hands."[134]

Questions about the relationship between conscience and law can arise in trials of dissenters when the trials are conducted within the framework of the rule of law and, even in rare instances such as More's trial, in partisan trials. Judge Thomsen commented to the defendants that:

> If you had done this thing in many countries of the world, you would not be standing here. You would have been in your coffins long ago. Now, nobody is going to draw and quarter you. You may be convicted by the jury, and if you are, I certainly propose to give you every opportunity to say what you want.[135]

In many political trials, getting to say what you want is the whole point.

Conclusion

Certain trials become fulcrums on which our public moral knowledge turns. These are the trials we first think of when we face conflicts of conscience. Dissent is powerful when, as illustrated by each of the trials in this chapter, the act is symbolic. Violence undermines the appeal to conscience. The striking similarity in such trials is how closely they resemble the trial of Socrates. He was accused of presenting a threat to Athens, not through violence, but by raising questions about its moral assumptions. The same can be said of More and the others.

The critical task in trials of dissenters, whether Socrates or an antiwar demonstrator of our time, is the attempt to convince a representative of society that the policy of the government is wrong. The prosecution in such trials seeks to prove to the same representative that the dissenter is not only mistaken but constitutes a threat. The representative may be the judge, the jury, the media, or, more commonly, all three at the same time. An appeal to conscience is an appeal to shared moral knowledge. In order for conscience to respond to conscience the trial must be public. Whatever the fate of the dissenter—whether death in the cases of Socrates and More, exile for Williams and Hutchinson, jail terms for many including most antiwar dissenters, or acquittal in the trials of Lilburne and Zenger—the aim of the trial from both sides is to influence and move the society by touching its sense of right and wrong. That is why the issue of jury nullification is present in one form or another in trials of dissenters. Perhaps the most dauntless appeal for a type of jury nullification comes from Socrates who, after he had been found guilty, proposed the penalty which would be his due: a pension for the rest of his life. He had spent his life teaching Athenians to seek virtue and wisdom, and he should be rewarded.[136] Those who have no hope of any jury nullification, such as More, Williams, or Hutchinson, nevertheless appeal to the wider jury. If the trial jury is rigged and the trial itself a partisan show, the verdict might be a long time in coming. While More was executed five days after his trial in 1535, four hundred years later he became a saint.

Dissenters take a risk in appealing to representatives of society. They may lose the immediate trial, but they are confident that once the conscience of society is touched, society will respond. Dissenters do not question the propriety of that conscience. Once society understands, dissenters believe, it will respond properly. Once the American people understand the wrongness of the Vietnam War, the unfairness of the draft, the madness of nuclear arms; once Christians understand the wrongness of a sovereign king controlling the church or the idolatry of forced orthodoxy; once Englishmen understand the folly of arbitrary rule by a king or the military grandees, or once the Athenians understand the rationality of living according to their conscience, then we will all live more just lives.

Not every dissenter can rightly claim that he or she appeals to conscience. Not every prosecutor of a dissenter is standing on the moral dark side of society and history. Not every judge and jury who convict a dissenter will have their verdicts reversed in time. Admittedly, the trials covered in this chapter have been selected because of the Socrates factor: the defendants have either been vindicated or stand in the likelihood of moral exoneration. The next chapter will concern itself with two dissenters who, in spite of their moral sincerity and fervor, have earned society's reproach. Fritz Adler assassinated the Austrian prime minister to protest World War I, and Karlton Armstrong blew up a building, killed one person, and injured several others to protest the Vietnam War. The Adler and Armstrong trials are, in short, fundamentally different from those covered in this chapter because the methods of dissent are different and the questions raised are inevitably different. They are notable because they do not follow the Socrates model.

Notes

1. Minneapolis *Star & Tribune*, August 13, 1982, p. 3A; *Mankato* (Minn.) *Free Press*, August 13, 1982, p. 4.
2. See Ronald Radosh and Joyce Milton, *The Rosenberg File: A Search for the Truth* (New York, Holt, Rinehart, & Winston, 1983), pp. 450-451.
3. *Ibid.*, Ch. 1. See also Walter Schneir and Miriam Schneir, *Invitation to an Inquest: Reopening the Rosenberg "Atom Spy" Case* (Baltimore, Penguin, 1973), Ch. 9.

4. Radosh and Milton, *Rosenberg File*, pp. 99-102, 448.

5. *Ibid.*, p. 284.

6. See Allen Weinstein, *Perjury: The Hiss-Chambers Case* (New York, Knopf, 1978). Weinstein, who concluded that Hiss was guilty of perjury, met with a strong reaction from Victor Navasky. See *Nation*, April 8, 1978, pp. 393-401; April 22, 1978, pp. 450-452; May 6, 1978, pp. 523-526; June 17, 1978, pp. 718-724; See also *New Republic*, April 8, 1978, pp. 27-29; April 29, 1978, pp. 16-21. A preview of the 1978 controversy can be found in the 1976 exchanges in *New York Review of Books*: April 1, 1976, pp. 14-20; May 27, 1976, pp. 32-48; September 16, 1976, pp. 52-61. A follow-up to the 1978 controversy is the petition for a writ of error, *In Re Alger Hiss*, which was denied in 1982, see: Edith Tiger, ed., *In Re Alger Hiss: Petition for a Writ of Error Coram Nobis* (New York, Hill & Wang, 1979); William A. Reuben, *Footnote on an Historic Case: In Re Alger Hiss* (New York, Nation Foundation, 1983); Fred J. Cook, "Alger Hiss: A New Ball Game," *Nation*, October 7, 1978, pp. 336-340.

7. See Louis Joughin and Edmund M. Morgan, *The Legacy of Sacco and Vanzetti* (New York, Harcourt Brace, 1948); Francis Russell, *Tragedy in Dedham: The Story of the Sacco-Vanzetti Case* (New York, McGraw-Hill, 1962); Herbert B. Ehrmann, *The Case That Will Not Die* (Boston, Little, Brown, 1969); Brian Jackson, *The Black Flag* (New York, Routledge & Kegan Paul, 1981).

8. See I. F. Stone, "I. F. Stone Breaks the Socrates Story," *New York Times Magazine*, April 8, 1979, pp. 22ff; A. E. Taylor, *Socrates* (London, Peter Davies, 1932), Ch. 3.

9. Arthur Koestler, *The Sleepwalkers: A History of Man's Changing Vision of the Universe* (New York, Macmillan, 1959), pp. 436ff.

10. See Karl Jaspers and Rudolf Bultmann, *Myth and Christianity: An Inquiry into the Possibility of Religion without Myth* (New York, Noonday, 1958); Rudolf Bultmann et al., *Kerygma and Myth: A Theological Debate* (New York, Harper Torchbooks, 1961).

11. *Newsweek*, October 31, 1983, p. 94; *Washington, Post*, October 22, 1983, p. Cl; Andrew Kopkind, "Passion Play," *Nation*, November 5, 1983, pp. 420-421.

12. Many of the cases taken by Clarence Darrow chronicle the rise of labor. See Irving Stone, *Clarence Darrow for the Defense* (New York, Doubleday, 1941); Arthur Weinberg, ed., *Attorney for the Damned* (New York, Simon & Schuster, 1957).

13. Elizabeth Cady Stanton, Susan B. Anthony, and Matilda Joslyn Gage, *History of Woman Suffrage*, 6 vols (New York, Source Book Press, 1970, originally 1861-1876), Vol. 2, pp. 687-689.

14. See David Karaner, *Debs: His Authorized Life and Letters* (New York, Boni & Liveright, 1919); *Eugene V. Debs, Writings and Speeches* (New York, Hermitage Press, 1948).

15. Daniel Berrigan, *The Trial of the Catonsville Nine* (Boston, Beacon, 1970); Wiliam VanEtten Casey, ed., *The Berrigans* (New York, Avon, 1971).

16. Martin Luther King, Jr., *Why We Can't Wait* (New York, Mentor, 1963), Ch. 5; Alan F. Weston and Barry Mahoney, *The Trial of Martin Luther King* (New York, Thomas Y. Crowell, 1974).

17. Plato, *Apology*, 20-21.

18. Stanton, Anthony, and Gage, *History of Woman Suffrage*, Vol. 2, p. 689.

19. Debs, *Writings and Speeches*, p. 434.

20. "Letter from Birmingham Jail"; *Why We Can't Wait*, pp. 79-80.

21. Plato, *Crito.*
22. Stanton, Anthony, and Gage, *History of Woman Suffrage*, Vol. 2, p. 688.
23. Karsner, *Debs*, p. 33.
24. E. E. Reynolds, *The Field Is Won: The Life and Death of St. Thomas More* (Milwaukee, Bruce, 1968), p. 246.
25. Richard Marius, *Thomas More* (New York, Knopf, 1985), Ch. 26.
26. J. Duncan M. Derrett, "The Trial of Sir Thomas More." *The English Historical Review*, 312 (July 1964), p. 459.
27. E. E. Reynolds, *The Trial of St. Thomas More* (London, Burns & Oates, 1964), pp. 70-77.
28. H. Maynard Smith, *Henry VIII and the Reformation* (New York, Russell & Russell, 1962), p. 27. See Henry Ansgar Kelly, *The Matrimonial Trials of Henry VIII* (Stanford, Stanford University Press, 1976).
29. G.R. Elton, *Policy and Police : The Enforcement of the Reformation in the Age of Thomas Cromwell* (Cambridge, Cambridge University Press 1972), p. 417.
30. Samuel Hugh Brockunier, *The Irrepressible Democrat: Roger Williams* (New York, Ronald, 1940), p. 13-15.
31. *Ibid.*, pp. 47-49.
32. *Ibid.*, pp. 59-60.
33. *Ibid.*, p. 68.
34. Selma R. Williams, *Divine Rebel: The Life of Anne Marbury Hutchinson* (New York, Holt, Rinehart, & Winston, 1981), Ch. 5; Richard B. Morris, *Fair Trial: Fourteen Who Stood Accused from Anne Hutchinson to Alger Hiss* (New York, Knopf, 1953), Ch. 1.
35. Williams, *Divine Rebel*, pp. 148-151.
36. Morris, *Fair Trial*, pp. 15-16.
37. Williams, *Divine Rebel*, p. 113.
38. Morris, *Fair Trial*, pp. 23-24.
39. *Ibid.*, p. 25.
40. *Ibid.*, p. 29.
41. Perry Miller, *Orthodoxy in Massachusetts, 1630-1650* (Boston, Beacon, 1959), pp. 250, 262.
42. "The Answer of Mr. John Cotton," in Roger Williams, *Complete Writings* (New York, Russell & Russell, 1963), Vol. 3, pp. 46-47.
43. Williams, To Mr. Daniel Abbot, *Ibid.*, Vol. 4. p. 401; Bloody Tenent, *Ibid.*, Vol. 3, p. 173.
44. Williams, Bloody Tenent Yet More Bloody, *Ibid.*, Vol. 4, p. 439.
45. Williams, The Examiner defended, *Ibid.*, Vol. 7, p. 263; Bloody Tenent, *Ibid.*, Vol. 3, p. 173.
46. Williams, Bloody Tenent Yet More, *Ibid.*, Vol. 4, p. 295; Bloody Tenent, *Ibid.*, Vol. 3, pp. 63-64.
47. Williams, Bloudy Tenent, *Ibid.*, Vol. 3, p. 83.
48. *Ibid.*, pp. 136-137.
49. *Ibid.*, pp. 81 and 217-218.
50. *Ibid.*, p. 136.
51. Williams, Bloody Tenent Yet More, *Ibid.*, Vol. 4, p. 207.
52. See Christopher Hill, *The World Turned Upside Down: Radical Ideas during the English Revolution* (New York, Viking, 1972); Michael Walzer, *The Revolution of the Saints: A Study in the Origins of Radical Politics* (New York, Atheneum, 1974).

53. Pauline Gregg, *Free-born John: A Biography of John Lilburne* (Westport, Conn., Greenwood, 1961), p. 53.
54. Edward Cheyney, "The Court of the Star Chamber," *American Historical Review* (July 1913), pp. 747-748; Harold W. Wolfram, "John Lilburne: Democracy's Pillar of Fire," *Syracuse Law Review* (Spring 1953), p. 216.
55. Wolfram, "Lilburne," p. 217.
56. Gregg, *Free-born John*, p. 56.
57. The same oath, however, had been refused over the years by Puritans called before the High Commission, the body which dealt with heretics as the Star Chamber dealt with seditious libelers and traitors.
58. Leonard W. Levy, *Origins of the Fifth Amendment: The Right against Self-Incrimination* (New York, Oxford University, 1968), pp. 275-278.
59. Wolfram, "Lilburne," pp. 220-221.
60. George Burton Adams and H. Morse Stephens, ed., *Selected Documents of English Constitutional History* (London, Macmillan, 1918), p. 342.
61. Levy, *Origins of the Fifth Amendment*, pp. 262-263.
62. *Dictionary of National Biography*, Vol. 11, pp. 1123-1124.
63. Don M. Wolfe, ed., *Leveller Manifestoes of the Puritan Revolution* (New York, Humanities Press, 1967), pp. 402-407. See George Burton Adams, *Constitutional History of England* (London, Jonathan Cape, 1921), p. 324.
64. *State Trials*, Vol. 4, pp. 1320-1321.
65. *Ibid.*, p. 1329.
66. *Ibid.*, p. 1324.
67. *Ibid.*, p. 1301.
68. *Ibid.*, p. 1300.
69. *Ibid.*, p. 1296.
70. *Ibid.*, p. 1297.
71. *Ibid.*, p. 1305.
72. *Ibid.*, p. 1317.
73. *Ibid.*, pp. 1289-1291.
74. *Ibid.*, p. 1340.
75. *Ibid.*, p. 1373.
76. *Ibid.*, pp. 1379-1380.
77. Levy, *Origins of the Fifth Amendment*, p. 315; William Holdsworth, *History of English Law* (London, Sweet & Maxwell, 1955), 7th ed., Vol. 1, pp. 344-345.
78. *State Trials*, Vol. 4, p. 1276.
79. *Ibid.*, p. 1279.
80. *Ibid.*, p. 1280.
81. *Ibid.*, pp. 1293, 1297, 1307, 1312.
82. *Ibid.*, p. 1373.
83. *Ibid.*, pp. 1349-1350.
84. *Ibid.*, p. 1352.
85. *Ibid.*, p. 1381.
86. *Ibid.*, p. 1405.
87. Quoted by Wolfram, "Lilburne," p. 254.
88. *Ibid.*, pp. 253-256.
89. *Ibid.* See also the *Dictionary of National Biography*, Vol. 11, pp. 1128-1129.
90. See Paul Finkelman, "The Zenger Case: Prototype of a Political Trial," in Michael R. Belknap, ed., *American Political Trials* (Westport, Conn., Greenwood Press, 1981), Ch. 1.

91. Stanley Nider Katz, "Introduction," James Alexander, *A Brief Narrative of the Case and Trial of John Peter Zenger* (Cambridge, Mass., Harvard University Press, 1963), p. 18.
92. *Ibid.*, p. 19.
93. *Ibid.*, p. 21.
94. Alexander, *Brief Narrative*, pp. 74-75.
95. Morris, *Fair Trial*, pp. 74-75.
96. Alexander, *Brief Narrative*, p. 111.
97. *Ibid.*, p. 221, note 6 by Stanley Nider Katz.
98. Holdsworth, *History of English Law*, Vol. 8, p. 336.
99. *New York Times v. Sullivan*, 376 US 254 at 270 (1964).
100. Alexander, *Brief Narrative*, p. 99.
101. Leonard W. Levy, *Freedom of Speech and Press in Early American History: Legacy of Suppression* (New York, Harper Torchbooks, 1963), p. 133.
102. Alexander, *Brief Narrative*, p. 100.
103. Art. 3, Sec. 3. See Irving Brant, *The Bill of Rights: Its Origin and Meaning* (New York, Mentor, 1965), Ch. 2; Bradley Chapin, *The American Law of Treason: Revolutionary and Early National Origins* (Seattle, University of Washington Press, 1964); Holdsworth, *History of English Law*, Vol. 3, pp. 287ff.
104. *Schenck v. United States*, 249 US 47 (1919).
105. Jessica Mitford, *The Trial of Dr. Spock* (New York, Alfred A. Knopf, 1969), pp. 255-259.
106. *United States v. Spock*, 416 F.2d 165 (1969), at 193-194.
107. *Ibid.*, 179.
108. *Ibid.*, 180.
109. Mitford, *Trial of Dr. Spock*, p. 198.
110. *U.S. v. Spock*, 181.
111. Mitford, *Trial of Dr. Spock*, pp. 232-234.
112. *Ibid.*, p. 235.
113. *United States v. Dougherty*, 473 F. 2d 1113, at 1132 (1972). See Lord Devlin, *Trial by Jury*, Chs. 4-5; Mortimer R. Kadish and Sanford H. Kadish, *Discretion to Disobey: A Study of Lawful Departures from Legal Rules* (Stanford, Stanford University Press, 1973), pp. 45-66.
114. *U.S. v. Dougherty*, 1135.
115. *Ibid.*, 1139.
116. *Ibid.*, 1139-1140.
117. *Ibid.*, 1140-1141.
118. *Ibid.*
119. *Ibid.*, 1136-1137.
120. *Ibid.*, 1143.
121. *Ibid.*, 1135.
122. Mitford, *Trial of Dr. Spock*, p. 179.
123. *Ibid.*, 185.
124. *Ibid.*, p. 184.
125. *Ibid.*, p. 188.
126. *Ibid.*, p. 190.
127. *Ibid.*, pp. 209-210.
128. See William O'Rourke, *The Harrisburg 7 and the New Catholic Left* (New York, Thomas Y. Crowell, 1972); Garry Wills, "Love on Trial: The Berrigan Case Reconsidered," *Harper's* (July 1972), pp. 63-71.

129. O'Rourke, *Harrisburg 7*, pp. 259-260.
130. Daniel Berrigan, *The Trial of the Catonsville Nine* (Boston, Beacon, 1970), p. 100.
131. *Ibid.*, pp. 103-104.
132. *Ibid.*, p. 105.
133. *Ibid.*, 114-115.
134. *Ibid.*
135. *Ibid.*, p. 114.
136. Plato, *Apology*, 36. For an analysis of the appeal to conscience in trials of Vietnam war protesters see John and Rosemary Bannan, *Law, Morality, and Vietnam: The Peace Militants and the Courts* (Bloomington, Indiana University Press, 1974). Chapter 9 contains some revealing anonymous interviews with judges who faced the issue of conscience in trials.

6

The Wisconsin Bomber:
Trial of a Frustrated Dissenter

Dissenters who commit violent acts expect the bombing or the assassination itself to demonstrate how wrong a policy is and how frustrated right-thinking people are becoming with it. The "propaganda of the deed" is an attempt to convince society that it needs a drastic change of direction and especially of rulers. Both of the trials of this chapter involve accused who committed violent acts out of frustration with a war policy.

Fritz Adler

In 1916 Friedrich Adler, a brilliant physicist who was also a leader of the Austrian Social Democrats and associate of the key European socialists, shot and killed Prime Minister Count Sturgkh. For Adler, the central issue of his trial was not his guilt or innocence, but whether his act had been justified. Although not allowed to introduce his position as evidence, Adler succeeded in putting it forth whenever he had the opportunity. When asked by the judge, "Doctor Friedrich Adler, please step forward. Do you plead guilty?" Adler startled the audience and the court by replying, "I am guilty to the same degree as every officer who has killed in a war or who has given the order to kill—no less and no more!"[1]

Adler distanced himself from his counsel, who would explain the assassination by saying he was insane: "The defense counsel, from the responsibilities of his office, has the duty of seeking to save my life. I have the duty of standing up for my beliefs, which are more important to me than whether during this war in Austria one more man will be hanged or not." Adler was tried before an especially moderate and untraditional judge who permitted him, when asked to present his version of the facts in the case, to analyze the indictment. The indictment stated that "the reprehensibility of murder as a political means cannot be a subject for debate among moral men in an orderly society." Adler attacked the assumption that Austria at war was an orderly society and cataloged the illegal acts of the government.

Throughout the trial Adler reversed the government case, constructing an indictment against the Austrian government, not for the court but for the public.

Although he frequently spoke his mind during the trial, working in his justification at every point, in his closing remarks Adler reasserted his indictment. Adler responded to the prosecutor's claim that vanity motivated the assassination by stating:

> The real reason I want to speak is that I must explain that the question of murder, for me, has always been a real moral question. . . . I have always believed that the violent killing of men was inhuman, and that it is because we live in an Age of Barbarism that we are reduced to killing men. I completely agree with my colleagues who argue: War is inhuman. And I will not deny: Revolution is also inhuman.

> When one comes to the historical realization that man cannot and should not be a true Christ in the Age of Barbarism, in the Age of Inhumanity, in the Age of Unkultur, in which we live, then there is only the alternative standpoint: If we must really kill and be killed, then murder cannot be a privilege of the rulers, we must also be ready to resort to force. If it is true that the Age of Humanity has still not come, then we should at least employ force only in the service of the idea of humanity.

> I have heard the war justified, and I have understood the arguments which justified the war.

> As they marched through Belgium and an innocent people fell as victims, as women and children were killed, they said: Necessity knows no commandments, it is war, there was no alternative.

> As the Lusitania sank, and a mass of innocent civilians were killed, again they said: It is war, there was no alternative. . . .

> We live in a time when battlefields are covered with hundreds of thousands of dead, when tens of thousands of men lie beneath the sea. It is war, it is necessity, they say to justify it.

> But if one man should fall, a man who has destroyed the constitution of Austria, who has trampled the laws of Austria into the ground, if the one man who is most guilty for these horrors should fall, then suddenly they confront me and say: Human life is sacred.[2]

Adler concluded by saying that he knew what the verdict would be, but, quoting poetry, "Not all are dead who are entombed,/ For you cannot kill the spirit, ye brethren!"[3] Adler was found guilty and sentenced to death. As he was escorted from the courtroom, he turned to the galleries and the windows and shouted, "Long live the International Revolutionary Social Democracy!" Since Austria lost the war, Adler was not executed, but had his sentence commuted to eighteen years imprisonment and finally was granted the amnesty extended to all political prisoners. By 1921 he was the organizer of a new international, the Social Workers International, and lived to be eighty-one years old.[4]

Bombing: Sterling Hall

In another trial of a war dissenter, the issue for the prosecution was again the method of dissent, while the issue for the defense was the war itself. Karl Armstrong bombed the Army Math Research Center at the University of Wisconsin in 1970, unintentionally killing a physics student and injuring five other persons. His sentencing hearing became a trial of the war in Vietnam.

Two hours before dawn on Monday, August 24, 1970, the Madison, Wisconsin police dispatcher heard the following message when he answered the phone: "Okay, pigs, now listen and listen good. There is a bomb in the Army Math Research Center, the University, set to go off in five minutes. Clear the building, get everyone out, warn the hospital. This is no bullshit, man."[5]

In less than three minutes the squad cars hurrying to the location were lifted off the ground by the force of an explosion, although they were several blocks away. Sterling Hall, which on its upper floors held the Army Math Research Center (AMRC), was in flames. The bomb had been located in a Ford Econoline van parked next to the basement on a ramp outside the Physics Department labs. The explosion drove the van's rear axle through eight inches of reinforced concrete on the ramp and three feet into the ground below. Pieces of the van, bricks, and debris were blown three blocks away. Four researchers and a night watchman in the physics lab and offices were severely injured, and Dr. Robert Fassnacht, working late on his project in low temperature electricity so that he and his family could leave on a vacation, was killed.[6]

Karl Armstrong, who placed the phone call to the police and lit the fuse, had driven the van gingerly through the streets of Madison and had parked it on the ramp next to what he thought was the army's computer center. After the explosion he, his brother, and a friend fled in the Armstrong family's 1966 yellow Corvair. When stopped for speeding, they explained to the deputy sheriff that they were on their way to Devil's Lake State Park to do some camping. Although they did check in at Devil's Lake and registered for a campsite, they hurried back to Madison to return the car on time, as Mr. and Mrs. Armstrong expected their boys would. After having breakfast with his folks, Karl started east. In New York City he abandoned the Plymouth he had taken in Madison and, in a stolen Pontiac, headed for Canada. In upstate New York a patrolman stopped him for a noisy muffler, but erroneously transposed digits in his report. Consequently, the computer did not identify the car as stolen, and Karl continued on. He was arrested a year and a half later in Toronto. An informant tipped off the police and collected a $25,000 reward.[7]

Karl Armstrong

Although the AMRC bombing was his largest effort, it was not the first bomb built by the 23-year-old former University of Wisconsin student. Nor was it the only bombing Karl Armstrong had bungled. In a stolen plane on New Year's Day, 1970, he had attempted an aerial bombing of the Badger Ordnance owned by the Olin Corporation near Madison at Baraboo, but the mission was a dud. Twice he had thrown firebombs into what he thought were the offices of the army ROTC, but the first time he hit a classroom and the second time he burned out the armory basketball court. The next night, after his second ROTC error, he made another bomb, walked to the corner of Orchard and Regent, and threw the container into what he thought was the Selective Service Office. Over the radio, after he returned to his apartment, he learned that he had the right corner but the wrong address and that he had firebombed the Primate Research Center. A second assault on Badger Ordnance was made on Washington's Birthday, 1970; this time by land and after considerable preparation. Around midnight Karl and a friend took thirteen sticks of dynamite to the Prairie du Sac electrical substation which provides electricity for the Badger Ordnance plant. But after they had the dynamite in place and were stringing out the wire, they were spotted by an employee and forced to make a getaway. Police found Karl's fingerprints on the abandoned materials and the dynamite.[8]

After his arrest in Toronto in March 1972, Karl Armstrong resisted a return to Wisconsin for a year because the United States treaty with Canada does not allow extradition for political crimes. But after the Canadian courts decided that bombing was not a political act, he was returned to Madison in March 1973. In a letter to the judge, signed "Karlton Lewis Armstrong, P.O.W." and "Power to the People!" he protested that he "was kidnapped and held for ransom by the State of Wisconsin."[9] When arraigned he stood mute, and a first-degree murder trial date was set. After visits in jail from, among others, Philip Berrigan, and after plea bargaining, Karl Armstrong pled guilty on September 28 to second-degree murder, to four counts of arson, and to transporting explosives with intent to commit a crime. The trial of Karl Armstrong was in actuality a sentencing hearing covering not only the bombing of the Math Research Center and the death of Robert Fassnacht but also the burning of the Primate Lab, the ROTC classroom and basketball court, and the attempt to blow up the electrical substation. Although he referred to the event in his own testimony, the attempted aerial strike against Badger Ordnance was not included in the state case because it was on army property and was part of the federal case.

In the two-week sentencing hearing, which began on his twenty-seventh birthday, Karl Armstrong emphasized that his bombings were acts of protest against the Vietnam War, that other nonviolent protests were not affecting the conduct of the war, and that he had not intended to injure or kill anyone, only destroy property. He had been born, he pointed out, on the day the convicted Nazi leaders were executed, October 15, 1946. He and his father later discussed Nuremberg and attempted to understand how Hitler had come to power without German resistance. "I resolved that nothing like that, as long as I was alive, would happen in America. That's probably the only real resolution I ever made about my whole life—that I would be prepared to give up my life so that wouldn't happen here in America."[10]

The Armstrong family lived in a housing project next to Truax Field, an Air Force base near Madison. Karl, his older sister, and younger brother, grew up seeing military people daily but fearing that if they went near the barracks they would be shot on the spot. Karl was a member of the Madison's Boy's Choir, a Boy Scout who enjoyed camping, and a good athlete. From the stand he observed, "I felt very wholesome when I was a child."[11]

The Vietnam War and the 1968 Democratic Convention disillusioned Karl Armstrong as they did many Americans. In 1964, when he was eighteen, he worked for Lyndon Johnson's election because Johnson had said that he would not commit more troops to Vietnam. When the war escalated during the next year, Karl said, "I felt betrayed by the president of the United States. I felt like a fool."[12] This made Karl question everything about America. While Karl was a student at the University of Wisconsin, his father warned him not to join civil rights or peace demonstrations: "Don't get involved in anything political because you're going to get destroyed. Either you won't get a job or you'll be put on black lists; they'll find some way of destroying you."[13]

Karl participated in dozens of demonstrations at the university, the first in 1965 at Peterson Hall to protest the university's complicity with Selective Service, and the largest in 1967 against Dow Chemical, a demonstration which turned into a riot. In 1968 he quit his job with Graber's Drapery Fixtures to hitchhike to Chicago for the Democratic Convention protests. He had just arrived at 5 P.M. when someone, probably seeing his long hair, asked him if he was a Yippie. "I wasn't and didn't know what a Yippie was. But I said, 'Well, this is a free country; if I want to be a Yippie, I can be a Yippie.' I said, "Yeh, I'm a Yippie.'"[14] He was then thrown into the Chicago River. Cold and soaking wet, Karl went to Lincoln Park where he listened to Allen Ginsberg and other speakers. He had no place to sleep, but at a campfire on the side of a hill he found "a real sense of solidarity" with the other demonstrators, including members of the Blackstone Rangers. Later he was chased through the streets—all the time carrying his wet sleeping bag—and was involved in the Grant Park battle and the march on the Conrad Hilton Hotel. These were his first contacts with police provocation. "I said to myself, 'Karl Armstrong, you are such a stupid person. Stupid and naive to think that these people care about civil disobedience or anything of that sort?"[15]

After his radicalizing experience in Chicago, Karl began to wrestle with the ethics of political violence. Although a marginal student at the University, having been dropped for poor grades three times, he did receive a grade of A, ironically, in Social Disorganization. His interest was American history, especially the American Revolution. He concluded that "any sort of social progress in class society takes place because there are people who are willing finally to use violence to change the conditions of their life."[16] In 1969 the focus of attention on campus turned toward the connections the university had with the military, especially the Army Math Research Center. At the end of the year Karl began to plan his firebombing campaign, feeling a "horror and complete revulsion for war" yet sensing that because most of the American people were against the war, the democratic institutions had failed. "I am a very nonviolent person, basically. Even when I was firebombing ROTC facilities and conducted the aerial bombing of Badger Ordnance I felt alienated by the violence I was using. And all the time I was wishing that there was some other way to stop the war."[17]

Following the invasion of Cambodia and the Kent State killings, when the University of Wisconsin continued to ignore the demands by protestors that the AMRC be closed down, Karl began preparations for the big AMRC bombing. He stockpiled explosives, primacord, ammonium nitrate fertilizer, and fuel oil in his uncle's basement in Minneapolis. Some of the explosives and primacord had been stolen from northern Minnesota. He began reading books on explosives, and he cut his shoulder-length hair short and shaved off his beard. In mid-August he rented a U-Haul trailer from a Madison station, using his own driver's license as identification and the Armstrong family Corvair. From a construction site he took six 55-gallon drums and purchased 1,700 pounds of ammonium nitrate fertilizer, using an alias and telling the salesperson he was a farm worker. All the materials were collected on a site outside Madison where the bomb was constructed inside a van stolen from a professor.[18]

Around 2 A.M. on the morning of the AMRC bombing, witnesses testified that they saw a yellow Corvair and a white Ford van carefully making their way down Pennsylvania Avenue and onto Johnson Street in Madison.

The van slowed to a crawl as it crossed the railroad tracks near Johnson and First streets. At 3:40 A.M. the enormous explosion shook the area around Sterling Hall, awakened people throughout Madison and for miles around, including Karl's father who asked his wife the next morning if she had heard what sounded like an earthquake.[19]

Sentencing Hearing: Trial of the War

Because jury trial procedures restrict the presentation of issues, Karl decided to plead guilty in order to deal more fully with the reasons for his acts in a sentencing hearing. There he would "reach everyone's hearts and minds and . . . . reveal the impelling reasons which made my acts necessary. I in no way regard these acts as crimes." In fact, he continued in his statement when he pleaded guilty:

> These proceedings demonstrate the utmost hypocrisy of a government which I and the greater part of humanity deem to be criminal. The acts with which I have been credited were undertaken with a purpose of crippling the efforts of the American government to wage an illegal, criminal and aggressive war against the Indochinese people, to prevent there the further loss of life, devastation and suffering. I have acted out of a sense of moral responsibility and felt for me not to have taken concrete actions against this war would have been criminally irresponsible. I am not happy about the death of a human being and the suffering suffered by others as a result of these actions. These actions were intended as an affirmation of life, and great precautions were taken to prevent injury to human life.
>
> [applause]
>
> COURT: There will be order in this court. No demonstrations from the audience of any kind.[20]

William Kunstler began the sentencing hearing on Karl's behalf promising that "for the general public this will be a unique educational experience." Issues such as the illegality of the Vietnam War and how the AMRC became a symbol at the university for the resistance to the war, all of which would be ruled immaterial in a regular trial, would be presented. This is the same kind of opportunity Clarence Darrow used successfully in the Leopold and Loeb case to demonstrate that the young men had been carried away by an insane philosophy when they killed Bobby Franks and that they should be spared. "In this case we want to show that Karl Armstrong was carried away by nothing more than an absolute abhorrence to what was being done in Southeast Asia. He was carried away by an idealism that was of, I think, the finest and truest nature, that he did what he did with compassion, with an attempt to spare anyone's life," Kunstler emphasized. While Armstrong bore the legal responsibility for the death of one person, Kunstler urged, the moral responsibility rested in the White House, Congress, Pentagon, and finally in "an American population which somehow couldn't understand that it was being made into a replica of Germans two generations back, who would sit by and let things happen in their name without understanding their own power and what to do about it until it was much too late for anyone." Armstrong is in court to be judged "when those who plunged us into this indecent tragedy walk the earth unpunished and unjudged."[21]

The forty-one witnesses called by the defense included Vietnam veterans, who related experiences of the brutal and indiscriminate killing of civilians; experts on warfare, who told about military tactics and weapons; a leading psychiatrist, a former United States senator, an expert on international law, and several historians, who set Karl's act in the emotional context of war as the others questioned its legality and affirmed the rightness of resistance to it. The director of the AMRC was called, as were its critics and leading antiwar activists from Madison and the rest of the country. Finally, Karl and his parents were called. With witnesses like Robert Jay Lifton, Senator Ernest Gruening, Richard Falk, Philip Berrigan, Daniel Ellsberg, Harvey Goldberg, Gabriel Kolko, and Howard Zinn, what ordinarily would be a routine sentencing hearing became, as the *New York Times* called it, "a full-scale evocation of the Vietnam war — its morality, its impact on American youth and the climate of protest it engendered."[22]

Six Vietnam veterans testified that the atrocities against civilians were commonplace. Charles Piper, the first witness, a recently discharged Marine, Armstrong's age and also from Madison, served as a legal clerk and reporter in thirty to forty court martial cases, a quarter of which involved crimes against civilians. One of the five cases he told about involved crimes by a "killer team" which had murdered fourteen villagers, including women, children, an infant, the blind, and the crippled. Of the five tried, only one soldier was convicted. Although that one was sentenced to life imprisonment, the division commander cut it to a year, and when he was released from prison, he was given a hero's welcome in his West Virginia hometown, the key to the city, and a job in a mill. In another case a staff sergeant was accused of manslaughter for dumping gasoline on an old man and igniting it. The court martial found him not guilty. The conclusion from these and other cases is that if a soldier deliberately killed a Vietnamese civilian, he had a good chance of "beating the rap."[23]

Among the experts who testified about military tactics and weapons was Kenneth Osborn. He told about the CIA's Phoenix program which employed such torture techniques as pushing detainees out of helicopters or driving dowels into their ears, killing some 43,000 people suspected of being Viet Cong sympathizers.[24] Egbert Pfeiffer, author of *Harvest of*

Death, recounted evidence of the effects of the chemical Agent Orange in Cambodia as early as November 1969, months before the administration admitted its "incursion."[25]

Robert Jay Lifton, the Yale psychologist who in 1973 had just finished the highly regarded study of Vietnam veterans entitled *Home from the War,* painted a portrait of the emotions and attitudes produced in the war. When GIs, who after arrival in Vietnam were at first confused, then saw their buddies killed, they felt guilty because they had survived. Overwhelmed with rage and unable to take out their emotions against an unseen enemy on fixed battlefields, they developed a "kill everyone and everything attitude. There developed in Vietnam an atrocity-making situation which became the norm and everyday way of life."[26] A leading authority on international law, Richard Falk of Princeton, invoked the Nuremberg precedent to argue that there is a right of individuals to stop crime "even by creating a lesser crime." The principle is that "individuals are accountable for the laws of war in every situation." This means, he suggested, that American leaders are just as "indictable" as were the World War II German and Japanese leaders.[27]

Former senator Ernest Gruening of Alaska, one of the two senators to vote against the Bay of Tonkin Resolution, eighty-six years old and a publicity director for Robert LaFollette's 1924 presidential campaign, proclaimed that "resistance to this war is not only an obligation but a solemn duty of the American people. The people who have had the courage to fight this war deserve not castigation but accolades. It took courage to say 'I will not fight in this obscene war.'"[28] Seven Madison activists took the stand to trace the path of protest from peaceful dissent to violent resistance, explaining their growing frustration especially when the university insulted the students by refusing to take action against the AMRC.[29]

The AMRC itself was the center of testimony for one day when Dean Stephen Kleene of the College of Letters and Sciences and R. Creigton Buck, acting director of the AMRC, claimed that none of the material in the center was classified. "Mathematics is a very ambiguous subject," Buck remarked. "There is no such thing as Army math, any more than there is Jewish math or British math." Joseph Bowman, however, who assisted in writing *The AMRC Papers,* which were critical of the university's sponsorship of the AMRC, cited instances of research for the army which suggested that as much as half of the AMRC research was done for the army and much of that would have application to the Vietnam War. He pointed out that although the University officials were technically correct to claim that the AMRC research was nonclassified, this would apply only to the math problems themselves, whereas the applications of the problems to the Vietnam War would be classified.[30]

Daniel Ellsberg, who had been scheduled to testify, became ill and was forced to send a tape recording. On it he admitted that he had never met Armstrong and that he did not condone his actions. If he had been present he would have opposed his doing it. Nevertheless, he continued, "I am applying standards to which I aspire. I would like to live in a society in which the use of dynamite or explosives is condemned. But this is not the society we live in." Ellsberg said he would gladly testify at a trial of President Nixon, who "has exploded more dynamite than any other individual in history."[31] Ellsberg's co-defendant in the Pentagon Papers conspiracy case, Anthony Russo, told a hushed courtroom how he had been sent to Vietnam by the Rand Corporation to do a study and returned with the realization that most of those being killed were civilians and that the Viet Cong were the defenders of the nation.

> I never before said this publicly. I brought back a grenade from Vietnam. I walked down the halls at Rand and I wanted to throw it into the computer room. I had it with me, but I thought I would come back when all of the people were gone. I wanted to blow up the computers for the benefit of man. I thank God I didn't. I walked out on the Santa Monica pier and threw it into the ocean. Had I been younger I would have done it.[32]

Former priest Philip Berrigan had been one of the Baltimore Four convicted in 1967 for pouring blood over draft records, the Catonsville Nine convicted in 1968 for destroying draft records, and the Harrisburg Seven convicted in a 1972 conspiracy trial for smuggling letters out of prison. He sketched his own involvement in the antiwar movement and his attempt to understand the role Christians must play in a nation which wages war. He defended Armstrong's action, saying that the death of Fassnacht "has to be balanced against the calculated deaths of millions" in Indochina.[33]

Karlton's parents, Donald and Ruth, testified on the final day of the sentencing hearing, as did Karlton himself. Karlton detailed the precautions he took to make sure that no one would be in the AMRC when he bombed it. He decided that during semester break at predawn on a Monday would be the time when there would least likely be anyone in the building. He watched for lights in Sterling Hall the weekend before the bombing, and he saw none. He counted auto and pedestrian traffic, and he kept a careful log. He also tested the length of time it would take to phone the police. On the night of the bombing, when he drove the van to Sterling Hall, he was upset to see a car parked there and lights on in what he thought was the AMRC computer room. "I would have to honestly say that—that there probably—you know, the probability was that there was someone in the computer room." He looked in the window, could see about three-quarters of the room, and noticed no one. Then he lit the fuse, returned to the window, and still saw no one in the room. He made the phone call to the police and the bomb blew up shortly after he placed the call. The early morning radio news reported that someone had been killed in the bombing of Sterling Hall.

> And—I don't know—that—that really destroyed me. Because—because in my own mind I didn't think that there was any way that the death could be justified. And the explosion had—you know, the news of the death had had such an effect on me that—that I didn't think I could even explain why—at that point—why Army Math was even destroyed. I don't know, I guess you'd say I was in shock.[34]

Armstrong's bomb did succeed in destroying the Army Math Research Center and much of the rest of the new six-story wing of Sterling Hall, but that was because the bomb was as powerful as it was, not because Armstrong had placed it accurately. The AMRC was on the third floor, and the Physics Department occupied the basement and the first floor. Armstrong had parked the bomb-laden van on a ramp outside the office of physicist Dr. David Schuster. The lighted room Armstrong thought was the AMRC computer room when he peered in the window was really the Physics Department's accelerator room, a place which was in use twenty-four hours every day. Robert Fassnacht had his coat on and was on his way out of the building, only pausing in the hall to talk to Norbert Sutter, the security guard. Schuster had briefly left the accelerator room in search of some reading material and had just passed Fassnacht and Sutter in the hall when the bomb blew.[35] The bomb was powerful enough that, in addition to destruction of much of Sterling Hall, other buildings—chemistry and pharmacy—including the University Hospital and its cardiac care wing 500 feet away, suffered damages.

Ruth Armstrong, Karlton's mother, was the final witness to take the stand. She expressed sorrow for the Fassnacht family and recalled how her son had always been conscientious and fond of people. From his earnings at Gardner's Bakery, she mentioned, he saved every check for his schooling. Her concluding comment drew applause: "There would have been no bombing if people my age got up and done something beside letting our children do it for us."[36]

The defense introduced, in addition to the forty-plus witnesses, more than sixty exhibits. Among the exhibits were two critiques of the AMRC; part of the Pentagon Papers; the book by Richard Falk, Gabriel Kolko, and Robert Jay Lifton, *Crimes of War*; and photos of Vietnam atrocities.

Prosecution Case

Compared to the defense, the prosecution did little: no witnesses called, no exhibits introduced. The prosecution team of lawyers did not cross examine the defense witnesses extensively, mainly asking if the witness had ever met Karlton Armstrong and establishing that, except for his parents, only three of the more than forty had met Karlton and even they had little to say about him. The renowned experts, the prosecution claimed, were testifying *for* Karlton rather than *about* him.[37]

The major presentation by the prosecution, in addition to the statement of facts submitted in support of Armstrong's guilty plea, was the state's summary. Michael Zaleski, an assistant attorney general for Wisconsin, reviewed Karlton's actions and their ramifications. His several bombings caused $2.6 million damage to twenty-six buildings. Five persons were injured in Sterling Hall—none of them connected to the AMRC—and one person was injured in the Hospital nearby. Many years of research were destroyed. Robert Fassnacht, a 33-year-old postdoctoral physicist studying problems of electrical conductors, was killed, leaving a wife, a three-year-old son, and one-year-old twin daughters. Zaleski argued that, contrary to Armstrong's testimony, he had not been careful. If the defense portrayed Armstrong as an idealist frustrated by the manipulations of the war machine, Zaleski painted a picture of an egotistical loser so stultified by his desire for recognition that he would rally to any cause. "He had to excel and be recognized, and the only way he could do it was to make a bigger bomb than the next guy, and he did it." As an example of his egoism, Zaleski pointed out that when someone yawned during Armstrong's testimony on the stand he called the court's attention to it. He wanted every word of his etched in slate for future generations, Zaleski concluded, but, in fact, Armstrong's words which should be so etched are, "I am not repentent. I'd do it again."[38]

The court was asked to condone Armstrong's actions, Zaleski suggested, by giving him a mere slap on the wrist. "Imagine the society we'd have if every time a person felt morally committed to a cause he could throw around one-ton bombs. I suppose if Karl felt firmly committed to zero-population growth, he'd think he was morally justified in playing King Herod." Although Armstrong condemns the government, says it is immoral and should be overthrown, Zaleski observed, the conduct of Agnew and the Watergate defendants is the same as his: "It is the same old thing that when you feel justified—even if it is illegal—go ahead and act. He condemns these people, but he thinks he should go free." That is the anarchical law of the lynch mob, taking the law into our own hands.[39]

Final Arguments

In his short final argument for the defense William Kunstler quoted Thomas Jefferson: "I tremble for my country because I know that God is just" and referred to the "good Germans" who refused to oppose or question those in authority. He pointed to the difficult position Judge Horton was in when he resisted community and political pressure in the heated environment of the Scottsboro trial as he strove to see that justice was done to the eight Blacks accused of rape in Alabama. Kunstler urged that Judge Sachtjen follow the lead of Judge John Curtin in Western New York who gave a one-year suspended sentence to five Roman Catholics who bombed a draft board destroying property, although not taking a life. "They were luckier than Karl Armstrong. But someone could have been in the building." Kunstler drew the attention of the court to, of all things, Michaelangelo's sculpture of David. Unlike other portrayals of David, which show his foot on the severed head, Michaelangelo was not concerned with triumph but endeavored to capture the thoughts of a man about to do something which would jeopardize himself, not knowing the outcome of what he was about to do. Was Kunstler suggesting that Armstrong attempted to slay the military Goliath? That was implied perhaps, but Kunstler stressed the internal torment of Judge Sachtjen as he faced the decision on sentencing Armstrong. "How are you going to tell millions of little children here and in Southeast Asia that their fathers, brothers, sisters, mothers, uncles, grandparents, friends and neighbors won't be home because some maniacs blew up their country? That's the question before you, not the tragic death of Robert Fassnacht."[40]

Although Armstrong faced a possible imprisonment of ninety-five years on the state charges and seventy years on the federal charges, in the plea bargaining the prosecution agreed not to ask for more than a maximum of twenty-five years on both to run concurrently. While not bound to such a bargain, Judge Sachtjen sentenced Armstrong to fifteen years on each of four arson charges, to ten years on the possession of explosives, and to twenty-three years on the second-degree murder charge, all to run concurrently.

Federal Hearing

At a shorter sentencing hearing in April 1974 in the federal District Court across the street from the Dane County Courthouse in Madison, Karlton Armstrong faced the court concerning the attempted aerial bombing of the Badger Army Ammunition Plant near Baraboo as well as the AMRC bombing. He had the opportunity in his second hearing to answer the arguments, first, that his actions led to anarchy and, second, that he felt no remorse. The former, he maintained, "is just another variation of the 'red herring' used to destroy or repress opposition to government policy in the past. The anarchy the prosecution speaks of was already being perpetrated by his client in Indo-China." His actions threatened a governmental policy in the interest of a very few, while it is "the duty of every person in this country to try to decide if the government's acts are 'intelligent' and 'moral' and to change or stop the government's acts if they are not so." When all democratic and legal means have been exhausted, "then that person must decide whether the use of violence is justified to end the government's crimes." The Watergate events and the Pentagon Papers case reveal how the government acted illegally, abused and manipulated the processes of democracy, and suppressed opposition to the war. "This same government is now asking for more blood, mine, to try to cover its own crimes by trying to make those who resisted them criminals."[41]

As for remorse, Armstrong maintained that the prosecutor must not have listened at the mitigation hearing. He did bear full responsibility for the death and injuries as a result of the AMRC bombing. "What I am *not* remorseful about is the remorse which the prosecutor really speaks of— remorse for trying to destroy war facilities. My acts did not intend that anyone die; they were intended to save untold lives and stop the suffering of Third World people." That remorse "will never be forthcoming; no matter how severely the prosecutor would have me punished." He concluded by saying that he would not be rehabilitated in prison. "No sentence is going to deter anyone who acts from their conscience and love for life." He signed his statement to the court, "Karl Armstrong, P.O.W., Waupun Prison."[42]

Recognizing that he was dealing with the "bitter fruit of a bitter season in the history of our country," Federal Judge James E. Doyle considered that the American people had made the judgment that both the military action in Southeast Asia and Armstrong's actions were wrong. Judge Doyle rejected punishment for vengeance or for retribution, but gave consideration to questions of what sentence would deter others, how the community could be protected from Armstrong, and the type of sentence needed, if any, for his rehabilitation. Avowing that his best practical judgment led him to believe in general deterrence, Judge Doyle suggested that fringe sympathizers with militant groups might be deterred by the knowledge that they would be punished if they attempted, as Armstrong did, to use violence in imposing their will on others. Likewise, he pointed out, given a similar set of circumstances, perhaps United States military action in Palestine or South Africa, Armstrong might be deterred from attempting to use violence to win his point. Discounting the bravado of Armstrong's statement as understandable in light of seeing "his 1970 moment on center-stage drown in the relentless torrent of 1974's new crimes in the United States and in the world, it would be natural to assert rather stridently one's political immortality." It would be reasonable to expect that further violence from Armstrong is unlikely.[43]

As for Armstrong's rehabilitation, Judge Doyle admitted that if it meant conditioning him to a proestablishment philosophy, the government had no right to do it, and if it meant developing a perspective skeptical of slogans and movement, although he was in need of it, prison was not the place. Judge Doyle concluded by recognizing general deterrence as the primary consideration, but, with due respect to the state court, twenty-five years seemed an extravagant response to the need for general deterrence. Consequently, he made the federal sentence a term of ten years, made it concurrent with the state sentence, and gave the federal parole board complete discretion over the sentence.[44]

In September 1976, while in prison, Karlton Armstrong married Naomi Wall from Toronto. She greeted him at the gates of the Wisconsin State Prison at Waupun when he was released on parole in the spring of 1980. His brother Dwight was arrested in Toronto in April 1977, sentenced to seven years in prison on a charge of second-degree murder, and released on parole in May 1980. David Fine was arrested in San Raphael, California, in 1976, sentenced to seven years, and paroled August 1979. The final member of the AMRC bombing team, Leo Burt, is still at large.[45]

Conclusion

Both Adler and Armstrong turned to violence after becoming frustrated with democratic methods. Adler had watched his father, Victor Adler, spend years leading the Austrian Social Democrats against war. In 1914 the senior Adler, then a member of the Austrian Parliament, began to support and justify the war. Listening to his father rationalizing the abandonment of his "war against war" rhetoric, Friedrich felt his "whole life plans and life work had been wrecked."[46] Hence, Friedrich resolved to oppose the war as an individual and began planning the assassination of the prime minister.

Armstrong had participated in various demonstrations against the Vietnam War, but his experiences at the 1968 Democratic Convention in Chicago convinced him that nonviolent demonstrations would not stop the war. The trials of Adler and Armstrong confronted society with dissenters who maintained that a selective act of violence was morally right in order to halt war's wholesale killing. The state, on the other hand, naturally drew the public's attention to the violent acts and the consequences for society if those who commit them receive a light punishment.

Violence wipes away the persuasive argument of conscience. It is difficult to convince a judge, jury, or the public that an act of dissent was morally justified when someone is killed, whether that someone is directly involved like the Austrian prime minister, or an innocent bystander like Robert Fassnacht, Armstrong's victim. The position of conscience is powerful when, as in the case of Thomas More or the Berrigan brothers, the acts are symbolic. In the long run, society responds to an appeal to conscience, just as in the short run it reacts against violence. Law evolves, and the rule of law is strengthened by the one type of dissent, as law and the rule of law are undermined by the other.

Notes

1. Ronald Florence, *Fritz: The Story of a Political Assassin* (New York, Dial Press, 1971), p. 221. Emphasis in original.
2. *Ibid.*, pp. 263-265. Emphasis in original.
3. *Ibid.*, p. 266.
4. *Ibid.*, pp. 263-265, 276, 302, 317.
5. Statement of Facts in Support of Submission of Guilty Plea, transcript, *Wisconsin v. Karlton Armstrong*, September 28, 1973, p. 25.
6. David Schuster, interview, January 23, 1981, and *Capital Times* (Madison), August 25, 1970, p. 1.
7. Statement of Facts, Transcript, September 28, 1973, p. 27-28; *Capital Times*, October 10, 1973, p. 9; and October 13, 1973, p. 11.
8. Statement of Facts, Transcript, September 28, 1973, p. 32-41; Testimony of Karl Armstrong, Transcript of Sentencing Hearing, *Wisconsin v. Armstrong*, October 26, 1973, Vol. 10, p. 90; Henry Schipper, "A Trapped Generation on Trial," *The Progressive*, 38 (January 1974), p. 45.
9. Karl Armstrong, letter to the Court, May 27, 1973.
10. Karl Armstrong, Transcript of Sentencing Hearing, October 26, 1973, Vol. 10, p. 61.
11. *Ibid.*, p. 65.
12. *Ibid.*, p. 72.
13. *Ibid.*, p. 74.
14. *Ibid.*, p. 81.
15. *Ibid.*, p. 85.
16. *Ibid.*, p. 67.
17. *Ibid.*, p. 90.
18. Statement of Facts, Transcript, September 28, 1973, pp. 18-24.
19. *Ibid.*, pp. 25-26; *Capital Times*, October 10, 1973, p. 1.
20. Transcript of Proceedings, September 28, 1973, pp. 42-43.
21. Transcript of Sentencing Hearing, October 15, 1973, Vol 1, pp. 7, 11-12.
22. *New York Times*, October 16, 1973, p. 12.
23. Transcript of Sentencing Hearing, October 15, 1973, Vol. 1, pp. 7, 15-30.
24. Transcript, October 16, 1973, Vol. 2, pp. 110-152; *Capital Times*, October 17, 1973, p. 4.
25. Transcript, October 18, 1973, Vol. 4, pp. 13-60.
26. *Capital Times*, October 17, pp. 1, 4; Transcript, October 17, 1973, Vol. 3, pp. 6-63.
27. *Capital Times*, October 19, 1973, pp. 1, 4; Transcript, October 19, 1973, Vol. 5, p. 3ff.
28. *Capital Times*, October 20, 1973, p. 11; Transcript, October 19, 1973, Vol. 5, p. 62ff.

29. *Capital Times*, October 23, 1973, p. 23; Transcript, October 22, 1973, Vol. 6.
30. *Capital Times*, October 24, 1973, p. 27; Transcript, October 23, 1973, Vol. 7.
31. *Capital Times*, October 24, p. 27.
32. *Capital Times*, October 25, 1973; Transcript, October 24, 1973, Vol. 8, p. 60ff.
33. *Capital Times*, October 25, 1973, p. 27; Transcript, October 24, 1973, p. 111ff.
34. Transcript, October 26, 1973, pp. 57-59.
35. David Schuster, interview, January 23, 1981.
36. Transcript, October 26, 1973, Vol. 10. p. 97.
37. Transcript, November 1, 1973, Vol. 11, p. 17.
38. *Ibid.*, pp. 4-7, 16.
39. *Ibid.*, p. 11.
40. *Ibid.*, pp. 90-91.
41. Karlton Armstrong, Statement, United States District Court for the Western District of Wisconsin, filed April 16, 1974.
42. *Ibid.*
43. Judge James E. Doyle, Statement, United States District Court for the Western District of Wisconsin, April 18, 1974.
44. *Ibid.*
45. *Capital Times*, May 1, 1980, p. 6.
46. Florence, *Fritz*, p. 133.

7

Trials of Nationalists:
The Question of Representation

Nationalist trials raise the same questions that religious trials raised before the advent of nationalism. Religion, until modern times, roughly since the sixteenth century, served to unify society, just as nationalism does today. Nationalism is as much our political bond as religion once was.

Religious trials before modern times and nationalist trials today are, at their core, trials over the issue of representation. Who speaks for God's people? Who dares to claim that he or she, this group or that imperium possesses a will that is God's will? The Roman emperor? The priestly theocracy? The pope? The king? Today, in spite of all that has changed, we can notice that in trials of nationalists the question of representation remains. Just as heresy trials for centuries involved more than a dispute over matters of doctrine, so nationalist trials touch deeper into our political identity than differences over public policy. Does the government represent all the people, or does it represent one people yet rule another? Who speaks, for instance, for the American Indian: the United States government's Bureau of Indian Affairs (BIA), the tribal councils, or the American Indian Movement (AIM)? The same basic question arises in all precincts of the world, and it has for a long time.

The Roman Empire

To Christians no trial could be more important than the trial of Jesus. Its theological significance makes it difficult to see its other aspects. What we know of Jesus' trial, to name but one difficulty, comes from the Gospel writers who wanted to tell about the trial to demonstrate the fulfillment of prophecy and to introduce the passion story.[1] The earliest Gospel, Mark, was written at the time of the destruction of the Temple and of Jerusalem itself by Roman troops in 70 AD. This catastrophe came after a nationalist group, the Zealots, succeeded in gaining power in Jerusalem. The hometown Christians who had not fled were among those exterminated in the

Roman siege of Jerusalem. With them all of the records were destroyed. The Gospels were written with a desire to underplay the fact that Jesus had been tried and executed as a Zealot.[2]

While the judgment was unjust—Jesus was not a Zealot—to the Roman authorities and the theocratic judges of the Jewish Sanhedrin close was bad enough. Jesus presented a danger to their control over a volatile territory and that was what mattered. Roman rule over Judaea, Samaria, and Galilee was as tenuous then as Soviet rule of Poland and Eastern Europe is now. Risings against Rome had taken place in 4 BC when Rome's ruler of the Jews, Herod the Great, died and an imperial procurator moved in to establish direct rule. With the suppression of the rebellion 2,000 Jewish insurgents were crucified in reprisal.[3] To continue the guerrilla resistance against the Romans and the Jewish priestly aristocracy, especially the Sadducees who collaborated with the Romans, the Zealots were founded by Judas of Galilee.[4]

From what Jesus said, from those with whom he chose to associate, and from his actions during Passover, the Romans might have had good reason to suspect that he was a Zealot. He was a follower of the apocalyptic John the Baptist, and he preached that the kingdom of God was at hand. That sounded like rebellion. He was from Galilee, where Zealotism was born. Among those he picked for his disciples one was a known Zealot, Simon, and four others were perhaps Zealots, probably fellow-travellers of Zealotism: Peter, Judas Iscariot, and the sons of Zebedee, James and John.[5] That, if nothing else, looked like seditious company to keep. During Passover Jesus attacked the center of authority for the priestly aristocracy and the focus of Jewish ritual, the Temple of Jerusalem. Moreover, he made the attack not merely as a prophet with some measure of popular support but as the Messiah of Israel, the Son of God.[6] That had, at least, the appearance of insurrection.

Then, consider the events of his final days. If Judas Iscariot was a Zealot, his betrayal makes sense as his attempt to force Jesus' hand by putting him in such a desperate position that Jesus would have to make use of his supernatural powers. Or, maybe the betrayal, together with Peter's denials, was born of a disillusionment that Jesus was not living up to the Zealots' expectations. Jesus' arrest and interrogation took place at night, as they might in any authoritarian state then or now. Before the Sanhedrin, which met in extraordinary session at the home of the high priest, Jesus faced the community leaders. Among the charges, which were the product of conflicting false witnesses, was that Jesus had claimed he would destroy the Temple, which had been made with hands, and within three days build another "made without hands."[7] To this charge and others Jesus said nothing. But when he was asked if he was "the Christ, the Son of the

Blessed," Jesus replied "I am: and ye shall see the Son of Man sitting on the right hand of power, and coming in the clouds of heaven."[8] That did it. He was condemned: guilty of blasphemy.

The second phase of Jesus' trial came in the morning when he was taken to the Roman governor, Pontius Pilate. Here the charge was sedition. Pilate asked Jesus, "Art thou the King of the Jews?" Jesus replied, "Thou sayest it."[9] To the other charges Jesus refused to respond. Barabbas, who also had been condemned by the Romans as a Zealot, was in fact the true leader of the insurrection. Jesus, on the other hand, was not a Zealot.[10] When the crowd picked Barabbas instead of Jesus to be spared, it might have been a clever political choice. Jesus, not Barabbas, was sent to be crucified and he was condemned not because he had led a rebellion but because he claimed to be the King of the Jews. Whatever the mistakes might have been, the short of it is that Jesus was tried and executed by the Romans for being a nationalist. If he represented the Jews, Rome could not.

For several centuries after Jesus, Romans persecuted Christians. Then, when the religious tables were turned, Christians controlling Rome persecuted pagans. Throughout, Jews were persecuted by both. The issue in all such persecutions is representation. The persecution of Christians during the first three centuries after Christ, especially during the Great Persecution (303-311) of Emperor Diocletian, and the persecution of pagans and heretics, especially the Donatists, after 364 A.D. share this: The persecutions were carried out by those in power intent on maintaining the unity of the state against those determined to remain separate. That is the theme too of centuries of anti-Semitism.

Emperor Diocletian, facing military threats on the vast Roman frontiers as well as anarchy all around him at home, sought stability in restoration. Rome would be revived by returning to the traditional Roman values, in particular Roman majesty. He claimed that as emperor he not only ruled "by consent of the gods," but he was the incarnation of Jupiter.[11] Christians, however, refused to participate in the ceremonies of this new emperor worship, out of concern for idolatry. They were charged in one edict with "the wickedness of attempting to undo past tradition." This made it necessary "to punish the obstinacy of the perverted mentality of these most evil men." The Diocletian persecution, W. H. C. Frend observes, aimed to show that Christianity was "self-contradictory and woven around an individual who on close investigation turned out to be merely a minor rebel chieftain in Palestine."[12] Jesus' trial as a nationalist was paying off for Rome three centuries later.

The payoff for Rome was short-lived. The Great Persecution, while torturing and martyring thousands of Christians, weakened the resolve of the persecutors while strengthening that of the Christians. Within a generation the Roman Empire moved from the terror of the Great Persecution of the Christians, to the general toleration granted to all religions in the Edict of Milan (313), to the official establishment of Christianity under Emperor Constantine, to the persecution of pagans, schismatic Donatists, and heretical Arians in the name of Christianity.

Not long after Emperor Constantine saw the political futility of persecuting the determined Christians, he realized the advantages of religious toleration. The Edict of Milan propounded that "we have been watchful not to deny freedom of worship . . . [and] to secure reverence for the Divinity . . . so that whatever there be of the divine and celestial might be favoring and propitious to us and to all those living under our rule." The thinking behind the edict was familiar: toleration was necessary in order to gain favor and success from the gods. This was the same reasoning which motivated the persecutions. "In the ebb and flow of Christianity and paganism," Ramsay MacMullen observes, "this was the point of slack tide."[13] Constantine worked out a compromise between Christianity and pagan religions. He is famous in history for what he did for Christianity: founding Constantinople, building basilicas throughout the empire, and presiding over the Council of Nicaea where orthodoxy was defined. Yet he continued as the head of the established state cults because it was an ancient custom of his office as emperor. As a statesman concerned about unity, Constantine employed religion as needed.

If the spirit of Constantine was toleration, it did not last. The thinking soon prevailed that to make the world safe for Christendom it had to be rendered immune to Christianity. The switch-about in religion meant that the trial of Jesus had to be reinterpreted. In the fourth century Pilate was seen as sympathetic to Jesus while Jews became the villains responsible for the trial and crucifixion. The most vicious attack on the Jews came from St. John Chrysostom (344-407) who railed against their "odious assassination of Christ" and claimed that there would be no end to God's vengeance, "no expiation possible, no indulgence, no pardon."[14]

The most famous contemporary of Chrysostom was the Bishop of Hippo, St. Augustine, who directed his energy toward putting down a number of heretical movements. The rebellious Donatists were his major challenge. Just as before Emperor Constantine Christians were persecuted because they lacked a religion which expressed civic loyalty, so after Constantine the Donatists were persecuted for the same reason. In Africa, where Augustine had his jurisdiction as bishop, the Donatists resembled the Zealots. They maintained a purist standard for the church and a militant one for politics. They argued that the validity of the sacraments depended on the morality of the priest. If the priest had compromised with the Roman emperor by surrendering the Scriptures to avoid the Diocletian persecution, he had cut himself off from Christianity, according to the Donatist ideology, an would need rebaptism by a legitimate, Donatist priest.[15]

Faced with the overt persecution carried out by the Donatists against Catholics, Augustine developed his own theory of persecution. It was based on the fact that Christ had not merely said "blessed are they who are persecuted" but added "for righteousness' sake."[16] Not only were the Donatists who suffffered false martyrs because they did not suffer for righteousness, but the church could, Augustine argued, actively persecute them in the name of righteousness. For Augustine the distinguishing feature is the intention of the agents of persecution, making some wrong and some right: "The former doing harm by their unrighteousness, the latter seeking to do good by the administration of discipline; the former with cruelty, the latter with moderation; the former impelled by lust, but is not careful how he wounds, but he whose aim is to cure is cautious with his lancet; for the one seeks to destroy what is sound, the other that which is decaying."[17] As much as the Donatists might think that the compulsory measures taken against them by Rome was persecution, in reality the decrees, trials, and punishments were "their truest friends" since by such means they were delivered from "ruinous madness."[18] Augustine's strictures against the Donatists read, with a few word changes to bring them up to date, like the closing arguments of many prosecutors in political trials, especially of nationalists. Chrysostom's anti-Semitic rhetoric would find a modern parallel in the most extreme partisan show trials, but Augustine's correction of the Donatists fits the pattern of argument found in many prosecutions in nationalist's trials.

Augustine's dominant analogy was the parable of the householder who prepared a banquet—read, state representing a people. When the invited guests made excuses, the householder (ruler) instructed his servant to "go out to the highways and hedges and compel them to come in, that my house may be filled" (Luke 14:23). The parable, as Augustine used it, is a figure for the unity of the church and the "power which the Church has received by divine appointment in its due season, through the religious character and the faith of kings" to be the instrument by which heresies and schisms are compelled to come in.[19] The householder represents all who are in society and can compel unity.

The message in Augustine's political thought as a whole is that the true bond of unity is the love of God and that human society is unified when it gives up the idolatries of the earthly city in favor of the City of God.[20] But when it comes to those such as the Donatists, Augustine stresses the use fear might have as a bond of unity. Like a prosecutor stressing to the jury that ordinary citizens obey laws because they respect their duty as citizens but that the defendant has no such respect, Augustine urged that genuine persuasion was preferable but that the Donatists were different because they compelled their adherents by fear. Fear of punishment, therefore, might release some from the fear of the fanatic Donatists and others from their frenzy as Donatists.[21] Fear itself may not change a person from evil, but it can serve as a warning to compel him to examine the truth.[22]

What is sought by persecution, according to Augustine, is neither the Donatists' possessions nor their death but "by the help of the terror of judges and of laws" their deliverance from error and their unity with the church. Augustine developed the idea of persecution out of love, making analogies to the parent correcting a child and extending it to weighing the suffering of a few in error against the benefits for the rest of society. "What then is the function of brotherly love? Does it, because it fears the short-lived fires of the furnace for a few, therefore abandon all to the eternal fires of hell?" It follows that if those who persecute are acting out of love, those who resist are acting on selfish motives. The Donatists prefer "their own contentions" to the "testimonies of Holy Writ," and "they must impudently venture in the madness of their vanity" to assert the truth of their doctrines.[23] In fact, it follows, the Donatists are the true authors of their own suffering. As the proverb says, "he that prepareth a pit for his neighbor shall himself most justly fall into it." By their own free will they have chosen "a pernicious error" by which they become the enemies of their own souls. The Donatists have severed themselves from the body of the church, "have usurped the sacraments of the Church outside the Church and in hostility to the Church, and have fought against us in a kind of civil war."[24]

Political habits change slowly. While in our day religious toleration is not at odds with religious establishment, as England and the Scandinavian countries illustrate, ancient tradition in the Roman Empire held that a unified civil religion was necessary for political success. Rousseau, like Augustine, argued that religious unity was a political prerequisite. But Rousseau, in contrast to Augustine, maintained that Christianity undermined political unity. No state, Rousseau pointed out, had ever been founded without a religious basis, but "the law of Christianity at bottom does more by weakening than good by strengthening the constitution of the State."[25] Rousseau urged a return to the Roman variety of civil religion. Nationalism, with Rousseau's enthusiastic approval, provided a substitute religion, accomplishing for every nation what Constantine had hoped to achieve in Rome. The demands for unity and the benefits of seeing the opposition defeated lead to an exclusive state religion. As Gibbon put it: "The enthusiasm which inspired the troops, and perhaps the emperor himself, had sharpened their swords while it satisfied their conscience. They marched to battle with the full assurance that the same God who had formerly opened a passage to the Israelites through the waters of Jordan, and had thrown down the walls of Jericho at the sound of the trumpets of Joshua, would display his visible majesty and power in the victory of Constantine."[26]

In the empire's persecution of nationalists and in Augustine's persecution of Donatists we have prototypes for the justification of later persecutions, national and religious. Groups that desire to remain separate threaten the larger unity. Yet their identity demands that they remain apart. Those who compel them to come in act as deputies for the larger society on behalf of public goals. To these deputies the separate groups appear to act from selfish goals for their own private advantage. The unity of the Roman Empire or the unity of Christian society demanded that the disruptive Zealots or Donatists be brought back into the fold or suffer the consequences. At stake in such prosecutions, whether in the Roman Empire or in our own day, is the nature of representation. This becomes even clearer in the trials of the fifteenth and sixteenth centuries, which present further parallels for our times.

Joan of Arc and the Spanish Inquisition

After Joan of Arc had turned the tide of war in favor of France, she was captured by the Burgundians, sold on a bribe to their English allies, and tried in 1431 by the Inquisition. Both the English and the church had reasons to try her. The English recognized that Joan represented the threat of a unified France. The Earl of Warwick held her as an English prisoner instead of turning her over to the bishop. He surrounded the court of the Inquisition with English soldiers, threatened and otherwise influenced the judges to condemn her, and organized her burning immediately after the verdict.[27]

The church also saw Joan as a challenge to its unified authority. For months she was questioned by experts in theology and law. She impressed them with her simple piety but, as well, with her astute replies to their ensnaring questions. She had heard voices and appealed to God and to the saints. Further, she was reluctant to give full obedience to the pope and the church hierarchy by admitting that the voice of the men in the court she faced was the voice of God. At the time the church was engaged in a campaign of major proportions against those who claimed supernatural powers and magic. Unless Joan agreed that the church, Christ's vicar on earth, could override her voices, they would have to condemn her. Even when she was offered the possibility of having her case heard by the pope, which would free her from English control, she refused. She could not recognize the pope's authority over her voices, only over matters of faith.[28] To the Inquisition, as to many involved in trials of nationalists in any age, this spelled anarchy. Augustine would have sided with the Inquisition's duty to correct Joan, and, given a change of language and context, so would many in our time.

The Inquisition came in two separate editions, medieval and Spanish. The medieval Inquisition had been established two centuries before Joan's trial by Pope Gregory IX in 1233 to bring unified authority to the church. The Spanish Inquisition operated independently of the papacy as an arm of the secular rulers to unify Spain, not the church. Granted, it would be difficult to classify the medieval Inquisition as a system of trials within the rule of law. It had replaced the episcopal courts which had operated under an equitable process in Roman law.[29] But the Spanish Inquisition is an extreme example of expediency made legal. It was a tribunal of Spanish nationalism.

Although the Spanish Inquisition lasted for more than three centuries, it was at the height of its terror when Ferdinand and Isabella employed it to unify their rule. Jews had suffered persecution in Spain long before Aragon and Castile were joined in 1479 under Ferdinand and Isabella. The Muslims persecuted both Jews and Christians. Later, beginning in the thirteenth century, Christians persecuted both Jews and Muslims, especially Jews. Pogroms in 1391 wiped out the Jewish ghettos, murdering 4,000 in Seville alone, and compelling the rest into baptism.[30]

Under Ferdinand and Isabella the Inquisition accelerated with such ardor that Pope Sixtus IV, who had earlier authorized the rulers to name the priests of the Inquisition, rebuked it saying that:

> The Inquisition has for some time been moved not by zeal for the faith and salvation of souls, but by lust for wealth, and . . . many true and faithful Christians, on the testimony of enemies, rivals, slaves and other lower and even less proper persons, have without any legitimate proof been thrust into secular prisons, tortured and condemned as relapsed heretics, deprived of their goods and property and handed over to the secular arm to be executed, to the peril of souls, setting a pernicious example, and causing disgust to many.[31]

This strong papal admonition, far from cooling the Inquisition, only inflamed Ferdinand's determination. Pope Sixtus, after hearing from Ferdinand, agreed to suspend the bull, giving the Inquisition under Ferdinand's direction a green light. More significantly for the development of the totalitarian regime which the Spanish Inquisition became, Pope Sixtus in 1483 agreed to the appointment of Tomás de Torquemada as inquisitor general, uniting the tribunal directly under the crown.[32]

Baptized Jews (*conversos*) and Muslims (*moriscos*) were persecuted by the Inquisition on the slightest pretext for relapsing into their old faith. After the Reformation began, Christians likewise were persecuted for heresy. Unbaptized Jews and Muslims were forced to leave Spain, an exodus of several million. In all, the terror of the Spanish Inquisition unified the new national state. The state, in turn, confiscated the property of its victims and achieved a rigid rule over an orthodox society. Spain was purified, but more important, it was unified. The price in human suffering was high.

Punishment by the Spanish Inquisition took a variety of forms. The mildest was a penance such as wearing a yellow garment called a *sanbenito*. It was a smock with a diagonal cross on it, worn as a mark of infamy for a few months or for life. It had to be worn by those condemned whenever they went out in public. Imprisonment could be decreed by the Inquisition for a short time or, in the case of heresies deemed "perpetual and irremissible," for life. Scourging by being "whipped through the streets," while passers-by and children threw stones to show their hatred for heresy, was another form. Confiscation of property was imposed whenever possible. Since informers received a percentage of the confiscated property, the temptation to inform was heightened, but the temptation was even greater for the government, which received most of the confiscated property. Wealth confiscated by the Inquisition was used to fight the war in Granada against the Muslims and some of it was used to finance a risky expedition proposed by an Italian, Christopher Columbus.[33]

The ultimate penalty of the Inquisition was burning at the stake. This was reserved for those who failed to confess before punishment was pronounced or for those who did confess in time but had relapsed into heresy. The Inquisition professed that it never killed. The heretic was surrendered, or, as the Inquisitorial jargon had it, "relaxed" to the secular arm which would hold the public ceremony of burning heretics, or, to use the euphemism, carry out an *auto-da-fé*, an act of faith.

What about the Jews who remained Jews? Torquemada had a plan which would bring national unity to Spain by ridding it of all Jews. He convinced Ferdinand and Isabella in March 1492 to sign a decree forcing all Jews of whatever age or condition to leave Spain by the end of July. They could take with them only what they could carry but no money, silver, or gold. Over 100,000 Jews, as a result of Torquemada's plan, disposed of their homes and all they possessed in order to leave Spain on pain of death. It is said that as Columbus set out for the unknown, his three ships passed several vessels carrying Spanish Jews away from Spain toward exile and dispersion.[34]

Martin Luther

The 1521 trial of Martin Luther involves considerable drama and two agendas: religious and political. A theological conflict certainly, it was also a trial testing the national spirit of Germany. Like the trial of Joan of Arc and the Inquisition in Spain, although in differing degrees, the trial of Luther was infused with the requisites of national politics.

Luther's revolt began with his objection to the fund-raising technique of selling papal indulgences, the subject of his ninety-five Theses in 1517. He was spared extradition to Rome by the protection which Elector Frederick of Saxony extended to this monk and theology professor at Wittenberg University. When the papal legate Cardinal Cajetan at a hearing concerning Luther's case decided that Frederick must either send Luther to Rome or banish him, Frederick, although in a tight position and troubled by the charge that he might be harboring a heretic, again refused to turn Luther over to Rome until he had been declared a heretic.[35]

Luther's revolt swept into history on the incoming tide of nationalism. He was able to ignore the 1520 papal bull condemning his writings to be burned and requiring him to submit within sixty days or be excommunicated and declared anathema. Luther not only withstood this strongest of papal condemnations, but he burned the papal bull. His reply in his *Address to the German Nobility* was worded in strong language:

> If ninety-nine per cent. of the papal court were abolished and only one per cent. were left, it would still be large enough to deal with questions of Christian faith. At present there is a crawling mass of reptiles, all claiming to pay allegiance to the pope, but Babylon never saw the like of these miscreants. The pope has more than 3,000 secretaries alone, and no one can count the others he employs, as the posts are so numerous. It is hardly possible to number all those that lie in wait for the institutions and benefices of Germany, like wolves for the sheep. I fear that Germany today is giving far more to the pope in Rome than she used to give formerly to the emperors. Some have estimated that more than 300,000 guilders go annually from Germany to Rome, quite uselessly and to no purpose, while we get nothing in return except contempt and scorn. It is not at all astonishing if princes, aristrocracy, towns, institutions, country, and people grow poor. We ought to marvel that we still have anything left to eat.

> Now that we have come to close quarters, let us pause a while to consider whether the Germans are quite such simpletons as not to grasp or understand the Romish game. For the moment, I shall say nothing by way of deploring the fact that God's commandments and Christian justice are despised in Rome. The state of Christendom, especially in Rome, is not so happy that we should risk calling such exalted matters into question at the present time. Nor am I objecting that natural or secular right and reason are of no avail.

The root of the trouble goes altogether deeper. My complaint is that the Romanists do not observe the very canon law which they themselves have devised, though this in itself is simply a piece of tyranny, avarice, and worldly pomp rather than law.[36]

Luther got away with saying this because he was protected by the German princes, especially Frederick of Saxony. Frederick was able to protect Luther because he had among his own people the support of a growing German national resentment against Rome. In spite of his opinions which resembled the heresy of John Hus, Luther was not burned as Hus had been a century earlier. Nor was Luther subject to the Inquisition as were secret Lutherans in Spain, because, unlike Ferdinand and Isabella, Frederick did not make the Inquisition an instrument of national unity. Instead, Luther was the instrument of nationalism in Germany.

The break from Rome was made final with the Diet of Worms in 1521, before the nobles and representatives of cities in the Holy Roman Empire and under the authority of Emperor Charles V, where Luther was called upon by a representative of the archbishop to retract the heresies in his writings: "Your plea to be heard from Scripture is the one always made by heretics. You do nothing but renew the errors of Wyclif and Hus. . . . Martin, how can you assume that you are the only one to understand the sense of Scripture? Would you put your judgment above that of so many famous men and claim that you know more than they all?" The question, in other words, concerned representation. Augustine would probably not have agreed with Luther's answer.

Luther's reply came in German, not Latin: "Since then Your Majesty and your lordships desire a simple reply, I will answer without horns and without teeth. Unless I am convinced by Scripture and plain reason—I do not accept the authority of popes and councils, for they have contradicted each other—my conscience is captive to the Word of God. I cannot and I will not recant anything, for to go against conscience is neither right nor safe. God help me. Amen." He might also have spoken the famous words of the Reformation: "Here I stand, I cannot do otherwise."[37]

When Emperor Charles called in the electors he stressed the issue of representation. He told them that he, following in the steps of the long line of emperors and kings from whom he was descended, intended to be faithful to the Church of Rome and defend the Catholic faith: "A single friar who goes counter to all Christianity for a thousand years must be wrong." Four of the six agreed to declare Luther a "notorious heretic," but the elector of the palatinate and Frederick of Saxony refused. For Luther's safety Frederick hid him at Wartburg castle.[38]

Luther's trial in the Diet at Worms drove the question of representation in several directions: Was God represented by the pope, by councils, by tradition, or by Scripture and conscience? Was the German nation better represented by Luther's doctrine and the princes or by Catholicism and the papacy? Did Luther preach German freedom from Roman tyranny and Christian freedom in the priesthood of all believers? Or, was his position, as the Edict of Worms declared, a denial of "the power of the keys" and an encouragement for "the laity to wash their hands in the blood of the clergy" in "rebellion, division, war, murder, robbery, arson, and the collapse of Christendom"?[39] Was it, in sort, tyranny with Rome and order under German princes? Or was it anarchy with Luther and order with Rome?

Variations of these same questions arise in all nationalist trials. As viewed from one side, the rebels are not representative but are irresponsible harbingers of chaos and anarchy. Luther had, after all, called the pope "the adversary of Christ and the apostle of the Devil." He in turn, was called by the Edict of Worms a "devil in the habit of a monk" who "brought together ancient errors into one stinking puddle and . . . invented new ones." As Augustine established a theoretical framework for justifying the trial of heretics and schismatics who destroy unity, so Luther provided a theory of resistance for those whose identity lies in being separate. Whatever Augustine and Luther might share in theology, probably much, on the issue of representation they are the two opposite sides of the question.

Irish Nationalists

A nation and its nationalism are tied together, but they are different and should not be confused with one another. Each of us is born into a nation. We speak the nation's language from birth and it is the sine qua non of national identity. Nationalism, however, is learned. It is an ideology which, like Roman civil religion, has a unifying role. Members of a nation might speak the same language and yet have different nationalist civil religions. Nationalists are not born but made. If language brings an identity of nationhood, nationalism carries with it a superconsciousness of a nation's mission in history.[40] Trials of nationalists call into question both the unity of a society and the capacity of either the government or the nationalist to speak for the people. A clear example lies in the struggle of the Irish nationalists. The Irish/English conflict has been of such long duration that it is a permanent fixture of history. At the many trials involving Irish nationalists neither side has lacked articulate and outspoken representatives.

The clash of nationalists over Ireland—Irish nationalists confronting their English problem and English nationalists encountering their Irish problem—demonstrates the basic patterns of nationalism. Irish nationalist strategy has been characterized as "England's difficulty [being] Ireland's opportunity." As shown in the potato famine of the 1840s, when the policy of laissez faire led to massive death and a change in the land distribution from subdivision toward consolidation, the English did not ignore the inverse: Ireland's difficulties could be England's opportunity.[41]

On each side the nationalists of the other persuasion are portrayed as acting from selfish motives, misleading the gullible people of the opposite side. Throughout the writings of Wolfe Tone, for instance, the policies of Britain are at every juncture characterized as tyrannical and sinister. "Every talent which gives dignity to the human species," Tone charged, "has been not only disregarded, but discouraged, as destructive to the interest of Britain. . . . Even that branch of trade which consists of the manufactory of the raw materials produced on her own soil, is denied to Ireland, and absorbed by England. Her raw hides, and her wool, in the state of yarn, which part of the labor demands many hands, and is not paid one hundreth part of the profit, can only be sent to the English gulph."[42]

Likewise, when Irish nationalists have been tried, the English prosecution has sought to demonstrate that a Wolfe Tone, a Robert Emmet, Padric Pearse, James Connolly, or Roger Casement represented not the Irish people but a foreign power. Granted, when Tone insisted on appearing at his trial wearing the full-dress French military uniform, he put himself at a disadvantage for claiming that his cause was Ireland's and not France's. Nevertheless, to assert that the loyalty of an Irish nationalist to Ireland is in any measure diminished because of an alliance with England's enemy, whether France or Germany, is to fly in the face of all common sense and evidence about the intensity of the nationalist's attachment to the nation.

Nationalism and religion have always been inseparable. Either they will knit together, as they have today in Spain, Israel, South Africa, Iran, or Nicaragua, or they will stand opposed but in their opposition become dependent upon, even imitate, each other. During the French Revolution, for instance, the Roman Catholic Church was unseated from its privileged position, but under the Civil Constitution of the Clergy the churches were turned into civil temples, the Declaration of the Rights of Man and of the Citizen was declared a national catechism, and national rites, hymns, and prayers were introduced. Abbe Raynal claimed that "the state . . . is not made for religion, but religion is made for the state. . . . The state has supremacy in everything."[43]

The Irish nationalist cause is Catholic, and the Orange Unionist cause is Protestant. To each side the negative is as important as the positive: the Irish nationalist anti-British feelings and the Orange anti-Catholic. The Reformation continues to be fought out in Northern Ireland. If some suggest that the real issues in Northern Ireland are not religious, that can be admitted only to the extent that the real issues of the Reformation were not religious either. Since nationalism and religion are so closely tied together, it makes little sense to distinguish between them.

The Unionists, especially the Rev. Ian Paisley, blast Roman Catholicism as the Anti-Christ and call upon their supporters to "Remember 1690" when William of Orange defeated the Catholic Irish at the battle of the Boyne and established a protestant ascendancy. The ascendancy meant the confiscation of Catholic Irish land, legal discrimination against Catholics, and the supremacy of the Protestants who would insist upon English rights and English protection. Irish nationalist resistance to this was not generally understood among the British. "English officials would concede to the Irish," observes historian Patrick O'Farrell, "no principles, no impulses, other than those of treachery and rebelliousness: claims for religious freedom and individual liberty were a mere pretence."[44]

To the British the issue has been political, not religious. Henry VIII's break with Rome turned all Catholics into potential traitors, and when the Inquisition in 1570 found Queen Elizabeth guilty of heresy and excommunicated her, devout Catholics found it impossible to be loyal to the Queen. An act of 1571, in reply, made it high treason to allege that Elizabeth was a heretic or schismatic.[45] Under Cromwell in the next century, while Catholics were tolerated within England, the Irish Catholics suffered massacres at Drogheda and Wexford which have been compared in their savagery to the horrors of the German Thirty Years' War. Cromwell told the Irish that he intended to enforce the Tudor act which made the Mass illegal.[46] Until 1766 Irish Catholics, especially the clergy, were further suspect by the English because the pope continued to recognize the Stuart Pretender to the English throne rather than the Hanoverians.[47] Throughout the seventeenth century and far beyond, the Gunpower Plot of 1605 was used to discredit Catholics.

In 1796, with the wars of the French Revolution, Irish patriots looked to France for liberation. France, however, looked upon Ireland only as a possible conquest and blow at England. In mid-December an armada of thirty-five French ships and 12,000 men evaded the British blockade and arrived at Bantry Bay, County Cork, ready to invade Ireland, establish a friendly but independent Irish republic, and then prepare to conquer England.[48] Wolfe Tone, aboard the flagship, had spent five years organizing the United Irish Society, a forerunner of today's Irish Republican Army (IRA). The aim of the United Irish Society was, in Tone's words, "to subvert the tyranny of our execrable government, to break the connection with England, the never-ending source of all our political evils, and to assert the independence of my country."[49] When Tone had been expelled from Ireland for his organizational activities, he had gone to the United States where he met with and was encouraged by the French minister, who sent him on to

France. The French Directory was, after some delay, persuaded of the worth of Tone's liberation expedition and appointed none other than the commander-in-chief, General Lazare Hoche, to the Irish project. Tone was made a *chef de brigade* and given a French uniform. After reaching Irish shores, however, the armada met with hurricane-force winds, preventing a landing and driving it out to open sea. Again, as with the 1588 Spanish Armada, England escaped an invasion thanks to the weather at sea.

Two years later, in 1798, another French invasion was planned, this one to coincide with an Irish rebellion. But because of French involvement in Egypt and poorly coordinated uprisings in Connaught, Wexford, and Dublin, along with insufficient support, the Irish rebels experienced nothing but failure. Most of the Irish rebellion erupted in May and was crushed by September. In the meantime, at the mouth of the Nile, Admiral Nelson decisively defeated Napoleon. Later, in exile, Napoleon speculated that if he had gone to Ireland instead of Egypt (somewhat like Hitler's second-guessing his decision to move against Russia), he might have defeated England. By mid-October the British intercepted the French fleet heading for Ireland. They captured most of the French; with them was Wolfe Tone, *chef de brigade*.[50]

When he was charged with high treason before the court martial in Dublin a month later, Tone's appearance was not calculated to impress his judges favorably, nor were his words. He was dressed in his French uniform, complete with "a large and fiercely cocked hat, with a broad gold lace, and the tri-coloured cockade, a blue uniform coat, with gold and embroidered collar, and two large gold epaulets, blue pantaloons with gold laced garters at the knees." When asked how he pleaded, Tone replied, "Guilty! for I have never in my life stooped to a prevarication."[51]

His trial became the occasion for Tone not merely to explain his own actions but to level an indictment against the British. "What I have done has been purely from principle and the fullest conviction of its rectitude," Tone claimed. "The favourite object of my life has been the independence of my country, and to that object I have made every sacrifice. . . . The connection of England I have ever considered as the bane of Ireland, and have done everything in my power to break it, and to raise three million of my countrymen to the rank of citizens." Here the court stopped Tone, but, after some discussion, allowed him to continue. Tone did not deny that he sought the assistance of France—hardly, as he stood in the dock wearing his French uniform:

> In my efforts to accomplish the freedom of my country, I never have had recourse to any other than open and manly war. . . . In the glorious race of patriotism, I have pursued the path chalked out by Washington in America,

and Kosciusco in Poland. Like the latter, I have failed to emancipate my country; and, unlike both, I have forfeited my life—I have done my duty, and I have no doubt the Court will do their's [sic]—I have only to add, that a man who has thought and acted as I have done, should be armed against the fear of death.[52]

After receiving the death sentence, Wolfe Tone took his own life before he could be executed.

The Irish nationalist revolutionary tradition had its beginnings in the 1798 rebellion and Wolfe Tone's ideology. Trials of Irish nationalists after Tone's trial often feature what is known as the "Irish speech from the dock." When the 24-year-old Robert Emmet traveled to Europe in 1802 seeking support for another expected uprising in Ireland, he spoke with Napoleon and Talleyrand but returned to Dublin with nothing more than promises from France to help if the rebellion were successful. Although Emmet and a few hundred supporters, dressed in green, began the rebellion, killed the lord chief justice and several others, the Emmet forces were soon in dissarray, their leader arrested. During his trial for treason and after he had been judged guilty, the judge asked Emmet what he had to say about why he should not be sentenced to death. "Why the sentence of the law should not be passed upon me," he replied, "I have nothing to say. Why the sentence which in the public mind is usually attached to that of the law, ought to be reversed, I have much to say."

Emmet then launched into an eloquent refutation of the charge that he conspired to join Ireland to France. His cause was "not for France, but for liberty." He admitted communication with France, but "God forbid that I should see my country under the hands of a foreign power. . . . If the French came as a foreign power, Oh, my countrymen! meet them on the shore with a torch in one hand—a sword in the other—receive them with all the destruction of war—immolate them in their boats before our native soil shall be polluted by a foreign foe." When he proclaimed that his true cause was not France but Ireland, "to effect a separation from England," the judge interrupted Emmet to remind him that he was called upon to tell the court why the death sentence should not be pronounced, but instead "you are making an avowal of dreadful treasons." The judge admonished Emmet: "You should make some better atonement to expiate your own crimes and alleviate the misfortunes you have brought upon your country." Emmet answered that his motive resulted from "an ardent attachment to my country, from a sense of public duty." If he were not permitted to vindicate his cause and character, then, he told the court, "Let it remain in silence—in charitable silence. . . . I am going to my cold grave. I have one request to make. Let there be no inscription upon my tomb. Let no man write my epitaph. . . . Let my character and my motives repose in obscurity and peace, till other times and other men can do them justice; *Then* shall my character be vindicated. *Then* may my epitaph be written."[53]

During the nineteenth century, after the 1801 Act of Union merging Ireland with Great Britain and after the catastrophic famine of the 1840s— which the Irish saw as directly related to the union—the secret Fenian Brotherhood was founded "to keep alive a spirit of hatred to the British Crown and Government."[54] A spy and provocateur, Pierce Nagle, who worked in the editorial offices of the Fenian weekly *The Irish People*, supplied the police with information about the editors. John O'Leary and the other editors were arrested, tried, and convicted in 1865 for treason. The prosecution was based in large part on letters they had received from Irish nationalist zealots. One letter, from a "half-crazed" man named O'Keeffe, urged that "the French exterminated their aristocracy, and every honest revolution must imitate that of France. We must do the same." This led the government to charge that "the operation of this revolution, as it is called, [was] to be commenced by an indiscriminate massacre—by the assassination of all those above the lower classes, including the Roman Catholic clergy, against whom their animosity appears, from their writings, to be especially directed."[55]

In his speech from the dock O'Leary asked the meaning of treason. "Treason is a foul crime. The poet Dante consigned traitors to, I believe, the ninth circle of hell, but what kind of traitors? Traitors against king, against country, against friends and benefactors. England is not my country; I have betrayed no friend, no benefactor." O'Leary pointed out that Algernon Sidney would be a legal traitor because he was convicted by the infamous hanging judge, George Jeffreys. So would Robert Emmet. Yet Jeffreys and the judge who tried Emmet, Lord Norbury, would be loyal men under the law.[56] With his reductio ad absurdum of treason and loyalty, which was absurd to the thinking of an Irish nationalist but probably made good sense to an English nationalist, O'Leary finished his speech and received a sentence of twenty years of penal servitude.

The 1916 Easter Rising in Dublin, another rebellion prompted by an English war in Europe, was put down within a week. Fifteen leaders, including Padraic Pearse, Sean MacDermott, and James Connolly, were arrested, given a hearing before a court martial, and shot. Connolly's statement to the court summarized their position: "Believing that the British Government has no right in Ireland, never had any right in Ireland, and never can have any right in Ireland, the presence in any one generation of Irishmen of even a respectable minority ready to die to affirm that truth makes that government for ever an usurpation and a crime against human progress."[57] Pearse in his statement made an effort to emphasize that their cause was Ireland, not Germany, that they were not German agents financed with German gold:

> I repudiate the assertion of the prosecutor that I sought to aid and abet England's enemy, Germany. Germany is no more to me than England is. . . . My aim was to win Irish freedom; we struck the first blow ourselves but I should have been glad of an ally's aid. I assume I am speaking to Englishmen who value their own freedom, and who profess to be fighting for the freedom of Belgium and Serbia. Believe that we too love freedom and desire it. . . . If you strike us down now we shall rise again and renew the fight. You cannot conquer Ireland; you cannot extinguish the Irish passion for freedom; if our deed has not been sufficient to win freedom then our children will win it by a better deed.[58]

Likewise, when Sir Roger Casement was tried in the Old Bailey for going to Germany and returning to Ireland in a German submarine in time for the Easter rising, he ordered his counsel not to attempt to clear him but rather "to defend and make clear an extreme Irish Nationalist's standpoint—that I wanted to put up a straight fight for Ireland," that he was not an English traitor, not a dreamer, and not a fool, but an Irish patriot. Casement told the jury that "the rebellion was not made in Germany, and that not one penny of German gold went to finance it." He said he had never sold himself to any government, but he always claimed that an Irishman "has no right to fight for any land but Ireland. . . . From the first moment I landed on the Continent until I came home again to Ireland I never asked for nor accepted a single penny of foreign money . . . for only the money of Irishmen."[59] He like the others in 1916 was executed as a traitor.

By itself the Easter Rising did little to attain Irish independence. Few Irish became involved. The nationalst leaders seized the Dublin Post Office and fought valiantly, but the Irish people only watched with interest. What kindled the real rebellion and civil war was the court martial and execution of the Easter Rising leaders. From that followed the formation of the Irish Republican Army and the creation in 1921 of the Free State. What was "a harebrained romantic adventure," as it was called by George Bernard Shaw, was turned by the British trials and executions into a "heroic episode in the struggle for Irish freedom." "Those who were executed," Shaw observed, "accordingly became not only national heroes, but the martyrs whose blood was the seed of the present Irish Free State. . . . Nothing more blindly savage, stupid, and terror-mad could have been devised by England's worst enemies."[60] Within a few weeks after the executions the mood of Ireland changed. Picture postcards of the executed leaders were displayed and copies of the "last and inspiring" speeches were sold on the streets.[61] What the Rising failed to achieve the English court martials and executions clinched.

In each of the Irish nationalist trials the accused, instead of denying the charges, affirmed them and indicted the British with the real wrongdoing: ruling the Irish. From the dock they insisted that they, not the British, represented the Irish people. Whether in fact that was true at the time of their trials is another matter. Tone, Emmet, O'Leary, and the 1916 leaders presumed to speak for the Irish people. The trial gave each of the nationalists a retrospective mantle of authority to speak in the name of the Irish nation. Whether or not they genuinely possessed that authority at the time they were tried, they possess it now.

A contrasting strategy is illustrated by the 1980 trial of the Provisional IRA's director of operations, Brian Keenan. The British authorities claimed that his capture was one of the biggest catches ever made by the security forces. Keenan was arrested outside Belfast, flown to London, and tried in the Old Bailey for conspiracy in a series of Provo IRA terrorist activities in London. These included a series of bombings and murders which took the lives of eight people in 1976, including a police officer who was trying to defuse a bomb, a cancer researcher, Prof. Gordon Hamilton-Fairley, and the editor of the *Guinness Book of World Records*, Ross McWhirter.[62] Most of the bombing victims were random, but McWhirter was shot when he answered his doorbell shortly after he had announced that he would offer a substantial reward for the capture of the persons responsible for the wave of bombings.

Four Provo IRA men, the Balcombe Street-Four, were tried and convicted for the actual bombings and murders. Keenan was charged with being the architect of the terror. A diary found on Keenan when he was arrested, which included phone numbers of terrorist groups in the Middle East and Japan as well as Libyan bank notes torn in half, coded messages and false identity papers, could have proved his high position in the Provos. It was not, however, allowed to be presented as evidence. The judge did allow the introduction of fingerprint evidence which connected Keenan with the three apartments where the bombs were constructed. The judge also allowed the introduction of several crossword puzzle solutions, also found in the apartments, which matched Keenan's handwriting. In a statement from the dock Keenan maintained that "to me all the evidence is circumstantial. I'm not part of any conspiracy to cause explosions." He told the jury that while in London to buy a taxi to take back to Belfast he had visited friends not knowing they were terrorists.[63] Although the jury learned nothing of his IRA career, Keenan was convicted and sentenced to eighteen years in prison. Unlike Tone, Emmet, O'Leary, and the 1916 Irish nationalists, who openly fought the English, Keenan's method was terror. In the courtroom the other nationalists presented stirring speeches which have become part of the Irish nationalist heritage. Emmet's "let no man write my epitaph" is the very stuff of Irish nationalist feeling. Keenan, by contrast, inspired few.

Gandhi

The 1922 trial of Mohandas Gandhi is as classic a nationalist trial as can be found. Gandhi was charged with "an attempt to excite disaffection towards Government . . . to excite political discontent and alienate the people from their allegiance" to His Majesty's Government established by law in India.[64] His offense was writing three articles for *Young India*. In the first, "Tampering wth Loyalty," Gandhi made common cause with two Muslems [Mussulmans], the Ali brothers, who had been charged with sedition. "Only a Mussulman divine can speak for Islam," Gandhi wrote, "but speaking for Hinduism and speaking for nationalism, I have no hesitation in saying, that it is sinful for anyone, either as soldier or civilian, to serve this Government which has proved treacherous to the Mussulmans of India and which has been guilty of the inhumanities of the Punjab." He advised the Indian soldiers in British service to "leave at once."[65]

When Lord Reading said that he was "puzzled and perplexed" by those who commit "flagrant breaches of the law" in order to challenge the government and compel arrest, Gandhi wrote "A Puzzle and Its Solution" to enlighten the noble lord: "We seek arrest because the so-called freedom is slavery. We are challenging the might of this Government because we consider its activity to be wholly evil. We want to overthrow the Government. We want to compel its submission to the people's will. We desire to show that the Government exists to serve the people, not the people the Government."[66]

Gandhi's third offending article which was part of the indictment, titled "Shaking the Manes," was an answer to Lord Birkenhead who reminded Indians that Britain had lost none of its "'hard fibre.'" Gandhi asked: "How can there be any compromise whilst the British Lion continues to shake his gory claws in our faces?" Gandhi told him that the British "'hard fibre' will have to be spent in India in a vain effort to crush the spirit that has risen and that will neither bend nor break." While the Indians might lack "hard fibre," nevertheless, "the rice-eating, puny millions of India seem to have resolved upon achieving their own destiny without any further tutelage and without arms."[67]

Gandhi pleaded guilty, but the prosecutor requested that, in order that the facts be fully known, the trial proceed. The judge agreed to hear each side. Sir J. Strangman, for the crown, documented the articles Gandhi had written, summarizing those which were "preaching disaffection towards the existing government and preparing the country for civil disobedience."

Gandhi, who had a legal education among the finest available and was a barrister who had been admitted to an Inn of Court in London, undertook his own defense. He answered by not only admitting all that the prosecutor had said, but corrected him: "It commenced much earlier." He then set about to "explain why, from a staunch loyalist and co-operator, I have become an uncompromising disaffectionist and non-co-operator."

After describing his life in South Africa and India, giving a strong indictment of British rule in both places, Gandhi outlined his theory of non-cooperation: "non-co-operation with evil is as much a duty as is co-operation with good. But, in the past, non-co-operation has been deliberately expressed in violence to the evil-doer. I am endeavouring to show to my countrymen that violent non-co-operation only multiplies evil and that, as evil can only be sustained by violence, withdrawal of support of evil requires complete abstention from violence. Non-violence implies voluntary submission to the penalty for non-co-operation with evil." He ended his statement by telling the judge that, as such, he could either "resign your post and thus dissociate yourself from evil" or "inflict on me the severest penalty."[68]

In his judgment Judge R. S. Broomfield told Gandhi that "the law is no respecter of persons. Nevertheless, it will be impossible to ignore the fact that you are in a different category from any person I have ever tried or am likely to have to try. It would be impossible to ignore the fact that, in the eyes of millions of your countrymen, you are a great patriot and a great leader." He acknowledged that Gandhi had constantly preached against violence, but he could not understand how Gandhi continued to believe that violence would not be the inevitable consequence of his political teaching. Judge Broomfield said he would follow the case of Ganhadhar Tilak in passing sentence, giving him two years imprisonment on each count, six years total. Gandhi responded by saying he considered it to be "the proudest privilege and honour to be associated" with a patriot such as Tilak.[69] The transcript of Gandhi's trial cannot be read without sensing that it was really the British who were on trial.

The Black Panthers and Angela Davis

Few organizations in American political life have been as flamboyant as the Black Panthers. Few political trials have been so filled with drama as the Panther trials in the late 1960s and early 1970s. The Panthers were nationalists like the Irish nationalists, rather than dissenters, because they saw themselves as representing a distinct people not represented by the government. Unlike Martin Luther King's Southern Christian Leadership Conference, the NAACP, or other civil rights organizations, the Panthers did not seek merely to challenge and correct racial discrimination. They aimed to destroy what they viewed as a White capitalist colonial system dominating Black people in America as severely as any colonial regime ruled India, Ireland, or Africa.

The Black Panther Party Platform and Program, *What We Want, What We Believe*, stated their position in its first article: "We want freedom. We want power to determine the destiny of our Black Community. We believe that black people will not be free until we are able to determine our destiny." The tenth and final article stated that the "major political objective" of the party is a "United Nations-supervised plebiscite to be held throughout the black colony in which only black colonial subjects will be allowed to participate, for the purpose of determining the will of black people as to their national destiny."[70] It is this quest for national destiny that links the Panthers to other nationalists.

A notable characteristic of the Panther trials, in contrast to the Irish nationalists' trials, is how few convictions resulted. The Panthers' reputation was fearsome. Yet, in spite of sensational trials where Panthers were charged with the most serious crimes, only a handful of Panthers were convicted. Most were either found guilty on substantially reduced charges, which amounted to near-acquittals, were set free after a deadlocked jury produced a mistrial, or were found not guilty.

One of the Panther cofounders, Huey Newton, was charged with the murder of an Oakland Patrolman, John Frey, but he was convicted in 1968 of voluntary manslaughter. After serving nearly two years of his sentence, Newton was freed by the California Supreme Court on the ground that the jury had not been properly instructed. He was retried twice, both times in 1971, for the Frey killing. Both the second and third trials ended with a deadlocked jury and a mistrial. After the third trial the charges against Newton were dropped.[71]

The New York Panther Twenty-One (actually thirteen were tried) were indicted for conspiracy to attack a police station, murder policemen, and bomb five department stores. They were found guilty. In another trial three Panthers had been arrested while passengers in a car driven by a fourth, who was an undercover policeman. The three, Alfred Cain, Ricardo DeLeón, and Jerome West, faced their driver in court where he provided all the evidence against them, just as earlier he had provided the car and a map drawn for a hotel robbery. One trial ended in a hung jury, and the second acquitted the three of conspiracy to commit robbery, although it convicted them of unlawful possession of weapons.[72]

Another of the Panther cofounders, Bobby Seale, was tried in New Haven for the murder of Alex Rackley. Earlier Lonnie McLucas had been found guilty of conspiring to murder Rackley, although acquitted on even more serious kidnapping charges. George Sams and Warren Kimbo, who pleaded guilty and testified for the prosecution, were given life sentences for the murder. But the trial of Seale and Erika Huggins for the same crime resulted in a dismissal of the charges after the jury deadlocked.[73]

Panthers in Los Angeles, Detroit, and New Orleans were acquitted in 1971 on charges of murder in attacks on policemen, although convicted of possession of illegal weapons or of assault in two trials while found not guilty in the third.[74]

In two trials related to the Panthers, verdicts of not guilty were returned: the Soledad Brothers' trial for the murder of a prison guard and Angela Davis's trial for supplying weapons in a Marin County kidnapping which resulted in the death of a judge and three others. In all, of seventeen important trials of Black Panthers or nationalists identified with the Panthers, juries returned with full guilty verdicts against only three defendants: against Charles Bursey and Warren Wells in 1969 for a shootout in Oakland and against Mark Holder in 1972 for the murder of Panther Samuel Napier which grew out of a factional feud between the Newton and the Cleaver followers.[75] The Panthers could claim victory in all the rest of the trials.

Murray Kempton, in titling his book about the 1971 New York Panther Twenty-One trial *The Briar Patch*, put his finger on a characteristic of many nationalist political trials. Each side wants to throw the other into the briar patch, yet each gets ensnared in a genuine briar patch in the trial. The New York Panthers were charged with plotting a series of terrorist events: bombing police stations, department stores, railroads, and the Bronx Botanical Gardens, and the murder of police. If all these guerrilla activities had taken place, and not merely been talked about, New York would have been thrown into chaos. But they did not happen. Was an immense plot nipped in the bud? Or was the Panthers' bluff called? Perhaps some of both? The seeds of actual terrorist activities had been planted, but whether they grew faster and larger in the imagination of the police or the Panthers is unclear. The bombing of the 24th and the 44th Precinct Police Stations was a genuine terrorist plot which was put into operation. But because of skillful undercover police work, such as replacing dynamite with an oatmeal-clay mixture, the Panthers' raid on these two police stations was a dud. The trial, which might have concluded with a conviction of those involved in this conspiracy, instead trapped the prosecution. Yet, if the purpose of the prosecution was to break and finish off the Panthers as an organization, perhaps the trial did contribute to this end even though those put on trial were acquitted.

More than two years of proceedings in the New York Panther Twenty-One case, including an eight-month trial which involved six weeks of jury selection and six months of presenting evidence to the jury, all boiled down to less than three hours of jury deliberation (perhaps, after time for lunch and the jury's housekeeping details are subtracted, twenty minutes of deliberation) and a verdict of not guilty repeated 156 times. If the jury had listened to evidence and arguments from October to May, it might seem poor form for them to dispose of it all so quickly in a single afternoon. But, as Murray Kempton observed, "the swiftness of their course was itself an insistence on form, its speed being one point of its affirmation."[76]

The decisive not guilty verdict was not an instance of jury nullification. The jury had not balked at applying the law. Nor did the jury reject the evidence presented to them. Rather, the prosecution in the Panther Twenty-One trial overplayed its hand and drew out the jury's trump.

As Peter Zimroth demonstrates, and as the prosecutor apparently failed to do, the Panther Twenty-One trial involved real crimes with real intended victims. Several of the defendants had planned a coordinated bombing and long-range rifle attack on the 44th Precinct Police Station in the Bronx, the 24th Precinct Police Station in Manhattan, and the Queens Board of Education office, all at 9 P.M. on Friday, January 17, 1969. Dynamite had been placed in the three locations. However, the sticks at the 44th Precinct Station had been switched with phonies so that only a blasting cap exploded. At the 24th Precinct Station the fuse on the phony sticks had been improperly lit. At the Queens school the real dynamite (from a source other than the undercover police) blew a hole in the side of the building. Near the 44th Precinct Station, after some shooting, one Panther (nineteen-year old Joan Bird) was arrested while two men escaped. They left behind a long-range rifle with which they had planned to shoot at the police as they rushed out of the burning building after the explosion.[77] These are crimes, and the Panthers had been caught in the act. That no one had been injured and that property damage had been small is due to clever police work, hardly to a lack of intention or effort on the part of the Panthers. Yet the verdict was clearly *not guilty*.

What went wrong for the prosecution, to put it briefly, was that the Panther Twenty-One trial backfired. As Zimroth, who observed the trial and had come from a background which made him sympathic with the prosecution, concluded:

> And so, after more than two years of fighting, the prosecutor lost the propaganda war he started. He wanted to convince the jurors, and beyond them the

public, that the Black Panther Party was dangerous; that it believed "the only good pig is a dead pig"; that its members shot at cops and blew up buildings; that they "iced" suspected police informants like Alex Rackley; that the Party strove to overthrow the "establishment" as the Algerian rebels had done; that it led the urban guerrilla warfare being waged all over the country; that it symbolized the chaos of radical dissent. He wanted the jurors to see the events charged in the indictment as part of a broader history of violence on the Left.

Instead, by the end of the trial, the prosecutor had convinced most of the jurors not that the defendants were dangerous, but that the District Attorney and Judge were . . . .

These jurors saw the prosecution as part of the history of government repression; and they did not want to be part of that history.[78]

This is hardly to suggest that the defense in the Panther Twenty-One trial was passive. The proceedings before the trial began were notable for disruptions and are used as one of several prime examples in a major study of courtroom disorder. Some of the flavor of these hearings is provided in the following exchange:

The Court: Do the defendants want to enter pleas?

A Defendant: You can take the indictment, you can take the entire Nixon Administration and stick it up your ass. We're not willing to . . . .

Another Defendant: You think we got contempt for your court? You're absolutely right. It's nothing but a joke. It's a class institution that upholds your class. You going to put me in jail? I've been in jail almost a year. You're going to put me in jail, punk.

The Court: Be seated.

A Defendant: You white-haired rascist [sic] pig.

Another Defendant: This is toilet paper.

The Court: And you will be seated, too.

Another Defendant: Why don't you shut up?[79]

Finally, after three weeks of such pretrial hearings and outbursts, Judge Murtagh ordered the defendants out of the courtroom and indefinitely recessed the proceedings, leaving the defendants facing an indefinite stay in jail. The impasse broke when the Supreme Court in *Illinois v. Allen* permitted judges to remove defendants who misbehaved. This decision gave Judge Murtagh the authority to continue the hearings in the absence of the defendants if they had to be removed for disorderly conduct. It worked; the thirteen Panthers agreed to behave in court, and the hearings then progressed toward the trial.[80]

Both sides in the New York Panther Twenty-One (or thirteen) trial played by a political agenda in the case. As Murray Kempton put it, "counsel on all sides would begin with the same misconception: Mr. Phillips thought he was prosecuting the armed revolution and his opponents thought they were defending it. Mr. Phillips thought these were the worst and Mr. Lefcourt, the best, of revolutionaries."[81]

The jurors soon saw that the indictment was inflated beyond the facts, that the government put out what appeared to be hysterical publicity, that the defendants were held on unusually high bail, that the police and their undercover agents had gathered evidence with considerable, perhaps excessive, zeal, and that the prosecutor and judge appeared to be working together. "After hearing all the evidence and everything," a juror said later, "I came to the conclusion myself that the whole thing was a conspiracy to eliminate the Panthers as a whole."[82] Given that perception, which was shared by the other jurors, the defense would have wide latitude to operate from their political agenda. The defense had the tactical advantage, as Murray Kempton put it, "that belongs to the lawyer who had learned that he is not defending the Viet Cong and is opposed by judge and prosecution who go on assuming that they are trying the Viet Cong. The most difficult task in any argument is to convince by hyperbole."[83]

An irony in the Panther Twenty-One trial is that, while the overblown indictment portrayed the defendants as major conspirators in the assault on the White capitalist establishment, a picture which Panther rhetoric encouraged, the facts supported little of it. As their collective autobiography illustrates, they envisioned themselves as the vanguard of the "worldwide people's struggle against the worldwide racist, fascist, capitalistic, greed-filled pigs." Yet they had done next to nothing to initiate the revolutionary upheaval. This was a source of embarassment. As Murray Kempton speculated, for their pride it would have been better "if the defendants would all confess to having done what they had not done rather than let everyone see that they had done so little and, then, their reputation for *badness* restored, try to persuade the jury that it was a fine thing for them to have done what they had not done."[84]

The prosecution, for all of its effort (rather because of it), lost the jury and the trial. But the Panthers, because of the time, money, and energy diverted from their organizational and political activities into the defense effort at the trial, lost the war and were virtually eliminated. Because the two founders, Newton and Seale, were also on trial and their trials were deemed more important than the New York trial, the national Panthers Party did not assist the New York Panther Twenty-One. This contributed to the split between the Newton-Seale and the Cleaver factions, as well as to the murders of Robert Webb, who was loyal to Cleaver, and Samuel Napier, loyal to Newton, by the opposite sides. In the end both factions and all others involved had been caught in a briar patch.

The 1972 trial of Angela Davis parallels the Panther Twenty-One trial. There was, to begin with, a serious crime. In 1970 Jonathan Jackson entered a Marin County courtroom and at gunpoint took hostages, including Judge Haley. In the shootout which followed, Jackson, two San Quentin convicts, and the judge were killed. Angela Davis—a friend of George Jackson, one of the Soledad Brothers and Jonathan's older brother—was arrested and charged with murder, kidnapping, and conspiracy. The link was that the guns Jonathan used were Angela Davis's. The prosecution attempted to convince the jury that Davis had engineered the plot as a means of freeing the Soledad Brothers. "Passionate love" was the motive suggested by the prosecution. Davis's political views, radical in all directions, were not far below the surface in the trial. She was an active Communist, a Black revolutionary, and a militant feminist. At the time of the shootout she was the center of California attention when Governor Reagan attacked her for being a Communist and got her fired from a teaching position in the Philosophy Department at UCLA, an action which earned UCLA the censure of the American Association of University Professors (AAUP). The regents refused to reappoint her because her speeches were "so extreme, so antithetical to the protection of academic freedom and so obviously, deliberately false in several respects as to be inconsistent with the qualifications for appointment to the faculty of the University of California."[85]

If the purpose of the prosecution at her 1972 trial was to prove to the world that Angela Davis was a dangerous person who masterminded the 1970 courthouse shootout, they failed to convince the all-White jury which heard the evidence. They found her not guilty. When she was asked after the trial whether her opinion of the American system of justice had changed, she replied: "No, my opinion is not changed. . . . The very fact that I was acquitted shows not that I had a fair trial, but that I shouldn't have been tried at all."[86]

Conclusion

Questions about representation raised in trials of nationalists reach beyond the answers the trials provide. When, as the Panthers' trials demonstrate, the indictment is broad and ideological, the trial is less likely to suggest a clear answer than when the charges are narrow and singularly criminal. Yet if the focus is circumscribed by specific statutes and rules of evidence, as in the Keenan trial, the broader issue of nationalism may be avoided. Either way, trials of nationalists may become catalysts for political questions, although the opportunity may be missed.

Even if the transcript of a nationalist's trial yields no exchange on the basic question of representation, the trial itself may press the issue in the public's mind and in the judgment of history. The tension built into such trials is between the unity necessary to hold society together and the separate identity required for human dignity. Those who stand with the Romans in the trials of Jesus and the early Christians; with Augustine, the Inquisition, and the Holy Roman Empire in the "correction" of the Donatists, of Joan of Arc, and of Martin Luther; with the British in the trials of Irish nationalists or Gandhi; with the prosecution in the Black Panthers' trials, even with Torquemada; all share a fundamental position which, at least in the abstract, is respectable: the unity of society requires common shared values. As Justice Felix Frankfurter said in his 1940 opinion in the first flag salute case: "The ultimate foundation of a free society is the binding tie of cohesive sentiment."[87] This, at its best, is the core of the prosecution's case in every nationalist trial. It is not always pursued at its best.

Nationalists, on the other hand, do not accept the assumption that the values and the voice of the government represent the values and voice of the whole society. In his 1962 trial for inciting South African workers to strike, Nelson Mandela, a lawyer and leader of the African National Congress (ANC) who is still imprisoned following a 1964 trial, expressed the feelings of all nationalists who are on trial:

> The white man makes all the laws, he drags us before his courts and accuses us, and he sits in judgment over us. In this courtroom I face a white magistrate, I am confronted by a white prosecutor, and I am escorted into the dock by a white orderly. The atmosphere of white domination lurks all around in the courtroom. It reminds me that I am voteless because there is a Parliament in this country that is white-controlled. I am without land because the white minority has taken a lion's share of my country and forced my people to occupy poverty-stricken reserves, overpopulated and overstocked, in which we are ravaged by starvation and disease. These courts are not impartial tribunals dispensing justice but instruments used by the white man to punish those among us who clamor for deliverance from white rule.
>
> Any thinking African in this country is driven continuously to a conflict between his conscience and the law.[88]

This is the nationalist's argument at its best, although not in every such trial is it expressed at its best. What Mandela says is also the nub of the problem each nationalist faces.

Many nationalists have had an experience in the outside before rejoining their nation. When they return to the fold they often become leaders and are arrested and tried for their work in the cause. Gandhi was a barrister at home on Chancery Lane and in the Inns of Court, until he felt the injustice of racial discrimination in British-ruled Natal, South Africa. Wolfe Tone and Padraic Pearse, two more barrister-revolutionaries, along with Sir Roger Casement, all had careers which were, to say the least, nonrevolutionary before they joined the Irish cause and became leaders. Tone was a British soldier, Pearse a reviver of Gaelic language and Irish legends, and Casement a British diplomat. Russell Means, whom we will consider in the next chapter, although born not far from Wounded Knee, was an accountant in Oakland and Cleveland before becoming an AIM leader.

Whatever their personal origins and ties with the nation, nationalists presume to speak for an entire people. Their leadership is dependent on those who follow them and for whom they speak, a reciprocal relationship. Their presumption of this is important. Nationalists who merely reflect the values and political awareness of their nation are seldom put on trial and are generally castigated as betrayers, ironically, by the militant nationalists. Those who run afoul of the law and are tried in nation-shaking cases are the nationalists who, to use James MacGregor Burns's terms, are *transforming* instead of merely *transactional* leaders.[89] While the transactional leaders seek accommodation, the transforming leaders "raise" their followers up and are likely to get into trouble as they do. They might look back only to find that few are following. The Irish nationalists have had that experience more than once. Yet that is precisely when a trial serves a political purpose: creating the very bond with their followers which the nationalists claimed existed from the start. The presumption that they speak for the people is made true because of the trial. One of the planners of the 1916 Easter Rising, Sean MacDermott, who was among those executed immediately after the insurrection failed, observed, "We'll hold Dublin for a week, but we'll save Ireland."[90]

The problem is an old one—the relationship of the part to the whole. Can law and politics establish a bond representative of both the whole and the part? This question will be explored in a detailed investigation of the 1974 Wounded Knee trial in the next chapter. The trial of Dennis Banks and Russell Means provides a clear instance of the tension between the requirements of unity within a democratic society and the demands for national identity and dignity.

Notes

1. See Donald Juel, *Messiah and Temple: The Trial of Jesus in the Gospel of Mark* (Missoula, Mont., Scholars Press, 1977).

2. Oscar Cullmann, *The State in the New Testament* (New York, Charles Scribner's Sons, 1956), pp. 11-13; S. G. F. Brandon, *The Trial of Jesus of Nazareth* (New York, Stein & Day, 1968), Chs. 4-5.
3. Brandon, *Trial of Jesus*, pp. 25-27.
4. *Ibid.*, pp. 28-29; Cullmann, *State in the New Testament*, pp. 9-10.
5. Brandon, *Trial of Jesus*, p. 144; Cullmann, *State in the New Testament*, pp. 15-16.
6. Mark 11.
7. Mark 14:58. Juel suggests that, instead of charging Jesus with magic in claiming to rebuild the Temple in three days, Mark includes this charge against Jesus to emphasize that the new temple is the Christian community and that Jesus as the Messiah will build it. Juel, *Messiah and Temple*, Chs. 5, 10.
8. Mark 14:62.
9. Mark 15:2.
10. Cullmann, *State in the New Testament*, pp. 48-49; Brandon, *Trial of Jesus*, pp. 102-103.
11. W. H. C. Frend, *Martyrdom and Persecution in the Early Church* (Garden City, Doubleday, 1967), p. 352.
12. *Ibid.*, pp. 369-370.
13. Ramsay MacMullen, *Constantine* (New York, Dial Press, 1969), pp. 93-95.
14. Edward H. Flannery, *The Anguish of the Jews: Twenty-three Centuries of Anti-Semitism* (New York, Macmillan, 1965), p. 48.
15. G. G. Willis, *Saint Augustine and the Donatist Controversy* (London, S.P.C.K., 1950), Ch. 1-2; W. H. C. Frend, *The Donatist Church: A Movement of Protest in Roman North Africa* (New York, Oxford, 1952).
16. Philip Schaff, ed., *A Select Library of the Nicene and Post-Nicene Fathers of the Christian Church* (Buffalo, Christian Literature, 1886), Letter 86, Vol. 1, p. 367.
17. *Ibid*, Letter 93, p. 385.
18. "The Correction of the Donatists," *Ibid.*, Vol. 4, p. 635.
19. *Ibid.*, p. 642. See also Letters 93, 173, 208, Vol. 1, pp. 383, 547, 559.
20. See *The City of God*, Bk. 14, 28, and Bk, 19, 14-17.
21. Herbert A. Deane, *The Political and Social Ideas of St. Augustine* (New York, Columbia University Press, 1963), p. 194.
22. *Nicene and Post-Nicene Fathers*, Vol. 1, Letter 93, p. 388.
23. "The Correction of the Donatists," *Ibid.*, Vol. 4, p. 634, 6 37.
24. *Ibid.*, p. 649.
25. J.-J. Rousseau, *The Social Contract*, trans. by G. D. H. Cole (London, Everyman's Library, 1941, originally published 1762), Bk. 4, Ch. 8, p. 117.
26. Edward Gibbon, *The Decline and Fall of the Roman Empire* (New York, Modern Library, n.d., originally published 1776), Vol. 1, Ch. 20, p. 644.
27. G. G. Coulton, *Inquisition and Liberty* (Boston, Beacon Presss, 1938), Ch. 23; Frances Gies, *Joan of Arc: The Legend and the Reality* (New York, Harper, 1981), Chs. 11-12; Marina Warner, *Joan of Arc: The Image of Female Heroism* (New York, Knopf, 1981).
28. W. P. Barrett, *The Trial of Jeanne d'Arc: A Complete Translation of the Text of the original Documents* (London, George Routledge, 1931), pp. 270-279; Albert Bigelow Paine, *Joan of Arc: Maid of France*, 2 vols. (New York, Macmillan, 1925), Vol. 2, Pt. 9, Chs. 1-27.
29. H. C. Lea, *The Inquisition of the Middle Ages: Its Organization and Operation* (New York, Harper Torchbooks, 1963, originally published 1887), p. 152.

30. Henry Kamen, *The Spanish Inquisition* (New York, Mentor, 1965), pp. 22-23.
31. *Ibid.*, pp. 47-48.
32. *Ibid.*, pp. 48-49.
33. *Ibid.*, pp. 37, 148-156.
34. Roland H. Bainton, *The Travail of Religious Liberty* (New York, Harper Torchbooks, 1951), p. 52.
35. Roland H. Bainton, *Here I Stand: A Life of Martin Luther* (New York, Mentor, 1950), Ch. 5.
36. John Dillenberger, ed., *Martin Luther: Selections from His Writings* (Garden City, Anchor Books, 1961), pp. 420-421.
37. Bainton, *Here I Stand*, pp. 143-144.
38. *Ibid.*, Ch. 10.
39. *Ibid.*, p. 147.
40. See Salo Wittmayer Baron, *Modern Nationalism and Religion* (New York, Meridian, 1960), Ch. 1.
41. See Patrick O'Farrell, *Ireland's English Question: Anglo-Irish Relations, 1534-1970* (New York, Schocken Books, 1971); *England and Ireland since 1800* (New York, Oxford University Press, 1975), pp. 29-31.
42. William Theobald Wolfe Tone, *Life of Theobald Wolfe Tone*, 2 vols. (Washington, Gales and Seaton, 1826), Address to the People of Ireland, Vol. 2, p. 299.
43. Quoted by Carleton J. H. Hayes, *Essays on Nationalism* (New York, Macmillan, 1928), p. 101.
44. O'Farrell, *Ireland's English Question*, p. 43.
45. Levy, *Origins of the Fifth Amendment*, pp. 89-90.
46. Christopher Hill, *God's Englishman: Oliver Cromwell and the English Revolution* (New York, Harper Torchbook, 1970), pp. 116-122.
47. O'Farrell, *Ireland's English Question*, p. 46.
48. Thomas Pakenham, *The Year of Liberty: The Story of the Great Irish Rebellion of 1798* (Englewood Cliffs, N. J., Prentice-Hall, 1969).
49. *Dictionary of National Biography*, Vol. 19, p. 951.
50. Pakenham, *Year of Liberty*, pp. 336-338.
51. *State Trials*, Vol. 27, pp. 616-617.
52. *Ibid.*, p. 621.
53. *State Trials*, Vol. 28, p. 1177.
54. O'Farrell, *Ireland's English Question*, p. 139.
55. Malcolm Brown, *The Politics of Irish Literature: From Thomas Davis to W. B. Yeats* (Seattle, University of Washington Press, 1972), p. 187.
56. John O'Leary, *Fenians and Fenianism*, 2 vols. (New York, Barnes & Noble, 1968, originally published 1896), Vol. 2, p. 224.
57. Edward MacLysaght, "Larkin, Connolly, and the Labour Movement," in F. X. Martin, ed., *Leaders and Men of the Easter Rising: Dublin, 1916* (Ithaca, Cornell University Press, 1967), p. 132.
58. Max Caulfield, "The Executions," in Roger McHugh, ed, *Dublin, 1916* (New York, Hawthorn Books, 1966), p. 261.
59. B. L. Reid, *The Lives of Roger Casement* (New Haven, Yale University Press, 1976), pp. 399-400.
60. Quoted in McHugh, *Dublin 1916*, pp. 360-361.
61. Jacqueline Van Voris, *Constance de Markievicz: In the Cause of Ireland* (Amherst, University of Massachusetts Press, 1967), p. 200.

62. *The Guardian*, June 26, 1980, pp. 1, 17; also notes taken during the Keenan trial by the author, June 9-26, 1980.

63. *Ibid.*, June 19, 1980, p. 3; June 20, 1980, p. 4.

64. *The Collected Works of Mahatma Gandhi* (Publications Division, Ministry of Information and Broadcasting, Government of India), Vol. 23, p. 111.

65. *Ibid.*, Vol. 21, p. 221.

66. *Ibid.*, Vol. 22, p. 28.

67. *Ibid.*, pp. 457-458.

68. *Ibid.*, Vol. 23, pp. 114-119.

69. *Ibid.*, pp. 119-120. Tilak had been tried for sedition in 1908. *Dictionary of Indian History* (1972).

70. Sara Blackburn, ed., *White Justice: Black Experience Today in America's Courtrooms* (New York, Harper Colophon, 1977), pp. xxi-xxiv.

71. Huey P. Newton, *Revolutionary Suicide* (New York, Harcourt, Brace, Jovanovich, 1973), Chs. 26, 31; Edward Keating, *Free Huey* (Berkeley, Ramparts Press, 1971); *New York Times*, September 9, 1968, 1:4, June 29, 1971, 14:4; December 10, 1971, 63:4.

72. Blackburn, *White Justice*, Ch. 5; *New York Times*, May 23, 1970, 44:5; September 27, 1970, 72:3.

73. Donald Freed, *Agony in New Haven: The Trial of Bobby Seale, Ericka Huggins, and the Black Panther Party* (New York, Simon & Schuster, 1973); *New York Times*, August 20, 1970, 1:6; August 23, 1970, Sec. 4, p. 4; May 30, Sec. 4, p. 6; Blackburn, *White Justice*, Ch. 6.

74. In Los Angeles Elmer Pratt and twelve others were charged with conspiracy to murder as a result of a police shootout. They were acquitted of the murder conspiracy charge, although eight were found guilty of conspiracy to possess illegal weapons. *New York Times*, December 24, 1971, 14:2. In Detroit twelve Panthers were acquitted of murdering a policeman, although three were convicted of felonious assault. *New York Times*, July 1, 1971, 38:2. Twelve Panthers in New Orleans were found not guilty of attempted murder of a policeman. *New York Times*, August 8, Sec. 4, 3:7.

75. Blackburn, *White Justice*, Chs. 3, 4; *New York Times*, April 14, 1972, 48:6.

76. Murray Kempton, *The Briar Patch: The People of the State of New York v. Lumumba Shaker et al.* (New York, Delta, 1973), p. 278.

77. Peter Zimroth, *Perversions of Justice: The Prosecution and Acquittal of the Panther 21* (New York, Viking, 1974), pp. 6-7.

78. *Ibid.*, p. 397.

79. Norman Dorsen and Leon Friedman, *Disorder in the Court: Report of the Association of the Bar of the City of New York Special Committee on Courtroom Conduct* (New York, Pantheon, 1973), pp. 65-66.

80. Zimroth, *Perversions of Justice*, Ch. 4; Kempton, *Briar Patch*, Ch. 4.

81. Kempton, *Briar Patch*, p. 140.

82. Zimroth, *Perversions of Justice*, p. 396.

83. Kempton, *Briar Patch*, p. 218.

84. *Ibid.*, p. 217.

85. Charles R. Ashman, *The People vs. Angela Davis* (New York, Pinnacle Books, 1972), pp. 24-25.

86. *Ibid.*, p. 158.

87. *Minersville School District v. Gobitis*, 310 U.S. 596 (1940).
88. Quoted by Donald Woods, *Biko* (New York, Paddington Books, 1978), p. 22.
89. James MacGregor Burns, *Leadership* (New York, Harper & Row, 1978), p. 426.
90. Martin, *Leaders and Men of the Easter Rising*, p. 251.

8

The Wounded Knee Trial: A Trial of Nationalists

When about 200 militant Indians took over the tiny settlement of Wounded Knee, South Dakota, for seventy-one days between late February and early May 1973, they proclaimed it a free nation. When 300 federal agents surrounded the occupied town, they designated the situation a terrorist takeover. Everyone agreed that the American Indian Movement (AIM), especially Dennis Banks and Russell Means, led the occupiers. How responsible Banks and Means were for what happened was the theme of their trial a year later. But the story begins earlier.

The full story, naturally, had begun a century before with the conflict between the westward moving settlers and the plains Indians. But the immediate story began in St. Paul, Minnesota, in October 1972, during the presidential campaign when AIM organized the Trail of Broken Treaties, a march to the Washington headquarters of the Bureau of Indian Affairs. The marchers had carefully prepared a list of twenty grievances based on broken treaties. As the group was leaving the BIA building, guards pushed some of the Indians. This scuffle escalated into a seizure of the building by AIM and a week-long occupation that was terminated when the administration agreed to respond to the twenty points. The "response" came in January, but it was in the form of a press release citing Nixon administration accomplishments and promising to make even more advances in the second term. The AIM leaders were outraged.[1]

Another portion of the immediate background involved the killing of two Indians and what many others saw as insensitivity by local officials toward the killings. In both instances AIM led protests. In February 1972, Raymond Yellow Thunder, a young Sioux, had been seized, stripped naked from the waist down, and shoved onto a dance floor in Gordon, Nebraska. He was found dead in a used car lot. Five persons, all White, were charged, not with murder, but with manslaughter.[2] AIM led 300 Sioux to Wounded Knee where the trading post was sacked. A second killing of a Sioux, twenty-year-old Bad Heart Bull, in January 1973, in Buffalo Gap, South Dakota, and the charging of a White suspect with second-degree manslaughter instead of first-degree murder, prompted AIM to hold a protest meeting. Riots broke out during which the Chamber of Commerce building in Custer, South Dakota, was burned to the ground and the courthouse was set afire, the National Guard called in, twenty people injured, and forty arrested.[3]

During the week before the Wounded Knee occupation, public attention on the Pine Ridge Reservation was drawn to impeachment hearings concerning the tribal chairman, Richard Wilson. Gladys Bissonette, one of his accusers, a 56-year-old leader of the Oglala Sioux Civil Rights Organization, charged Wilson with building a "goon squad" of toughs to "terrorize and intimidate the Indians and harass them and beat them," using the goons and the BIA to protect bootleggers. At the impeachment hearing, as Bissonette saw it, Wilson dominated the acting chairman, Vincent Thunderbolt, and intimidated witnesses. The hearing broke up when three council members walked out and the goons and the BIA police rushed in.[4]

As at a meeting of the Third Estate, the 400–500 members of the Oglala Sioux Civil Rights Organization left the tribal government hall and walked to a community building, the Calico Hall. Gladys Bissonette spoke to the crowd: "I told the Indian people that there was nowhere we could turn for help; we could not go to our tribal chairman; we could not go to the BIA superintendent; we couldn't even call into Washington, D. C. any more for any help; the corruption was too great and all our power was in Dick Wilson's hands, so we had to do something."[5] By a show of hands they voted to call in AIM.

On the next night, February 26, nine elderly chiefs and head men made their way to Calico Hall to decide whether AIM should be invited in. At this second meeting, also a gathering of 500, the chiefs and head men withdrew to a basement room for their decision. When they returned upstairs after an hour, Chief Fools Crow announced that they had come to the decision that AIM should be asked to give its support. Russell Means, who was an Oglala Sioux and was at the Calico Hall meeting, "did not have a choice," according to Bissonette, "he had no alternative but to listen to the chiefs. We went back to our chiefs because no one listened to us."[6]

A third meeting, this one even larger, about 600 participants, was held the next day. Means introduced Dennis Banks, who was a Chippewa from Minnesota, and Chief Fools Crow welcomed him, urging him to stay and help. After a pow-wow, Vern Long of the Oglala Sioux Civil Rights Organization suggested that a larger meeting place was needed, perhaps the Porcupine community hall. The journey from Pine Ridge to Porcupine, about fifteen miles, would take the caravan of cars through Wounded Knee.

Occupation of Wounded Knee

When and how the decision was made to stop and take over the village of Wounded Knee is unclear, but the residents who were taken hostage testified about the circumstances. Agnes Gildersleeve, a seventy-year-old Chippewa who grew up in Minnesota and married a White trader, had operated the trading post in Wounded Knee with her husband since 1934. Next to the general store/trading post they had built a museum for Indian artifacts. On February 27, she told the court, everything was normal, except that two cameramen sat around the trading post most of the day and left when it was locked up at 6 P.M. This suggests, naturally, that AIM had planned to take over and had tipped off the press. In the evening she saw the caravan arrive and exclaimed, "My God, AIM is here again."[7]

Mrs. Gildersleeve watched from her front window as the street lights and gasoline pump lights were shot out by those arriving with the caravan and as guns, groceries, and other articles were carried out of the trading post across the road from her home. She turned out the lights, got down on the floor, crawled into the bedroom, and phoned the BIA, the FBI, the U.S. marshals, and the fire departments of nearby Gordon and Rushville, Nebraska. Two hours had passed but no help had arrived when someone with a gun came to the door and announced: "Regard yourselves as hostages and political prisoners."[8]

Father Paul Manhart saw the caravan arrive. Manhart, priest at Sacred Heart Catholic Church on the hill near the trading post, had been on the Pine Ridge Reservation since 1952. Five young men drove up to the church and one approached Fr. Manhart, who was outside the church. "I greeted him, and he said nothing," Fr. Manhart related. "Almost at that very moment the front door of the church was opened . . . [by] a young man who stood rather tall carrying a large shotgun." After they all went into the church, Russell Means arrived. "I said to him, 'Russell, do you know that this is a sacred place that you're in?'. . . . He said, 'I've heard enough of that sort of stuff.'"[9] Fr. Manhart was tied up and taken to the church balcony where he spent the night. In the morning he was taken to the Gildersleeve home which served as a gathering place for the eleven hostages. Manhart later reported that Dennis Banks told them they should not consider themselves hostages, perhaps political prisoners, perhaps not even that, and they should feel free to leave at any time they wanted. Since they lived in Wounded Knee, they refused to leave.[10]

During the day following the takeover, some 100 federal agents surrounded Wounded Knee, closing it off. Gunfire was exchanged. The seige was on. Discussions between AIM and the government began when South Dakota senators George McGovern and James Abourezk arrived and received a list of demands, among which were that the Senate Foreign Relations Committee investigate the election of Oglala Sioux officials and consider the details of some 371 broken treaties. Federal officials replied that they would negotiate only their terms of surrender. Negotiations, nevertheless, did begin. AIM demanded that the Tribal Council and Richard Wilson be suspended and new tribal elections be held. The Interior Department responded that such a suspension would threaten the basic political structure established by the Indian Reorganization Act in 1934. That was the exact consequence the AIM leaders desired. Russell Means proclaimed secession of Wounded Knee from the United States and announced that any foreign official representing a foreign power, especially the United States, would be regarded as a war agent.[11]

Members of the Oglala Sioux Tribal Council and Richard Wilson attacked the ministers from the National Council of Churches, who had come as mediators, for their "aiding and abetting the criminals in Wounded Knee."[12] Throughout the occupation and seige of Wounded Knee, Wilson was vituperative: working to prevent food from entering, criticizing governmental inaction, and calling upon the Justice Department to end negotiations so that Wounded Knee could be taken by force.

The confrontation broke into fierce fighting several times, especially at the end of March and in mid-April. Frank Clearwater, an Apache who had come to join the militants, was shot April 17 and died a week later. His burial became a major issue when the Tribal Council refused permission for him, because he was non-Sioux, to be buried on the reservation. The heated dispute was resolved when Leonard Crow Dog, a Sioux medicine man, offered to have Clearwater buried in his family plot.[13] Louis Lamont, a Sioux from the Pine Ridge Reservation, was shot and killed in an April 27 exchange of gunfire. U.S. Marshal Lloyd Grimm was wounded seriously enough to remain paralyzed from the waist down. FBI agent Curtis Fitzgerald was shot but less seriously wounded, and we do not know how many Indians were wounded in the gunfights.

Indictment and Trial Beginnings

Russell Means and Dennis Banks were indicted for burglary of the Wounded Knee Trading Post; theft of the Gildersleeves' 1970 Dodge; assault with a gun against FBI agent Joanne Pierce; aiding and abetting the assault against FBI special agent Curtis Fitzgerald and U.S. Marshal Lloyd Grimm; obstructing, impeding, and interfering with U.S. marshals and the FBI by blocking roads, placing armed guards at roadblocks, and constructing trenches and bunkers; unlawfully possessing firearms and Molotov cocktails; and finally, conspiring with others to do all of the above and much more. The conspiracy charge repeated the substantive charges and added such matters as the seizing of the Sacred Heart Catholic Church, homes, and trailers which were used by the occupiers for sleeping and eating. The overt acts necessary to prove the existence of a conspiracy included driving a caravan from Calico to Wounded Knee and giving the government a list of demands.[14]

The trial began January 8, 1974, in Federal Courtroom Number 3 in St. Paul, Minnesota, with Judge Fred Nichol from the Western District of South Dakota presiding. The trial was moved from South Dakota because potential jury members there had more knowledge of and possible bias about the case than Minnesotans. The defense team was headed by William Kunstler, who had been an attorney for Martin Luther King, the Freedom Riders, Stokely Carmichael, Adam Clayton Powell, the Berrigan brothers, and, of course, the Chicago Seven. Another nationally known lawyer, Mark Lane, who had written *Rush to Judgment* in criticism of the Warren Report on President Kennedy's assassination, joined Kunstler and Kenneth Tilsen of St. Paul, a leading civil rights/civil liberties lawyer in Minnesota, as attorneys for Russell Means. Douglas Hall of Minneapolis, a civil rights lawyer who had worked for Minnesota Indians in earlier cases, was joined by Larry Leventhal, also of Minneapolis, and Indian lawyer Ramon Roubideaux of Rapid City, to represent Dennis Banks. The United States was represented by William Clayton, the District Attorney for South Dakota, R. D. Hurd and David Gienapp, the assistant U.S. attorneys, and Earl Kaplan from the Justice Department. Hurd did most of the courtroom work.

After eighteen days (January 8 to February 5) of questioning 133 prospective jurors, a jury was in place and the trial could begin. The jury was relatively young and composed of nine women and three men. (See Appendix on jury selection.) No one thought the trial would last until mid-September, although it was expected to take several months. Before the end of the more than 100-day trial, considerably longer than the occupation itself, the jury would hear the testimony of ninety-four witnesses and the 21,765-page transcript would fill 118 volumes. After all the testimony and arguments were presented, after Judge Nichol had presented an 82-point instruction to the jury, and after the jury had deliberated for more than eight hours, the judge delivered a one-hour blistering rebuke to the FBI and the Justice Department for their conduct and admonished the prosecution lawyers for their part in deceiving the court. He then dismissed all the charges against Means and Banks, excused the jury, and adjourned court.

Opening Statements

The opening statements on February 12 illustrate two opposing attitudes toward the law. R. D. Hurd told the jury that the government would present evidence showing Means and Banks wanted to attract public attention to their grievances, make demands upon, and extort confessions from the United States. To accomplish these aims they used arms to seize the village of Wounded Knee; broke into the trading post, looting it, the post office, and the Catholic church; forced their way into private homes driving the residents out, and shot at law enforcement officials and private citizens. Hurd quoted the AIM leaders as saying that there were only two options open for the United States at Wounded Knee: either "wipe out all of the old people, women, children, and men by shooting and attacking us" or negotiate the AIM demands.[15]

By contrast, Russell Means, who along with Dennis Banks opened for the defense, set a distinctly different mood in his opening statement. He began with a greeting, "Hau mi tok pi," and explained that he was a Lakota, that the word *Sioux* is French meaning "cut throat," and that *Lakota* in their own language means "allies." He told the jury that the defense would produce evidence showing that the real case was not the United States v. Russell Means and Dennis Banks but in fact the United States v. the Oglala Lakota and all Indian people. Means, like many defendants in political trials, reversed the indictment, indicting the government, especially the Interior Department, the BIA, and the FBI, for harassing and intimidating Indians, dominating the tribal government under the heel of the BIA, and forcing Indians to go underground in order to maintain their traditional religion. The Oglala Lakota, he maintained, have always lived with a communal government, respecting traditional chiefs and head men, but the BIA and their police based in the town of Pine Ridge are a puppet government which in no way represents the people of the reservation. The United States, he charged, is "in a concerted effort and conspiracy to destroy our culture."[16]

Means gave the jury a lengthy portrayal of Indian life and the differences between the value system the jury knows and the Indian value system. "You will find out that Indian people have respect for our brother's vision. We do not have missionaries to change Crows to Siouxs."[17] The core of the value system is the belief that "all living things come from our sacred mother earth—green things, winged things, four-leggeds, things that crawl and swim, and of course two-leggeds—all are related and have to treat one another with the respect and reverence that we would our own blood relatives." We, the two-leggeds, are the weakest because "we have no direction." We have built our civilization to compensate for what the green things, the eagle, dove, raccoon, spider, and the snake have. A second essential to the value system is the knowledge "we knew eons before Christopher Columbus got lost," that everything is round: the stars, sun, moon, trees, you and

I, and those things held sacred—the drum, the sweat lodge, and the sacred pipe.[18]

Means continued, drawing the attention of the jury to the circumstances of the 1868 Treaty which, he claimed, in this case the government was violating, in spite of treaties having legal status equal to the Constitution. He related how he and others had gone to the U.S. attorney's office in November 1972 and asked for intervention in the tribal government because the tribal court had issued restraining orders preventing Means from attending meetings and religious events or any gathering of more than three people, a clear violation of the First Amendment. But the Attorney, William Clayton, present in court after having just delivered one of the opening statements for the government, had responded that this was an internal matter for the tribe. All their letters to the president and Congress about the deprecation of rights on the reservation went unanswered.[19]

To the Indian male, Means continued in his opening statement, there are only five options for expressing his manhood: participate in athletics; put on a uniform and join the service; grab the bottle; mistreat his wife; or cut his hair, put on a tie, and "become a facsimile of the white man." Means mentioned that he had taken the latter course earlier, but in the Lakota way if a man cuts his hair it means he is in mourning. "With cut hair I was mistaken for a Chicano, Hawaiian, Pakistanian, everything but an American Indian. I am proud to be Lakota, and when I walk down the street, I want people to know I am Indian." Now, he asserted, there was another option for Indians, the Lakota way, AIM.[20]

In the final portion of his opening presentation Means told about the Wounded Knee occupation. The trading post, he charged, had been operating for twelve years illegally, without a license, keeping people on the reservation in economic bondage through the trader system, and violating the Truth in Lending Act, usury laws, and postal regulations. As for the FBI agents and U.S. marshals, they had been illegally invited to the reservation by Richard Wilson without consent of the tribal council. The BIA and Wilson's tribal government were corrupt, Means contended. As an example of corruption, Means cited a man who had worked in the realty division of the BIA for twenty-three years and now, together with his children, was the largest landowner on the reservation. Traders and government employees have acquired land illegally, but the Indian people do not have the right to make decisions concerning their own land. While the Indians had lived up to the 1868 Treaty, AIM by taking over Wounded Knee was asking the government to live up to its part. Means compared AIM with the early Christian movement and with the early days of the labor movement. The occupation was not the work of outside agitators but of Oglala.

The Oglala people called in AIM after having "the door slammed in our face" by the tribal council, the BIA, federal judge, and the U.S. attorney. Means concluded by quoting Chief Joseph: "Give me the right to choose my own teachers; give me the right to practice a religion of my fathers; give me the right to travel and come and go as I please, and do business with whom I please; give me the right to follow the ways of my fathers, and I will obey every law or submit to the penalty."[21]

The only objection the prosecution made to the opening statement by Means came at its completion when Kunstler embraced and patted him on the back. Out of the presence of the jury Hurd wanted the record to show that the gesture was "inappropriate behavior for an attorney in the courtroom." Lane wanted the record to show that Kunstler did not rise rapidly or step forward and expressed the opinion that it was a natural reaction.[22]

Dennis Banks's opening statement, by comparison, precipitated acrimony. He began by telling the jury that the reason for a change of venue to Minnesota was, as it had been put by Judge Nichol, that the people of South Dakota "would rather line us up and shoot us all dead."

Court: Now, I never said that I felt that was . . .

Banks: One of the reasons we asked for the change of venue . . .

Court: Wait a minute, Mr. Banks . . .

Banks: Was because the prosecutions from South Dakota . . .

Court: Mr. Banks, I'm going to ask the marshals . . .

Banks: who have never seen . . .

Court: Mr. Banks. Marshall, will you take him and sit him down. Now Mr. Banks if you want to make an opening statement under the same rules as Mr. Means did, you may, but I'm not going to permit you to make an opening statement of this nature.

During a conference at the bench Judge Nichol told the defense that Banks was misquoting him and that the change of venue has nothing to do with the defendants' guilt or innocence. He sustained the prosecution's objection.[23]

A few minutes later Banks claimed that the BIA failed to respond to the request by the family of Raymond Yellow Thunder that his death in Gordon, Nebraska, be investigated. William Clayton objected for the prosecution.

Court: "Yes, I think you have been very patient, Mr. Clayton, in not objecting before." Lane responded that everything Banks had said would be presented, but Judge Nichol replied that nothing to do with Gordon, Nebraska, would be received as evidence. Lane argued that the defense would show how Banks became involved in the affairs of the Oglala Sioux, but Judge Nichol admonished him, "I don't want to sit here and listen to another argument. Please sit down."

Lane: Except the Court . . .

Court: Mr. Lane, I'm going to have you removed . . . if you keep on taking exceptions to my rulings.

When Lane and Kunstler objected, Judge Nichol had marshals remove them, called a recess, and met the attorneys in his chambers. When everyone returned to the courtroom the Judge explained to the jury that in chambers he had learned that Lane was taking exception not to him but to Clayton's manner of objecting to Banks. "I guess I wasn't listening very carefully."[24] In spite of the lucidity and and eloquence of Russell Means, the press coverage of the first day of argument stressed, nearly exclusively, the courtroom skirmishes, with such headlines as "Lawyers Ousted at Wounded Knee Trial."[25]

Government Witnesses

Although Means and Banks spent more than twice the amount of time that the prosecution did in opening statements, the government on February 12 began testimony which took ninety-eight days to unfold, while the defense called witnesses and rested its case all in three days. The lead-off prosecution witnesses were two BIA clerks who brought in tribal records to show that Dennis Banks was of ¾ Indian blood and enrolled with the Chippewa tribe, while Means was of $^{15}/_{32}$ Indian Blood and enrolled with the Oglala Sioux.[26] The prosecution seemed to be off to a slow start.

Within the first week the government called two FBI agents who were not of Indian blood but pretended to be: Agent Stanley Keel (alias "Richard Roundtree") and Agent Charles Stephenson (alias "Charles Lightfoot") who had infiltrated AIM meetings. A week before the Wounded Knee occupation had begun, Keel and Stephenson were assigned by the FBI to conduct surveillance of AIM by posing as genuinely interested Indians. Dressed in rough clothes, driving an old and dirty car in poor running condition, and holding South Dakota drivers' permits, Social Security cards, and Air Force discharge papers all falsely made out in their assumed Indian names, they went to the Mother Butler Center in Rapid City where they met Banks, Means, and Vernon Bellecourt. Stephenson told the AIM leaders that he and his friend had recently been discharged from the military after having been in Vietnam and were bumming around the country. "Well, you fought one war," Bellecourt responded. "Now you have one more war to fight for your people." When Stephenson inquired, "We would like to support AIM. How can we help in the support?" Bellecourt replied, "Well, I just told you."[27]

The conversation between the AIM leaders and the FBI agents disguised as Indians turned to the plans AIM had, as Stephenson put it, that "50 or 60 AIM individuals would go to Pine Ridges to observe the impeachment against Wilson, the current chief of the Oglala Sioux." AIM, he said, had been invited for the anticipated victory celebration and would assist in jailing U.S. marshals and other federal officials on the reservations once Wilson was deposed. Over 2,000 Indians on the reservation, he was told, were waiting the AIM call.

Note should be taken that Stephenson employed FBI bureaucratic jargon in his testimony, for instance, "AIM individuals," and how he revealed an appalling ignorance of the situation a full year later by referring in his testimony to Wilson as the Oglala "chief." While he might have dropped the jargon during his surreptitious activities, one wonders how he could carry on a conversation of any length with the three AIM leaders when he thought that Wilson was a chief. Even more surprising is that a year later, after all the Wounded Knee events, he continued to think Wilson was a chief.

When the priest of the Sacred Heart Catholic Church in Wounded Knee, Father Paul Manhart, testified, he was engaged by Kunstler during cross-examination in a classic exchange over the nature of religion and the church. In Kunstler's questions we can see the rational lawyer viewing religion as ideology and the church as an arm of a dominant culture, while in Fr. Manhart's answers we find a priest believing religion to be a mystery and the church an institution needed and loved by the people in whose midst it lives.

Q.[Kunstler] Is there a feeling among some Indians on the Pine Ridge Reservation that they would prefer the traditional Indian religion to any non-Indian religion?

A. [Manhart] What is known as the traditional religion is commonly felt and thought to be consistent enough with the Christian religion as to be integrated with it, some of it. . . .

Q. Are there some who don't want an integration of these religious concepts, who want their own traditional Indian religion, without any embracement by other religions?

A. I cannot state for another religion exactly their position. . . . The general thinking of the Indian people, and particularly those who are strong in their knowledge of the past, the traditional, [is] that there is a reconciliation somehow between what they know as real solid traditional religion and the Christian faith.... [They are] able and willing to accept that as a proposition, but this is speaking in terms of integration, not antagonism....

Q. Is one of your duties to attempt to convert Indians to Catholicism?

A. I don't understand ... can't answer question when based upon my convincing anybody.... Half of the people on the Pine Ridge Reservation are Catholic, and my involvement is deeply with them. Now as far as describing some sort of convincing technique in my mind as a missionary, this does not make sense.... [It is] too much for me to answer.... As a priest, as a minister of Christ, I am interested in sharing with others what I have. Now if you describe that as conversion, all right.

Q. Do you persuade Indians?

A. Nobody becomes a Christian by persuasion. That is the reason I cannot answer your question.

Q. Is it conversion from an ecclesiastical point of view?

A. It rests upon sharing, not trying to convince. It is a work of the grace of God, whatever that change is that takes place which we are defining as conversion and that work, that is God's work, not my work.

Q. Is not one of those functions [as a priest] to assist in or assist non-Christian Indians where the soil is ripe?

A. To assist?

Q. Coming into the Catholic Church?

A. To assist anybody.

Q. I know that, but I am limiting the question to non-Christian Indians.

A. In Wounded Knee? In Wounded Knee I don't know any who are non-Christian Indians.

Q. Is it your testimony that everybody in Wounded Knee is a Christian? Every Indian living within the boundry of that hamlet?

A. Very nearly all, yes.

Q. Are there some who are not?

A. That I don't know how to verify exactly.

Q. Well, how do you verify those who are Christians outside of the ones who attend Sacred Heart?

A. Well, we know a very large proportion are Catholics and Episcopalian. That is almost all of them. Then there are a few Presbyterians; there are a few Body of Christ which are Christians. There are a few Native Americans, and I would call them Christians. I don't know who else I can find there.

Q. Let me put it this way. Have you yourself officiated in any conversion ceremonies while you have been on the Pine Ridge Reservation of Indians?

A. I assist in no conversions. Only God assists in that.

Q. I use the term officiate.

A. If I celebrate it, that is a different thing.

Q. I will use the term celebrate. Have you celebrated the conversion of non-Christian Indians on the Pine Ridge Reservation during your pastorate?

A. Not that I can recall.

Q. Never once?

A. Some were already of another denomination. I have assisted some of them into communion with the church.

Kunstler then turned to questions about the Sun Dance ceremony, which Father Manhart said the church did not oppose; "we favor the good that is there and foster it and develop it." Father Manhart was asked about the Indian drum and the pow-wow, and he agreed that they are parallel to Christian concepts. Kunstler began a line of questioning into whether Father Manhart considered Rose Shot legally married to Ben White Butterfly. He did not. He was asked whether he knew they were married by an Indian ceremony. "I know of no celebration of that union that way."

Q. Do you believe Rose Shot and Ben White Butterfly are living in any form of sin?

A. That's between themselves and God.[28]

The most effective prosecution witness was not from the multitude of BIA officials or FBI agents, who heaped testimony upon weary testimony, but from Agnes Gildersleeve, who with her husband had run the trading post in Wounded Knee for nearly forty years. After she described in vivid terms what the occupation had meant for the residents of Wounded Knee, who had seen the caravan arrive, the trading post and museum looted, and AIM members take over their homes, she told how she had confronted Banks with the question: "Why did you attack these innocent people?" According to Gildersleeve, Banks replied, "You had the food, you had the ammunition; we needed it, and we took it."

Hurd: Did he say anything else at that time you recall?

Gildersleeve: Well, I was crying around about the Trading Post and he said, what are you crying about a few groceries for? Banks told her that she had undone all the good she had done before by telling senators McGovern and Abourezk that she was still a hostage.

Hurd: Did Banks or Means tell you that because of what you had done you would have to do anything else?

Gildersleeve: Go to the checkpoint and talk to Mr. Clayton, tell him we were no longer hostages.

Hurd: After they told you you were no longer a hostage, did you leave Wounded
    Knee?

Gildersleeve: "No."

When Hurd asked her why, she said that she "wanted to save what was left;
our little home, that's all we had left. They had taken everything else; the
store, the museum, and they were started on the garage where we had put
all our savings of things all through the years, and we had to store them
there, and they were started on that."[29]

In a conference at the bench Kunstler pointed out to Judge Nichol that
the Gildersleeves had been operating without a license, violating both
criminal and civil statutes. Judge Nichol asked, "You mean if I don't have a
license on my home and I don't pay taxes on my home, somebody could
come in and loot it?" Kunstler responded, "In the regulation it states that
without a license the goods which they are selling shall be forfeited to the
Indians." Hurd pointed out that this was a matter of law for the court, not
the jury, and Judge Nichol agreed that it should be outside the hearing of
the jury.[30]

In cross-examination Mrs. Gildersleeve claimed that she was not prejudiced against AIM, "only what they stand for—destruction and razing,
rioting and things like that." When Kunstler asked her if she remembered
accusing AIM of being a Communist organization, she replied, "Yes, sir.
Their gaurd told us that they adopted communist tactics, Chinese tactics
and Negro tactics, and that composes AIM."

Kunstler inquired about a letter she had written to a congressman, telling him that AIM indoctrinated young Indians "so there would be no living
with them," that AIM had set the Sioux back fifty years, and that "before
AIM ever came to the Reservation we all lived peacefully, happily; children
were all going to school; Indians were going to and from their work, getting
paid regularly and living very well like any other community." She admitted that was what she had written: "Yes, . . . I just felt sorry for the local
Indians that had to readjust their lives after AIM came in."[31]

The progress of the trial was sidetracked between mid-March and mid-
April for an extensive evidentiary hearing, without the jury, on a defense
motion to dismiss the indictments because, as they learned, the FBI had
secretly monitored conversations on a Wounded Knee telephone during
the takeover. The director of the Minnesota and Dakotas division of the
FBI, Joseph Trimbach, knew about such monitoring, but the FBI had failed
to comply with Judge Nichol's discovery order to make evidence available
to the defense. In addition, the U.S. marshals denied that they had made
logs of intercepted radio messages, only to have them surface during testimony. Aerial photos were not turned over until it was proved that they

existed. Various other pieces of evidence, letters, and documents were not produced by the prosecution.

The defense argued that just as Judge Matthew Byrne had terminated the Daniel Ellsberg trial, Judge Nichol should dismiss this trial because of general misconduct and dishonesty. Although Judge Nichol refused to grant the defense motion, he characterized the behavior of the FBI as "negligent at best," but he could not attribute to them a purposeful intent to obstruct the judicial process. Without dismissing the case, because that would have been the last resort, Judge Nichol said he had come to the brink of dismissal and admonished the government "that this court will continue to be acutely aware of its compliance, or lack thereof, with this court's discovery order and with the rules of law."[32] In May, two months before the Supreme Court handed down its decision in *United States v. Nixon*, which led to Nixon's resignation, Judge Nichol, at the request of the defense, signed a subpoena for the White House to deliver any tapes containing conversations which might be related to the Wounded Knee case. Although the issue dragged on for months, the tapes never came.[33]

Defense Witnesses

In contrast to the cavalcade of witnesses brought forth by the prosecution, the defense called only five and did it in three days. The first was writer and lawyer Vine Deloria, author of *Custer Died for Your Sins*, who was currently writing a study of Indian treaties (*Behind the Trail of Broken Treaties*). He was a Standing Rock Sioux from North Dakota who had grown up on the Pine Ridge Reservation between 1933 and 1951. After he told the jury about the "radical difference" between the way Indians look at the world and the way non-Indians do and about the Indians' use of humor as a means of avoiding tragedy, he talked about the problem of stereotyping minorities in a nation of large technology and instantaneous communication.

Defense attorney Larry Leventhal then asked Deloria if the Sioux people were generally familiar with the 1868 Treaty, bringing an objection by Hurd which was sustained by Judge Nichol. Leventhal then tried a slightly different question: Did Deloria in conversation find the Sioux people were generally familiar with the 1868 Treaty? Yes, he answered, some were intimately familiar with it, while others had a general knowledge of the oral tradition to the effect that the government had not kept the treaty. Judge Nichol allowed the 1868 Treaty to be introduced as a defense exhibit, which introduced a lengthy argument, with the jury and Deloria excused over the meaning of the treaty and its relevance for the trial. Judge Nichol regarded the motivation of the defendants. When Deloria was back on the witness stand, in spite of frequent objections by Hurd sustained by Judge Nichol, he was allowed to tell how the Sioux people understood the 1868 Treaty. He told of an "overwhelming consensus" of Indians who "take it literally," understanding that it means what it says, considering it a sacred document with its interpretation a religious issue.[34]

Dee Brown, the author of the mostly widely read recent book about Indians, *Bury My Heart at Wounded Knee,* was the second defense witness. When the questioning by Kunstler turned to the 1868 Treaty, Hurd, predictably, was on his feet with objections. Judge Nichol ruled that questions about the opinions held concerning the treaty would be permitted. This allowed Kunstler to bring Brown through a series of questions in which the historian gave his judgment that when the Indians signed a treaty it "was a holy thing, [which] meant we will not break the treaty." He mentioned that the federal government "violated almost all of the treaties and still is violating all of the treaties that today's activities would impinge upon." Hurd instantly moved to strike the portion "still is violating" and was sustained by Judge Nichol. Brown was allowed, however, to give examples of how Indians tried to bring the federal government's attention to the facts of the violations: they wrote letters, which went unanswered; they went to Washington, but were ignored; and when they used other than normal channels, such as forcefully confining an agent to his own house, the military was brought in against them.

When Kunstler started questions about massacres, Hurd raised objections that were sustained. On the ground that Brown was an expert, Judge Nichol did allow Kunstler to ask what effect massacres at Wounded Knee and Sand Creek had on Indians. Brown replied that there was a "path of destruction across the West, one massacre following another to forty or fifty years" endangering the very survival of the Indian peoples. When Kunstler inquired whether the fear of massacre persisted to that day, Brown responded that psychology was not his field, although he admitted that while talking about history with Indians the topic did come up. He had noticed a change of attitude: "When I began to meet Indians forty years ago, most did not want to be known as Indians. Today almost all Indians are proud to be Indians."[35]

In cross-examination, Hurd revealed some surprising gaps in Brown's knowledge of Indian history. Asked if he was aware that since the 1920s there had been a special place in the judicial branch for Indian claims and that between 1920 and 1946 the Sioux filed eleven claims, Brown replied, "No, I didn't know that."

Hurd asked if he was aware of a new avenue since 1946, the Indian Claims Commission.

A. No, sir, I'm a historian of the 19th century.

Q. In other words, you don't know what has been done in the 20th century, of avenues opened up for Indians to satisfy grievances under claims?

A. No, sir.

Q. You don't know at present that there are seven pending dockets before the Indian Claims Commission involving the Sioux that haven't been decided yet?

A. No.

Q. Your opinion that the United States failed to live up to treaties is based on what took place prior to 1900?

A. Well, I know that most of South Dakota does not belong to the Lakota Indians.

Q. Are you aware these treaties were changed at numerous times by subsequent agreements—between Indians or by Acts of Congress after 1900?

A. I know nothing about the laws after 1900.

Q. In order to say that at the present time treaties are not being honored, you would have to say that's based upon what you know about what occurred prior to 1900?

A. Yes.

Q. You are not aware of various programs and funding that Congress made for tribes in effort to fulfill the 1868 Treaty in the last twenty-five years?

A. Not in detail, no.

Hurd then turned the questions in a direction which, if he wanted to keep the attention of the jury focused on the events of the Wounded Knee takeover instead of wider issues, was dangerous prosecution territory: historical justification. He asked Brown whether he believed that "the commission of a crime can be justified on the basis of what was done to somebody else at a different time and in a different place?" For the answer Brown gave—"There have been cases in history where violence was necessary to keep a group of people from being destroyed; it would depend entirely on the circumstances"—Hurd must have regretted raising the topic of historical justification. Kunstler in his redirect examination of Brown naturally pursued the topic by asking if the Boston Tea Party was historically justified. Hurd rose in objection. Kunstler replied: "He's opened that door, Judge, historical justification." Although Judge Nichol sustained Hurd's objection, Kunstler persisted with further questions about the American Revolution, and Hurd objected to each, with Judge Nichol sustaining the objections until on a question about the forthcoming bicentennial celebration he granted that "it leads to something, and I don't know what, but I will overrule the objection." Kunstler then asked Brown if he thought "the bicentennial celebration should be cancelled because the people involved on the colonists' side were committing crimes." Brown did not, and Kunstler carried the questioning further by asking if Brown thought a long history of deprivation would provide motivation for the use of violence. Brown replied that every example had to be considered on its own: the Boston Tea Party, Hiroshima, the Warsaw Ghetto.

Hurd, in a re-cross-examination of Brown, continued the historical justification topic by asking if Brown thought it would be historically justified to use violence because of long-standing social and economic problems.

Brown: I think so. . . . Personally I don't like violence but . . . [there] are times in a people's history when the only way to survive is by violence, and if this is the case where the people, the tribe's existence was threatened, then I would say they would have to use violence.[36]

The third defense witness was 81-year-old Frank Kills Enemy, who understood English but used an interpreter for nuances. He had lived on the Pine Ridge Reservation near Wounded Knee all his life and was the grandson of Red War Bonnet, one of the signers of the 1868 Treaty. When defense attorney Douglas Hall asked him what his opinion was of the 1934 law setting up the tribal council, he replied that it was "all wrong from the start up to this present time." He explained that when the Indians signed the treaty they did so with the "peace pipe, and this peace pipe is sacred. Therefore, the people cannot lie, so they think the white man who made the treaty as it's written here . . . they think what they say is true."

Hall explored with Kills Enemy the contrast between the traditional Lakota governance and that established by the 1934 act. Under the old system mixed-bloods and women were not allowed to vote. The head men called meetings and advised the people and, presumably, acted between the people and the chiefs. Kills Enemy had been chosen and served as a head man in the 1960s.

Hall: Who is the chief of the Oglala Sioux Tribe now?

Kills Enemy: Red Cloud.

Hall: Who is Dick Wilson?

Kills Enemy: He's a mixed-blood. He's not an Indian.

Hall: What position does he hold?

Kills Enemy: Oglala Sioux Tribal Council.

Hall: The council was set up under the 1934 Act?

Kills Enemy: Yes.

Hall: Tell us about life before the 1934 Act.

Kills Enemy: Before 1934, the people had cattle, horses, chickens, hogs. We were well off. Especially my father. We were three boys and four girls. We had hogs, chickens, cattle and horses at that time.

When Hall asked him what changes he has seen since 1934, Hurd objected, but Judge Nichol overruled his objection commenting that "we've got to find if there were changes."

Kills Enemy: It's bad. . . . So we have the Oglala Sioux Tribal Council. The self-government is supposed to be for the full-blooded Indians, according to the law. . . . After the '34 Act, the government came in and it was made into units. Therefore, we cannot use our land.

Under Hall's questioning Kills Enemy explained that White ranchers received leases on the Indian land from the BIA. When others came to him and he complained to the superintendent, nothing was done and conditions did not change. "We've been fighting the '68 Treaty for many years, and now we want help. We can't turn to nobody for help. We got no supreme laws of the land, and we're discriminated from everything on the Pine Ridge Reservation, so we want help on our treaty."[37]

The most impressive defense witness was Gladys Bissonette, an aunt of both Buddy LaMonte, who had been killed during the takeover, and Pedro Bissonette, who had been killed by police in October after the takeover. Mark Lane questioned her about the events before and during the occupation, particularly the meeting at which AIM was invited to provide leadership. While testifying she held her grandfather's peace pipe, which "was a rock given by Mother Earth, which means life, hope, and is to be upheld by the Indian people, and it is a very sacred thing to us Indian people." She told how she held the pipe up after Richard Wilson's "goons" stormed the meeting hall at the impeachment hearings, and, as she stood in the center of the room with the pipe, "you could hear a pin drop throughout the whole hall. None of the BIA policemen who had run in from behind me did dare go beyond me, and everything came to a halt in there. This is why I know my pipe is sacred."

She reinforced what Kills Enemy had pointed out, that the major grievance derived from the 1934 Indian Reorganization Act which enrolled nonmembers into the tribe, depriving "the grass roots people of our reservation" by controlling the allotted land and putting the reservation in the hands of "these new people . . . such as Dick Wilson and the rest of the people who work for the BIA." With them, she asserted, came legalized beatings, murder, bootleggers, corruption throughout the reservation."[38]

During an intense cross-examination, Hurd zeroed in on Bissonette's attitudes toward "half-breeds." "Ever since I was a child," she observed,

"the mixed-bloods were upheld. It's the very same thing going on today. . . .
They originally don't—do not belong on our reservation." Before the 1934
Act, she explained, full-bloods were in a better position on the reservation
than were the mixed-bloods. The mixed-bloods left the reservation, giving
up their Indian rights. But, thanks to the 1934 Act, they were brought back
and given land.

Hurd asked her pointed questions about the guns at Wounded Knee and
the inclination toward violence by AIM leaders. When she was read the
words of Banks to the effect that AIM was going to win the war at Wounded
Knee and that this confrontation was only the beginning, she responded by
saying: "I would say that this was not the beginning of a war between the
United States government and the Indians. We've been at war with the
government all our lives." She described leaving Calico Hall on February
26 and driving to Pine Ridge where she saw men, "all over the top of the
BIA building," marshals and FBI men packing sandbags and erecting machine guns. Hurd asked her if she knew that the marshals on Pine Ridge
were under an obligation by law to protect federal property because, as
happened in Washington, D.C., there might be an attempt to seize the BIA
building. "I would like to know," she responded, "why they would shoot us
Indians down just to save a building. Take human lives to save a building?
How greedy can you get?"[39]

When Bissonette's testimony was concluded, Means stood and stated:
"We believe that the story has been told. We stand on our treaty rights. The
defense rests.[40]

Louis Moves Camp

The trial's most dramatic witness, in a surprise appearance as a rebuttal
witness for the government, was a 22-year-old near full-blood, Louis Moves
Camp. He had grown up on the Pine Ridge Reservation and was a member
of both the Oglala Sioux Civil Rights Organization and AIM. He had
joined AIM in the aftermath of the killing of Raymond Yellow Thunder.
But because he was "tired of the American Indian Movement ripping off
the Indian people, abusing the Indian people," he had gone to the FBI just
two weeks earlier, early in August, since he felt "it would be better for my
people if I came and testified."

At the bench Tilsen told Judge Nichol that the defense had had no idea
that this witness was coming. Moves Camp testified that at meetings in
Rapid City the week before the Wounded Knee takeover, AIM leaders
Means, Banks, and the Bellecourt brothers, Vernon and Clyde, used the
term, "get it on," which meant to fight with weapons. He said that he saw
Banks at Wounded Knee handle a Russian AK-47 and heard Means say

"get it on" before firing at an armored personnel carrier. He claimed that he was a witness to Means's and Banks's taking items out of the trading post and to their taking of hostages. Banks, he charged, had argued for the formation of a "suicide squad" to do such things as start fires, and, in fact, after statements by Means and Banks, the Coates ranch was burned down and the cattle killed. When the news came into Wounded Knee that a U.S. marshal had been injured, Moves Camp narrated, "well, Mr. Means stood up, and he was—you know, very happy that the marshal had got shot. You know, he was in serious condition, you know, they were saying that was right on, you know, going through—I don't know, hysteria or something, I don't know."[41] The marshal whom Moves Camp referred to was Lloyd Grimm, who a month earlier had testified from a wheelchair because he had been left paralyzed from the waist down by the injury at Wounded Knee.

In short, Moves Camp was the perfect prosecution witness. His testimony connected Means and Banks to most of the charges and, as a former AIM member, he was not, like some of the other prosecution witnesses, unsympathetic to the Indian people. Furthermore, unlike most of the prosecution witnesses, Moves Camp could say that he was on the spot at all the crucial times, linking Means and Banks with the plans to occupy Wounded Knee and quoting Means as saying that they "should go to Wounded Knee and take it over." Other witnesses said they saw Means and Banks with trading post merchandise, but Moves Camps claimed he took about $1,000 from the safe and gave it directly to Means and Banks. Moves Camp made the same direct connections between the defendants and the shooting of FBI agent Curtis Fitzgerald, the order to build bunkers and roadblocks, and the order to make Molotov cocktails.[42]

At one point in Moves Camp's startling testimony, just as Judge Nichol announced a morning recess, Ellen Moves Camp, Louis's mother, stood up in the back of the courtroom and rushed forward toward her son shouting, "Your Honor, I want to talk to my son. You butcher. Lie. What did they do to you so you're lying? Get your hands off me. Don't do it. They're lying to you. They're going to bury you. You're lying, Louie. Leave me alone. You marshals, FBI, what are you doing to my son?"[43] Judge Nichol ordered the marshals to take her into custody and called the attorneys into his chambers where he accused the defense lawyers of staging the incident. He was so angry that at first he could not talk with them, and later he could be heard shouting at them while pounding on his desk.[44]

After the stormy morning recess, instead of returning to Moves Camp for cross-examination by Kunstler, a second rebuttal witness was introduced by the government. Edgar Red Cloud, a 77-year-old grandson of the famous Chief Red Cloud, confounded the testimony of Frank Kills Enemy and Gladys Bissonette. He favored the 1934 law. He was present at the critical Calico Hall meeting, but he was not consulted about taking over Wounded Knee. He went to the meeting "for the sole purpose to sing, and I didn't go back there the next day." When asked by Hurd if he thought the takeover of Wounded Knee helped or hurt the Indian people, Red Cloud answered that it "may have been good for the people who done it, but for us on the outside, we were hurt by it."[45] The defense had no questions.

In his cross-examination of Moves Camp, Kunstler asked a series of questions which produced apparent contradictions. When Kunstler pointed them out, Moves Camp, perhaps feeling caught by his own words, retorted: "Now, maybe I did state that Russell had said that at the time and like you got me so confused right now with the little show you put on before we recessed before noon bringing up my own mother in here . . ."

Kunstler: Your Honor, I ask that . . .

Moves Camp: You made her come here. You people . . .

Kunstler: . . . for that untrue statement.

Judge Nichol: Wait. I'm not sure that it's an untrue statement.

Kunstler: Your Honor. I think your remark is prejudicial.

This prompted Judge Nichol to order the marshal to clear the courtroom of all persons wearing AIM insignias because "they are the ones that are creating disturbance," while Kunstler responded by suggesting that Judge Nichol's remark was reversible error.[46]

Kunstler continued the cross-examination of Moves Camp, especially asking him about the statement he wrote for the government in which he claimed that the AIM leaders had meetings with representatives of various countries in an attempt to gain financial help and weapons. Moves Camp maintained that he had been directly outside the door where he overheard the representatives who posed as reporters. Kunstler asked him which nations were represented. Red China, Czechoslovakia, the Soviet Union, East and West Germany, Italy, he recalled, but he could not remember when the meeting took place, whether at the beginning, the middle, or the end of the occupation, nor did he recollect any of the names of the foreign visitors.

Kunstler: And both East and West Germany were of the same opinion?

Moves Camp: Yes.

Kunstler: That they were going to help out, or have another meeting to help out?

Moves Camp: Yes.

Kunstler: Do you know that's the first time that East and West Germany have sat down together and agreed on something?[47]

At this point, as Hurd rose to object, laughter broke out and Judge Nichol ordered the third row of spectators, where the laughter came from, removed from the courtroom. Vernon and Clyde Bellecourt refused to leave and were carried out. When a fight broke out between a spectator and a marshal, another marshal sprayed mace. This prompted Kunstler to comment that all this had happened because of a laugh. Judge Nichol took exception to his comment, saying, "Mr. Kunstler, one more word, and you are going to join him." Kunstler threw his pencil to the floor exclaiming, "I don't care whether I do or not, judge." Judge Nichol ordered a marshal to take him out, and when Lane objected, he was sent out too. Both attorneys spent the night in jail and were released the next day, Saturday, after they and Judge Nichol agreed upon a joint statement to the jury on Monday expressing their regret at what happened.[48]

Louis Moves Camp's mother, Ellen, was introduced by the defense as a rebuttal witness. Judge Nichol had met with her following her outburst and commented to the press that in accusing the defense he "was really wrong in blaming them for the incident." Mary Hall, a University of Minnesota clinical psychology professor and wife of defense attorney Douglas Hall, had suggested to the judge that he should talk with Mrs. Moves Camp who had been sitting near her. Hall told the press that she was convinced the incident had not been planned, that Mrs. Moves Camp had been trembling during her son's testimony trying to restrain herself. In an interview with the press Mrs. Moves Camp said she told Judge Nichol "I was sorry about the outburst. I didn't mean to do it. I was so angry that he was lying that it just happened." She told the press that she thought the FBI had bribed her son. "I know how they work. I know they're brainwashing him. That's not Louis sitting up there. He doesn't talk that way. He doesn't say 'Indian'; he says 'redskin.' He's using words he doesn't usually use. Everything I've heard him say so far is a lie."[49] On the stand under questioning by Tilsen in cross-examination by Hurd, Mrs. Moves Camp maintained that Louis was not at the Calico Hall meeting February 27, as he claimed, and that, while she had been in Wounded Knee from the beginning of the occupation until near its end, her son left Wounded Knee after eleven or twelve days and never returned. Hurd asked her if she had seen weapons in Wounded Knee. She denied seeing any. He then produced a photograph of Mrs. Moves Camp in a group of fifty people, many of them holding weapons. "I never noticed those guns," she commented.[50]

Louis Moves Camp's stunning testimony collapsed nearly as rapidly as it happened. He had asserted that he was in Wounded Knee from the beginning of the takeover until May 1, six days before the end. During that time he had been, presumably, standing in all the right places to become a witness to all the acts of Means and Banks which were mentioned in the indictment. However, a series of defense rebuttal witnesses were as dramatic in destroying Moves Camp's claims as he had been in making them. Three witnesses put Moves Camp in San Francisco as early as St. Patrick's Day, 1973, in San Jose early in April, and in Monterey late in April. An AIM member told how he and Moves Camp worked to organize support for AIM up and down California. A BIA employee testified that she had hired Moves Camp as a security guard at a San Jose high school Indian Culture Day. The president of a Monterey TV station brought logs showing that Moves Camp appeared live on a program April 23.[51] Finally, Gaylene Moves Camp, Louis's nineteen-year-old wife and mother of their nine-month-old baby, testified about an assault charge pending against her husband in Rapid City and she said he was concerned that he might be "set up" for a few years. He told her early in August that he was going to the FBI. "He told me that they would give him a house wherever he wanted it. They gave him $200 a week and then the case is dropped—the assault charges, they would find some way to drop it. . . . They would find him a job so that he would have a coverup for the money."[52]

The Louis Moves Camp dimension of the case took yet another bizarre turn when it came to light that two weeks earlier, August 14 and 15, a week before he testified and while he was being watched by two FBI agents, Moves Camp was accused of raping a high-school girl in River Falls, Wisconsin, and that perhaps the FBI had convinced the local police to drop the charges against their star witness. During *in camera* testimony FBI agent Ronald Williams explained how he and agent David Price had been assigned to protect Moves Camp. They took him to the J & R Ranch, a resort motel near Hudson, Wisconsin, about twenty miles from St. Paul. Moves Camp and the two FBI agents went bar-hopping in nearby River Falls. Louis announced to the two agents that he planned to take a certain girl back to their motel. She, on the other hand, wanted Louis to leave with her and her friends, saying as she hugged him, "Come home with me." The FBI agents told Moves Camp that they would not allow him to return with the girl. Finally, they parted, with the agents going back to the J & R Ranch and Moves Camp leaving with his new friend. The transcript does not make it clear how the protecting agents thought Moves Camp would be able to return to Hudson after they had left with the car. The next communication that the agents had from Moves Camp was an 8 A.M. phone call awakening them with the news that their witness had been charged with rape. Agent Price hurried to the River Falls police station where he spent three hours. Later in the week the River Falls Police informed Price that no charges would be filed against Moves Camp.[53]

Final Arguments

During the clash of closing summaries in all trials, but especially in political trials, the opposition over the nature of law appears most clearly. These addresses to the jury are not merely summaries. They put before the jury more than a recitation of facts. They offer a whole theory of law. Each side tells the jury not only how the evidence should be interpreted, but the lawyers show the members of the jury a picture of law and life itself. In the closing arguments the lawyers assume the role of a guide at Plato's cave, pointing out that the opposition case is little more than flickering shadows on the dark cave wall and leading the jury members up and out of the cave to the clear light of the real world.

Hurd's theme was that the Wounded Knee trial was a criminal trial only. In his view, the jury's duty was limited to deciding whether or not Means and Banks were guilty of certain specific crimes: participating in the theft of merchandise from the trading post, assaulting three federal agents, and conspiring to disobey or disregard the law. It was not for them to decide, Hurd told the jury, whether the government had violated the 1868 Treaty or if the 1934 law was wise. Nor should the jury consider whether or not mixed-bloods should have the same rights as full-blooded Indians. Since no one can invite another to commit a crime and, thereby, excuse the crime, the jury is not faced with a question of whether the defendants were invited into Wounded Knee. Likewise, Hurd asserted that the case for the jury did not concern whether Means and Banks were motivated to reestablish their treaty rights. It is not "a philosophical dispute as to whether or not crimes may be committed in order to right past wrongs or bring about an ultimate good." All these aspects were raised in the trial and permitted by the court to provide a broad background for understanding why the defendants acted as they did.

But the question for the jury, Hurd emphasized, remained confined to the criminal charges. "I don't care and it doesn't make any difference if conditions on the Pine Ridge Indian Reservation are good or bad. Conditions everywhere should be improved. . . . I don't care if the 1868 Treaty was violated or was not violated by the United States. In our society we have methods and means of redress. Primarily there are two. There is the courts, and there is the ballot box." Problems which the nation has not yet solved exist, "but if people in their vigor can inflict violence on innocent people, can commit crimes, then a system of democracy cannot exist. It's anarchy. That's saying that because my end is right, any means are justified. The theory that the end justifies the means is as old as history, but every civilized country has rejected it. To do otherwise is to destroy the very fabric that holds any society together."[54] Thus, although he stressed to the jury that they should not look beyond the specific criminal liability in the case, Hurd also told them that their decision would involve civilization itself.

Defense attorneys Larry Leventhal and Douglas Hall picked up Hurd's "I don't care" phrases and turned them against the prosecution by emphasizing that they illustrated the government's attitude toward Indians for the past two centuries. Whenever Indians attempted to use the proper channels to bring about a change of conditions, the government's response was "I don't care."[55] In general, the defense encouraged the jury to take a broad look at the trial, to see it as part of a long-standing struggle waged by the Indians. While acknowledging that the trading post was looted, although not conceding that Means and Banks were involved, Kunstler emphasized in his closing argument that "this was an upheaval. This was a straining and a new experience. This was one of those occasions in history when human beings and social issues were in motion." He made an analogy to a 1933 strike in Flint, Michigan, when the Plymouth auto workers took over the plant and refused to allow the owners in, temporarily held the managers hostages, and faced the National Guard which surrounded the plant. Walter Ruether and the United Auto Workers negotiated this strike into an agreement. "There was some violence around it, of course. . . . There were no charges filed against the occupiers of the Plymouth works in Flint, and it was negotiated into a new era for the labor movement."[56]

Both the defense and the government warned the jury to guard against the thirteenth juror, prejudice. If any fellow juror made a comment which seemed inappropriate, Tilsen cautioned, it should be called to his or her attention.[57] Kunstler confessed that at age fifty-five he was beginning to understand himself a little and know that as a White person, deep down, he could not stand in front of his Maker and say he was a person without prejudice. All that is asked of anyone on a jury is that they attempt to suppress prejudice as much as possible while trying to grow and develop away from prejudice.[58]

Hurd also warned against prejudice, the prejudice of the voice which declares, "'Look at what's happened to the American Indian for 400 years,' and these are people that represent all the American Indians, and to find against them would be to find against all the American Indians." The tragedy in the case, he stressed, would be for the jury to endorse the crimes committed at Wounded Knee because they thought Means and Banks represented all American Indians.[59] By putting the jury on guard against the "prejudice" of seeing the AIM leaders as representative of all Indians, Hurd parried Kunstler's comparison of the Wounded Knee takeover with the Flint strike led by Ruether and the UAW.

Both sides told the jury that the conspiracy charge was a matter of common sense. Hurd emphasized that when crimes were committed with a mutual understanding to disobey or disregard the law, no matter how informal or subtly agreed upon, that was conspiracy. The many overt acts, such as the meeting in Calico Hall, the lists of grievances and demands, need not be crimes in themselves merely because they documented the intent to advance willfully the purposes of the conspiracy. The jury system, he reminded them, was designed to invoke "good, old fashioned common sense," and they should draw appropriate inferences. Breaking into and looting the trading post, for instance, were part of the larger plan to occupy the town of Wounded Knee.[60]

Conspiracy law, the defense argued, was tricky. Even the judge did not like it, Kunstler suggested. "He told you so. He said 'I might also add that I don't care much for the conspiracy charge in the first place, and I think this isn't the first time I have said so,' but he will also tell you it is the law, and I tell you it is the law as well." Nevertheless, conspiracy is the charge that has always been used against movements, Kunstler pointed out, whether it was the Chicago Seven, Father Philip Berrigan, the Viet Nam Veterans against the War, the Black Panthers, or Angela Davis. Conspiracy charges are used because they are easiest to prove. That is, the jury is asked to consider a great deal of hearsay evidence which would ordinarily not be admitted. The evidence is allowed to be presented to the jury "on the feeling there is a conspiracy, and then you reason from the evidence that gets before you backwards that there was a conspiracy. It's a nebulous and dangerous doctrine."

The word *conspiracy*, Kunstler continued, has itself been given a sinister tone, suggesting "dubious and daring plots." But the reality at Wounded Knee is that in the first days there was confusion, as in any social cataclysm, where some people lose their heads. If they are people who have had very little in their lives and then see a whole trading post open to them, they are tempted. But where, Kunstler asked, is the proof that Means and Banks planned and ordered the looting? The real evidence, apart from the discredited word of Moves Camp, Kunstler recalled, shows Dennis Banks seeking out and returning a treasured antique family clock to Mrs. Gildersleeve and Means ordering that artifacts from the museum be safeguarded in the church.[61]

If the jury used common sense in the way that the defense would advise, they would reject the notion that conspiracy is a mystical agreement given evidence to by circumstances alone. "The theory of conspiracy," Kunstler put to the jury, "is that if you find these things were done, there must have been an agreement to do it. It takes all the heart out of a social upheaval."[62] Quoting Tolstoy, Tilsen argued that events have a history of their own quite apart from what any individual may have intended. The Kerner Commission report on the disorders of the 1960s, for instance, refuted the conspiracy theory and demonstrated that the riots arose not out of an agreement by a handful of leaders but from the life of poverty.[63]

Hurd argued that the grand plan behind Banks and Means's conspiracy was to turn the reservation into a sovereign state. After success in South Dakota, AIM would take the revolution on to Arizona and Oklahoma. Finally they would return Indians to the old days before the 1934 Act and before the Congress and the Supreme Court modified the 1868 Treaty, a time controlled by the full-bloods.[64] Kunstler contended that, on the contrary, the defendants were attempting "to secure some reason for remaining alive; some reason so that Indian children didn't have the highest suicide rate in the nation. That's what was at stake in this courtroom. That's what was at stake in Wounded Knee."[65]

Dismissal

On Thursday, September 12, Judge Nichol gave his instructions to the jury, covering eighty-two points of law which had been submitted by both sides, touching the role of the jury as well as the details of the five charges. When he had finished he dismissed the alternate jurors and sent the twelve jurors out to deliberate. All four alternates were willing to give their opinions to the press and three said they would have voted for acquittal.[66]

The jury deliberated for eight hours and retired for the night in a St. Paul hotel shortly before 10 P.M.. Before they could resume their consideration on Friday, one juror, Therese C., suffered a mild stroke. Judge Nichol visited her in the hospital, met with three doctors, and announced that she would not be able to continue on the jury.[67] The government refused to accept a verdict by the remaining eleven jurors. "I am powerless to do anything more than ask or suggest," Judge Nichol angrily told those assembled in the courtroom on Monday. After a trial of nine months "that has involved the lives of at least a hundred families, if you include witnesses, counsel, marshals, members of my staff, other persons here in the district of Minnesota that have been necessary attendants in this Court, it seems to me that it's almost incredible that it cannot be agreed that this case could proceed to verdict."[68]

Judge Nichol had once been the assistant U.S. attorney for South Dakota, Hurd's current position. This gave Nichol an understanding of the dilemma Hurd faced: How could Hurd fulfill his duty to the court when he must carry out the instruction of the Justice Department? The only good thing Judge Nichol could find to say about the instruction was that Hurd had received it without the usual wait of several weeks. Nichol sharply criticized the directive as contrary to the obligation of the government. As servant of the law, government should see not merely that prosecution be earnest and vigorous but that justice be done.[69]

The defense filed a motion for a judgment of acquittal. Judge Nichol pointed out that the difference between acquittal and dismissal was slight, that acquittal could not be appealed and dismissal could. The Court of Appeal, however, is at liberty to treat a judgment for dismissal as one for acquittal. He then revealed his decision. He recalled that in April when deciding the motion to dismiss he had said that he was "at the brink of dismissal. I think it's only fair to say, and you will see the reasons very shortly, I am now over the brink." Since the decision in April, he continued, four serious matters drove him over the brink: (1) the entire testimony of a sixteen-year-old government witness had to be striken from the record because of a government misconduct in failing to furnish the defense with a document revealing that he had been in jail, contrary to his testimony, when he had claimed to be at Wounded Knee; (2) the Louis Moves Camp matter, "a most serious misconduct," which involved Hurd's helping a cover-up; (3) the illegal use of the military to quell the occupation; (4) and the final blow, the refusal by the government to permit the case to go to a verdict.[70]

One of the reasons Judge Nichol wanted a jury verdict in this case was that there were trials of other AIM leaders involved in the Wounded Knee takeover pending in Lincoln, Nebraska. He told the jury that they would soon learn how the alternates would have decided, albeit without deliberation, but "if the government could not produce sufficient evidence in nearly eight months of trial to convince you that the two persons, who were the sort of self-appointed leaders of the whole thing," were guilty, then should the others be tried? It resembles, Judge Nichol noted, the situation of the Nixon aides facing trial after Ford had pardoned Nixon, an event which had happened the previous week.

Judge Nichol had sharp criticism of the FBI. Its manner of operating had "certainly deteriorated," particularly when FBI agents went bar-hopping with Moves Camp, "let him have all the liquor he wanted . . . [but] did a pretty good job of trying to keep up with him." Even more serious, as Judge Nichol saw it, was the conduct of the prosecutor: "I don't think Mr. Hurd is going to like this. Maybe our relationship is going to be different from now on . . . [but] Mr. Hurd deceived the Court up here at the Bench in connection with the Moves Camp incident in Wisconsin. It hurts me deeply. It's going to take me a long time to forget it." When he had told Judge Nichol that the charges in River Falls were nothing more than ordinary public intoxication, Hurd knew in fact that they involved rape. When the defense asked for a lie dectector test on Moves Camp, the head of the FBI in Minnesota and the Dakotas, not the prosecution, said no. "Since when does the FBI start telling the prosecution that they can't have a lie dectector test if they want to?" Nor was there anything to prevent Hurd from checking Move Camp's California story himself. "I say that Mr. Hurd's errors have been errors of judgment, negligence that could have been avoided, had he been half as thorough, checked half as hard as counsel for the defendants did in this case. I think the negligence on the part of the government has been to such an extent in this case that it involves governmental misconduct; and I'm rather ashamed that our government was not represented better in the trial of this case."[71]

Finally, Judge Nichol turned to the military involvement, a violation of the tradition of civilian government. "I was proud to serve in World War II, but we don't have the military running the civilian affairs and particularly we don't want the military running the FBI and marshals or any part in the execution of laws." Although U.S. marshals were never trained to handle a situation like Wounded Knee, and in spite of the evidence that Col. Warner exercised a restraining influence in his advice to the FBI, the Justice Department, and the marshals, telling them to "cool it," nevertheless the government should have gotten a presidential proclamation to allow the military to assist. With that Judge Nichol thanked the jury, excused them, discharged the bonds on Means and Banks, and adjourned court.[72]

Reactions to the conclusion of the Wounded Knee trial were varied, but one in particular deserves note. When he learned about the result of the trial, Richard Wilson called it "a total breakdown of the judicial system."[73] Had the jury been allowed to come to a verdict, what might the result have been? There are two indications. On the larceny charge, in ballots taken before one juror had a stroke, the jury had stood 11-1 for acquittal of Banks and 8-4 for acquittal of Means. On the charge of conspiracy the jury had voted at first 8-3, then unanimously for acquittal of both Banks and Means. A verdict, had it been reached, would not have answered the dilemma of the trial any better than the dismissal which did result.

This dilemma is: How can the integrity of the rule of law be preserved when social movements protest injustices of the established order? The question infused the trial from beginning to end. If it was not answered, it was at least clarified. The contention between the American Indians of AIM persuasion and the rest of American society, as represented by BIA or other government agencies, was dramatized by the trial. Drama is our best way of understanding difficult questions, those we may never answer but must face. The trial, whatever its outcome, set before us in a public forum a contradiction we might not be able to resolve but which we must understand if we are to maintain a vital society and a democratic government. Both the rule of law and social justice are essential. We cannot allow any faction, even that of a democratically responsive government, to claim in triumph that one determines the other.

Notes

1. Vine Deloria, *Behind the Trail of Broken Treaties: An Indian Declaration of Independence* (New York, Delacorte Press, 1974), pp. 48-60.

2. *New York Times*, March 9, 1972, p. 15.
3. *Ibid.*, February 8, 1973, p. 32.
4. Transcript of Trial Proceedings, *United States v. Dennis Banks and Russell Means*, U.S. District Court, District of South Dakota, Western Division (referred to hereafter as Trial Transcript), Vol. 103, p. 19085.
5. *Ibid.*, p. 19089.
6. *Ibid.*, Vol. 104, p. 19114.
7. *New York Times*, March 10, 1974, p. 25.
8. Trial Transcript, Vol. 65, pp. 12722-12731.
9. *Ibid.*, Vol. 31, p. 5924.
10. *Ibid.*, Vol. 32, p. 5957.
11. *New York Times*, March 7, 1973, p. 30; March 12, 1973, p. 1.
12. *Ibid.*, March 18, 1973, p. 42.
13. *Ibid.*, April 30, 1973, p. 14.
14. Judge Fred Nichol, summary of indictment for prospective jurors, Trial Transcript, Vol. 1, pp. 8-15.
15. *Ibid.*, Vol. 21, pp. 3894-3897.
16. *Ibid.*, p. 3911.
17. *Ibid.*
18. *Ibid.*, p. 3916.
19. *Ibid.*, pp. 3919-3920.
20. *Ibid.*, p. 3922.
21. *Ibid.*, pp. 3933-3936.
22. *Ibid.*, pp. 3938-3939.
23. *Ibid.*, pp. 3942-3948. Banks, in fact, had quoted Judge Nichol correctly, not from a decision but from a January 7 meeting with reporters in which he said a friend had made the comment. *Minneapolis Tribune*, February 13, 1974, p. 4A.
24. Trial Transcript, Vol. 21, pp. 3958-3962; *Minneapolis Tribune*, February 13, 1974, pp. 1A, 4A.
25. *Minneapolis Tribune*, February 13, 1974, p. 1A.
26. Trial Transcript, Vol. 22, pp. 4020-4035.
27. *Ibid.*, Vol. 25, p. 4614.
28. *Ibid.*, Vol. 32, pp. 6064-6109.
29. *Ibid.*, Vol. 65, pp. 12740-12749.
30. *Ibid.*, p. 12830.
31. *Ibid.*, pp. 12838-12850.
32. *United States v. Banks*, 374 F. Supp. 321, at 335 (1974).
33. *New York Times*, May 4, 1974, p. 9. Judge Nichol signed another order on August 15 concerning the White House tapes. When the dispute arose over whether the government or former president Nixon owned the tapes, Kunstler expressed concern that the relevant tapes might disappear. Nichol signed an order that the White House retain the tapes until it was determined whether they contained conversations bearing on the trial. *Ibid.*, August 16, 1974. p. 34. Judge Nichol said of the order, "I can't see any harm in signing the simple order that you're talking about. It may be ineffective." Trial Transcript, Vol. 103, p. 18912.
34. Trial Transcript, Vol. 102, pp. 18703-18807.
35. *Ibid.*, pp. 18826-18862.
36. *Ibid.*, pp. 18876-18897.
37. *Ibid.*, Vol. 103, pp. 18919-19009.
38. *Ibid.*, pp. 19050-19090.

39. *Ibid.*, Vol. 104, pp. 19218-19231.
40. *Minneapolis Tribune*, August 17, 1974, p. 4A.
41. Trial Transcript, Vol. 106, pp. 19419-19426.
42. *Minneapolis Tribune*, August 22, 1974, pp. 1A, 11A.
43. Trial Transcript, Vol. 106, pp. 19472-19473.
44. *Minneapolis Tribune*, August 23, 1974, pp. 1A, 9A.
45. Trial Transcript, Vol. 106, pp. 19476-19490.
46. *Ibid.*, pp. 19506-19508.
47. *Ibid.*, Vol. pp. 19698-19709.
48. *Minneapolis Tribune*, August 24, 1974, pp. 1A, 4A; August 25, 1974, pp. 1A, 8A, Trial Transcript, Vol. 107, 19701-19714.
49. *Minneapolis Tribune*, August 23, 1974, pp. 1A, 9A.
50. Trial Testimony, Vol. 110, pp. 20160-20216; *Minneapolis Tribune*, August 29, 1974, p. 2B.
51. Trial Transcript, Vol. 110, pp. 20120-20127; Vol. 111A, pp. 20487-20494.
52. *Ibid.*, Vol. 114, pp. 21041-21053. The jury was told the details of the payments of $1990.50 to Moves Camp as follows: $36 per day as a witness, August 8 to 14, plus transportation ($350.50); $32 per day, August 8 to 28, under the government's Witness Security Program for subsistence ($640); $1000 for relocation expenses. In addition, Moves Camp received an $84 one-way airline ticket to his chosen relocation. Trial Transcript, Vol. 115, pp. 21112-21113.
53. *Ibid.*, Vol. 111, pp. 20317-20338. See also *Minneapolis Tribune*, August 31, 1974, pp. 1A, 5A.
54. Trial Transcript, Vol. 116, pp. 21128-21133, p. 21490.
55. *Ibid.*, Vol. 116, pp. 21312ff, 21342ff.
56. *Ibid.*, Vol. 117, pp. 21421-21422.
57. *Ibid.*, Vol. 116, p. 21311.
58. *Ibid.*, Vol. 117, pp. 21459-21460.
59. *Ibid.*, p. 21560.
60. *Ibid.*, Vol. 116, pp. 21133-211139, 21151-21152.
61. *Ibid.*, Vol. 117, pp. 21424-21436.
62. *Ibid.*, p. 21434.
63. *Ibid.*, Vol. 116, pp. 21288-21289.
64. *Ibid.*, p. 21148; Vol. 117, p. 21531.
65. *Ibid.*, p. 21454.
66. *Minneapolis Tribune*, September 13, 1974, p. 1A.
67. *Ibid.*, September 14, 1974, p. 1A.
68. Trial Transcript, Vol. 118, pp. 21723-21724.
69. *Ibid.*, pp. 21722-21728.
70. *Ibid.*, pp. 21731-21735.
71. *Ibid.*, pp. 21743-21755.
72. *Ibid.*, pp. 21755-21765.
73. *Minneapolis Tribune*, September 17, 1974, pp. 1A, 7A, 10A. In 1980 the Sioux "won" a U.S. Supreme Court case based on the 1868 Treaty and were awarded $106 million. See *United States v. Sioux Nation*, 448 U.S. 371 (1980). Because they wanted the land, not the money, AIM under the leadership of Bill Means, Russell's brother, occupied an 800-acre campsite in the Black Hills named Camp Yellow Thunder for Raymond Yellow Thunder who had been killed in 1972. See Peter Matthiessen, *In the Spirit of Crazy Horse* (New York, Viking Press, 1983), Ch. 19. See also Jim Messerschmidt, *The Trial of Leonard Peltier* (Boston, South End Press, 1983).

9

Trials of Regimes:
The Question of Legitimacy

Are law and revolution on opposite ends of a seesaw? When one is riding high, is the other down? Whether the ancien régime tries the revolutionaries or, after the revolution, is tried by them, to the defendants the judge represents not the law but merely the powers that be. Yet to the prosecution, whether of the old or the new order, the legitimacy of the law is at stake in the trial of those who have not only "taken the law into their own hands" but have grabbed for much more: the authority to make law, substituting their power interest for law itself. Can this contradiction be resolved?

Are the rule of law and revolution incompatible? They appear to operate from hostile premises: Law seems to begin with the assumption that justice results from following precedent, and revolutions seem to start from the idea that justice demands the destruction of precedent and the creation of a new order. This puts us face-to-face with the fundamental question of jurisprudence: What is law? If we examine several trials conducted during revolutions for what they say about the basic questions of the law, we can shed some light on this basic question.

The most difficult of all types of political trials is the trial of one regime by another. In such a hot crucible the elements of law and politics clearly separate. Every revolution, sooner or later, seems to initiate trials to discredit the regime they have triumphed over. The Gang of Four trial in China and the Iranian Tribunal are recent examples. But our own generation is always in a mist. We can see the past more clearly than the present. If we take certain seventeenth- and eighteenth-century trials, especially those of Charles I (1649) and Louis XVI (1792), we will have a better opportunity to understand the nature of political trials in revolutions than we would by attempting to be up to date with China or Iran.

Trials of the English Revolution

Without recounting the battles of the English Civil War or the moves made by the royalists and the forces opposed to the king, we might consider three trials conducted during the revolution. The first two, those of Strafford and Laud, were rehearsals for the third and major trial, that of Charles I. These three provide insight into the conflict of power and law during a revolution.

Thomas Wentworth, Earl of Strafford and commander of the largest body of the royal army, was tried by Parliament in 1641 under a bill of attainder for the treason of advising Charles I that "he was now absolved from law" and of inviting an Irish invasion.[1] William Laud, Archbishop of Canterbury and the orthodox zealot who oversaw a religious persecution of Puritans, was tried in 1644 for the treason of "his endeavour to introduce into this kingdom an arbitrary power of Government, without any limitation or rules of law.[2] Together Strafford and Laud represent the two edges of the sword of royal authority—the army and the church.

The trial of the king speaks for itself in importance, a head-on courtroom collision of two powerful authorities—the king and the revolutionary army. As we saw in chapter 5, not long after Charles had been tried and executed, John Lilburne, a dissenter who had objected to the trial of Charles and to the high-handed authority exercised by Cromwell and the army, was tried in a classic legal tussle which crystallizes the other side of the revolution. While Cromwell's regime advanced against the king, judging him for his abuse of authority and disregard for the law, Lilburne's dissent and trial is a rearguard legal action, challenging the Cromwell regime for the same abuses.

Since 1351 and until the Tudors, Edward III's treason statute kept the law bound closely to offenses against the king's person. It declared that treason consisted of compassing or imagining the death of the king, levying war against him, or adhering to his enemies.[3] Under the Tudors, treason was expanded to include writing, printing, and other acts which would create internal disorder. Even more, the currency of treason was cheapened by Henry VIII's convoluted treason statutes which reflected his matrimonial windings and turnings. It was made treasonous, to take only one example, for an unchaste woman (read, Catherine Howard) to marry the king without revealing the fact of her unchastity. More statutes made it treasonable to assert the invalidity of various of the king's marriages at the wrong time or, equally treasonable, to assert their validity at other times. To complicate the picture of treason under the Tudors further, religion entangled the law of treason in its establishment, which went from Roman Catholic under Henry VII to Henry VIII's break-away version to a Protestant version under Edward VI to a fully Roman Catholic version with Mary and a fully Protestant establishment under Elizabeth. Treason statutes, together with acts about heresy and royal supremacy in the church, were passed and repealed and passed again as the official establishment switched.[4] These Tudor changeabouts in what treason meant, depending on which wife and heir and which religion were current, would have no lasting significance except that they depreciated the concept of treason. Their effect was felt in the reign of Charles I.

In addition to the offenses against the person of the king, which were those of Edward III's statute, treason would include causing a division between the king and his people. Strafford's trial gave yet a new direction to this addition to the treason law. For both sides, the Tudor-Stuart autocracy and the Parliamentary, unity was an obsession. Strafford was charged with making such a political division that a rebellion and civil war would threaten the king's life. This doctrine of constructive treason was used in the Strafford indictment, but it did not originate with his trial. The new element was the accusation that the division would be permanent, a perpetual change in the constitutional order.[5] John Pym, the Commons leader, for contrast, mentioned the murder of Henry IV of France and the attempts against Queen Elizabeth, "but [Strafford's] treason, if it had taken effect, was to be a standing perpetual treason, which would have been in continual act, not determined within one time or age, but transmitted to posterity, even from one generation to another."[6] Here the trial of Strafford takes on attributes of a revolutionary trial, one regime trying another by calling into question its legitimacy. Treason, as an act against the king, can happen in any time. The Tudors may have cast the net wide to catch those who questioned the royal marriages or religion and called it treason. But in Strafford's trial by elevating the charge from compassing the king's death, to dividing the king and the people, to permanently undermining the constitutional order, legitimacy, not ordinary traitorship, became the issue.

Also characteristic of revolutionary trials, the indictment could easily cut both ways. Pym, it could be demonstrated equally well, was threatening the king's life by rising up against Strafford. This, comments Conrad Russell, "made it a dangerously double-edged doctrine. It was quite true that the constitution in which they all believed (there are fewer differences between Pym and Strafford than is commonly supposed) could not function if there was division between the king and the Parliament. Serious division meant danger of civil war, and in a civil war the king's life was endangered. But it takes two to make a division, and it was quite open to somebody who thought Strafford was right and Pym was wrong to maintain that Pym was making a division, making a civil war likely, and thereby compassing the king's death." Legitimacy, in the same way, could be denied Parliament, just as it could be denied Strafford's government. Beyond the question of legitimacy, as revolutions demonstrate, is our fear of chaos. Both sides in the English Revolution, as Russell shows, realized that: "If the king and his parliament could not agree, government had to be altered somehow. If government were altered, everyone, Pym and Strafford equally, feared that something like Hobbes's state of nature would follow."[7]

During the trial of Strafford, after the evidence for and against him had been placed before the House of Lords, Commons abandoned the impeachment of Strafford, in favor of a bill of attainder. This shift, a move Raoul Berger says "remains an unsolved puzzle," was opposed by the leaders in Commons, Pym and John Hampden, and served to deeply annoy the majority of the House of Lords, and required, unlike an impeachment, the consent of Charles I.[8] "If the issue of guilt was indeed for the Lords 'a judicial question, which must be judicially proved,'" Berger observes, "it does them little credit to attribute to them a readiness to acquit after a full-dress trial only to turn and join in a legislative lynching."[9] Ostensibly, Commons saw that Charles could more easily be pressured into abandoning his former advisor, complying with the attainder and the execution of Strafford, than the Lords could be expected to give up on a proof of guilt and the procedure of establishing it in an impeachment trial. This moving from impeachment to attainder, in short, is a clear instance of the political agenda supplanting the legal agenda.

If part of the charge against Strafford was treason for his advice to Charles that "you have an army in Ireland you may employ here to reduce this kingdom,"[10] the members of Parliament were aware that Strafford, if he had the chance, would charge them with complicity with the Scots. After Strafford had served as the Lord Deputy of Ireland, he was put in charge of the army in the North to oppose the Scots. It was the dispute with Parliament over money to pay these troops which led to Charles's conflict with the Short Parliament and the arbitrary imprisonment of Pym, Hampden, and the other Parliamentary leaders, events which led directly to the outbreak of the revolution and civil war. But it was Strafford, not Pym and Hampden, who was in the Tower, although had the circumstances been reversed, the high treason charges would have been flying in the opposite direction. Charles had plans to rescue his advisor, but they failed. One was to bring the army down from the North, but it was discontented from lack of pay. Another was a dramatic rescue, involving a plot to seize the Tower, but it was foiled by a betrayal. Finally, with an armed mob outside Whitehall, Charles abandoned Strafford and gave his royal assent to the attainder bill. He was executed two days later.[11]

As Strafford walked to his execution his former colleague, William Laud, watching, raised his hand in a blessing from his own Tower cell. Two years later he was also tried for high treason. As the Archbishop of Canterbury, Laud was impeached for, among other matters, having "traitorously endeavoured to subvert the fundamental laws and government of this kingdom; and instead thereof, to introduce an arbitrary and tyrannical Government against law: And to that end hath wickedly and traitorously advised his majesty, that he might, at his own will and pleasure, levy and take Money of his subjects without their consent in parliament. And this, he affirmed, was warrantable by the law of God." The fourteen-point indictment further accused Laud of defending absolute power by his sermons and writings, of obstructing justice and selling justice, of robbing the king of his supremacy in assuming for "himself a papal and tyrannical Power," of altering and subverting "God's true Religion by law established in this realm; and instead thereof, to set up Popish Superstition and Idolatry" which he defended in sermons and writings, of employing "for the same traitorous and wicked intent . . . such men to be his own domestical Chaplains, whom he knew to be notoriously disaffected to the Reformed Religion, grossly addicted to popish Superstition, and erroneous and unsound both in judgment and practice; by which means divers false and superstitious Books have been published, to the great scandal of Religion, and to the seducing of many of his majesty's subjects," of seeking to "stir up War and Enmity betwixt his majesty's two kingdoms of England and Scotland, and, finally, of working to subvert the rights of Parliament."[12] With an indictment worded as this one was, the prosecutor had little more to do than paraphrase it and make comments. The legitimacy of the Stuart regime was again on trial.

Laud stressed in his own defense that he was guided by the law and was in conscience bound to keep it. He denied any intention of introducing an arbitrary government, which he maintained he had always hated. With Aristotle, Laud said, he believed it is a "very dangerous thing to trust the Will of the Judge, rather than the written law."[13]

"As for Religion," Laud told the lords sitting as his judges, "I was born and bred up in and under the Church of England, as it yet stands established by Law. I have, by God's blessing, and the favor of my prince, grown up in it to the years which are now upon me, and to the place of preferment which I yet bear: And in this Church, by the grace and goodness of God, I resolve to die." He told them that he might have easily "slid through all the difficulties" in the recent years, but "of all diseases, I have ever hated a palsy in religion." He worked to preserve the external public worship of God with decency and uniformity, but the unity of the church cannot continue "where Uniformity is shut out at the churchdoor." He saw the public neglect of God's service, "the nasty lying of many places dedicated to that Service, and almost cast a damp upon the true and inward Worship of God."[14]

Laud denied acquaintance with any recusants or any endeavor to advance the Church of Rome. What, then, he asked, kept him in his office where he had "fallen into a great deal of obloquy in matter of Religion, . . . to endure the libels and the slanders, and the base usage of all kinds, which have been put upon me"? Not because of a pledge to any in the world who would sway him against his conscience. He had no wife or children "to cry out upon me to stay with them." Nor was he at all loath to leave the honor, profit, and ease of living in his office. He scorned honor and pride, and could have lived at much better ease and have avoided the "barbarous libelings and other bitter and grievous scorns" elsewhere. "Nay, my Lords, I am an innocent in this business of Religion, as free from all practice, or so much as thought of practice for any alteration to Popery, or any way blemishing the true Protestant Religion established in the Church of England, as I was when my mother first bare me into the world." Lastly, he named some twenty people who had been seduced by the Church of Rome that he "settled in the true Protestant Religion established in England."[15]

If Strafford represented the military side of Charles's rule, Laud was Charles's Torquemada. The High Commission had conducted an inquisition, under Archbishop Laud, suppressing the Puritans in England and imposing the Church of England on the Presbyterians in Scotland, both prompting rebellion. Laud's High Commission, according to Leonard Levy, was "suddenly very active, merciless, and formidable. It prosecuted Nonconformists as if to extirpate them, and it was everywhere."[16] His impeachment, like Strafford's, can only be understood against the political background of the preceding decade.

Yet both trials had substantial legal consequences as well. James Madison and the Founders were well aware of the trials and the legal battles fought in England.[17] They learned the same lesson from both the Stuart autocracy and parliamentary triumphancy. One of the consequences of the Strafford trial, Charles McIlwain observes, is that from it "it is but a step to the declaration that 'no Bill of Attainder or *ex post facto* Law shall be passed.'"[18] As McIlwain demonstrates, such cases also led the American Founder to reject a rigid doctrine of parliamentary supremacy.[19] Likewise, the U.S. Constitution narrows the definition of treason to such a degree that constructive treason is not recognized, that retroactive declarations of treason are impossible, and all that Strafford and Laud were tried for could not be called treason in the United States.[20]

Colonel Thomas Pride purged Parliament of its Presbyterian members who had defied the army over the question of reaching a settlement with the king, excluding ninety-six members and arresting forty-seven. The rest, an oligarchy called the Rump Parliament, serving as the voice of the army but purporting to represent the nation, established a court to try the king.[21] The Resolution creating the High Court of Justice for Trial of the King, which was not agreed to by the House of Lords, read: "Resolved, That the people are (under God) the original of all just powers. That themselves, being chosen by and representing the people, have the Supreme Power in the nation. That whatsoever is enacted or declared for law by the Commons in parliament, hath the force of a law, and the people concluded thereby, though consent of King and Peers be not had thereunto."[22]

Cromwell's initial concern was the trial, not the execution. Compelling Charles to answer for his high crimes before the bar of Parliament would suffice to topple royal legitimacy. But before the trial began Cromwell changed his attitude and answered, when Algernon Sidney protested against the validity of the court, "I tell you we will cut off his head with the crown on it."[23]

Sidney's defection from the enterprise of bringing the king to trial was not the only break within the revolutionary ranks, only the most dramatic. Sir Henry Vane, the leader of the Independents in the House of Commons, Lord Thomas Fairfax, the lord general and commander-in-chief of the army, as well as the chief justices and most of the lawyers, including Oliver St. John who had prosecuted Strafford, all withdrew and stayed away.[24] What Cromwell had wanted to avoid happened. Parliament's authority to bring down the king in a trial shrank to the point that royalists could charge that the king was murdered by a group of rogues and knaves. To the royalists it was a partisan trial—regicide. Everyone could see that the Rump Parliament had lost those members who disagreed with the army. Those few left in the House of Lords had refused to agree to the bill authorizing the trial of the king, and the Rump went ahead without the Lords, abolishing, in fact, the upper house. Could a High Court established under such circumstances lay claim to legitimacy? With this question in mind, perhaps more as a symptom of the trouble, the regime designed a new Great Seal, replacing the one bearing the name and face of Charles with a seal showing only one house, Commons, in debate encircled by the words: "1651 in the Third Year of Freedom by God's Blessing restored."[25]

Cromwell recognized that the key question in a trial of the king would be the authority of the High Court: "I desire ye to let us resolve here what answers we shall give the king when he comes before us, for the first question that he will ask us will be by what authority and commission do we try him." Henry Marten, a radical, gave the revolutionary answer: "In the name of the Commons and Parliament assembled and all the good people of England."[26] For Cromwell a higher authority supported the trial: "If any man hath carried on the design of deposing the King and disinheriting his posterity . . . he should be the greatest rebel and traitor in the world, but, since the Providence of God hath cast this upon us, I cannot but submit to Providence, though I am not yet provided to give you advice."[27]

The High Court of Justice assembled in Westminster Hall January 20, 1649 to try the king. Of the designated 150 members only fifty-eight formed the procession to march into the crowded hall.[28] Later, after the trial, fifty-nine signed the death warrant. About this group C. V. Wedgewood says: "Some were no better than the Royalists thought them—scoundrels scrambling for the spoils of war and the seats of power. But the majority acted from a sincere conviction that no other course was opened to them as God-fearing Christians and lovers of their country. Between thirty and forty men gave character, solidarity, and strength to the High Court of Justice."[29]

The indictment drawn up by the Rump Parliament made it clear, in language which resembles Jefferson's in the Declaration of Independence a century and a quarter later, that King Charles ruled illegitimately:

> Whereas it is notorious, That Charles Stuart, the now king of England, not content with those many encroachments which his predecessors had made upon the people in their rights and freedoms, hath had a wicked design totally to subvert the ancient and fundamental laws and liberties of this nation, and in their place to introduce an arbitrary and tyrannical government; and that besides all other evil ways and means to bring this design to pass, he hath prosecuted it with fire and sword, levied and maintained a cruel war in the land, against the parliament and kingdom, whereby the country hath been miserably wasted, the public treasure exhausted, trade decayed, thousands of people murdered, and infinite other mischiefs committed.[30]

For such "high and treasonable offences" Charles was before the High Court. Under the old idea of treason, stemming from Edward III's statute, it would have been difficult to charge Charles with treason since the crime had to be in every way directed against the person of the king. But after Strafford and Laud had been convicted of treason and executed, the charge that Charles had subverted the fundamental constitutional order and introduced his own tyrannical government could hold.

The first and only response Charles made when he appeared in Westminster Hall was, as Cromwell had anticipated, to challenge the authority of the court:

> Now I would know by what authority, I mean lawful; there are many unlawful authorities in the world, thieves and robbers by the highways; but I would know by what authority I was brought from thence, and carried from place to place, and I know not what; and when I know what lawful authority, I shall answer. Remember I am your king, your lawful king, and what sins you bring upon your heads, and the judgment of God upon this land; think well upon it, I say, think well upon it, before you go further from one sin to a greater; therefore let me know by what lawful authority I am seated here, and I shall not be unwilling to answer. In the mean time, I shall not betray my trust; I have a trust committed to me by God, by old and lawful descent; I will not betray it, to answer to a new unlawful authority; therefore resolve me that, and you shall hear more of me.[31]

Lord President John Bradshaw replied that the court held its authority "in the name of the people of England, of which you were elected king." Charles shot back that he denied it because "England was never an elective kingdom, but an hereditary kingdom for near these thousand years." He said he would "stand as much for the privilege of the house of commons, rightly understood, as any man here" but saw no House of Lords, nor king, giving authority to call "the king to his parliament." When he saw "a legal authority warranted by the Word of God, the Scriptures, or warranted by the Constitutions of the kingdom," he would answer.[32]

The sparring between Charles and Bradshaw continued over several sessions. When Charles said he required to know the authority of the court, Bradshaw informed him that "it is not for Prisoners to require." "Prisoners!" Charles rejoined, "Sir, I am not an ordinary prisoner." He maintained that the Commons was never a court of judicature and asked how it could become one. Bradshaw told him he could not give such discourses and asked that he be taken away. "Well, Sir, remember that the king is not suffered to give in his Reasons for the liberty and Freedom of all his Subjects," Charles said before being led away. "Sir," Bradshaw told Charles, "you are not to have Liberty to use this language: How great a friend you have been to the Laws and Liberties of the people, let all England and the world judge."[33]

Finally, Bradshaw required that Charles, "in plain terms, for Justice knows no respect of persons; you are to give your positive and final Answer in plain English, whether you be Guilty or Not Guilty of these Treasons." Charles replied that he did not know how he could answer: "For the Charge, I value it not a rush; it is the Liberty of the People of England that I stand for." Bradshaw told Charles in a lenghty discourse of his own that "as the Law is your Superior, so truly, Sir, there is something that is superior to the Law, and that is indeed the Parent or Author of the law, and that is the people of England." The end of all governors, "of having kings," is justice. Consequently, if the king "will go contrary to that end, . . . he must understand that he is but an officer in trust." Parliaments, Bradshaw instructed Charles, "were ordained for that purpose, to redress the Grievances of the people; that was their main end."[34]

Bradshaw employed an ominous image when, in his lecture on the law to Charles, he compared Charles to Emperor Caligula who had said he wished the people of Rome had but one neck so that in one blow he might cut it off. "And your proceedings have been somewhat like to this: for the body of the people of England hath been (and where else) represented but in the Parliament; and could you but have confounded that, you had at one blow cut off the neck of England. But God hath reserved better things for us, and hath pleased for to confound your designs, and to break your forces, and to bring your persons into custody, that you might be responsible to justice."[35]

As for the stories of Scottish and English kings, Bradshaw reminded Charles that he was the 109th king of Scotland, and that since the first,

Fergus, was elected, "no kingdom hath yielded more plentiful experience than that your native kingdom of Scotland hath done concerning the Deposition and the Punishment of their offending and transgressing kings," with his grandmother (Mary, Queen of Scots) as a fine example: set aside and replaced with his father, James, an infant. In England Edward II and Richard II were deposed by Parliament. In fact, Bradshaw told Charles, "you are the twenty-fourth king from William called the Conqueror, you shall find one half of them to come merely from the state, and not merely upon the point of descent." The oath and the coronation "doth shew plainly, that the kings of England, although it is true, by the law the next person in blood is designed; yet if there were just cause to refuse him, the People of England might do it. For there is a Contract and a Bargain made between the King and his People." Because the bond is reciprocal, according to Bradshaw, "if this bond be once broken, farewell sovereignty!"[36] The arguments soon ended, and Charles was declared to be a "Traitor, Tyrant, a Murderer, and a public Enemy to the Country." The High Court established by the Rump oligarchy had tried, convicted, sentenced, and executed Charles I all within the month of January 1649.

What can we make of these trials held during the English Revolution? The trials of Strafford and Laud prepared the way for two important changes in the law. First, they set the legal stage for the trial of Charles. Just as the Tudors had diluted the treason law sufficiently to try and convict not only those who threatened the king but the king's own closest advisors who together represented both sides of royal authority, the sword and the bishop's staff, so their trials watered down the legitimacy of the Stuart regime enough that the king himself might be tried. Second, the Strafford and Laud trials, by way of negative example, influenced James Madison and the American Founders to write a tightly worded treason clause, provide against bills of attainder and ex post facto laws, and incline against parliamentary supremacy.

The trial of Charles I pits two regimes, two claims to sovereignty, directly against each other. Three views of the law emerge during this clash. First, the royalist position of sovereignty based on divine right: No court had authority to judge the king. A second position, held mainly by members of the bar and bench, opposed the king's prerogative and the High Court's claim because both lacked positive legal authority. Many, such as Algernon Sidney, were strong republicans, but they walked out on the deliberations about the king's trial because they saw nothing in the written or common law providing for it. Finally, Cromwell and Bradshaw introduced the higher authority of God's Providence and natural law to give legitimacy to the trial of the king. This was also Lilburne's position, but he wanted a more legitimate source to give voice to this higher law than the army's Rump Parliament, and he insisted that if the king were to be tried for violating basic principle, he could not be subjected to a court which denied him such fundamentals as a trial by jury.

The Trial of Louis XVI

Louis was put on trial at roughly the same stage in the French Revolution as Charles had been in the English. The moderates had, in both, suffered defeat, and the radicals were feeling their first triumph. In England the king had been captured in August 1648, the Parliament later purged by the army, and the king brought to trial and executed in January. In France the August 10, 1792, insurrection with the storming of the Tuileries resulted in the suspension of the monarchy and in the king's being put under house arrest. LaFayette, identified with the Declaration of the Rights of Man and the Citizen and a leader of the first revolution, was forced to flee the country as the Paris Commune came to power and the second revolution began. The September Massacres, a slaughter of aristocrats en masse, proved to be only a harbinger of the Reign of Terror which began a year later. In the meantime, the deputies of the National Convention had to decide what they were going to do with their prisoner, the king.[37]

In the month before Louis's trial the National Convention engaged in a debate which revealed three positions on the place of law in a revolution. Charles Morisson, the only deputy who expressed a position close to Louis's defense, expressed his feeling that he would like to see the "bloody monster" pay for his crimes, but, although such retribution was his first response, reason and respect for the law must prevail. The penal code made no provision for judging Louis. Despite the enormity of his crimes and the blood of his victims which demanded that France avenge what Louis did, the law said nothing. In this silence, Morisson suggested, the National Convention could legally denounce Louis for his treason and despotism, recognize in a resolution that "strict justice" would "cause Louis XVI to expiate his crimes on the scaffold," and then forever banish Louis from France under penalty of death if he were ever to return. But Louis could not be tried.[38]

The Marquis de Condorcet, one of the leading embodiments of the French Enlightenment and a Girondin at the National Convention, took a middle position. If the law was silent on the question of judging the king, that silence was an unfortunate consequence, he maintained, of the king's own power, not a reflection of the principles of reason and equity. The 1791 Constitution and the penal code, as positive law, were applications of natural law. The king and the National Convention itself were responsible to the nation, and the nation was accountable to mankind and to the posterity.

The nation, in Condorcet's view, could judge the king under the law, could change the law, but it could not violate the law. Instead of being tried by the National Convention, which would then be legislator, accuser, and judge, Condorcet proposed the creation of a special tribunal, with members named by the departments, which would make a judgment independent of the National Convention.[39]

The third position on whether Louis could be tried is represented with articulate clarity by Louis-Antoine-Léon St. Just and Maximilien Robespierre, two leaders of the Jacobin Mountain. St. Just argued that laws and courts were intended for citizens, not kings. Louis, as a king, was a rebel, an alien, a prisoner of war who waged war against the people and lost. Only the law of nations, not the law for citizens, could apply to Louis. "No man can reign innocently. The folly is all too evident. Every king is a rebel and an usurper." Louis was guilty of being king. He must either reign or die, but he could not be judged.[40]

Robespierre followed the same logic by denying that the proceeding of the National Convention against Louis was a trial, that Louis was an accused, or that the deputies were his judges:

> You are, and you can only be, statesmen and representatives of the nation. You do not have a verdict to give for or against a man, but a measure to take for the public safety, a precautionary act to execute for the nation. A deposed king in a Republic is good only for two things; either to trouble the tranquility of the state and to undermine liberty, or to strengthen both.[41]

The victory of the revolution was, in Robespierre's reasoning, the verdict condemning Louis. Putting Louis on trial would be "counter-revolutionary since it would bring the revolution itself before the court." The people do not judge as a court of law. They do not hand down sentences or condemn kings; they hurl down thunderbolts to plunge kings into an abyss.[42]

If Morisson found law only in reading the statutes, Condorcet saw such positive law as an application of natural law. Where the positive law of the penal code is silent, principles provide direction. If the code says nothing about the king's responsibility to the law, we cannot fill the gap with the idea that the king rules with impunity and cannot be tried. St. Just and Robespierre approached law from a position of radical popular sovereignty. The only sacred principles were not those of the bar but, according to Robespierre, "the spontaneous and universal movement of a people weary of the tyranny which oppresses it," which is the "most equitable of all judgments."[43] Yet, in spite of his populist position on the source of law, Robespierre opposed appealing the fate of Louis to the people. That, he argued, would create stormy arenas for and against Louis in which bad citizens, moderates, aristocrats, and long-winded lawyers would "create pity for the tyrant in the hearts of simple men who cannot see the political consequences of so fateful an indulgence or so unconsidered a decision."[44] The general will, which for St. Just and Robespierre in their faithful application of Rousseau's ideas was the absolute sovereign, would speak through the National Convention, not in a vote of the people themselves. But after the Girondins opposed the Jacobins and had to be purged in the Reign of Terror and Virtue, Robespierre and St. Just would hear the general will only in the Committee of Public Safety. They present us with a transparent case for the logic of power upon which the justification for modern totalitarian rule has been built.[45]

On December 10 and 11, 1792, Louis XVI was summoned by the National Convention to the building that had been his riding arena, in order to face the accusation. He pleaded innocent to the charges. There were no laws on some of the issues, such as suspending the meetings of the Estates-General; he had no intention of shedding blood, as when the troops marched on Paris, and much of what he was accused of was the responsibility of his ministers. In a reverse of the Nuremberg trial, where the ministers blamed Hitler, Louis blamed his ministers: "I executed all the orders proposed to me by the ministers."[46] Instead of pleading the doctrine of superior orders, Louis plead inferior orders.

With the example of Charles I before him, Louis faced three choices.[47] He could, like Charles, refuse to recognize the authority of the court to try the king. For this, as Morisson's argument suggests, he had good legal ground since the Constitution of 1791 provided that "the person of the king is inviolable and sacred." Yes, but it also stated that no authority in France is superior to the law, that the "King reigns only by it; and it is only in the name of the law that he can require obedience." If the king were to use the army against the nation, the Constitution provided, he would be held to have abdicated. After abdication "the king shall be in the class of citizens, and may be accused and tried like them, for acts posterior to this abdication."[48] Louis had accepted the 1791 Constitution and was willing to be held responsible for his actions under it, as a constitutional monarch, but not prior to it or apart from it. Yet he was called to answer to the National Convention itself, not a special court such as Charles I had, and the revolutionaries were in control. He had no hope of winning a challenge to its authority. For the same reason he had to reject his second choice, throwing himself on the mercy of the court. There would be little mercy, and it, like his first choice, would be a step toward the guillotine.[49]

The only real choice Louis had was to put up a vigorous defense, although thereby recognizing the right of the National Convention to try him. But if his chances of not being executed were slim, he would have a day in court and a chance for a moral victory. "By insisting on a fair trial," David Jordan observes, "he would compel his accusers to live up to their supposed admiration for the law. Let them give me a fair trial, he thought, and he would be exonerated. Unlike Mary, Queen of Scots, unlike Charles I, Louis thought this moral victory worth fighting for, and he certainly had no interest in the glories of martyrdom. He would appear in court protected only by the law. He would neither beg for his life nor try to overawe his judges. He would appear before the Convention as a man unjustly charged, as a man who had not violated the laws of men or God. He was neither a criminal nor a tyrant. He dared his accusers to *prove* him guilty."[50]

Although not allowed a lawyer at his interrogation, the Convention decided he could be represented at his trial. That gave Louis two weeks to find lawyers and prepare his defense. Of Louis's three hastily assembled lawyers, Raymond DeSeze, the youngest, presented the king's defense before the Convention on December 26, 1792. DeSeze's first argument was that as king Louis was inviolable under the 1791 Constitution unless he was forced to abdicate, and in that situation, he could be tried, but not for what he had done as king. What he had done before 1791 did not apply, and neither the 1791 Constitution nor any statute law could be legally used against Louis. DeSeze even quoted the patron saint of the Revolution, J.-J. Rousseau, for authority to argue that the general will could not pronounce upon a specific person. If, then, the king was immune from all positive law, and natural law in the form of the general will could not apply to an individual, what then, was left on which to try Louis? Only force, DeSeze replied. While the Convention possessed unequalled power, "there is a power you do not have: it is that of not being just."[51] Louis was innocent because he was immune.

DeSeze's second argument in Louis's case was an attack on the legal procedure. He directed his attention at the moderates, the Girondians, and gave up on the radical Jacobins, led by Robespierre and St. Just, who were intent on executing Louis without a trial. The moderates might be persuaded that the trial was unfair if DeSeze could do it without attacking the legitimacy of the Convention itself. "Citizens," he urged, "I will speak to you here with the frankness of a free man. I search among you for judges, and I see only accusers. . . . You want to pronounce on Louis's fate, and your opinions are disseminated throughout Europe."[52] In all of France Louis is the only person who has the benefits of neither the new nor the old state, "neither the rights of a citizen nor the prerogatives of a king!"[53]

DeSeze concluded with an attempt to move those who could be moved by compassion. When Louis took the throne at age twenty he was "an example of character," without "wicked weaknesses" or "corrupting passions." As king he proved himself to be "the constant friend of the people. The people wanted the abolition of servitude. He began by abolishing it on his own lands. The people asked for reforms in the criminal law . . . he carried out these reforms. *The people wanted liberty: he gave it to them*."[54] This assertion created a sensational stir in the Convention. An indiscretion, it became useful to the king's foes.

Louis spoke briefly, declaring that his conscience reproached him for nothing, that his heart was torn with the accusation that he wanted to shed the blood of the people, and that he had no fear in exposing himself to danger to spare the people's blood and "to remove forever such an imputation." The key to what effectiveness Louis's defense had was neither the legal brief of his lawyers nor the oratorical power of DeSeze's presentation but, instead, the pathos of Louis himself. "His composure and dignity," Jordan comments, "the inevitable symbolism of a great man brought low, made more of an impression on contemporaries than did arid legal arguments." His character and presence made him a sympathetic, even tragic, figure.[55]

The Convention took three votes: Was Louis guilty? Should the decision be submitted to the ratification of the people? What punishment should Louis suffer? Louis struck out on all three: 693 to 0 for guilty; 424 to 283 against an appeal to the people; 361 for death without conditions, 34 for death with various conditions (such as delay), and 321 for imprisonment.[56] Louis XVI was executed on January 21, 1793.

Nuremberg

The most important political trial of our century was the Nuremberg trial. It raised the same questions other trials of regimes do: Was the Nazi regime legitimate? Was the International Military Tribunal legitimate? Except for Article 3 of the tribunal's Constitution, which disallowed any challenges to the tribunal's authority, the Nazi leaders might have taken the position Charles I took. On the other side, Justice Robert Jackson, chief prosecutor for the United States, began his opening address by justifying the tribunal's authority:

> The wrongs which we seek to condemn and punish have been so calculated, so malignant, and so devastating, that civilization cannot tolerate their being ignored, because it cannot survive their being repeated. That four great nations, flushed with victory and stung with injury stay the hand of vengeance and voluntarily submit their captive enemies to the judgment of the law is one of the most significant tributes that Power has ever paid to Reason.[57]

Jackson went on to acknowledge that the trial was unprecedented and that, unfortunately, the nature of the crimes was such that "both prosecution and judgment must be by victor nations over vanquished foes." The accused were given a fair opportunity to defend themselves and, despite a public opinion which condemned their acts, a presumption of innocence.[58]

Was the Nuremberg trial within the rule of law? From a position of positivist jurisprudence it decidedly was not within the rule of law. No international code outlawed "crimes against humanity" and, therefore, the indictment was new law and the trial ex post facto. Likewise, the Nazi leaders were charged with conspiracy, an Anglo-American legal concept unknown in either Europe or international law. Two other charges, on the other hand, could be understood as defined by the Hague and Geneva Conventions (war crimes, "violations of the laws or customs of war") and the Kellogg-Briand Pact (crimes against peace, "planning, preparation, initiation, or waging of aggression"). Nevertheless, a positivist would not accept the notion that aggressive war was a crime.

There were other serious flaws in the Nuremberg trial. Francis Biddle, the senior American tribunal member, sat as judge, although he had helped plan the trial. The Soviets blamed the Nazis for the Katyn massacre of Polish officers; the massacre was a Soviet act. As prosecutor, Jackson asserted that the same law would be applied to all, but the tribunal did not allow the defendants to cite Allied misdeeds, which were considerable. The London Charter of June 1945 resembled a bill of attainder singling out individuals for prosecution. Finally, planning for the trial was rushed, creating several blunders: the elderly Gustav Krupp, who was not competent to stand trial, was indicted instead of his son, Alfred. Julius Stricher was hanged, but Rudolf Hoess, the commandant of Auschwitz, was used as a prosecution witness. Otto Dietrich, second to Goebbels in the propaganda heirarchy, was not prosecuted, while Hans Fritzsche, a mere radio announcer, was prosecuted.[59]

Nevertheless, while admitting how deeply flawed the Nuremberg trial was, compelling reasons can lead us to say that, on balance, it was within the rule of law. First, the tribunal possessed judicial independence. Both the British and the American judges insisted on this principle, and the French judges exhibited their independence from the French government. Only the presence of the Soviet members, taking a hard line, serves to raise questions about the degree of their independence from Stalin's policy. As Bradley Smith shows, evidence indicates that, given the interaction among the judges especially during deliberations, "all in all, it is reasonable to conclude that, although there were different degrees of independence granted to the Tribunal members, and although the individual judges made different use of their prerogatives, the defendants faced a court surprisingly free from outside control."[60]

Another important consideration in assessing the Nuremberg trial is to assess the main alternative. In the United States, President Roosevelt faced the Morgenthau Plan which, among other suggestions, contained a simple proposal: Compile a list of the Nazi criminals for the Allied military to identify and shoot as soon as they were captured.[61] The trial and the deliberations associated with it, Bradley Smith points out, may have forestalled a bloodbath. By establishing what procedural protections there were in the trial, the Nuremberg tribunal also avoided becoming merely a pro forma trial, a partisan trial as a wartime precedent.[62]

Finally, the Nuremberg trial strengthened the rule of law at the international level by enforcing what has come to be known as the Nuremberg Principle: "Individuals have international duties which transcend the national obligations of obedience imposed by the individual state. He who violates the laws of war cannot obtain immunity while acting in pursuance of the authority of the state if the state in authorizing action moves outside its competence under international law."[63]

Conclusion: Revolution and Jurisprudence

The lawyer's adage, "Hard cases make bad law," seems especially apt during a revolution. Certainly revolutions produce hard cases, but do they result in bad law? Granted, the law coming out of partisan trials—the revolutionary tribunals set up in the shadow of a scaffold—is bad law, rather, the worst that law can offer because it is nonlaw. But what of the cases of the English and French revolutions, Strafford, Laud, Charles I, and Louis XVI? Hard cases, admittedly, but partisan ones with bad law?

Revolutions inevitably bring forth political trials. The law cannot be carried on in its ordinary fashion during the upheaval. Those persons caught up in the whirl and brought to trial will be tried by a court operating on an agenda of power as well as an agenda of positive law. But such trials can be within the rule of law. Lilburne's trial, which we looked at in chapter 5, has no resemblance to the trials which followed the trial and execution of Louis in France, the tribunal of the 1793-1794 Reign of Terror which continued and intensified the September Massacres with a phoney legal cover. There the only agenda was power and the one aim expediency. Lilburne's trial was a genuine contest. Was it, however, a contest on the legal agenda as well as the power agenda? As much as the judges might be favorable to the prosecution side and the army, Lilburne had the crowd and, more importantly, the jury on his side. The accused in partisan trials never wins. But if we are to remove Lilburne's trial from the category of partisan trials because he won, we are only attending to the agenda of power. Is it possible to make a judgment about trials in revolutions on the agenda of law?

In all revolutions a stage is reached where the society has, in effect, dual governments.[64] At that point the revolutionaries have both enough power and authority to offer an alternative rule. Double governments become mirror-like reversals of each other. That point seems to have been reached in the English Revolution with the opening of the Long Parliament in 1640, certainly with the trial of Strafford in 1641, and in the French Revolution with the August insurrection and September Massacres in 1792. In such crises what becomes of the rule of law? In 1943 the Gestapo killed all the wedding guests at a celebration in Poland, except the bride and groom who were away at the photographer's. The Polish underground held a court, passed the death sentence against the Gestapo leader, Fuldner, who had overseen the murders, and executed him in the presence of Nazi officials who were released and told to report the execution to their leaders. The underground then radioed the news to London.[65] Can we say the underground court in this instance acted according to the rule of law? If not, does the rule of law have any meaning in a revolution? If yes, would we then say the same about other underground trials by, for instance, the Red Brigade or the IRA?

In revolutions, especially when a regime is put on trial, law is taken back to its origins in self-help. Self-help is the opposite of the rule of law. "The first business of the law, and more especially of the law of crime and tort," William Holdsworth writes, "is to suppress self-help."[66] Holdsworth finds that in fifth-century Salic law, for example, the effort was made to induce people to submit to the decisions of a court instead of seeking to help themselves to what they deemed their rights and continuing the feud cycle. Early law, especially early procedure, is a rigid series of rules. The rules would spell out, for instance, the precise conditions under which a creditor might help himself to the property of a debtor. Each party in a dispute would follow the rules to the letter. A mistake would be fatal.[67] The same seems to happen in revolutions. The dual governments cannot last for long. In both the English and French revolutions the radicals triumphed but then faced the most basic of problems: kindling a compliance with the law in such a way that it becomes second nature. Their beginnings, like Salic law, saw the enforcement of a rigid code of rules. On whatever else they might differ, the English Puritans, Robespierre's Jacobins, and Khomeini's Shiites would understand each other on the necessity for a literal reading of the rules and a rigid enforcement.[68]

The next step in moving a revolution from disorderly self-help to the rule of law is to engage a civil religion. Robespierre provides the best example, but the Puritans, Lenin (and, after his death, the cult *of* Lenin), and Kho-meini all illustrate the same use of revolutionary symbols and myths of history. The new French calendar based on nature began the day after the abolition of the monarchy (September 22, 1792, or Vendemiaire 1st, Year I); a new trinity of Equality, Liberty, and Fraternity; the *bonnet rouge* for citizens; the Marseillaise; the gospel according to the new saint, J.-J. Rousseau; the martyr Marat; Jacques David's art and festivals celebrating the revolution; and Robespierre's massive Festival of the Supreme Being (June 8, 1794, or 20 Prairial, Year II).[69] All these changes served to create a civil religion to provide the new order and its rule of law with legitimacy.

A trial of the former regime, whether in the person of powerful figures near the sovereign, such as Strafford and Laud, or personified in the sovereign himself, provides a new regime with an incomparable opportunity to elicit support. In such a trial the old regime can be separated from the people. As employed in the trials of Strafford and Laud and then in the trial of Charles, treason came to mean the creation of a permanent division between the rulers and the people. Evidence can be presented that this separation is the fault of the accused, an enemy of the people, who is motivated by private-interest goals. The public world is protected from this misuse of power by the unselfish devotion of the prosecutors who act out of public-interest motives as deputies for the people. The army in England and the Jacobins in France thought of themselves as not only representing but actually embodying the public goals. For St. Just and Robespierre this was so clear in their minds that a trial of the king was not necessary, only the public execution. The trial and execution established the new order with a legitimate title to rule.

What gives legitimate title to any regime? This question brings to the surface three positions in jurisprudence. The composition of the rule of law, whether or not a given trial is a partisan trial, and what is legitimate in a regime depend on one of three sources of the law: tradition, a sovereign lawmaker, or natural law.[70] The view of the law profession generally is the first position, that the source of legitimate law is tradition. Judith Shklar calls this "legalism." It involves, she maintains, the "tendency to think of law as 'there' as a discrete entity, discernibly different from morals and politics," and it means its adherents will fight to the death against arguments based on expediency, the public interest, or the social good.[71] Charles Morisson, the deputy who called Louis XVI a "bloody monster" but nevertheless argued that he could not be tried because the penal code had no provision for such a trial, and the judges and lawyers who were active in the movement against Charles I but stayed away from the trial, represent this view of the law. For them the trial of the king was partisan. Likewise, from this viewpoint the Nuremberg trial was outside the rule of law because there was no international code outlawing "crimes against humanity" and, therefore, the indictment was new law and the trial ex post facto.

A second position on the question of legitimacy and the rule of law is that law has its source in the will of a lawmaker, a sovereign. This viewpoint in its purest form also separates law from morals and all policy considerations. That would be how John Austin or Hans Kelsen and the analytical positivists might see the law, a tendency toward formalism with the law a set of rules. Thomas Hobbes and Jeremy Bentham, two of the giants in this school, infused the law at every point with a rigid moralism: security in one case and utilitarianism in the other. St. Just and Robespierre, but also Charles I, give expression to this dogma on the law. Either the voice of the sovereign people was heard in the revolution, making the trial superfluous, or there existed no authority to judge the king, making the trial a partisan travesty. The Morgenthau Plan for the summary execution of the Nazi leaders, a plan given preliminary approval at the 1944 Quebec conference, and also the defense of Hermann Goering that "Germany was a soverign state, and that her legislation within the German nation was not subject to the jurisdiction of foreign countries,"[72] illustrate the clash of sovereign law.

The third school of jurisprudence understands law as legitimate when it reflects a higher or natural law. Condorcet in the French Revolution presents a clear-cut example of this view, and it is represented in the English Revolution by Cromwell, Bradshaw, and Lilburne. The test of whether or not a given trial was within the rule of law or was partisan would depend upon whether certain translegal standards were satisfied. This is reflected in Justice Jackson's positon on the law at the Nuremberg trial and in the document which was an indirect result of that trial: The Universal Declaration of Human Rights.

Each of the three schools of jurisprudence can summon forth imposing authorities in its behalf. Edward Coke, William Blackstone, and, in our time, Oliver Wendell Holmes and Felix Frankfurter would defend the position that, however much we might disagree with those in power, the courts cannot be employed to bring them down unless the established law provides for it. This is eloquently expressed in Robert Bolt's play *A Man for All Seasons*, when William Roper implores Lord Chancellor Thomas More to arrest Richard Rich. More's wife, Alice, and daughter, Margaret, urged Rich's arrest because "that man's bad." More replied that there was no law against being bad.

Roper: There is! God's law!

More: Then God can arrest him.

Roper: Sophistication upon sophistication!

More: No, sheer simplicity. The law, Roper, the law. I know what's legal not what's right. And I'll stick to what's legal.

Roper: Then you set man's law above God's!

More: No, far below; but let *me* draw your attention to a fact—I'm not God. The currents and eddies of right and wrong, which you find such plain sailing, I can't navigate. I'm no voyager. But in the thickets of the law, oh, there I'm a forester. I doubt if there's a man alive who could follow me there, thank God.

Alice: While you talk, he's gone!

More: And go he should, if he was the Devil himself, until he broke the law!

Roper: So now you'd give the Devil benefit of law!

More: Yes. What would you do? Cut a great road through the law to get after the Devil?

Roper: I'd cut down every law in England to do that!

More: Oh? And when the last law was down, and the Devil turned round on you—where would you hide, Roper, the laws all being flat? This country's planted thick with laws from coast to coast—man's laws, not God's—and if you cut them down—and you're just the man to do it—d'you really think you could stand upright in the winds that would blow then? Yes, I'd give the Devil benefit of law, for my own safety's sake.[73]

No thinker has made a more compelling case for sovereignty than Thomas Hobbes, and his view that the source of law is the will of a sovereign lawmaker is the foundation for thinkers as diverse as Rousseau, Bentham, Marx, and Austin. Hobbes wrote during the English Revolution, rejecting the Puritan position as dangerous yet not accepting divine right. Hobbes begins with the circumstance of self-help, where each person seeks to enforce his/her natural right to do everything deemed necessary for self-defense. The solution is a covenant creating a sovereign who represents the public conscience of each person. The sovereign will is our will, and our obligation to obey is identical to our self-interest, i.e. our security.[74] To presume to judge the sovereign, then, is an absurdity, or, to say the same thing, those who judge are sovereign. Whoever denies the authority of the sovereign is no longer a citizen but an enemy of the commonwealth, beyond the law and relapsed into a condition of war.[75] This was the view that Charles I had of the Puritans and that St. Just and Robespierre had of Louis XVI.

A long tradition in political thought holds that the worst form of government is tryanny. The natural law view of jurisprudence is most definitely expressed by Thomas Aquinas. Tyrannical rule is unjust because, according to Aquinas, it is not directed to the common good. It does injury to the public welfare in doing benefit to the private welfare of the ruler. "Consequently the overthrowing of such government is not strictly sedition;

except perhaps in the case that it is accompanied by such disorder that the community suffers greater harm from the consequent disturbances than it would from a continuance of the former rule." The tyrant is responsible for sedition when he spreads discord among the people in the hope of controlling them more easily.[76] John Locke, approaching law from the liberal position of natural rights, sees government as created by trust and limited by human rights including the right of resistance to arbitrary rulers,[77] a position reflected in the Declaration of Independence.

This brings us back to the dilemma presented by hard cases. "Great cases like hard cases make bad law," wrote Justice Oliver Wendell Holmes. "For great cases are called great not by reason of their real importance in shaping the law of the future, but because of some accident of immediate overwhelming interest which appeals to the feelings and distorts the judgment. These immediate interests exercise a kind of hydraulic pressure which makes what previously was clear seem doubtful and before which even well-settled principles of law will bend."[78] Trials in revolutions are likely to be hard, and trials of regimes are of necessity both hard and great. What is a society to do when the hydraulic pressure of revolution forces such cases into the court? If such trials are the product of "immediate overwhelming interest which appeals to the feelings and distorts the judgment," that is merely good evidence that the law and the courts cannot escape working amidst the conflicts of society and shaping history by making decisions.

Although in ordinary cases and most of the time, decisions in the law are not hard and great, when they are, even if such times are rare, our understanding of what the law is should go beyond what we might find in a law user's manual, even if it does have the imposing title of *Corpus Juris*. If we assume that the rule of law is fully embraced by the maxim, "We are a government of laws, not men," we ignore the responsibility decision makers have for interpreting the written and case law, applying the requirements of principle and justice, as well as facing the perversities of human nature and the ceaseless transformations of history, all of which are elements of the law itself. But—and this is the point—the rule of law is not a legalism, not a formula, not the same as the rules of law. While revolutions and the rule of law might begin as hostile foes, the rule of law can be strengthened by revolution. Revolutions do for law what the scientific revolutions—Copernican, Newtonian, and Einsteinian—have done for science. A new paradigm of legitimacy replaces the old one.[79] Political trials of regime become the fulcrums in revolution by which the old dispensation in legitimate rule is pushed down and a new dispensation rises.

Notes

1. Raoul Berger, *Impeachment: The Constitutional Problems* (New York, Bantam Books, 1974), p. 33. See also C.V. Wedgwood, *The King's Peace: 1637-1641* (New York, Macmillan, 1956), Ch. 5.
2. Thomas B. Howell, comp., *A Complete Collection of State Trials and Proceedings for High Treason and Other Crimes and Misdemeanors from the Earliest Period to the Year 1783*, 35 Vols. (London, R. Bagshaw, 1809-1826), Vol. 4, p. 321. Hearafter cited as *State Trials*.
3. Holdsworth, *History of English Law*, Vol. 2, pp. 449-450.
4. *Ibid.*, Vol. 4, pp. 493-496.
5. Conrad Russell, "The Theory of Treason in the Trial of Strafford," *English Historical Review* 80 (1965), pp. 30-50.
6. *Ibid.*, p. 34.
7. *Ibid.*, p. 46-47.
8. Berger, *Impeachment*, p. 37.
9. *Ibid.*, p. 38.
10. Wedgwood, *King's Peace*, p. 328.
11. *Ibid.*, pp. 421-428.
12. *State Trials*, Vol. 4, pp. 326-329.
13. *Ibid.*, pp. 358-359.
14. *Ibid.*
15. *Ibid.*, pp. 361-363.
16. Leonard W. Levy, *Origins of the Fifth Amendment: The Right against Self-Incrimination* (London, Oxford University Press, 1968), p. 267.
17. *Ibid.*, Chs. 12-30. Irving Brant, *The Bill of Rights: Its Origin and Meaning* (New York, New American Library, 1965).
18. Charles McIlwain, *The High Court of Parliament and Its Supremacy* (New Haven, Yale University Press, 1910), p. 153.
19. *Ibid.*, p. 386.
20. Brant, *Bill of Rights*, Ch. 2.
21. C.V. Wedgwood concludes that Cromwell knew nothing of Pride's Purge before it occured, since he was in the North, but that he gave his approval because "it was too late for any redeeming maneuver and Cromwell accepted with a good grace a situation which he could not alter." Wedgwood, *The Trial of Charles I* (London, Collins, 1964), p. 43.
22. *State Trials*, Vol. 4, pp. 990-994.
23. Roger Howell, *Cromwell* (Boston, Little, Brown, 1977), pp. 122-123.
24. Wedgwood, *Trial of Charles I*, pp. 98-100.
25. *Ibid.*, p. 96. Although the new Great Seal bears the date 1651, it was ordered made at the time Charles's trial was in preparation, 1648.
26. Howell, *Cromwell*, pp. 123-124.
27. Esme Wingfield-Stratford, *King Charles the Martyr, 1643-1649* (Westport, Conn., Greenwood Press, 1975), p. 312.
28. Wedgwood, *Trial of Charles I*, p. 123.
29. *Ibid.*, p. 102.
30. *State Trials*, Vol. 4, pp. 1045-1048.
31. *Ibid.*, pp. 995-996.
32. *Ibid.*, p. 996.
33. *Ibid.*, pp. 999-1000.

34. *Ibid.*, pp. 1009-1010.
35. *Ibid.*, p. 1011.
36. *Ibid.*, pp. 1012-1013.
37. See George Lefebvre, *The French Revolution* (New York, Columbia University Press, 1962), 2 Vols., Vol. 1, Chs. 13-15.
38. Michael Walzer, ed., *Regicide and Revolution: Speeches at the Trial of Louis XVI* (Cambridge, Cambridge University Press, 1974), pp. 110-114.
39. *Ibid.*, pp. 139-157. Condorcet's views were circulated in a pamphlet.
40. *Ibid.*, pp. 121-126.
41. *Ibid.*, p. 131.
42. *Ibid.*, pp. 132-133.
43. *Ibid.*, p. 178.
44. *Ibid.*, p. 183.
45. See Albert Camus, *The Rebel: An Essay on Man in Revolt* (New York, Vintage, 1956), Ch. 3; J.L. Talmon, *The Origins of Totalitarian Democracy* (New York, Praeger, 1960), pp. 78-98.
46. David P. Jordan, *The King's Trial: The French Revolution vs. Louis XVI* (Berkeley, University of California Press, 1979), p. 109.
47. *Ibid.*, p. 113.
48. Constitution of 1791, Pt. 3, Ch. 2, Sec. 1, in Walzer, *Regicide and Revolution*, Appendix, pp. 215-216.
49. Jordan, *King's Trial*, p. 113.
50. *Ibid.*, pp. 114-115.
51. *Ibid.*, pp. 130-131.
52. *Ibid.*, pp. 131-132.
53. *Ibid.*
54. *Ibid.*, p. 135.
55. *Ibid.*, pp. 137-141.
56. *Ibid.*, pp. 172, 176, 190.
57. *Trial of the Major War Criminals before the International Military Tribunal* (Nuremberg, 1947), 42 Vols., Vol. 2, pp. 98-99.
58. *Ibid.*, pp. 100-102.
59. Bradley F. Smith, *Reaching Judgment at Nuremberg* (New York, New American Library, 1979), pp. 9,33,43,71,81,104,203,293.
60. *Ibid.*, p. 8. See also pp. 77, 144, 160, 215, 267, 291, 303-304.
61. *Ibid.*, pp. 23-24.
62. *Ibid.*, p. 303.
63. Telford Taylor, *Nuremberg and Vietnam: An American Tragedy* (New York, Quadrangle, 1970), p. 84.
64. See Leon Trotsky, *The Russian Revolution*, trans. by Max Eastman (Garden City, Doubleday Anchor, 1959), pp. 199 ff; Crane Brinton, *The Anatomy of Revolution* (New York, Vintage, 1958), pp. 139 ff.
65. Feliks Gross, in *Assassination and Political Violence: A Report to the National Commission on the Causes and Prevention of Violence*, ed. by James F. Kuhhan, Shelden G. Levy, and William J. Crotty (New York, Praeger, 1970), p. 578.
66. Holdsworth, *History of English Law*, Vol. 3, p. 278.
67. *Ibid.*, Vol. 2, pp. 99-100.
68. See Michael Walzer, *The Revolution of the Saints: A Study in the Origins of Radical Politics* (New York, Atheneum, 1974), Graeme Newman, "Khomeini

and Criminal Justice: Notes on Crime and Culture," *Journal of Criminal Law and Criminology* 73 (1982), pp. 561-581.

69. See Brinton, *Anatomy of Revolution*, pp. 192-207; Christopher Dawson, *The Gods of Revolution: An Analysis of the French Revolution* (New York, Minerva Press, 1972), Chs. 5-7; Lefebvre, *French Revolution*, Vol. 2, Ch. 2.

70. The three sources of law, or three schools of jurisprudence, seem to have been established by a variety of thinkers. Max Weber's well-known classification of the three types of legitimate authority is (1) traditional, (2) charismatic, and (3) rational, H. H. Gerth and C. Wright Mills, eds., *From Max Weber: Essays in Sociology* (New York, Oxford University Press, 1958), pp. 78-79, 295 ff. Roscoe Pound, *Introduction to the Philosophy of Law* (New Haven, Yale University Press, 1954), Ch. 2, sees the growth of law coming from historical assimilation (tradition), legislation (sovereignty), and philosophical theory (juristic). Judith Shklar (*Legalism*, pp. 6 ff.) finds legalism, analytical positivism, and natural law.

71. Shklar, *Legalism*, p. 9.

72. *Trial of the Major War Criminals*, Vol. 22, p. 367. See Bradley F. Smith, *The Road to Nuremberg* (New York, Basic Books, 1981) for the Morgenthau Plan and its politics, Chs. 1-2.

73. Robert Bolt, *A Man for All Seasons* (New York, Vintage, 1960), pp. 37-38.

74. Thomas Hobbes, *Leviathan* (Oxford, Blackwell, 1957), Ch. 17.

75. *Ibid.*, Chs. 28-29.

76. Thomas Aquinas, *Summa Theologica*, Secunda Secundae, Question 42, in A. P. D'Entreves, ed., *Aquinas: Selected Political Writings* (Oxford, Blackwell, 1954), p. 161.

77. John Locke, *Two Treatises of Government*, ed. by Peter Laslett (New York, Mentor, 1960), Second Treatise, sections 203-209, 220-222.

78. *Northern Securities Company v. United States*, 193 U.S. 197, at 400 (1904).

79. See Thomas S. Kuhn, *The Structure of Scientific Revolutions*, 2nd ed. (Chicago, University of Chicago Press, 1970); Harold J. Berman, *Law and Revolution: The Formation of the Western Legal Tradition* (Cambridge, Mass., Harvard Universtiy Press, 1983), Introduction.

10

Conclusion: Do Hard Cases Make Bad Law?

A political trial falls between politics and law. In politics, justice and the legal bounds of the rule of law are embarrassments to the realist. In law, the legalist cannot acknowledge public influence and the political consequences of judgments by courts. The realist would have us believe that, as the world goes, all trials are political, just as the legalist would have it that, properly, none are political. Is the rule of law identical with the rules of law? Or is it a cover for power? If the former, as legalists would have it, we can learn nothing from difficult political trials because the legal agenda is the only agenda. The Gordian knot in such trials must be cut with the legal sword. If the realists are right in saying that law is merely an extension of politics, again we will learn nothing because the Gordian knot will be sliced by a sword held by the powers that be. Yet it is evident that trials can be fair without being rule-bound, and they can be political without being partisan. The Nuremberg trial cannot be equated with the trial of Louis XVI; the Wounded Knee trial was different in kind from a South African Terrorism Law trial such as the SWAPO trial; what Karl Armstrong or the Berrigan brothers experienced in their trials bears no resemblance to the experiences of those tried by the Stalin regime.

If law and politics were thought of as two completely separate realms in our public life, political trials would not cease to exist. We might, however, deny that they exist by defining them away. The lofty pedestal of legalism encourages us to mistake the rules of law for the rule of law. We see the rules so clearly that we miss the principles on which they stand. An introduction of such issues as the rightness of policy or the representativeness of government, from this perspective, is rejected as contrary to the rules of law, as a "political defense." The problem with this critique of political trials is that while a "political defense" is castigated, a "political prosecution" might slip past us unnoticed. While William Kunstler might be accused of introducing matters of social justice to sway a jury by appealing to their conscience, every prosecutor who jumps from the narrow confines of an indictment to warn the jury that the defendant is a harbinger of anarchy taking the law into his own hands is doing for his side what Kunstler does for the defense. Clarence Darrow won acquittals for many of his clients accused of conspiracy by convincing the jury that a worse conspiracy was represented at the prosecution table by those who were using the "law for the purpose of bringing righteous ones to death or to jail."[1]

Still, unless law and politics are separate, unless a respectful distance is maintained between them, law will become an instrument of expediency. We have enough evidence in partisan trials to see this danger. If believing that law and politics can be totally separate is an illusion, thinking that law is politics by another means imperils those very rights which in a free and democratic society are the purpose of politics. An independent judiciary keeps constitutional politics honest by holding to the rule of law.

The dilemma of a political trial is contained in the phrase *law and order*. The two are identical only to the legalist and the realist, who think that law is a system of rules and that either all order is obtained through law or all law is a pageant for those who impose order. For others order is larger than law and the law is more than rules.[2] When legal and political agendas clash in a political trial, the legalist and the realist will see this conflict as a failure of the rules to clarify what conduct is required or as a refusal by certain people to obey. A political trial, from such viewpoints, represents either a blunder in which the law did not do its job or a mutiny by those who challenge the law's authority. Such positions lead rapidly to the conclusion that a political trial is either all law or all politics—the mere application of rules or the elimination of opponents. This is the standard assumption many make about political trials, that either no trials are political or that all are what have been called here partisan trials. The source of the confusion is in the meaning of "law and order."

A dissenter, such as a John Lilburne or a Daniel Berrigan, has a clear understanding of both *law* and *order*, an understanding which is not irresponsible. A criminal, intent on taking advantage of society, may have an irresponsible notion but not a dissenter. The D.A. prosecuting a dissenter may have as clear an understanding of both law and order as the dissenter, but it would be sharply different. The Irish nationalist might see true order for Ireland in its independence from England and view all laws which tie them together as tyranny, just as an English prosecutor would have no doubt that Irish violence disrupts civilized order and that prosecution for resistance activities is enforcement of the law. Granted, they differ, but their differences can be circumscribed by procedures of a trial.

The function of a political trial is to clarify for society the practical meaning of *law* and of *order*. What emerges will not be a logician's delight, but it can be a workable understanding. Charles I and the Cromwellites each had a firm notion of what *law* and *order* meant for England in the seventeenth century, and John Lilburne had his. For the king, the crown was the restorer of legitimate order because it was the ancient order, and an alternative was not merely unacceptable, it was unthinkable. For the Puritans, the Parliament was the voice of the people and they, the Puritans (or the New Model Army), were the voice of God. The royalists, in Puritan eyes, were as far from true order and its law as was the Roman Catholic Church, which for the Puritans was the force of disorder and tyranny. Finding his foundations in old English law, mainly the Magna Carta, in Scripture, and in popular will, John Lilburne is something of a compromise between the tradition-laden royalists and the revolutionary Puritans. He rejected the authoritarianism of both sides, which explains his many trials. The evolution of what *law* and what *order* mean emerges out of such trials.

Political trials are society's own judicial review. How it is exercised depends upon society's understanding of *law* and *order*, and it in turn shapes society's understanding. In partisan trials society imposes its power for revenge, to eliminate unpopular opponents, to dominate ethnic groups, or to establish victor's justice. If the trials are within the rule of law, society can explore the issues of responsibility, rightness of policy and dissent, representation and legtimacy. The Supreme Court can use judicial review to do the same. A political trial, like judicial review, can both reflect society and educate it. What Robert McCloskey concluded in his history of judicial review applies to political trials: "The judges have often agreed with the main current of public sentiment because they were themselves part of that current, and not because they feared to disagree with it. But the salient fact, whatever the explanation, is that the Court has seldom lagged far behind or forged far ahead of America."[3] Political trials are in the same current.

In political trials, where society can observe and be prompted to rethink basic concepts, the opposing sides take symbolic positions, and the trial encloses a form of existential representation.[4] Dennis Banks and Russell Means represent the American Indians in their struggle with the United States government and the BIA, but they also represent all Americans in an attempt to insure the rights guaranteed by the Constitution and treaties, and, further, they represent the fulfillment of human dignity which applies to all peoples. From the other side in the trial, Banks and Means represent a militant group (AIM) which desires to gain power easily and violently, but they also represent a challenge to the Constitution when they hold a town hostage, and they, like all terrorists, represent a threat to civilized society. Both viewpoints have not only solid evidence to present but respectable positions to argue, although they are opposites. The Wounded Knee trial emerges as an occasion for society to face the contradiction which in American history did not begin with the 1973 takeover of a tiny South Dakota town.

Alasdair MacIntyre observes in *After Virtue*: "Man is in his actions and practice, as well as in his fictions, essentially a story-telling animal. He is not essentialy, but becomes through history, a teller of stories that aspire to truth. But the key question for man is not about their own authorship; I can only answer the question 'What am I to do?' if I can answer the prior question 'Of what story or stories do I find myself a part?'"[5] Every trial is a story, but every political trial is a story with special claims upon society. The questions it raises touch each citizen twice, once because every citizen is involved in the responsible enforcement of law to achieve justice and again because of the issues with which it challenges society as a whole. Specific events set the legal agenda of a political trial while the wider stories of those involved, both victim and defendant, determine the political agenda. Dennis Banks and Russell Means, for instance, were tried for burglary, theft, assault, and possession of firearms in the 1973 takeover of Wounded Knee, but in addition to this legal agenda both the prosecution and defense raised a political agenda that involved the issue of representation: Who can speak for the American Indians?

The political agenda contains the stories which strike home with each of us as citizens. If the legal agenda focuses on incidents which can be dated and located, the political agenda calls up analogies from the depths of our culture that are difficult to delineate. If the legal agenda depends on a rational-analysis, the political agenda summons our empathy. Both sides can invoke the political agenda. The prosecution might, for example, tell the story of the victim—such as the residents of Wounded Knee, the owners of the trading post, and the priest of the Sacred Heart Catholic Church—while the defense might embrace the tale of the American Indians as victims of American history. The same dual agenda can be found in the trials of other defendants from Socrates and Jesus to the Rosenbergs and Berrigans. Their separate stories were shaped by the trials concerning specific events, but the stories reach further than the events to our common need to understand ourselves as a society with a history and an identity.

As the trial and the story of Joan of Arc demonstrate, we have difficulty knowing Joan. Three major playwrights, to take an obvious and perhaps extreme example, Shakespeare, Shaw, and Brecht, present Joan as a "witch" and "damned sorceress," (William Shakespeare, I *Henry VI*, Act III, scene 2); as "the queerest fish among the eccentric worthies of the Middle Ages," the "first Protestant martyr," one of the "first apostles of Nationalism, and . . . of Napoleonic realism in warfare," a "pioneer of rational dressing for women," a "born boss," (G. B. Shaw, *Saint Joan*, Preface); and as a proletarian martyr (Bertolt Brecht, *Saint Joan of the Stockyards*). If we were to survey the biographers and historians—French, English, and ecclesiastical—we would undoubtedly find several more

Joans. Naturally, the historical events and the real Joan matter. But at the same time, the story of Joan and the myth surrounding her life and trial have an importance which extends beyond the facts. Just as the events which lead to political trials, and the trials themselves as events, are part of the larger stories, so the stories participate in more universal myths. What we understand from the trials and stories shape the myths. Unlike the facts in the legal agenda, the myths are beyond proof, but they are not beyond understanding. Not only do the trials and the stories give the myths believability, but the myths, in turn, undergird the political trials and stories with universal significance. More, the trials-cum-stories-cum-myths stimulate our thought about fundamental public conflicts and assist in developing our sense of identity as a public.[6]

The political and legal issues which become the Gordian knots in certain trials are cut decisively, not untied. The Catonsville Nine and most of the Nuremberg Twenty-One were tried and judged guilty, while Angela Davis, John Zenger, and John Lilburne were tried and found not guilty. The verdicts may have settled the matter for the defendants and for society at the time but not definitively. In certain cases the trial is not over when the verdict is reached. The dialog on the issues may continue for centuries.

The head-on collision of values is most apparent, as I hope this book has demonstrated, in political trials within the rule of law. Yet as is equally clear, some trials in all countries and, sadly, all trials in some countries are partisan prescriptions of expediency. We learn from them, too, but they are negative examples. What happened to Socrates and Jesus at the hand of the state, to Joan of Arc and the victims of the Inquisition, to Thomas More, Alfred Dreyfus, Sacco and Vanzetti, and members of SWAPO demonstrates far more about the human spirit and the rule of law than many other trials within the rule of law. Nevertheless, from partisan trials we learn in spite, not because, of the law. To law and politics the rule of law is a moral consensus necessary for the peaceful resolution of fundamental conflicts. Its framework pemits hostile encounters over the nature of public responsibility, such as in the Watergate and the Hinckley trials, over the rightness of policy and the methods of dissent, as in the trials of Lilburne or Karl Armstrong, over the nature of representation, as in the trials of nationalists, and even over the questions of legitimate rule, as when regimes themselves are tried.

Normal trials follow a route similar to that which Thomas Kuhn sees normal science following: puzzle-solving and mopping-up operations.[7] Political trials, by contrast, engage those paradigmatic myths that are prior to the rules governing normal trials. The legal agenda can handle normal trials, but in political trials the dual agendas—political as well as legal— raise questions which bear upon the primary stories which the rules of law clarify and modify. During crises when normal trials might break down and the paradigms blur, political trials challenge the assumptions of both law and politics. The myths that are at the core of our understanding are given new meaning when a Socrates or a John Zenger is mentioned as the representative dissenter or a Joan of Arc, Robert Emmet, or Nelson Mandela is held up to represent all nationalists.

Political trials within the rule of law provide society with the occasion to examine, and perhaps redefine, itself. Such trials do not, perhaps cannot, resolve the tensions forever. The Berrigans did not stop the draft, nor did the federal government halt anti-Vietnam protests with the Catonsville Nine trials. The issues about the immorality of the war and the proper methods of dissent were not given a definitive answer. They were clarified, however. The trial for the occupation of Wounded Knee neither restored to the Sioux the Black Hills guaranteed by the 1868 Treaty nor reconciled AIM and its supporters to the BIA and the tribal council. The issue of who speaks for the American Indians, or even the Lakota, remains, as does the larger issue of the place of the American Indian in American society. The Wounded Knee trial did, however, bring about a better understanding of the Sioux and the issues they have raised. Political trials confront tangled issues, tied in tight knots. While a trial might not untie the knot, but only cut it, our reflection on the knot in front of us will help us to understand the next one much better. Hard cases, the adage has it, make bad law. Nevertheless, hard political cases make a better understood society.

In every criminal trial, whether for prostitution, driving while intoxicated, theft, rape, or murder, public order is at stake, as is one individual's liberty. This tension between society and the individual is rooted in both criminal law and religion, twins at birth and throughout their growth. It is far from an accident that the Christian liturgy and courtroom ritual have so much in common: beginning with an invocation of authority, followed by the entrance of a judge or priest in a robe signifying a special office, continuing with indictments and proclamations, confession of transgressions, the central issue of guilt, reliance on oaths and witnesses to the truth, and concluding with judgments and sanctions. It is interesting to note that the word *sanction* in law means punishment, but that the religious roots of the word are in that which makes life holy, which occurs in a civic sense when a judge passes sentence. Naturally and fortunately, there are crucial differences between criminal law and religion, especially in the adversary system, but criminal law cannot deny its origin in expiation.

A political trial involves these tensions and much more. Its agenda (often more latent than manifest) includes, in addition to those inherent in the criminal law, the tensions of our public identity, our myth of history, and our sense of destiny. The contradictions which arise over these issues intensify from trials of corruption, to trials of dissenters, to trials of nationalists, and finally to trials of regimes. Like Charles I, no defendant in a political trial is an ordinary prisoner. The atonement sought by the public, represented by the judge, in a political trial reaches further than in an ordinary criminal trial. The fact that Otto Kerner was a judge and former governor rather than, for instance, an accountant, made his bribe-taking a threat to the integrity of the public realm. The court, in imposing sanctions of law, restored that integrity. Likewise, the contradictions represented in the Armstrong trial involved more than arson and second-degree murder, just as those in the Banks-Means trial went far beyond theft, disorderly conduct, and illegal possession of firearms. The added agenda in these, as in all political trials, touches the fundamental dilemmas of politics: the morality of war and of violent protest, the identity of a people and who can speak in its name.

All criminal trials touch society's fabric. Judgments about public order and individual liberty made in ordinary criminal trials involve everyone. The texture of civility in everyday life is woven from such decisions. Political trials go beyond this warp and woof of law to the pattern in the public tapestry itself. That pattern, with all its unresolved contradictions, is the reason political trials become central moments for understanding nations and entire civilizations. The trial of Socrates is the event through which we generally approach Athens and all ancient Greece. Socrates' "Apology" at his trial is one of the cornerstones in the tradition of enlightened thought and freedom of inquiry in the liberal tradition. The trial of Jesus is, likewise, central to Christianity, and a foundation for the strength of religious feeling. Who would write a history of France without devoting close attention to the trials of Joan, Louis XVI, and Alfred Dreyfus? Are not the trials of John Peter Zenger, John Brown, Sacco and Vanzetti, the Rosenbergs, the Chicago Seven, and the Berrigans equally important for understanding America? For an Irish nationalist, the words Robert Emmet spoke before he was sentenced to death have come to have the same meaning as the Gettysburg Address does to an American.[8]

"The ultimate foundation of a free society," in the words of Justice Felix Frankfurter, "is the binding tie of cohesive sentiment. . . . We live by symbols."[9] Political trials serve a free society by bringing together for public consideration the basic contradictions which arise from the clash of conflicting values and loyalties. The tensions over the relationship of the private to the public realms, the rightness of police and of dissent, the nature of representation, and the legitimacy of government are all present in any political system. Especially in crises, these tensions must be faced. Although the judgments in political trials do not resolve these contradictions, it is important that they be raised. Generally, if either side of the tension were to win and dominate, we would all lose. This much we have known about such fundamental contradictions at least since Aeschylus wrote his *Oresteia*. In the three plays of this cycle justice is found neither completely on the side of the accused Orestes nor completely on the side of the accusing Furies. Orestes was guilty of murdering his mother, and Athena knew it, but Athena also knew that the angry vengeance of the Furies would not guarantee justice. She ended the cycle of blood revenge in the House of Artreus by establishing a court of law. In short and in conclusion, political trials within the rule of law, while not resolving cntradictions about the nature of society and history, do bring them into clear focus, and open the way for us to see and accept the ironies of law, politics, and history.

Notes

1. Irving Stone, *Clarence Darrow for the Defense* (New York, New American Library, 1969), p. 130.
2. For a discussion of the relationship between law and order by two of the others see Lon L. Fuller, *The Morality of Law* (New Haven, Yale University Press, 1964), Ch. 2, "The Morality that Makes Law Possible;" Lon L. Fuller, "Two Principles of Human Association," in Kenneth I. Winston, ed., *The Principles of Social Order: Selected Essays of Lon L. Fuller* (Durham, Duke University Press, 1981); Roberto Mangabeira Unger, *Law in Modern Society: Toward a Criticism of Social Theory* (New York, Free Press, 1976), Ch. 2, "Law and the Forms of Society."
3. Robert McCloskey, *The American Supreme Court* (Chicago, University of Chicago Press, 1960), p. 224.
4. See Eric Voegelin, *The New Science of Politics* (Chicago, University of Chicago Press, 1952), Ch. 1, "Representation and Existence," pp. 27ff. See also John T. Noonan, Jr., *Persons and the Masks of the Law: Cardozo, Holmes, Jefferson, and Wythe as Makers of the Masks* (New York, Farrar, Straus, & Giroux, 1976), Ch. 1, "The Masks of the Participants."
5. Alasdair MacIntyre, *After Virtue: A Study in Moral Theory* (Notre Dame, University of Notre Dame Press, 1981), p. 201.
6. For an analysis of stories and myths in society see G. S. Kirk, *The Nature of Greek Myths* (Penguin, 1974), Pt. 1; Ernst Cassirer, *The Myth of the State* (New Haven, Yale University Press, 1946), Pt. 1.
7. Thomas S. Kuhn, *The Structure of Scientific Revolution* (Chicago, University of Chicago Press, 1970), p. 24, Ch. 5.
8. Malcolm Brown, *The Politics of Irish Literature: From Thomas Davis to W. B. Yeates* (Seattle, University of Washington Press, 1972), p. 22.
9. *Minersville School District v. Gobitis*, 310 U.S. 586, 596 (1940).

Appendix A:

Jury Selection in the Wounded Knee Trial

Attention was drawn to the Wounded Knee trial not only for its well-known defendants and striking issues but also because a term of social scientists assisted the defense in jury selection. Jay Schulman and Richard Christie, who served as similar consultants for the defense in the Harrisburg Seven, Camden Twenty-Five, and Gainesville Eight trials, began to work two months before the trial opened, aided by some fifty volunteers. They developed a sociological profile of the community from which the potential jurors would be drawn by phoning 576 people at random with questions about attitudes toward, among others, Indians. Each of the 133 on the full panel was investigated, and ten observers during the *voir dire* questioning watched for emotional cues displayed by potential jurors through such signals as their body language and responses to authority by attention to the judge or by responding "Yes, sir" (*Time*, January 28, 1973, p. 60; Gordon Germant, "The Notion of Conspiracy Is Not Tasty to Americans: An Interview with June L. Tapp," *Psychology Today*, May, 1975, pp. 60-65).

To begin with, the full panel of 133 was a random sample of the voter registration lists and was representative of the community. These 133, as Table 1 shows, were equally divided between men and women and had an average age of 42. Judge Nichol asked questions of them which would, first, establish who among them could serve on the jury without hardship and second, based on questions from the attorneys, who could serve without bias. Of the 87 who were excused because of a hardship or dismissed because of a possible bias, 24 (28 percent) had family reasons and 26 (30 percent) had job reasons, while 20 (23 pecent) were dismissed for cause, 7 by the judge, 11 after defense challenges, and 2 from prosecution challenges. (See Table 2.)

The hardship excuses included 2 women who were expecting babies and the husband of an expectant mother, 10 people who were responsible for the care of small children, 4 who took care of spouses or elderly relatives, 3 who ran farms, 4 who were either self-employed or worked on a commis-

TABLE 1

	FULL PANEL (133)		TENTATIVE JURORS (46)		JURORS (16, incl. 4 alternates)	
Men	66	50%	21	46%	4	25%
Women	67	50%	25	54%	12	75%
AVERAGE AGE	. . . 42		. . 37		. 32	
over 70	3	2%	1	2%	--	--
60s	13	9%	4	9%	--	--
50s	19	14%	5	11%	2	13%
40s	22	17%	9	20%	3	19%
30s	19	14%	12	26%	3	19%
20s	21	16%	9	20%	7	44%
under 20	6	4%	4	9%	1	6%
no information	30	23%	2	4%	--	--
RESIDENCE						
St. Paul	51	38%	21	45%	6	37%
suburb	42	32%	16	35%	7	43%
small town	30	23%	9	20%	3	19%
farm	10	8%	--	--	--	--
OCCUPATION						
technical/skilled	30	22%	13	28%	4	25%
blue collar	31	23%	3	18%	3	18%
housewife	17	13%	5	11%	2	12.5%
sales	5	4%	5	11%	2	12.5%
secretary	14	11%	5	11%	2	12.5%
academic	5	4%	3	7%	2	12.5%
administrative	3	2%	3	7%	--	--
service	5	4%	2	4%	2	12.5%
retired	5	4%	2	4%	--	--
self-employed	10	8%	--	--	--	--
unspecified	1	1%	--	--	--	--
EDUCATION						
college plus			2	4%	--	--
college			9	20%	3	19%
high school plus			4	9%	4	25%
high school			4	9%	2	12.5%
less than high school			2	4%	2	12.5%
no information			25	54%	5	31%
POLITICS						
Democrat			16	35%	6	38%
Republican			2	4%	1	6%
Independent			10	22%	6	38%
no information			18	39%	3	19%
RELIGION						
Roman Catholic			19	41%	9	56%
Lutheran			11	24%	3	19%
Congregational			1	2%	1	6%
Episcopalian			2	4%	1	6%
Other Protestant			6	13%	0	--
Orthodox			1	2%	0	--
Mormon			1	2%	1	6%
agnostic			1	2%	1	6%
not asked/no religion			5	11%	0	--

TABLE 2

I --- <u>EXCUSED by JUDGE NICHOL</u> 74

    A. Hardship 67

                Family (24)

general	7
expecting or wife expecting	3
care of small children	10
care of other relative	4

                Job   (26)

general	8
farm	3
self-employed or working on a commission	4
essential to employer	3
jury duty will jeopardize job	4
will miss opportunity for promotion	1
financial hardship, e.g. house payments	3

                Health (4)

                Age   (2)

                Other Hardships (11)

nervous	3
sequestering would be a problem	3
a trip is pending	2
live further than 75 miles from St. Paul	3

    B. Cause 7

                Conflict of Interest (1)

                Bias (6)

believes defendant must prove innocence	4
cannot lay aside views	2

II --- <u>DEFENSE CHALLENGES for CAUSE</u>. 11

	accepted	denied
believes defendant must prove innocence	4	1
believes defendant should testify	3	
will believe police because they are police	1	1
strong opinions	1	
lied in <u>voir dire</u>	1	
other	1	3

III --- <u>PROSECUTION CHALLENGES for CAUSE</u> 2

    Total excused or dismissed for cause from full panel of 133. . . . . <u>87</u>

sion income, 7 who were essential to the employer or would jeopardize their job by serving on the jury, 3 who were visibly nervous, and 2 who were excused because of age (80 and 70). One spry woman of 81 who was active in civic affairs and well-read (she had read Dee Brown's *Bury My Heart at Wounded Knee* and subscribed to *Progressive*) was asked if she wanted to be excused, and replied that she would not, that she would serve if passed. After a long bench conference, during which Hurd expressed concern for the reading she had done, especially Brown's book, she was accepted as a potential juror without challenge (trial transcript, Vol. 4, pp. 660-698). Perhaps the most unusual hardship claim was made by the wife of a prominent St. Paul businessman who said that her son was soon to be married, her daughter was returning from a long voyage, she and her husband were planning a thirty-fifth anniversary vacation, and finally that her husband was "a brilliant person, but he doesn't know how to cook, and this, in itself, would be difficult for me." The Court: "Well, that sounds like there's some reason behind that. How about counsel?" Hurd for the prosecution requested that the judge inquire whether or not she preferred to be excused. She did. Kunstler said the defense had no objections. She was excused (trial transcript, Vol. 9, pp. 1539-1544).

Seven members of the panel of 133 were dismissed by Judge Nichol because they might prejudge the case, and he granted eleven challenges for cause by the defense and two by the prosecution. In most instances the prospective juror could not accept that the defendants did not have to prove their innocence. "Well, if they are entirely innocent they probably wouldn't even be here," replied a 37-year-old radar repair foreman (trial transcript, Vol. 16, p. 2906). Judge Nichol asked a 67-year-old semiretired farmer: "If your view of the law totally conflicted with what I instructed you the law was, would you still follow my view of the law?" He replied, "That is a hard one to answer, Your Honor." Court: "It is an important question. We need to know." Answer: "Your Honor, I wish you would reject me before I give you an answer on that one." He was excused (trial transcript, Vol. 10, p. 1888). A small-town police chief and a secretary for a law firm of prosecuting attorneys were both excused because they would be unable to set aside their prejudice in favor of the prosecution.

The extensive investigation by the defense team into the background of the prospective jurors revealed itself when a 46-year-old housewife and mother of three claimed that she attended the Methodist church regularly. Kenneth Tilsen told the judge at the bench that he had information that she had not been to church for two years because the minister was active in antiwar activities and race relations. When faced with her attendance record, she claimed that she had stopped going because "our church services have turned more into a civic meeting where the name of God was never mentioned." The challenge for cause by the defense was granted (trial transcript, Vol. 3, pp. 353-361).

After the 87 were excused for hardship or disqualified for cause, the remaining 46 constituted the tentative jurors. They were somewhat younger, more urban and suburban, and less small-town and rural than the full panel of 133. (See Table 1.) The 46 were composed of 38 possible jurors and 8 possible alternates who would be cut by the preemptory challenges by the attorneys (20 cuts by the defense and 6 by the prosecution; there was a similar proportion, 3 and 1, for the alternates).

The 12 jurors and 4 alternates selected to hear the case did not differ markedly from the tentative group of 46 except that all but 4 were women. Of the 16 people, the average age was 32. Eight were under 30, including one 19-year-old, and 5 were over 40, including two in their mid-50s. The 16 chosen for the jury box were slightly younger than the group of 46 over which the lawyers exercised their preemptory strikes. They were also more suburban and more Roman Catholic. (See Table 1.)

The 16 sworn in as the jury and alternates can be grouped into several occupational categories:

1. *Technically Skilled*

John K. (age 27). Chosen jury foreman; tool grinder from Red Wing (50 miles South of St. Paul); father of two small girls; Irish-German; 10th grade education; Democrat; president of his local machinists' union (for a term that included a 16-week strike; Vietnam naval veteran; married to an active Mormon, although not active himself; never reads newspapers and seldom watches the TV news, "just the weather report"; said about Wounded Knee: "I just knew it was happening, but I don't know anything about it. I didn't really pay attention to it" (trial transcript, Vol. 10, p. 2073).

Nancy C. (age 31). Degree in electrical engineering from the University of Wisconsin; both she and her husband work for Control Data; lives in suburb of White Bear Lake; German; Lutheran; Independent; reads *National Observer* but no other newspapers or magazines; does not watch TV news; never heard of Means, Banks, Kunstler, or Lane, the BIA or AIM, and did not recall much about Wounded Knee.

Theola D. (age 53). Research analyst for the Minnesota Highway Department; degree in Sociology from the University of Minnesota; single, lives in St. Paul with mother and sister; English; agnostic; Independent; avid reader including both St. Paul newspapers and news magazines; had been a juror in two prostitution cases with one conviction and one acquittal.

Fran A. (age 20). Technical illustrator with Honeywell; two years of vocational school; single, lives with parents in close-in suburb of Falcon Heights; father a Bell engineer; Scottish; Roman Catholic; not a union member; does not watch TV news; did not know who Means and Banks were and was not familiar wth Indian history.

2. *Blue Collar*

    Therese C. (age 53). Employed by the St. Paul Post Office; five children, two at home; three husbands, all in World War II, first died in war, divorced second; lives in suburb of Mahtomedi; Roman Catholic; Democrat; had been contacted in the random survey by the defense but declined to answer any questions about Wounded Knee because she had been called for jury duty.

    Richard G. (age 32). Phone installer; father of five children aged 4 to 13; Mexican-American, married a Mexican-American; lives in St. Paul; Roman Catholic; Independent; reads only St. Paul Sunday paper, no magazines; went to school with Indians.

    Patrick A. (age 24, alternate juror). Dockman for a trucking company; single; lives in St. Paul; grew up in the San Francisco area but attended school throughout California and also in Libya because his father was an engineer and his stepmother worked as a secretary in the embassy; nominal Roman Catholic; Independent; had been in air force but was released on a general discharge after going AWOL; college dropout; interested in motorcycles and science fiction; reads Minneapolis newspaper, *Time, Newsweek,* and *Psychology Today.*

3. *Housewives*

    Geraldine N. (age 42). Housewife with four children, including a married daughter and a son in his freshman year at Augsburg College; lives in St. Paul; Swedish; Lutheran; Independent with leanings toward Democrats; husband works as a maintenance supervisor at a refining plant; has heard of Kunstler, Means, Banks, and Wounded Knee; reads the St. Paul newspaper and *U.S. News.*

    Linda L. (age 26, alternate juror). Housewife and a night waitress at a pancake house where her boss is an Indian; mother of two, aged 3 and 5, who could be cared for by her mother; lives in Falcon Heights; Scandinavian; Congregational; member of Eastern Star; active Republican; was a delegate to the state convention; husband works at a garden center; reads St. Paul newspapers.

4. *Sales*

    Susan O. (age 19). Department store clerk; plans to return to college as a sophomore with a criminal justice major; lives in St. Paul with parents; father works at UNIVAC and mother is a high-school teacher; Roman Catholic; read part of *Bury My Heart at Wounded Knee.*

    Elaine G. (age 40, alternate juror). Clerk at Wards; mother of three (21, 20, and 14); husband an engineer at Control Data and World War II veteran; lives in White Bear Lake; French; Democrat; active in Missouri Lutheran Church; 10th grade education; reads the St. Paul newspaper.

5. *Secretarial*

    Louanne B. (age 42). Secretary in the Personnel Department of a manufacturing firm in Owatonna, 70 miles South of St. Paul; divorced and has custody of her five children, aged 13 to 22; German; Roman Catholic; Democrat; first cousin married an Indian; reads both Minneapolis and St. Paul newspapers and *Time*, but watches very little TV; recognized Kunstler as involved with the Chicago Seven trial.

6. *Academic*

Maureen C. (age 22). Librarian in West St. Paul; when a student at St. Catherine's College took a class in Indian culture and religion from a teacher who was an AIM member, but she said it did not deal with the BIA or treaties; "The only thing I can really remember discussing to any extent with anyone was the sweat lodge" (trial transcript, Vol. 7, p. 1164); lives in Mendota Heights, a suburb, with parents; father is a bank officer and brother a doctor; Scottish; Roman Catholic; Independent.

James P. (age 22). Student at Winona State College, arranged with the dean to make up classes missed; home is Rochester; works in Rochester State Hospital with mentally retarded during summers; Episcopalian; English; father a hotel bellman; mother active Republican; Eagle Scout; heard Kunstler speak two years earlier about Chicago Seven trial; "I shouldn't say I agreed with him, but I kind of felt that he was kind of right, in a way" (trial transcript, Vol. 9, p. 1554).

7. *Service*

Katherine V. (age 20). Nurse's aide in a nursing home; plans to enter convent; one year at junior college; lives with parents in suburb of Burnsville; father in sales at Honeywell; Independent; Roman Catholic but did not know who the Berrigan brothers were; does not read newspapers; did not know about Wounded Knee; brother killed in Vietnam three years earlier; when asked if she felt her brother's death had been a waste, she replied: "No, I don't think it was a waste. I think we have to trust that the governmennt is right just because, like in Vietnam . . . they were right in being in the war. But to complain and try to criticize the government isn't the way . . . to go about changing . . . making it better" (trial transcript, Vol. 14, p. 2693); challenged by the defense for cause but Judge Nichol denied the challenge.

Joyce S. (age 33, alternate juror). Safety officer at Macalester College (not a police position); lives in St. Paul; divorced, recently remarried; husband a machinist at Ford plant; five children (9 to 15); two years at junior college; Irish; Roman Catholic; Democrat; reads St. Paul newspapers and *Time*; recalls seeing Kunstler, Means, and Banks on TV.

Appendix B:
Possible Political Trials

The comments are intended for identification, not judgment.

Greek and Roman

Alcibiades (415 BC): Athenian general, sacrilege
Athenian Generals (406 BC): negligence; loss of 25 ships, 4,000 soldiers
Socrates (399 BC): corrupting the youth
Bacchanalia (186BC): secret cult among lower class and slaves; foreign and
    false religion
Gaius Verres (70 BC) misgovernment in Sicily, corruption
Lucius Catiline (63 BC): conspiracy, treason against Rome
Titus Milo (53 BC): killing of Claudius, a rival
Treason Trials (16-36 AD): Tiberius; *majestas* law prosecutions
Jesus (30 AD): blasphemy and sedition
Stephen (36 AD): blasphemy
Paul (56 AD): desecration of the Temple
Persecution of Christians: Nero (64-68), Trajan (98-117), Maximinus to
    Valerian (235-258), Diocletian (303-311)
Mani (276): founder of Manichaeism
Persecution of pagans and heretics (346-361, after 364)

Medieval to Sixteenth Century

Medieval Inquisition (thirteenth and fourteenth centuries): heresy
Jacques de Molay (1314): persecution of Knights Templars
Thomas, Earl of Lancaster (1322): rebellion
William Sawtre (1401): Lollard heretic, burned
John Hus (1415): Council of Constance; heresy
Joan of Arc (1431): heresy and witchcraft
Spanish Inquisition (from 1478): heresy
Girolamo Savonarola (1498): Florence, religious reformer; schism and
    heresy

Martin Luther (1521): Diet of Worms; heresy
Catherine of Aragon (1529): divorce from Henry VIII
John Lambert (1532): heresy
Thomas More (1535): treason; refusal to accept royal supremacy over church
Anne Boleyn (1536): adultery and incest
Anne Askew (1546): heresy; tortured and burned
Michael Servetus (1553): Calvin's Geneva; interpretation of the Trinity
John Philpot (1555): Anglican, Marian Inquisition
Marian Inquisition (1555-1558): against non-Catholics
Thomas Leigh (1568): contempt, habeas corpus
Thomas Howard, Duke of Norfolk (1572): Ridolfi plot against Elizabeth
Cuthbert Mayne (1575): Catholic priest, treason of propagating "Romanism"
Lord Vaux and Thomas Tresham (1580): refusal of oath that had not harbored Edward Campion
Edward Campion (1581): Jesuit, tortured, proselytism of "Romist religion"
Mary, Queen of Scots (1586): plot to assassinate Queen Elizabeth
John Udall (1590): authorship of Martin Marprelate tracts
Giordano Bruno (1591): Inquisition; heresy
John Penry (1593): Barrowist; seditious libel
Dr. Roderigo Lopez (1594): Spanish plot to poison Queen Elizabeth
Yorke, Williams, Young (1594): conspiracy to kill the queen and raise rebellion in Wales.

Seventeenth Century

Essex (1600): Robert Devereux, disobedience to Queen Elizabeth, attempted coup
Sir Walter Raleigh (1603): treason, intrigues with Spain
Guy Fawkes (1606): Gunpowder Plot to blow up king and Parliament
Henry Garnet (1606): Jesuit, accused in Gunpowder incident
Nicholas Fuller (1607): lawyer: condemnation of High Commission
Edward Peacham (1615): treason; calling the King a "whoremonger" and "drunkard"
Francis Bacon (1621): Lord Chancellor, accepting bribes
Five Knights (1628): opposition to Charles I
Galileo Galilei (1633): heresy; teaching that the earth moves around the sun
Roger Williams (1635): denied validity of Massachusetts Charter, freedom of conscience

John Lilburne (1637): treason for importing books which were "factious, scandalous"

Bastwick, Burton, and Prynne (1637): Puritan pamphleteers, sedition

John Wheelwright (1637): antinomian sermon in Massachusetts

John Hampton (1637): ship-money tax

Anne Hutchinson (1637): antinomian beliefs

Thomas Wentworth, Earl of Strafford (1641): attainder: chief advisor to Charles

Twelve Bishops (1642): treason; protested that laws of Parliament void

Samuel Gorton (1643): blasphemy in Boston; enemy "of all civil authority"

William Laud (1644): Archbishop of Canterbury; treason

John Lilburne (1645): libel of speaker of House

Charles I (1649): treason; levying war against Parliament

John Lilburne (1649): treason; writing *England's New Chains*

Robert Child and Samuel Maverick (1649): conspiracy to overthrow Massachusetts government and church

Christopher Love (1651): Presbyterian royalist plot

John Lilburne (1651): bill of attainder; summarily banished

John Lilburne (1653): returning from exile

Regicides (1660): sat in judgment of Charles I

John James (1661): Fifth Monarchy Man; treason

John Crook (1662): three Quakers; refusal of oaths of allegiance and supremacy

Henry Vane (1662): Parliamentary leader in Revolution; treason

Margaret Fell and George Fox (1664): Quakers; refusal of oath of obedience

Rose Cullender and Amy Duny (1665): witchcraft, Suffolk Co.

Edward Hyde, Earl of Clarendon (1667): Lord Chancellor, impeachment

Peter Messenger (1668): treason; tumultuous assembling, pulling down bawdy houses

William Penn (1670): unlawful preaching to street crowd

Francis Jenkes (1676): offensive political speech; led to Habeas Corpus Act

Bacon's Rebellion (1676): Virginia; insurrection

Anthony Ashley Cooper, Earl of Shaftsbury (1677): writ of habeas corpus

Popish Plot and Titus Oates (1678): anti-Catholic scare, Oates's perjury

Anthony Ashley Cooper, Earl of Shaftsbury (1681): treason; Monmouth rebellion

Algernon Sidney (1683): treason; implication in Rye House Plot to kill Charles II

Titus Oates (1685): perjury in Popish Plot

Alice Lisle (1685): treason; harboring regicides; Judge Jeffreys and Bloody Assize

Seven Bishops (1688): seditious libel; refusal to read James II's Declaration of Indulgence
Salem Witchcraft Trials (1692)
Thomas Maule (1695): Quaker critique of Salem witchcraft trials
John Fenwick (1697): plot to assassinate William II

Eighteenth Century

William Kidd (1701): piracy and murder
Nicholas Bayard (1702): treason; New York
Henry Sacheverell (1710): seditious libel for anti-Whig sermons
Robert Mortimer, Lord Oxford (1717): treason and other crimes
Prince Alexis (1718): treason; desiring death of his father, Peter the Great
Edward Arnold (1724): shooting Lord Onslow (insanity?)
Richard Franklin (1731): libel; Letter from Ghent
John Peter Zenger (1735): criticism of governor general, New York; seditious libel
Lord Lovat (1746): treason in cause of the Pretender
Admiral Byng (1757): court martial; neglect of duty
William Moore and William Smith (1758): criticism of apathetic effort in French-Indian war.
Jean Calas (1762): Toulouse: religious intolerance
John Wilkes (1764): seditious libel
Henry Laurens (1767): smuggling; South Carolina merchant
John Hancock (1768): smuggling; Boston merchant
Alexander McDougall (1770): seditious libel; author of Son of Liberty handbill
Boston Massacre Trial (1770): firing on mob, killing four
Johann F. Struensse (1772): Denmark; dictator overthrown by nobility
Silas Deane (1778): profiteering
John Roberts and Abraham Carlisle (1778): treason; Loyalists in American Revolution
Lord George Gordon (1781): No Popery riots, treason
Major John Andre (1780): British spy
Shays Rebellion (1786): insurrection
Lord George Gordon (1787): libel on judges and the Queen of France
Warren Hasting (1788): impeachment for treatment of Indians, India
Louis XVI (1792): treason
Tom Paine (1792): sedition; publishing The Rights of Man
James of Ankarstrom (1792): assassination of Swedish king Gustavus III
Marie Antoinette (1793): treason; conspiracy to cause civil war
Jacobin Tribunal (1793-1794): reign of terror and virtue, Robespierre

Charlotte Corday (1793): assassination of Marat
Thomas Hardy et al. (1794): treason; London Corresponding Society
Whiskey Rebellion (1794): treason
Gracchus Babeuf (1797): Conspiracy of Equals
John Fries (1798): armed insurrection against tax
Matthew Lyon (1798): Alien and Sedition Acts
Wolfe Tone (1798): Irish patriot; treason in service of France
Benedict Arnold (1799): court martial; use of military for private purposes
John Fries (1799): tax uprising in Pennsylvania; treason

Nineteenth Century-1920

James Hadfield (1800): attempted assassination of George III (insanity)
J. Thompson Callender (1800): newspaper editor; Sedition Act
Robert Emmet (1803): Irish patriot; conspiracy and rebellion
Duke of Enghien (1804): royalist conspiracy against Napoleon
Justice Samuel Chase (1804): impeachment trial, acquitted by Senate
Aaron Burr (1806): treason; plans to establish independent country
John Bellingham (1812): assassination of Prime Minister Spencer Perceval
General Andrew Jackson (1815): contempt of court; arrest of judge under
    martial law
Slagter's Nek rebellion (1815): South African frontier revolt against British
Peterloo Massacre cases (1820): Henry "Orator" Hunt arrested, crowd
    attacked
Arthur Thistlewood (1820): Cato St. conspiracy to assassinate Cabinet
Denmark Vesey (1822): slave rebellion
William Lloyd Garrison (1830): abolitionist; libel
Richard Lawrence (1835): attempted assassination of President Jackson
    (insanity)
Cinque and Amistad slaves (1839): slave mutiny; murder, piracy
John Frost (1839): Chartist; treason; leading mob
Edward Oxford (1840): attempted assassination of Queen Victoria (in-
    sanity)
Daniel McNaughtan (1843): assassination of prime minister's secretary (in-
    sanity)
Feargus O'Connor and fifty-eight others (1843): Chartists; seditious con-
    spiracy
Thomas Cooper (1843): Chartist; seditious conspiracy
Levi Williams, others (1845): accused assassins of Mormon leader Joseph
    Smith
Ferdinand Lassalle (1848): theft in the cause of Countess von Hatzfeldt
Dred Scott (1847): slavery

Karl Marx (1849): plotting against government; antitax proclamation

Ferdinand Lassalle (1849): plotting against government; antitax proclamation

Luther v. Borden (1849): Dorr rebellion in Rhode Island (1841)

Shadrach and Anthony Burns (1851, 1854): Fugitive Slave Law; mob rescues prisoner

Castner Hanway (1851): Fugitive Slave Law

Theodore Parker (1855): attempt to free fugitive slave

Felice Orsini (1858): attempt to assassinate Empress Eugenie and Emperor Napoleon III

John Brown (1859): slave rebellion

John Merryman (1861): suspension of habeas corpus; treason

Clement Vallandigham (1863): Ohio editor; court martial, sympathy for enemy

Ex Parte Milligan (1864): suspension of habeas corpus; treason

John O'Leary et al. (1865): treason; Fenians writing for *Irish People*

Mary Eugenia Surratt (1865): assassination of Lincoln

Henry Wirz (1865): Andersonville Prison deaths

John Surratt (1867): conspiracy to assassinate President Lincoln

General George Custer (1867): court martial; muddled Indian campaign

President Andrew Johnson (1868): impeachment

Robert Mitchell (1871): Ku Klux Klan leader; conspiracy to deny citizens the right to vote

William Tweed (1872): Boss Tweed; graft

Susan B. Anthony (1873): daring to attempt to vote

Langalibalele (1874): South African chief refused to register guns

Molly Maguires (1876): Irish Mafia; union activities v. Pinkertons; murder

Anne Besant (1877): publication of pamphlet on contraception

Vera Zasulich (1877): shooting of St. Petersburg chief of police

Charles Guiteau (1881): assassination of President Garfield

Louis Riel (1885): leader of Canadian rebellion

Haymarket Riot (1886): anarchists; conspiracy to commit murder

Davis v. Beason (1890): oath in order to vote; not belonging to organization (Mormon)

Alfred Dreyfus (1894): military secrets/anti-Semitism

Eugene Debs (1895): Pullman strike

Oscar Wilde (1895): homosexuality

Uitlanders (1896): South Africa; treason for support of Jameson raid

Emile Zola (1898): libel; accused army of covering up evidence in Dreyfus case

Caleb Powers (1900): assassination of candidate for Kentucky governor

Leon Czolgosz (1901): assassination of President McKinley

Cape and Natal rebels (1901): Afrikaners; treason for support of Boers
Leon Trotsky (1906): insurrection in Petrograd, 1905
Bill Haywood (1907): IWW leader; sedition, murder of Governor Steuuen-
    berg
Bal Gangadhar Tilak (1908): Indian nationalist; sedition
Francisco Ferrer (1909): complicity in attempt to kill Spanish king and
    queen
Dinizulu (1909): Zulu Chief; treason for Zulu rebellion
James McNamara (1910): murder, labor dispute
Lieutenant Adolf Hofrichter (1910): murder, poisoning of member of Gen-
    eral Staff (Austro-Hungarian Empire)
Arturo Giovannitti (1912): murder during strike (IWW)
Leo Frank (1913): murder, publicity, anti-Semitism
William Sulzer (1913): Governor of New York; impeachment, campaign
    contributions
Joe Hill (1914): IWW leader, murder, Salt Lake City
Henriette Caillaux (1914): murder of newspaper editor
Jopie Fourie (1914): Afrikaner rebellion
Nurse Edith Cavell (1915): Belgium; concealing French and English sol-
    diers
Warren Billings and Tom Mooney (1916): bomb in San Francisco parade
P.H.Pearse et al.(1916): Easter Rising in Dublin
Roger Casement (1916): Irish nationalist, hanged as traitor
Friedrich Adler (1917): assassination of Austro-Hungarian prime minister
Bill Haywood (1917): IWW leader, sedition
IWW 101 (1918): Chicago; sabotage and conspiracy to obstruct war
Eugene Debs (1918): sedition; denouncing prosecution of dissenters
IWW—Sacramento 46 (1918): bombing of governor's home
IWW—Wichita 34 (1918): oil strike
Roman Malinovsky (1918): agent provocateur in Russian Revolution
Scott Nearing (1919): obstructing recruiting and enlistment
Schenk v. U.S. & Abrams v. U.S. (1919): Espionage Act prosecutions
IWW—Centralia 11 (1920): murder
Joseph Calillaux (1920): French political leader; treason, opposition to war
William Bross Lloyd (1920): Chicago Communist trial
Benjamin Gitlow (1920): Red Scare; New York criminal anarchy law

1921-1944

World War I War crimes trials (1921): Leipzig
Nicola Sacco and Bartolomeo Vanzetti (1921): murder of payroll clerk;
    anarchists and immigrants

Mohandas K. Gandhi (1922): writing seditious articles for *Young India*
Matthias Erzberger (1922): libel case against Weimer minister
Taffy Long (1922): South African gold mine strike
Adolf Hitler (1924): Treason: Beer Hall Putsch
Friedrich Ebert (1924): libel suit of president of Weimar Republic
Leopold and Loeb (1924): murder ("the perfect crime")
Carl Magee (1924): Albuquerque editor; libel and contempt
Marcus Garvey (1925): back to African movement leader, mail fraud
John Scopes (1925): the "Monkey trial"
General Billy Mitchell (1925): court martial of WWI ace
D.C. Stephenson (1925): Grand Dragon of Ku Klux Klan accused of
    murder
Albert Fall (1925): Teapot Dome; bribery and conspiracy to defraud U.S.
Al Capone (1931): tax evasion
U.S. v. Douglas Macintosh (1931): denied U.S. citizenship: pacifism
Scottsboro (1931): rape
Near v. Minnesota (1931): gaglaw, prior restraint
Giuseppe Zangara (1933): shooting Chicago Mayor Cermak
Georgi Dimitrov (1933): Reichstag fire
Angelo Herndon (1933): insurrection; Communist organizer in Georgia
Samuel Insull (1934): utility millionaire, mail fraud
Ustachi Band (1935): assassination of King Alexander of Yugoslavia while
    in France
Bruno Hauptmann (1935): murder of Charles Lindbergh, Jr.
Leon Trotsky (1936): Stalin's purge
Harry Bridges (1938): attempt to deport labor leader
Bukharin, Rykov, Yagoda, et al. (1938): purge trial
Earl Browder (1940): American Communist; passport fraud
Flag Salute Cases (1940,1943): Jehovah's Witnesses
Hershel Grynszpan (1941): murder of German Diplomat
Dunne Brothers (1941): Minneapolis Teamsters, Trotskyites; sedition
Riom Trials (1942): Vichy France; responsibility for defeat
Guy Ballard (1944): I-Am movement; mail fraud
Nazi People's Court (1944): trial of those who attempted to kill Hitler
Korematsu v. U.S. (1944): relocation of American citizens of Japanese
    heritage
Nazi Sedition Trial (1944): thirty pro-Nazi leaders; Smith Act
Robby Liebbrandt (1944): Afrikaner; treason for pro-German activity

1945-1959

Vidkun Quisling (1945): Norway; treason

Marshal Henri Petain (1945): Vichy French government leader; treason

Pierre Leval (1945): Vichy vice-president; treason

William Joyce (1945): Lord Haw-Haw, German radio broadcasts to England

Ezra Pound (1945): treason; broadcasting Fascist propaganda (adjudged insane)

General Yamashita (1945): war crimes in the Philippines

Nuremberg (1945): Nazi leaders

Mikhailovitch Draja (1946): U.S.S.R.; treason and war crimes

Hollywood Ten (1947): Congressional investigation by HUAC

Mayor James Curley (1947): Boston; mail fraud

Douglas Chandler (1947): "Paul Revere"; treason for Nazi broadcasts

Tokyo War Crimes Trial (1948): Gen. Tojo and others; waging aggressive war

N.K. Godse (1948): assassination of Mohandas K. Gandhi

Caryl Chessman (1948): kidnapping, robbery

Robert Best (1948): treason; Nazi broadcasts

Cardinal Mindszenty (1949): Hungary; treason, opposition to Communism

Eugene Dennis (1949): Smith Act conviction of Communist Party leaders

Harry Sacher (1949): lawyer in Dennis case; contempt of court

Judith Coplon (1949): espionage

Alger Hiss (1949): State Department official; perjury

Mildred Gillars (1949): "Axis Sally"; treason for Nazi broadcasts

Iva Toguri d'Aquino (1949): "Tokyo Rose"; treason for WWII broadcasts

Klaus Fuchs (1950): atomic bomb secrets, England

William Remington (1950): Commerce Department employee; perjury

Abe Brothman and Miriam Moskowitz (1950): espionage, obstruction of justice

Oscar Collazo (1951): attempted assassination of President Truman; Puerto Rican nationalist

Julius and Ethel Rosenberg (1951): atom bomb espionage

Youngstown Sheet and Tube v. Sawyer (1952): President Truman's seizure of steel mills

House Un-American Activities Committee (from 1938) and Senator Joseph McCarthy's subcommittee (1950-1954): subversive activities

Jomo Kenyatta (1953): Kenya; conspiracy in Mau-Mau uprising

Owen Lattimore (1953): Senator McCarran's committee; perjury

J. Robert Oppenheimer (1954): suspended by Atomic Energy Commission as a security risk

Four Puerto Rican nationalists (1954): shooting in House of Representatives

Sam Sheppard (1954): pretrial publicity in murder trial
John Henry Faulk (1956): Columbia Broadcasting System (CBS) enter-
	tainer; libel, blacklisting by anti-communists
Wilhelm Reich (1956): leading psychologist; Food and Drug Act violation
Frank Costello (1956): denaturalization of gambler
Milovan Djilas (1956): Yugoslavia; spreading hostile propaganda
Treason Trial (1956-1961): South Africa; African National Congress (ANC)
Yates v. U.S. (1957): Communist Party members, Smith Act
James Hoffa (1957, 1964): teamsters union leader
Batista's Pilots (1959): Cuban revolutionary courts

1960-1969

Francis Gary Powers (1960): U-2 spy pilot shot down by U.S.S.R.
Francis Jeanson (1960): aid to Algerian FLN
Lady Chatterley's Lover (novel by D.H. Lawrence) (1960): England;
	obscenity
Adolf Eichmann (1961): Nazi, tried in Israel
Spiegel Affair (1962): German government crackdown against a newspaper
Ghana Treason Trials (1962): opposition to President Kwame Nkrumah
Chief Enahoro (1962): Nigerian opposition party leader
Iginuhit Ng Tadhana (1962): Phillipines campaign film and censors
Nelson Mandela (1962): incitement, leaving South Africa unlawfully
Martin Luther King (1963): Good Friday march in Birmingham; parade
	without a permit
O. V. Penkovsky and G. M. Wynne (1963): U.S.S.R.; spying for the West
Jack Ruby (1964): murder of Lee Harvey Oswald
Warren Commisssion (1964): Oswald was the lone assassin of President
	Kennedy
Keshav Singh (1964): India, contempt of the legislature
Rivonia Trial (1964): South African dissidents
Fanny Hill (1964): censorship
Norman Butler and Thomas Johnson (1965): assassination of Malcom X
Andrei Sinyavsky and Yuli Daniel (1965): Soviet authors
Arnold Rose v. Gerda Koch (1965): libel of professor by right-winger
David Henry Mitchell III (1965): refusing induction
Abram Fischer (1965): South African lawyer; sabotage
David John Miller (1966): draft card burning
Fort Hood Three (1966): refusing order for Vietnam duty
Barry Bonhus (1966): draft board raid (Big Lake One, Minn.)
David Gutknecht (1967): turning in draft card
Regis Debray (1967): guerrilla activity in Bolivia

Bobby Baker (1967): Senate majority secretary; larceny, tax evasion
Captain Howard Levy (1967): refusal to obey military order
International War Crimes Tribunal (1967): Jean-Paul Sartre and others indict U.S. concerning the Vietnam War
Baltimore Four (1967): pouring blood on draft records
Nambians (1967): SWAPO, terrorism
LeRoi Jones (1967): Black poet, Newark riots
Cecil Price and Sam Bowers (1967): conspiracy to murder civil rights workers—Schwerner, Chaney, Goodman
Orangeburg, S.C. Police (1968): shooting and killing three student demonstrators
Benjamin Spock and William Sloane Coffin (1968): darft resistance, Boston Five
Suzi Williams and Frank Femia (1968): draft board raid, Boston Two
Huey P. Newton (1968): Panther leader; murder, assault, kidnapping
James Lenkoe (1968): South Africa; death at police station
Milwaukee 14 (1968): draft board raid
Sirhan Sirhan (1968): assassination of Robert Kennedy
Oakland Seven (1968): conspiracy to trespass and resist arrest; stop the draft
Catonsville Nine (1968): the Berrigans; destruction of draft records
Pavel Litvinov (1968): denouncing U.S.S.R. invasion of Czechoslovakia, Moscow Five
Reies López Tijerina (1968): Hispanic raid on New Mexico courthouse
Adam Clayton Powell (1968): failure to obey subpoena
Clay Shaw (1969): possible conspiracy to assassinate President Kennedy
James Earl Ray, Jr. (1969): assassination of Martin Luther King, Jr.
Pasadena Three (1969): draft board raid
Chicago Fifteen (1969): draft board raid
Women against Daddy Warbucks (1969): Manhattan draft board raid
New York Eight (1969): draft board in Bronx
Beaver Fifty-five (actually eight) (1969): draft board raid, Indianapolis
Chicago Eight (1969): demonstrators at the 1968 Democratic National Convention
Charles Bursey and Warren Wells (1969): Panthers: Oakland shootout
Winnie Mandela et al. (1969): South Africans
Tinker v. Des Moines School District (1969): black arm bands in school to protest war
Algiers Motel (1969): Detroit policeman; killing three Black youths in 1967 riot

1970-1975

Basque Separatists (1970): murder of secret police inspector

Charles Manson (1970): Manson gang, murder of Sharon Tate and six others

Welsh Language Protesters (1970): disruption of court, contempt (England)

Dow Chemical Protesters (1970): unlawful entry, malicious destruction of property

Alfred Cain, Richard DeLeon, Jerome West (1970): Panthers; conspiracy to rob Harlem hotel

Minnesota Eight (1970): draft board raid

Lonnie McLucas (1970): murder, Panther

Lieutenant William Calley (1970): My Lai massacre, court martial

Seattle Eight (1970): demonstrations against Chicago Seven trial

Tacoma Seven (1970): Antiriot Act and contempt of court

Bobby Seale and Erika Huggins (1971): Panthers, murder, New Haven

Lumumba Shakur et al. (1971): New York Panthers Twenty-One; conspiracy to bomb police headquarters

Huey Newton (1971): second trial of Panther; killing policeman

Detroit Panthers Twenty-One (1971): murder of policeman

Baltimore Panthers (1971): murder of suspected informer

New Orleans Panthers Twelve (1971): police shootout; attempted murder

Los Angeles Panthers Thirteen (1971): police shootout; conspiracy to murder

Huey Newton (1971): third trial of Panther; killing policeman

Dean of Johannesburg (1971): possession of subversive pamphlets

Mangrove Nine (1971): making an affray, England

Aly Sabry (1971): high officials in Egypt; treason

Captain Ernest Medina (1971): My Lai massacre

Colonel Oran Henderson (1971): My Lai massacre

Quebec Separatists (1971): kidnapping, murder, seditious conspiracy

Gillette v. U.S. (1971): selective conscientious objection

New York Times v. U.S. (1971): Pentagon Papers censorship

Wilmington Ten (1972): Rev. Ben Chavis, others; firebombing White-owned grocery

Soledad Brothers (1972): murder of prison guard

Angela Davis (1972): Marin County Courthouse kidnapping and murder

Mark Holder (1972): Panther factional feud; murder

Edward Hanrahan (1972): Chicago state's attorney; conspiracy in killing of Panther leaders

Arthur Bremer (1972): shooting George Wallace

Harrisburg Seven (1972): conspiracy to kidnap Kissinger

Brittany Separatists (1972): Paris, terrorism

Wisconsin v. Yoder (1972): Amish v. public school

Daniel Ellsberg (1973): Pentagon papers; theft and leak

G. Gordon Liddy and James McCord (1973): Watergate break-in
Ervin Committee (1973): Senate Watergate hearings
Otto Kerner (1973): Illinois governor and federal judge; bribery, tax evasion, perjury
Camden Twenty-Eight (1973): draft card destruction
Gainsville Eight (1973): Vietnam Vets against the War; conspiracy to disrupt GOP Convention
Karlton Armstrong (1973): arson, murder: University of Wisconsin bombing
Tony Boyle (1974): UMW president; murder of rival Yablonski
Russell Means and Dennis Banks (1974): AIM leaders; Wounded Knee takeover
Maurice Stans and John Mitchell (1974): obstruction of justice, illegal campaign contributions from Robert Vesco
John Ehrlichman (1974): Plumbers' Trial; break-in at Ellsberg's psychiatrist's office
Richard Nixon (1974): impeachment hearings
John Mitchell et al. (1974): Watergate cover-up
Mikhail Stern (1974): Soviet Jewish doctor; sons' emigration to Israel
Joanne Little (1975): murder of jailer
Breyten Breytenbach (1975): Afrikaner poet; terrorism
Kim Chi Ha (1975): South Korean dissident poet
Lynette "Squeaky" Fromme (1975): attempt to assassinate President Ford
Beyers Naude (1975): refusal to testify before South African Commission
John Connally (1975): secretary of treasury; bribery
Baader-Meinhof Gang (1975): West German radicals; murder, bank robbery
Kent State (1975): Ohio governor and National Guard; responsible for shooting?
Kenneth Edelin (1975): is abortion manslaughter?
Russell Little (1975): Symbionese Liberation Army member; killing Oakland school superintendent

1976-1979

Aaron Mushimba et al. (1976): Namibia; SWAPO, assassination
SASO/BPC Leaders (1976): South Africa; organization of rally
Marvin Mandel (1976): Maryland governor; bribe in racetrack legislation
Bob Robideau and Dino Butler (1976): AIM members; murder of two FBI agents
Patty Hearst (1976): bank robbery
Emily and William Harris (1976): kidnapping of Patty Hearst

—

Balcombe Street Four (1977): IRA hit men; kidnapping, murder, and bombing in London
Leonard Peltier (1977): AIM member; murder of two FBI agents
Jacobo Timerman (1977): Argentina; military dictatorship v. editor
Frank Collin (1977): neo-Nazi rally in Skokie, Illinois
Ali Bhutto (1978): Pakistan's former president
Jonathan Nelson (1978): anti-Trident submarine demonstration
Anatol Shcharancky (1978): Soviet dissident
Daniel Flood (1979): Congressman; bribery and conspiracy
Iranian Revolutionary Tribunal (1979)
Dan White (1979): killing of Mayor Moscone and Supervisor Milk, San Francisco
Guillermo Novo and Alvin Ross (1979): assassination of Chilean ambassador Letelier
Jeremy Thorpe (1979): British Liberal Party leader; attempted murder
Progressive Magazine (1979): publication of H-bomb secrets
Dean and Robert Oeltjen (1979): Minnesota powerline opponents
William Kurykendall and James Merrill (1979): nuclear plant sabotage
Vaclav Havel et al. (1979): Czech human rights activists
Frank McGirl and Thomas McMahon (1979): IRA leaders; murder of Lord Mountbatten
MOVE (1979): Philadelphia radicals
Harry Hanson (1979): Minnesota Red Lake Indian Reservation; disturbances

1980—1985

Liberian Officers (1980): tribunal following coup; treason and corruption
Robert Garwood (1980): Vietnam vet; desertion, collaboration with enemy
Burt Lance (1980): bank fraud
Kim Jae Kyu (1980): South Korea; assassination of President Park
Kim Dae Jung (1980): South Korean opposition leader; sedition
Four Miami Policeman (1980): murder of Black insurance man, traffic violation
Brian Keenan (1980): IRA organizer; conspiracy, London bombings, murder of Ross McWhirter
Jiang Qing and the Gang of Four (1980): plotting assassination of Mao, persecuting officials, planning rebellion
Abscam (1980): congressmen; bribery
Nazi and KKK members (1980): Greensboro, N.C.; murder and rioting
Plowshares Eight (1981): Barrigans; damage to nuclear nose cone
Shipyard Bomb Conspiracy (1981): San Diego; plot to sabotage

Mehmet Ali Agca (1981): attempt to assassinate Pope John Paul
Larry Layton (1981): People's Temple; conspiracy to murder Representative Leo Ryan
Albanian Separatists (1981): Kosovo Province, Yugoslavia; nationalist riots
Egyptian fundamentalists (1981): assassination of President Anwar El Sadat
Eugene Tafoya (1981): shooting of dissident Libyan student
Creationist trial (1981): Arkansas; requirement of both creationist and evolutionist theory in school
Red Brigades (1982): kidnapping General James Dozier
Sadegh Gotbzadeh (1982): former Iranian foreign minister; plot against Khomeini
Mad Mike Hoare (1982): coup attempt in Seychelles
Sun Myung Moon (1982): tax fraud and conspiracy to obstruct justice
John Hinckley (1982): shooting President Reagan and others (insanity)
Joseph Franklin (1982): shooting Vernon Jordan
Enten Eiler and Benjamin Sasway (1982): failing to register for draft
Eddie Carthan (1982): Mayor of Tchula, Miss.; murder of political rival
Barbara Hogan (1982): South Africa; treason, membership in ANC, organizing boycott
Kakuei Tanaka (1982): former Japanese prime minister; bribe from Lockheed
Hugh Hamblelton (1982): England; Soviet spy
Red Brigades (1983): kidnapping and killing Aldo Moro
Yorie Kahl and Scott Faul (1983): tax protesters; killing two U.S. marshals
South African (Venda) Policemen (1983): police brutality, murder of lay preacher
Weather Underground and Black Liberation Army (1983): Goshen, N.Y.; Brink's heist
Edwin Wilson (1983): ex-CIA agent; attempted murder of witnesses
Major Zin Mo and Captain Kang (1983): North Koreans in Burma; bomb killed South Korean cabinet ministers
Yuri Sokolov (1983): death penalty for U.S.S.R. food store corruption
Carl Niehaus and Johanna Lourens (1983): South Africa; treason, working for ANC
Rita Lavelle (1983): EPA official; perjury and obstructing a congressional inquiry
Rose Harvey and Gerard Loughlin (1983): Belfast; IRA activities
Stacey Merkt (1984): sanctuary for illegal Salvadoran aliens
Nuns Case (1984): Salvadoran death squad; murder of four Americans
KKK in Greensboro (1984): second trial; murder of Communists
Yelena Bonner (1984): U.S.S.R.; slandering the state

Roland Hunter (1984): South Africa; treason, military intelligence
Operation Graylord (1984): Chicago; judges taking bribes
Argentine Generals (1984): disappearance of leftists
John LaForge and Barb Katt (1984): antinuclear protesters; damaging computer
Columbia Broadcasting System (CBS) (1984): libel; accused General Westmoreland of conspiracy to distort troop strength figures
Time (1984): libel; Ariel Sharon's role in Lebanon masssacre
Reverend Carl Kabat (1985): Kansas City Four; attempt to disarm Minuteman missile
Polish Secret Police Officers (1985): killing pro-Solidarity priest, Fr. Popieluszko
Polish Solidarity Leaders (1985): membership in an illegal organization and inciting unrest
General Ver (1985): Philippines; assassination of Benigno Aquino
Wilhelm Schmitt (1985): tax protester
Sergei Antonov et al. (1985): "Bulgarian Connection"; plot to assassinate Pope John Paul II
Richard Miller (1985): FBI agent; espionage
UDF leaders (1985): South Africa; two trials, distribution of antigovernment pamphlets and treason
The Order (1985): Nazi-like group; racketeering; murder of radio host
Governor Edwin Edwards (1985): Louisiana; racketeering
Sanctuary Trial (1985): Tucson; Central American refugees hidden in churches

Literary

Aeschylus: *Oresteia*
Bolt, Robert: *A Man for All Seasons*
Brecht, Bertolt: *Caucasian Chalk Circle*
Butler, Samuel: *Erewhon*
Carroll, Lewis: *Alice's Adventures in Wonderland*
Clark, Walter: *The Ox-Bow Incident*
Dickens, Charles: *A Tale of Two Cities*
Dostoevsky, Fyodor: *Crime and Punishment*
de Ghelderode, Michel: *Pantagleize*
Hawthorne, Nathaniel: *The Scarlet Letter*
Hugo, Victor: *Les Misérables*
Kafka, Franz: *The Trial*
Koestler, Arthur: *Darkness at Noon*
Lee, Harper: *To Kill a Mockingbird*

Levitt, Saul: *The Andersonville Trial*
Mazrui, Ali A.: *The Trial of Christopher Okigbo*
Melville, Herman: *Billy Budd*
Miller, Arthur: *The Crucible*
Sartre, Jean-Paul: *The Condemned of Altona*
Shakespeare, William: *Measure for Measure, The Merchant of Venice*
Shaw, George Bernard: *St. Joan*
Solzhenitsyn, Alexander: *Gulag Archipelago* (3 volumes)
Sophocles: *Antigone*
Tolstoy, Leo: *Resurrection*
Uris, Leon: *QB VII*
Wouk, Herman: *Caine Mutiny*
Wright, Richard: *Native Son*

Bibliography

Trial Transcripts

United States vs. Karleton Armstrong, U.S. District Court for the Western District of Wisconsin. Transcript. 1974.

Wisconsin vs. Karleton Armstrong, Dane County. Transcript. 1973.

United States vs. Dennis Banks and Russell Means, U.S. District Court for the Western Division of South Dakota. Transcript. 1974.

Charles Stuart, King of England (1649). Howell, Thomas. comp. *A Complete Collection of State Trials and Proceedings for High Treason and Other Crimes and Misdemeanors from the Earliest Period to the Year 1783.* London: R. Bagshaw, 1809-1826. Cited as *State Trials.*

Robert Emmet (1803). *State Trials*, Vol. 28.

Henry Garnet (1606). *State Trials*, Vol. 2.

Conspirators in the Gunpowder Plot (1606). *State Trials*, Vol. 2.

United States vs. John Hinckley, Jr., Criminal Docket, U.S. District Court for the District of Columbia. Transcript. 1982.

William Land, Archbishop of Canterbury (1644). *State Trials*, Vol. 4.

John Lilburne (1649). *State Trials*, Vol. 4.

State vs. Mushimba and Others. Trial Record. (South Africa, South West Africa Division) 1976.

Feargus O'Connor (1843), *Reports of States Trials, New Series*, Vol. 4. London: Professional Books, 1970 reprint. Cited in *State Trials, New Series.*

Daniel McNaughton (1843). *State Trials, New Series*, Vol. 4.

Wolfe Tone (1793). *State Trials*, Vol. 27.

Trial of the Major War Criminals before the International Military Tribunal. Nuremberg, 1947.

Court Opinions

Minersville School District vs. Gobitis. 310 U.S. 586 (1940).

New York Times vs. Sullivan, 376 U.S. 254 (1964).

Northern Securities Company vs. United States, 193 U.S. 197 (1904).

Olmstead vs. United States, 277 U.S. 438 (1928).

Rosenberg vs. United States, 346 U.S. 273 (1953).

Schenck vs. United States, 249 U.S. 47 (1919).

United States vs. Banks, 374 F. Supp. 321 (1974).

United States vs. Dougherty, 473 F. 2d 1113 (1972).

United States vs. Sioux Nation, 448 U.S. 371 (1980).

United States vs. Spock, 416 F. 2d 165 (1969).

Aaron Mushimba and Others vs. the State, Supreme Court of South Africa, South West Africa Division, 1976.

Newspapers and Magazines

Madison Capital Times (Wisconsin)
The Guardian (Manchester and London)
Mankato Free Press (Minnesota)
Nation
New Republic
Newsweek
New York Review of Books
Minneapolis Star-Tribune
New York Times
San Francisco Chronicle
Time
Washington Post

Other Sources

Adams, George Burton. *Constitutional History of England*. London: Jonathan Cape, 1921.

Adams, George Burton, and H. Morse Stephens, eds. *Selected Documents of English Constitutional History*. London: Macmillan, 1918.

Alexander, James. *A Brief Narrative of the Case and Trial of John Peter Zenger*. Cambridge: Harvard University Press, 1963.

Amnesty International Report, 1982. London: 1983.

Amnesty International. *Torture in the Eighties*. London: 1984.

Arendt, Hannah. *The Origins of Totalitarianism*. New York: Meridian, 1958.

Aristotle, *Politics*. trans. by Ernest Barker. New York: Oxford, 1958.

Ashman, Charles R. *The People vs. Angela Davis*. New York: Pinnacle Books, 1972.

Augustine, *The City of God*.

Bainton, Roland H. *Here I Stand: A Life of Martin Luther*. New York: Mentor, 1950.

Bainton, Roland H. *The Travail of Religious Liberty*. New York: Harper Torchbooks, 1951.

Bannan, John, and Rosemary Bannan. *Law, Morality, and Vietnam: The Peace Militants and the Courts*. Bloomington: Indiana University Press, 1974.

Baron, Salo Wittmayer. *Modern Nationalism and Religion*. New York: Meridian, 1960.

Barrett, W.P. *The Trial of Jeanne d'Arc: A Complete Translation of the Text of the Original Documents*. London: George Routledge, 1931.

Becker, Theodore, ed. *Political Trials*. Indianapolis: Bobbs-Merrill, 1971.

Belknap, Michal, ed. *American Political Trials*. Westport, Conn.: Greenwood, 1981.

Ben-Veniste, Richard, and George Frampton, Jr. *Stonewall: The Real Story of the Watergate Prosecutions*. New York: Simon & Schuster, 1977.

Berger, Raoul. *Impeachment: The Constitutional Problems*. New York: Bantam Books, 1974.

Berman, Harold J. *Law and Revolution: The Formation of the Western Legal Tradition.* Cambridge, Mass.: Harvard University Press, 1983.

Berrigan, Daniel. *The Trial of the Catonsville Nine.* Boston: Beacon, 1970.

Blackburn, Sara, ed. *White Justice: Black Experience Today in America's Courtrooms.* New York: Harper Colophon, 1977.

Bolt, Robert. *A Man for All Seasons.* New York: Vintage, 1960.

Bowen, Catherine Drinker. *Francis Bacon: The Temper of a Man.* Boston: Little, Brown, 1963.

Bowen, Catherine Drinker. *The Lion and the Throne: The Life and Times of Sir Edward Coke.* Boston: Little, Brown, 1956.

Brandon, S.G.F. *The Trial of Jesus of Nazareth.* New York: Stein & Day, 1968.

Brant, Irving. *The Bill of Rights: Its Origin and Meaning.* New York: Mentor, 1965.

Brinton, Crane. *The Anatomy of Revolution.* New York: Vintage, 1958.

Brockunier, Samuel Hugh. *The Irrepressible Democrat: Roger Williams.* New York: Ronald, 1940.

Brown, Malcolm. *The Politics of Irish Literature: From Thomas Davis to W. B. Yeats.* Seattle: University of Washington Press, 1972.

Bukovsky, Vladimir. *To Build a Castle: My Life as a Dissenter.* New York: Viking, 1979.

Bulfinch, Thomas. *Bulfinch's Mythology.* New York: Modern Library, n.d.

Bultmann, Rudolf, et al. *Kerygma and Myth: A Theological Debate.* New York: Harper Torchbooks, 1961.

Burns, James MacGregor. *Leadership.* New York: Harper & Row, 1978.

Camus, Albert. *The Rebel: An Essay on Man in Revolt.* New York: Vintage, 1956.

Caraman, Philip. *Henry Garnet, 1555-1606, and the Gunpowder Plot.* New York: Farrar, Straus, 1964.

Carswell, Donald, ed. *The Trial of Guy Fawkes and Others.* London: William Hodge, 1934.

Casey, William Van Etten, ed. *The Berrigans.* New York: Avon, 1971.

Cassirer, Ernst. *The Myth of the State.* New Haven: Yale University Press, 1946.

Chapin, Bradley. *The American Law of Treason: Revolutionary and Early National Origins.* Seattle: University of Washington Press, 1964.

Cheyney, Edward. "The Court of the Star Chamber." *American Historical Review* (July 1913): 747-748.

Churchill, Winston S. *A History of the English-Speaking Peoples.* 4 vols. New York: Dodd, Mead, 1956.

Clarke, James W. *American Assassins: The Darker Side of Politics.* Princeton: Princeton University Press, 1982.

Congressional Quarterly. *Watergate: Chronology of a Crisis.* Vol. 1. Washington: Congressional Quarterly, 1974.

Cook, Fred J. "Alger Hiss: A New Ball Game." *Nation* (October 7, 1978): 336-340.

Coulton, G. G. *Inquisition and Liberty.* Boston: Beacon Press, 1938.

Cullman, Oscar. *The State in the New Testament.* New York: Charles Scriber's Sons, 1956.

Dawson, Christopher. *The Gods of Revolution: An Analysis of the French Revolution.* New York: Minerva Press, 1972.

Dean, John. *Blind Ambition: The White House Years.* New York: Pocket Books, 1976.

Deane, Herbert A. *The Political and Social Ideas of St. Augustine.* New York: Columbia University Press, 1963.

Debs, Eugene V. *Writings and Speeches*. New York: Hermitage Press, 1948.

Deloria, Vine. *Behind the Trail of Broken Treaties: An Indian Declaration of Independence*. New York: Delacorte Press, 1974.

D'Entreves, A.P., ed. *Aquinas: Selected Political Writings*. Oxford: Blackwell, 1954.

Derrett, J. Duncan M. "The Trial of Sir Thomas More." *English Historical Review* 312 (July 1964): 459.

De Santillana, George. *The Crime of Galileo*. Chicago: University of Chicago Press, 1955.

Devlin, Lord Patrick. *Trial by Jury*. The Eighth Hamlyn Lecture, 1956. London: Stevens & Sons, 1966.

Dillenberger, John, ed. *Martin Luther: Selections from His Writings*. Garden City: Anchor Books, 1961.

Dimitrov, Georgi. *The Reichstag Fire Trial*. New York: Howard Fertig, 1969.

Dorsen, Norman, and Leon Friedman. *Disorder in the Court: Report of the Association of the Bar of the City of New York, Special Committee on Courtroom Conduct*. New York: Pantheon, 1973.

Dreyfus, Alfred, and Pierre Dreyfus. *The Dreyfus Case*. New Haven: Yale University, 1937.

Dugard, John. *Human Rights and the South African Legal Order*. Princeton: Princeton University, 1978.

Dworkin, Ronald. *Taking Rights Seriously*. Cambridge: Harvard University Press, 1977.

Ehrlichman, John. *Witness to Power: The Nixon Years*. New York: Simon & Schuster, 1982.

Ehrmann, Herbert B. *The Case That Will Not Die*. Boston: Little, Brown, 1969.

Elton, G. R. *Policy and Police: The Enforcement of the Reformation in the Age of Thomas Cromwell*. Cambridge: Cambridge University Press, 1972.

Fireside, Harvey. *Soviet Psychoprisons*. New York: Norton, 1979.

Flannery, Edward H. *The Anguish of the Jews: Twenty-Three Centuries of Anti-Semitism*. New York: Macmillan, 1965.

Florence, Ronald. *Fritz: The Story of a Political Assassin*. New York: Dial Press, 1971.

Fraenkel, Ernst. *The Dual State: A Contribution to the Theory of Dictatorship*. New York: Octagon, 1969.

Frankfurter, Felix. *The Case of Sacco and Vanzetti*. Boston: Little, Brown, 1962.

Freed, Donald. *Agony in New Havon: The Trial of Bobby Seale, Ericka Huggins, and the Black Panther Party*. New York: Simon & Schuster, 1973.

Frend, W.H.C. *The Donatist Church: A Movement of Protest in Roman North Africa*. New York: Oxford, 1952.

Frend, W.H.C. *Martyrdom and Persecution in the Early Church*. Garden City: Doubleday, 1967.

Froude, James Anthony. *The Reign of Henry the Eighth*. 3 vols. London: Dent, 1909.

Fuller, Lon L. *The Morality of Law*. New Haven, Yale University Press, 1964.

Fuller, Lon L. "Pashukanis and Vyshinsky: A Study in the Development of Marxian Legal Theory." *Michigan Law Review* 47 (1949): 1157-1166.

Fuller, Lon L. *Principles of Social Order: Selected Essays*. Ed. by Kenneth I. Winston. Durham: Duke University Press, 1981.

Gandhi, Mahatma *Collected Works*. Publications Division, Ministry of Information and Broadcasting, Government of India.

Gardiner, Samuel. *What Gunpowder Plot Was.* New York: Greenwood, 1969.

Gaylin, Willard. *The Killing of Bonnie Garland: A Question of Justice.* New York: Simon & Schuster, 1982.

Germant, Gordon. "The Notion of Conspiracy Is Not Tasty to Americans: An Interview with Jane L. Tapp." *Psychology Today* (May 1975).

Gerth, H. H., and C. Wright Mills, eds. *From Max Weber: Essays in Sociology.* New York: Oxford University Press, 1958.

Gibbon, Edward. *The Decline and Fall of the Roman Empire.* New York: Modern Library, n.d. (originally published 1776).

Gies, Frances. *Joan of Arc: The Legend and the Reality.* New York: Harper & Row, 1981.

Glueck, Sheldon. *Law and Psychiatry: Cold War or Entente Cordiale?* Baltimore: Johns Hopkins Press, 1962.

Gregg, Pauline. *Free-born John: A Biography of John Lilburne.* Westport, Conn.: Greenwood, 1961.

Hakman, Nathan. "Political Trials in the Legal Order: A Political Scientist's Perspective." *Journal of Public Law* 21 (1972): 73-125.

Halasz, Nicholas. *Captain Dreyfus: The Story of a Mass Hysteria.* New York: Simon & Schuster, 1955.

Harper, Fowler, and David Haber. "Lawyer Troubles in Political Trials." *Yale Law Journal* 60 (1951): 1-56.

Hart, H.L.A. *The Concept of Law.* Oxford: Clarendon, 1963.

Hayes, Carleton J. H. *Essays on Nationalism.* New York: Macmillan, 1928.

Hayward, Max, trans. and ed. *On Trial: The Soviet State versus "Abram Tertz" and "Nikolai Arzhak."* New York: Harper & Row, 1967.

Hill, Christopher. *"God's Englishman: Oliver Cromwell and the English Revolution.* New York: Harper Torchbooks, 1970.

Hill, Christopher. *The World Turned Upside Down: Radical Ideas during the English Revolution.* New York: Viking, 1972.

Hobbes, Thomas. *Leviathan.* Oxford: Blackwell, 1957.

Holdsworth, William. *History of English Law.* 17 volumes. London: Sweet & Maxwell, 1955.

Howell, Roger. *Cromwell.* Boston: Little, Brown, 1977.

Jackson, Brian. *The Black Flag.* New York: Routledge & Kegan Paul, 1981.

Jaspers, Karl, and Rudolf Bultmann. *Myth and Christianity: An Inquiry into the Possibility of Religion without Myth.* New York: Noonday, 1958.

Jordan, David P. *The King's Trial: The French Revolution vs. Louis XVI.* Berkeley: University of California Press, 1979.

Joughin, Louis, and Edmund M. Morgan. *The Legacy of Sacco and Vanzetti.* New York: Harcourt Brace, 1948.

Juel, Donald. *Messiah and Temple: The Trial of Jesus in the Gospel of Mark.* Missoula, Mont.: Scholars Press, 1977.

Kadish, Mortimer R., and Sanford H. *Discretion to Disobey: A Study of Lawful Departures from Legal Rules.* Stanford: Stanford University Press, 1973.

Kamen, Henry. *The Spanish Inquisition.* New York: Mentor, 1965.

Karsner, David. *Debs: His Authorized Life and Letters.* New York: Boni & Liveright, 1919.

Katkov, George. *The Trial of Bukharin.* New York: Stein & Day, 1969.

Keating, Edward. *Free Huey.* Berkeley: Ramparts Press, 1971.

Kelly, Henry Ansgar. *The Matrimonial Trials of Henry VIII.* Stanford: Stanford University Press, 1976.

Kempton, Murray. *The Briar Patch: The People of the State of New York vs. Lumumba Shaker et al.* New York: Delta, 1973.

King, Martin Luther Jr. *Why We Can't Wait.* New York: Mentor, 1963.

Kirchheimer, Otto. *Political Justice: The Use of Legal Procedure for Political Ends.* Princeton: Princeton University Press, 1961.

Kirk, G. S. *The Nature of Greek Myths.* Penguin, 1974.

Koestler, Arthur. *The Sleepwalkers: A History of Man's Changing Vision of the Universe.* New York: Macmillan, 1959.

Kopkind, Andrew. "Passion Play," *Nation* (November 5, 1983): 420-421.

Kuhhan, James F., Shelden G. Levy, and William J. Crotty, eds. *Assassination and Political Violence: A Report to the National Commission on the Causes and Prevention of Violence.* New York: Praeger, 1970.

Kuhn, Thomas S. *The Structure of Scientific Revolutions.* 2nd ed. Chicago: University of Chicago Press, 1970.

Kutler, Stanley I. *The American Inquisition: Justice and Injustice in the Cold War.* New York, Hill & Wang, 1982.

Lang, Gladys Engel, and Kurt Lang. *The Battle for Public Opinion: The President, the Press, and the Polls during Watergate.* New York: Columbia University Press, 1983.

Lea, H. C. *The Inquisition of the Middle Ages: Its Organization and Operation.* New York: Harper Torchbooks, 1963 (originally published 1887).

Lefebvre, Georges. *The French Revolution.* 2 volumes. New York: Columbia University Press, 1962.

Lerner, Max, ed. *The Mind and Faith of Justice Holmes: His Speeches, Essays, Letters, and Judicial Opinions.* New York: Modern Library, 1943.

Levy, Leonard W. *Freedom of Speech and Press in Early American History: Legacy of Suppression.* New York: Harper Torchbooks, 1963.

————. *Origins of the Fifth Amendment: The Right against Self-Incrimination.* London: Oxford University Press, 1968.

Liddy, Gordon G. *Will.* New York: St. Martin's, 1980.

Llewellyn, Karl. *The Bramble Bush.* New York: Oceana, 1960.

Locke, John. *Two Treatises of Government.* Peter Laslett, ed. New York: Mentor, 1960.

MacIntyre, Alasdair. *After Virtue: A Study in Moral Theory.* Notre Dame: University of Notre Dame Press, 1981.

MacMullen, Ramsay. *Constantine.* New York: Dial Press, 1969.

Magruder, Jeb Stuart. *An American Life: One Man's Road to Watergate.* New York: Antheneum, 1974.

Marius, Richard. *Thomas More.* New York: Knopf, 1985.

Martin, F. X., ed. *Leaders and Men of the Easter Rising: Dublin 1916.* Ithaca: Cornell University Press, 1967.

Marwil, Jonathan L. *The Trials of Counsel Francis Bacon in 1621.* Detroit: Wayne State University Press, 1976.

Mathews, Anthony. *Law, Order, and Liberty in South Africa.* Berkeley: University of California Press, 1972.

Matthiesson, Peter. *In the Spirit of Crazy Horse,* New York: Viking, 1983.

McCloskey, Robert. *The American Supreme Court.* Chicago: University of Chicago Press, 1960.

McHugh, Roger, ed. *Dublin 1916.* New York: Hawthorn Books, 1966.

McIlwain, Charles. *The High Court of Parliament and Its Supremacy.* New Haven: Yale University Press, 1910.

Medvedev, Zhores, and Roy Medvedev. *A Question of Madness.* New York: Knopf, 1971.

Messerschmidt, J. M., *The Trial of Leonard Peltier.* Boston: South End Press, 1983.

Miller, Perry. *Orthodoxy in Massachusetts, 1630-1650.* Boston: Beacon, 1959.

Mitford, Jessica. *The Trial of Dr. Spock.* New York: Alfred A. Knopf, 1969.

Moran, Richard. *Knowing Right from Wrong: The Insanity Defense of Daniel McNaughton.* New York: Free Press, 1981.

Morris, Norval. *Madness and the Criminal Law.* Chicago: University of Chicago Press, 1982.

Morris, Richard B. *Fair Trial: Fourteen Who Stood Accused from Anne Hutchinson to Alger Hiss.* New York: Knopf, 1953.

Newman, Graeme. "Khomeini and Criminal Justice: Notes on Crime and Culture." *Journal of Criminal Law and Criminology* 73 (1982): 561:581.

Newton, Huey P. *Revolutionary Suicide.* New York: Harcourt, Brace, Jovanovich, 1973.

Nixon, Richard. *RN: Memoirs.* New York: Warner, 1978.

Noonan, John T., Jr. *Persons and the Masks of the Law: Cardozo, Holmes, Jefferson, and Wythe as Makers of the Masks.* New York: Farrar, Straus, and Giroux, 1976.

O'Farrell, Patrick. *England and Ireland since 1800.* New York: Oxford University Press, 1975.

O'Farrell, Patrick. *Ireland's English Question: Anglo-Irish Relations 1534-1970.* New York: Schocken Books, 1971.

O'Leary, John. *Fenians and Fenianism.* 2 volumes. New York: Barnes & Noble, 1968 (originally published 1896).

O'Rourke, William. *The Harrisburg 7 and the New Catholic Left.* New York: Thomas Y. Crowell, 1972.

Paine, Albert Bigelow. *Joan of Arc: Maid of France.* 2 volumes. New York: Macmillan, 1925.

Pakenham, Thomas. *The Year of Liberty: The Story of the Great Irish Rebellion of 1798.* Englewood Cliffs, N.J.: Prentice-Hall, 1969.

Parkinson, C. Northcote. *Gunpowder, Treason, and Plot.* New York: St.. Martin's, 1976.

Plato. *Apology.*

Plato. *Crito.*

Plato. *The Republic.*

Pollock, (Sir) John. *The Popish Plot: A Study in the History of the Reign of Charles II.* Cambridge: Cambridge University Press, 1944.

Pound, Roscoe. *Introduction to the Philosophy of Law.* New Haven: Yale University Press, 1954.

Powell, Stephen J. "The Legal Nihilism of Pashukanis." *University of Florida Law Review* 20 (1967): 18-32.

Price, Raymond. *With Nixon.* New York: Viking, 1977.

Radosh, Ronald, and Joyce Milton. *The Rosenberg File: A Search for the Truth.* New York: Holt, Rinehart, & Winston, 1983.

Read, Donald, and Eric Glasgow. *Feargus O'Connor: Irishman and Chartist.* London: Edward Arnold, 1961.

Reich, Walter. "To Soviets, Sakharov Really Is Crazy." Minneapolis *Star-Tribune* (August 12, 1984): 27A.

Reid, B. L. *The Lives of Roger Casement.* New Haven: Yale University Press, 1976.

Reynolds, E. E. *The Field Is Won: The Life and Death of St. Thomas More*. Milwaukee: Bruce, 1968.

Reynolds, E. E. *The Trial of St. Thomas More*. London: Burnes & Oates, 1964.

Reuben, William A. *Footnote on an Historic Case: In Re Alger Hiss*. New York: Nation Foundation, 1983.

Rosenberg, Charles E. *The Trial of the Assassin Guiteau: Psychiatry and the Law in the Guilded Age*. Chicago: University of Chicago Press, 1968.

Rousseau, J.-J. *The Social Contract*. Trans. by G.D.H. Cole. London: Everyman's Library, 1941 (originally published 1762).

Russell, Conrad. "The Theory of Treason in the Trial of Strafford." *English Historical Review* 80 (1965): 30-50.

Russsell, Francis. *Tragedy in Dedham: The Story of the Sacco-Vanzetti Case*. New York: McGraw-Hill, 1962.

Sachs, Albie. *Justice in South Africa*. Berkeley: University of California Press, 1973.

Saffell, David C., ed. *Watergate: Its Effects on the American Political System*. Cambridge, Mass.: Winthrop, 1974.

Schafer, Stephen. *The Political Criminal: The Problem of Morality and Crime*. New York: Free Press, 1974.

Schaff, Philip, editor. *A Select Library of the Nicene and Post-Nicene Fathers of the Christian Church*. Buffalo: Christian Literature, 1886.

Schipper, Henry. "A Trapped Generation on Trial." *The Progressive XXXVIII* (January 1974): 45.

Schneir, Walter, and Miriam Schneir. *Invitation to an Inquest: Reopening the Rosenberg "Atom Spy" Case*. Baltimore: Penguin, 1973.

Schrag, Peter. *Test of Loyalty: Daniel Ellsberg and the Rituals of Secret Government*. New York: St. Martin's, 1980.

Shelley, Louise I. "Yelena Bonner Meets Soviet Justice System." Minneapolis *Star-Tribune* (September 21, 1984): 13A.

Shirer, William L. *The Rise and Fall of the Third Reich*. New York: Crest Books, 1959.

Shklar, Judith. *Legalism*. Cambridge, Mass.: Harvard University Press, 1964.

Sirica, John J. *To Set the Record Straight: The Break-in*, The Tapes, The Conspirators, The Pardon. New York: W. N. Norton, 1979.

Smith, Bradley F. *Reaching Judgment at Nuremberg*. New York: New American Library, 1979.

Smith, Bradley F. *The Road to Nuremberg*. New York: Basic Books, 1981.

Smith, H. Maynard. *Henry VIII and the Reformation*, New York: Russell & Russell, 1962.

Solzhenitsyn, Aleksandr I. *The Gulag Archipelago*. Vol. 1. Trans. by Thomas P. Whitney. New York: Harper & Row, 1973.

Stans, Maurice H. *The Terrors of Justice: The Untold Side of Watergate*. New York: Everest House, 1978.

Stanton, Elizabeth Cady, Susan B. Anthony, and Matilda Joslyn Gage. *History of Woman Suffrage*. 6 vols. New York: Source Book Press, 1970 (originally published 1861-1876).

Stone, I. F. "I. F. Stone Breaks the Socrates Story." *New York Times Magazine* (April 8, 1979): 22ff.

Stone, Irving. *Clarence Darrow for the Defense*. New York: Doubleday, 1941.

Stultz, Newell M. *Afrikaner Politics in South Africa, 1934-1948*. Berkeley: University of California Press, 1974.

Tallentrye, S. G. *The Life of Voltaire.* 2 vols. London: Smith, Elder, & Co., 1903.
Talmon, J. L. *The Origins of Totalitarian Democracy.* New York: Praeger, 1960.
Taylor, A. E. *Socrates.* London: Peter Davies, 1932.
Taylor, Telford. *Nuremberg and Vietnam: An American Tragedy.* New York: Quadrangle, 1970.
Thomson, David. *The Babeuf Plot: The Making of a Republican Legend.* Westport, Conn.: Greenwood, 1975.
Thucydides. *History of the Peloponnesian War.* Trans. by Rex Warner. Baltimore: Penguin, 1954.
Tiger, Edith, ed. *In Re Alger Hiss: Petition for a Writ of Error Coram Nobis.* New York: Hill & Wang, 1979.
Tobias, Fritz. *The Reichstag Fire.* New York: G. P. Putnam's Sons, 1964.
Tone, William Theobald Wolfe. *Life of Theobald Wolfe Tone.* 2 vols. Washington: Gales & Seaton, 1826.
Torrey, E. Fuller. *The Roots of Treason: Ezra Pound and the Secret of St. Elizabeths.* San Diego: Harcourt Brace Jovanovich, 1984.
Trial of the Major War Criminals before the International Military Tribunal. 42 vols. Nuremberg: 1947.
Trotsky, Leon. *The Russian Revolution.* Trans. by Max Eastmen. Garden City: Doubleday Anchor, 1959.
Tucker, Roboert C., and Stephen F. Cohen, eds. *The Great Purge Trial.* New York: Grosset & Dunlap, 1965.
Turk, Austin T. *Political Criminality: The Defiance and Defense of Authority.* Beverly Hills: Sage, 1982.
Unger, Roberto Mangabeira. *Law in Modern Society: Toward a Criticism of Social Theory.* New York: Free Press, 1976.
Van Voris, Jacqueline. *Constance de Markievicz: In the Case of Ireland.* Amherst: University of Massachusetts Press, 1967.
Voegelin, Eric. *The New Science of Politics.* Chicago: University of Chicago Press, 1952.
Walzer, Michael, ed. *Regicide and Revolution: Speeches at the Trial of Louis XVI.* Cambridge: Cambridge University Press, 1974.
Walzer, Michael. *The Revolution of the Saints: A Study in the Origins of Radical Politics.* New York: Antheneum, 1974.
Walker, Nigel. *Crime and Insanity in England.* Vol. 1, *The Historical Perspective.* Edinburgh: University Press, 1968.
Warner, Marina. *Joan of Arc: The Image of Female Heroism.* New York: Knopf, 1981.
Wedgewood, C. V. *The King's Peace, 1637-1641.* New York: Macmillan, 1956.
Wedgewood, C. V. *The Trial of Charles I.* London: Collins, 1964.
Weinberg, Arthur, ed.: *Attorney for the Damned.* New York: Simon & Schuster, 1957.
Weinstein, Allen. *Perjury: The Hiss-Chambers Case.* New York: Knopf, 1978.
Weiss, Mike. *Double Play: The San Francisco City Hall Killings.* Reading, Mass.: Addison-Wesley, 1984.
West, Rebecca. *The New Meaning of Treason.* New York: Viking, 1964.
Weston, Alan F., and Barry Mahoney. *The Trial of Martin Luther King.* New York: Thomas Y. Cromwell, 1974.
White, Charles. "When a Trial Becomes a Political Circus." *Update* 5 (Winter 1981).
———. "When Law Becomes a Political Football." *Update* 5 (Spring 1981).

_____. "What Is Justice?" *Update* 6 (Winter 1982).

White, Theodore H. *Breach of Faith: The Fall of Richard Nixon.* New York: Dell, 1975.

Williams, Roger. *Complete Writings.* New York: Russell & Russell, 1963.

Williams, Selma R. *Divine Rebel: The Life of Anne Marbury Hutchinson.* New York: Reinhart & Winston, 1981.

Willis, G. G. *Saint Augustine and the Donatist Controversy.* London: S.P.C.K., 1950.

Wills, Garry. "Love on Trial: The Berrigan Case Reconsidered." *Harper's* (July 1972): 63-71.

Wilson, Edmund. *To the Finland Station.* Garden City: Doubleday, 1953.

Wingfield-Stratford, Esme. *King Charles the Martyr, 1643-1649.* Westport, Conn.: Greenwood Press, 1975.

Wolfe, Don M., ed. *Leveller Manifestors of the Puritan Revolution.* New York: Humanities Press, 1967.

Wolfram, Harold W. "John Lilburne: Democracy's Pillar of Fire." *Syracuse Law Review* (Spring 1953): 216.

Woods, Donald. *Biko.* New York: Paddington, 1978.

Zimroth, Peter. *Perversions of Justice: The Prosecution and Acquittal of the Panther 21.* New York: Viking, 1974.

Index